Instructor's Manual With Test Bank To Accompany

Computers and Data Processing

CONCEPTS AND APPLICATIONS

Third Edition

WITH BASIC

Steven L. Mandell
Bowling Green State University

West Publishing Company
St. Paul   New York   Los Angeles   San Francisco

ISBN 0-314-87129-2

CONTENTS

The BASIC Supplement

CLASSROOM ADMINISTRATION

TEST BANK

INTRODUCTION

There are two primary goals associated with this instructor's manual: classroom guidance and test preparation. Every attempt has been made to provide the teacher with supporting materials so that concentration can be placed on the learning process. The manual has been segmented into four main parts: CLASSROOM ADMINISTRATION; ADDITIONAL APPLICATIONS; SCRIPT FOR SLIDE PRESENTATION; and TEST BANK.

The Classroom Administration section provides the fundamental support for classroom preparation. There are eight components for each corresponding text chapter: Learning Objectives; Outline; Answers to Review Questions; Answers to Discussion Points; Answers to even-numbered Study Guide Questions (odd-numbered answers appear in Study Guide); Additional Review Questions; Additional Discussion Points; and Enrichment Lectures.

There are three Additional Applications that can be used to support material in the text.

A Script for the slide presentation of a tour of a computer room is provided.

The Test Bank contains more than 1,200 multiple-choice questions suitable for machine scoring. These questions are organized by chapter and major headings within the chapter for convenience in designing individual exams. An answer key for the questions covering a particular chapter immediately follows that block of questions.

At the back of the manual is the BASIC Supplement. It includes Answers to Textbook Questions, Exercises, and Problems, and four Supplemental Programming Problems (along with solutions) for Sections IV - X. Also included are the answers to even-numbered Study Guide Problems (odd-numbered answers appear in the Study Guide). A Test Bank (with answer key) appears last.

Since there are so many possible variations in course structure, a standardized syllabus is impossible to develop. However, four general structures are provided that could be easily adjusted to almost any existing course.

	I	II	III	IV
Course Contact Hours:	30-40	30-40	45-60	45-60
BASIC Programming:	YES	NO	YES	NO
Chapter	Number of Class Hours Per Chapter			
1	1	1	1	1-2
2	1	1-2	2	2
3	2	2-3	3	3-4
4	1-2	1-2	2-3	2-3
5	1-2	1-2	2	2-3
6	2	2	2-3	3-4
7	1-2	2	2	2-3
8	2	2-3	2-3	3-4
9	1-2	2	2	2-3
10	2	2	2-3	3-4
11	1	1	1-2	2
12	2	2	2-3	3
13	2	2-3	3	3-4
14	2	2	2-3	3
15	1-2	2-4	3-5	4-6
16	1	2-3	2-3	3-4
17	2	1	1-2	1-2
18	1-2	2-3	3	3-4
BASIC	4-8	NA	8-12	NA

Although the text has been designed so that the sequence of chapters follows a logical approach, instructors may wish to modify certain placements. Whenever the BASIC language is employed, it is recommended that its coverage commence at the same time Section III (Programming) of the text is presented. This permits a marriage of the programming experience with the text coverage.

A special note of appreciation goes to Dr. Edward D. Fiscus for assisting with development of an educationally sound test bank.

Any suggestions for improving either the book or this instructor's manual will be greatly appreciated. Please address all correspondence to:

Dr. Steven L. Mandell
Associate Professor
Accounting and MIS Department
Bowling Green State University
Bowling Green, OH 43403

Introduction to Data Processing

LEARNING OBJECTIVES

Students should be able to:

- Identify the computer's basic functions and features
- Define the term data processing
- Distinguish between data and information
- Identify the steps involved in processing data
- Define the terms field, record, file, data base
- List some common applications in the government, education, and health-care fields

OUTLINE

I. Background: Most computers are general-purpose machines and cannot perform any task that a person has not predetermined.

    A. Computers can perform three basic functions:

        1. Arithmetic operations
        2. Comparison operations
        3. Storage and retrieval operations

        Instruction sets in the electronic circuitry of the computer are manipulated by specific programs to harness the computer's power for the desired purpose.

1

B.   Computers derive most of their power from three
     features: speed, accuracy, and memory.

  1.   Speed - expressed in units of time to perform one
       operation

     a.   Milisecond = one-thousandth (1/1,000)
          Microsecond = one-millionth (1/1,000,000)
          Nanosecond = one-billionth (1/1,000,000,000)
          Picosecond = one-trillionth (1/1,000,000,000,000)
     b.   Controlling factors: switching speed of the
          computer's electronic circuits and the dis-
          tances electric currents have to travel.

  2.   Accuracy - electronic circuits are inherently
       reliable. However, it is impossible for a computer
       to produce meaningful ouput from bad input or
       incorrect processing instructions. From this comes
       the phrase "garbage in-garbage out."
  3.   Memory - users can purchase memory capabilities to
       store any amount of data they wish to keep on hand.
       Once data is placed in the computer's memory, it
       can be retrieved for processing in a fraction of a
       second.

II.   Data Processing: Data processing is a method of
      collecting, manipulating, and distributing data to achieve
      certain objectives.

  A.   It has evolved from manual data processing to automatic
       data processing performed by machines to electronic
       data processing performed by computers.

  B.   The objective of data processing is to convert raw data
       to information, which can be used for decision-making.

    1.   Data refers to raw facts.
    2.   Information is data that has been organized and
         processed so it can be used to increase
         understanding and to make intelligent decisions.

  C.   To be useful to decision makers, information must be
       concise, timely, relevant, accurate, and complete.

  D.   The basic flow pattern for all computer processing is:
       input, processing, output.

1. Input involves

   a. Collecting
   b. Verifying
   c. Coding

2. Processing involves

   a. Classifying--categorizing data according to certain characteristics
   b. Sorting--arranging data into a predetermined sequence
   c. Calculating--performing arithmetic and/or logical manipulation
   d. Summarizing--reducing large amounts of data to a more concise and usable form
   e. Storing--keeping data for future reference

3. Output involves

   a. Retrieving previously stored data
   b. Converting information to human readable form
   c. Communicating the information to the right person at the right time

E. To achieve effective data processing, data is organized in the following manner:

   1. Field--an item of data
   2. Record--a collection of fields that relate to a single unit
   3. File--a collection of related records
   4. Data base--the structuring of information needs to satisfy a wide variety of user requirements

III. Data Processing Application: One common application of data procesing is payroll preparation.

A. This application is well adapted to electronic data processing (EDP) because it involves well defined, repetitive procedures and a large number of records.

B. In addition to preparing the paycheck for each employee, the computer can provide summarized information to aid management in its decision-making with respect to labor costs, cash flow planning, etc.

IV. Computer Impact: The computer revolution is characterized by the pervasiveness of computers in today's society.

A. The computer has perhaps had the greatest impact on business. Decisions on the allocation of scarce resources must be made in the face of uncertainty. The computer can enhance problem-solving capabilities by reducing the amount of uncertainty; and it can perform many tasks ranging from inventory control to market research.

B. Government makes extensive use of computers in clerical and administrative functions, military weapons and defense system development, health service, land resources, transportation planning, and police telecommunication systems.

C. Education applications include computer-assisted instruction and simulation.

D. In the health-care field, computers are used in medical diagnosis, patient monitoring, and maintaining medical histories.

E. Personal computers provide services ranging from thermostat regulation to menu planning.

ANSWERS TO REVIEW QUESTIONS

1.   The accuracy of a computer relates to internal operations, or the processing of the inputs. Inputs are fed into the computer by hand, which is when most errors occur. The computer can process only the data given to it and, in turn, will provide output based on that input. Since the computer has a zero IQ, it cannot upgrade or improve the accuracy of the input ("garbage in--garbage out").

The computer will follow exactly the instructions given to it; so bad processing instructions will result in bad output, too. The correctness of programs is, therefore, extremely important if output is to be accurate and relevant.

2.   Data refers to raw facts that, alone, have little meaning. Information is data that has been organized and processed so that it is meaningful. Note that what is information to one person may only be data to another. Data can be converted into information by classifying, sorting, calculating, summarizing, and storing.

For instance, sales data can be classified by customer, salesperson, or inventory type. Then the classified data can be stored by dollar values, activity levels, or another attribute desirable to the user. Calculations can then be performed, such as determining the commissions for each salesperson. Next, the data elements can be summarized and put into a form desired by the user, such as the total commissions for each salesperson. Finally, the data is stored for future use.

3.   Any category of data (e.g., employee's social security number) is called a field. A group, or collection, of fields that pertains to a single unit (e.g., an employee) is called a record. A field is a grouping of all related records (e.g., the records related to all employees). Data base refers to the structuring of data to satisfy a wider variety of information needs than can be supported by a single file.

4.   Some ways in which the computer has had impact on individuals are:

- banking functions, such as personal checking accounts, controlled by computer operations or automatic banking machines
- use of computers for faster telephone service
- bills prepared by computers, such as utility bills, or bills from credit card transactions.
- records stored on computers such as motor vehicle registration
- requirements by many schools and universities to learn about computers in order to survive in this generation of computers

5.   Problems created by computers include:

- worker displacement
- invasion of privacy
- depersonalization

6.   A wide variety of situations may be described. Responses should refer to improvements in speed, timeliness, accuracy, conciseness, and the relevance of the information involved.

Descriptions of impact on individuals may refer to depersonalization, displacement, and privacy invasion as well as the opportunity to learn and improve their decision-making capabilities.

ADDITIONAL REVIEW QUESTIONS

1.   Name the three basic functions that a computer can perform.
What is the only limitation pertaining to the combination of
instructions that a computer can perform?

2.   Compare the difference between data processing, automatic
data processing, and electronic data processing. What is the
objective of all data processing?

3.   Discuss the three elements of the basic flow pattern for
all data processing.

4.   What is the basic concept of memory? Explain.

5.   What are the two factors that affect the processing speed
of a computer? What is a nanosecond?

ANSWERS TO DISCUSSION POINTS

1.   Computer simulation training is especially beneficial when
procedures are too dangerous (either to persons or equipment) to
try in real life, when energy or fuel may be conserved, and when
insurance companies recognize its role in encouraging safety and
preventing accidents.

2.   Other applications for computer simulation training include
automobile driving, ship handling, chemical experimentation,
bridge and other complex construction projects.

ADDITIONAL DISCUSSION POINTS

1.   What types of computer simulation training might be
appropriate for use in the public schools?

2.   What types of people are likely to initiate and develop
ideas for computer simulation training programs?

ANSWER KEY TO STUDY GUIDE

True/False

2. T   4. F   6. T   8. F   10. T

Matching

2. i   4. b   6. f   8. j   10. h

Short Answer

2.   o switching speed of the electronic circuits
      o distance that electric currents have to travel

4.   The objective of all data processing is to convert raw data
      into information that can be used in decision making.

6.   input, processing, output

8.   Retrieve means the computer can access stored information
      for the user. Convert means the computer translates infor-
      mation into a form that humans can understand. Communicate
      means to send information to the right place at the right
      time.

10.   They are concerned about the problems that computers may
      create. Some of these problems are: worker displacement,
      invasion of privacy, and depersonalization in business
      operations.

ENRICHMENT LECTURE

Nondestructive Testing

Industry is just one area of modern life where computers have made an impact. In industry, quality control has long been a problem. Finding flaws or weaknesses in products is important to the successful operation of a company. If flawed products go out to the marketplace undetected, a company's reputation can quickly be destroyed. Because of the need to identify product flaws, nondestructive testing (NDT) is now a routine process in many industries.

Until recently, most companies had to be content with spotting flaws by visual inspection or physical stress tests of products. A visual inspection is effective only if the flaw is easily seen, and stress tests often destroy the object being tested. These two testing methods are being replaced in many companies by nondestructive testing.

NDT involves using x-rays, high frequency sound waves, or laser beams coupled with powerful microcomputers to inspect inside or beneath the surface of a product. NDT is used in a variety of ways. It is used to examine the interior of aircraft engines, check the condition of pressure valves, and monitor welds in pipelines, among other things.

One reason that NDT has grown in use has to do with the design of machines today. More and more machines are being designed to operate at levels close to the limits of physical tolerance.   If hidden flaws are not spotted in these machines, catastrophes could occur while the machines are in use.

Another reason for the increased use of NDT has to do with the use of untested new materials. New products can produce unanticipated problems and NDT can help identify possible problem areas. Some new ceramics currently on the market have created problems in quality control.

The ability to help differentiate between serious and minor flaws is an important part of nondestructive testing. It is important to find out about the size and shape of flaws in materials because some flaws are relatively harmless. Distinguishing between harmless and potentially dangerous flaws prevents needless waste of materials. A product that has a harmless minor flaw may at one time have been destroyed due to lack of adequate information about the nature of the flaw.

An ultrasonic scanning device is used by McDonnell Aircraft to inspect parts of the AV-8b Harrier jet. The computerized scanning device operates ten times faster than methods used in the past. It is also highly accurate in detecting either major or minor flaws.

Using computers to process signal data is a growing area of NDT. High-speed computers can process large volumes of infor-

mation that needs to be recorded, evaluated, and retrieved. In
one application, a nuclear reactor with over 2.5 million cubic
inches of metal is periodically checked for flaws by NDT techniques.

While several types of NDT tests are used in industry,
ultrasonics and radiography are the only two methods that can
detect flaws well below the surface of the object being tested.
Ultrasonic testing involves mounting transducers on the object
being tested. The sending transducer transmits a high-frequency
pulse which is reflected back to a receiving transducer when a
flaw is detected. The reflected pulse is sent to a receiving
amplifier which transmits the signal to a CRT screen for
display. The position of the reflected pulses on the CRT indicates the size and location of the flaw.

Radiography involves taking x-rays of an object. Radiation
passing through an object creates a two-dimensional image of the
object on film. Irregularities in the object being tested
appear as shadows on the film. Improvements in the x-ray process are producing more accurate results. Computers are used to
process the x-ray data that are collected. Some newer computerized systems produce images on a CRT screen and can even
follow movement in the tested object.

Computerized tomography (CT) has been used successfully in
the medical field for several years, and some people feel CT is
the next step in nondestructive testing. Tomography involves

reconstructing a two-dimensional cross section of an object. The cross-sectional image is created on a computer screen from information collected during multiple x-ray scans of an object. The x-rays are taken from different angles. The CT process produces high quality images from which more information can be derived than through normal x-ray techniques. Images reconstructed on the computer screen can also be manipulated by users. This capability allows detailed inspection of the object for tiny flaws.

Adapted from "Uncovering Hidden Flaws" by Carl Rain. <u>High Technology</u>, February 1984.

*Note: A transparency master is available for use with this lecture in your transparency packet that accompanies this textbook.

Suggestions For Discussion

1. Discuss the objects that affect our daily lives that may have undergone some form of nondestructive testing.

Some possible objects include: automobile tires, metal beams in bridges and buildings, airplanes, engine parts, and other machinery.

2. While nondestructive testing has grown in use in the past few years, the market for NDT systems has not increased as rapidly as systems like computer-aided design or computer-aided manufacturing. To what can you attribute the reluctance of some companies to implement NDT techniques?

Perhaps the biggest single reason is cost. Most manufacturers try to improve design techniques and produce cost-effective products, and NDT is expensive to implement.

The Evolution of Computers

LEARNING OBJECTIVES

Students should be able to:

- Outline the historical development of the computer from the abacus to the present
- Know the characteristics of first-, second-, and third-generation computers and their uses
- Discuss basic design features of computers

OUTLINE

I. Early Development: People have always needed to keep track of information throughout history; the concept of the computer developed over several centuries.

    A. One of the earliest computational devices was the abacus.

    B. John Napier and, later, Robert Bissaker, are two mathematicians who developed crude but effective manual calculators to help them work with logrithms.

    C. Blaise Pascal invented a mechanical adding machine in 1642. Gottfried von Leibnitz added multiplication, division, and square root capabilities 50 years later.

    D. The first use of punched cards was in the early 19th century when an automated loom was invented to speed up the weaving process.

E. Charles Babbage, the "father of the computer," invented
    the difference engine in 1812. Later he conceived the
    idea of a machine that could perform any calculation.
    The machine, called the analytical engine, contained
    many features similar to those found in today's com-
    puters.

F. Herman Hollerith used the punched card in a device that
    coded and sorted data for the 1890 census.

G. Further developments:

    1. Mark I, an electromechanical computer, was the
        first automatic calculator.
    2. The ENIAC was the first electronic computer.
    3. The EDSAC was the first stored-program computer.

II. First Generation--1951 through 1958: Began with the intro-
     duction of the first commercial electronic computer, the
     UNIVAC I. During this time, a few private businesses set
     up computers for their own purposes.

A. Vacuum tubes controlled internal operations; storage
    capacity was limited; punched cards were used for I/O
    operations.

B. First-generation computers were originally programmed
    in machine language.

    1. Machine language consists of a series of zeroes and
        ones representing a code specifying the electrical
        states of the computer's two-state internal cir-
        cuits and memory.
    2. Coding a program in machine language is extremely
        time-consuming.

C. Symbolic languages were developed so that programming
    would be more user-oriented; instructions were coded
    with symbolic names (mnemonics) rather than strings of
    zeroes and ones.

    1. To use symbolic codes, a method had to be found to
        translate the symbolic instructions into the
        machine code that the computer understood.
    2. Dr. Grace Hopper developed the first set of
        programs that could tell the computer how to
        translate mnemonic symbols into machine code.

III. Second Generation--1959 through 1964

A.   The development of transistors and their subsequent replacement of vacuum tubes resulted in computers that were smaller, more reliable, and faster.

B.   Storage capacity was significantly increased.

1.   Magnetic cores replaced magnetic drums as the primary medium of internal storage.
2   Magnetic tape began to be substituted for punched cards as auxiliary storage, thereby increasing input/output (I/O) processing speeds.

C.   Other significant changes were the development of disk storage, modular hardware, and improved I/O devices.

1.   Disks, which are similar to phonograph records, provide direct access to records in a file.
2.   The modular hardware concept involves design of electronic circuits in blocks, or modules, so that complete modules can be replaced in case of malfunction, or new modules can be added to expand capabilities.
3.   Improvements in I/O devices allowed them to be connected directly to the computer (online), without lowering the overall efficiency of the computer system.

D.   Second-generation computers were programmed in high-level languages which have a closer resemblance to English.

1.   These languages were standardized to be machine-independent and application- and problem-oriented.
2.   FORTRAN IV has been used for scientific purposes; COBOL, for business applications.

E.   Batch processing was used at this time. Data was collected over a period of time, put into a specific order, and input read into the computer in a group.

IV. Third Generation--1965 through 1971: IBM caused this transition when they introduced the versatile series of System/360 computers. Soon after, other companies followed suit.

A.   The development of integrated circuits and their subsequent replacement of transistors resulted in computers that were, once again, faster and less expensive.

B. Many hardware manufacturers began to provide operating systems with the computers they sold.

C. The software industry was born.

D. Other technological improvements:

    1. Increased storage capacity
    2. Operating-system software that automates many tasks previously handled by human operators
    3. Greater compatibility of components
    4. Use of communication channels providing remote I/O capabilities
    5. Ability to perform several operations simultaneously
    6. Capability to handle both scientific and business applications
    7. Use of remote terminals to communicate directly with a central computer
    8. Time-sharing capability in which many users are able to interact with the computer at the same time
    9. More sophisticated use of FORTRAN and COBOL for programming

V. Fourth Generation--1971 through ??: IBM once again paves the way for the transition to a new generation with its IBM System/370 Series.

    A. Large-scale integrated (LSI) circuit technology allows circuits containing thousands of transistors to be densely packed on a single silicon chip. As a result, today's computers have vastly enlarged storage capacity; they are miniaturized, speedier and highly reliable.

    B. Other technological improvements:

        1. Greater ease of use--"user friendly"
        2. Communication linkage capabilities, such as telephones
        3. Use of TV-like display screens
        4. Specialized equipment to capture data in machine-readable form at point of origin, (MICR, OCR, POS terminals)

    C. Microprocessors and microcomputers are becoming increasingly prevalant in private homes.

VI. An Historical Review of the Computer Industry

A. Mainframe computers

   1. Major competitors in this, the oldest, sector of
       the computer industry include IBM, Burroughs, DEC,
       CDC, and Amdahl.
   2. Appeal is to potential users of large, sophisti-
       cated computers.
   3. Huge capital investment is required to enter the
       market.
   4. Mainframe market is becoming saturated, because
       most companies that require the processing capabil-
       ities of large computers have had them for some
       time. Also, some companies are finding it more
       economical to purchase small computer systems.

B. Minicomputers

   1. Minicomputers were initially developed for specific
       applications such as process control and engi-
       neering calculations.
   2. The growth in minicomputer applications has led to
       the concept of distributed processing.
   3. Applications of minicomputers include time-sharing,
       numerical control of machine tools, industrial
       automation, and word processing.
   4. The minicomputer's popularity is due to its
       flexibility and its ability to be enlarged to meet
       the needs of growing organizations.
   5. The minicomputer industry has been growing at an
       annual rate of 35 to 40 percent; however, recently
       its growth rate has declined and may stabilize.

C. Microcomputers

   1. The rapid development of the microcomputer industry
       can be attributed to many ingenious and intriguing
       individuals.

       a. John Roach - Radio Shack and Tandy Corporation
       b. Jack Tramiel - Commodore PET
       c. Steven Jobs and Stephen Wozniak - Apple
           Computer Company
       d. Carole Ely and Lore Harp - Vector Graphics, Inc.
       e. Adam Osborne - Osborne Computer Corporation

   2. Nearly 200 manufacturers have entered the microcom-
       puter market where it is estimated that sales will
       reach $28 million for 1987.

3.   The microcomputer market is becoming increasingly competitive with the entrance of large corporations such as IBM.

ANSWERS TO REVIEW QUESTIONS

1.   The machine invented by Pascal and Leibnitz could perform only calculations. Not only can computers perform calculations, but they also can compare, store, and retrieve data. Computers also accomplish these operations much faster.

2.   Jacquard developed the concept of programmable instructions for machines. He used punched cards to provide instructions which were, in turn, "read" by the machine.

3.   Babbage developed the idea of an analytical engine which was too advanced for its time; the required parts could not be manufactured to produce it.

4.   The Mark I was the first automatic calculator. The Mark I was electromechanical--it used electromagnetic relays and mechanical counters. First-generation computers used vacuum tubes.

5.   See Table 201 in text.

	FIRST	SECOND	THIRD
STRUCTURE:	vacuum tubes	transistors	integrated circuits
INTERNAL STORAGE:	magnetic drum	magnetic core	magnetic core and solid-state

6.   LSI is a technological process that allows thousands of transistors to be densely packed on a single silicon chip. LSI has made computers much smaller, much faster, and has vastly increased their storage capacity, all at lower cost.

7.   Software developments in the second and third generation included:

   o versatile programs that automated many tasks previously handled by human operators
   o specialized programs for business and scientific applications
   o prewritten software packages that could be purchased from vendors and used immediately

Improvements in software were needed because in the early generations software packages were seldom reliable. In addition, third-generation computers had a different architecture (internal design) from second-generation computers so programs had to be rewritten.

8.   Jack Tramiel's strategy was to sell "to the masses, not the classes." Commodore introduced its new computer to the general public at an electronics show in 1977 without knowing specifically what the computer could be used for. The demand was so great that people were told to send their money in so that they could be placed on a waiting list for a computer. This strategy of selling to the general public was successful with over $3 million in orders for received in one month.

9.   Radio Shack was the first company to sell microcomputers through retail stores.

10.   After the large corporations entered the microcomputer market it has become extremely competitive. Smaller firms have been forced to declare bankruptcy. The companies with the lowest manufacturing costs or the greatest marketing strength are likely to succeed.

ADDITIONAL REVIEW QUESTIONS

1.   Discuss the limitations of punched-card devices.

2.   Name the first electronic digital computer and discuss its features.

3.   What are some of the advantages of second-generation computers in relation to first-generation? Third-generation in relation to second-generation?

4.   Why was the transition from second- to third-generation computers difficult? What made the transition to fourth-generation computers?

5.   Where do computers go from here? Discuss what you think will be some innovations in the fifth-generation of computers.

ANSWERS TO DISCUSSION POINTS

1.   Under the Whirlwind I Project, a scientific calculator called the NAREC was developed in 1952. Both the NAREC and the NORC typified first-generation computers. Both had internal storage capabilities consisting of electrostatic tubes and aux- iliary storage on magnetic drums.

2.   The main characteristic of third-generation computers that allowed them to be used in advanced applications (such as aircraft and weaponry control) was solid-state integrated cir- cuits. They reduced the size, increased the speed and reliabil- ity of computers, and combined with more sophisticated software, made artificial intelligence possible.

ADDITIONAL DISCUSSION POINTS

1.   What type of innovative concepts is the Office of Navy Research looking for?

2.   What technical areas has this search led them into?

ANSWER KEY TO STUDY GUIDE

True/False

2. F   4. T   6. F   8. T   10. F

Matching

2. f   4. b   6. g   8. c   10. a

Short Answer

2.   Third-generation computers required new operating systems. But the development of an operating system to accompany the IBM System/360 took several years to perfect. Because of the overwhelming need for reliable software, firms spe- cializing in the development of software began marketing software pacakges.

4.   ● transistors
      ● magnetic core memory
      ● faster input/output
      ● high-level programming languages

6. - introduction of microprocessors and microcomputers
    - sophisticated programs for special applications
    - versatility of input/output devices
    - increased storage capacity and speed

8. - flexible
    - can be plugged into standard outlets
    - do not require special facilities (air conditioning and water cooling)
    - can be enlarged to meet the needs of growing organizations.

10. - huge size
    - limited internal storage capacity
    - had to be programmed in machine language
    - unreliable due to breakdowns caused by excessive heat

ENRICHMENT LECTURE

William Shockley and the Transistor

Computers developed during the 1940s used mechanical relays that created a deafening clatter when the switches opened and closed. During the first generation of computers, vacuum tubes replaced mechanical relays and reduced the noise level, but the tubes generated so much heat that equipment malfunctions became commonplace. It took the inventive genius of William Shockley to help the development of computers take a giant step forward with the development of transistors.

William Shockley earned a doctorate in physics at MIT in 1936. Shortly after, he was hired to work as a physicist at Bell Labs in Murray Hill, New Jersey. Shockleys' main area of interest at Bell involved semiconductor research and studying the effect of impurities in semiconductor crystals. Semi-conductor crystals were capable of acting as a one-way conductor for electrical current. Shockley believed that the impurities, though present in only trace amounts, contained extra electrons that were needed to carry electrical currents. With the approval of Bell, Shockley assembled a research team whose focus was to study the impurities concept. Shockley's goal was to create a solid-state amplifier. Walter Brattain and John Bardeen were persuaded by Shockley to join in the research effort.

At first the team made no progress. Purdue University was conducting similar research and the Bell team observed the work at Purdue. Finally, Bardeen made a breakthrough. He discovered an inhibiting effect on the surface of the crystal that interfered with the flow of electrical current. An experiment performed by Brattain proved that the Bardeen theory was correct. The experiment took place two days before Christmas in 1947, the date attributed to the birth of transistors.

The transistor is sometimes referred to as "the invention of the century"--and it is no wonder! Transistors were smaller, faster, and more reliable than vacuum tubes. They generated little heat, and did not require massive air-conditioning systems. They truly revolutionized the development of computers. In spite of all the positive aspects of transistors, they did not receive much attention until Shockley, Bardeen, and Brattain received the Nobel Prize in 1956.

Shockley eventually left Bell Labs to set up his own semi conductor laboratory at the Beckman Institute. His lab is con sidered to be the first "Silicon Valley" company, and Shockley is known as the father of solid state electronics.

Adapted from "Fire in the Valley" by Paul Freiberger and Michael Swaine. _Popular Computing_, September 1984, and from an excerpt from _Introduction to Computers_ by Fred G. Harold.

*Note: A transparency master is available for use with this lecture in your transparency packet that accompanies this textbook.

Suggestions For Discussion

1. Discuss reasons why you think the development of the transistor did not reach widespread use until the late 1950s.

Possible reasons include: lack of publicity prior to Shockley's research team winning the Nobel Prize and the slow evolution of thought that often accompanies new scientific developments.

2. The development of transistors came primarily from efforts funded by Bell Labs. Do you think that the private sector can continue to finance the research necessary to continue future technological developments?

Answers will based on personal opinion, but students should be able to support their opinions.

Hardware

LEARNING OBJECTIVES

Students should be able to:

- Describe the components of a computer system and their functions
- Explain how instructions are stored and processed by the computer
- Identify the different types of internal memory and the advantages and disadvantages of each
- Explain how data is represented to permit communication with the computer
- Describe various classifications of computer systems

OUTLINE

I.   The Central Processing Unit: The CPU, also known as the "main frame" on large systems, is the heart of the computer system. It is composed of three sections: control unit, arithmetic/logic unit (ALU), and primary storage.

    A.   The control unit directs the sequence of operations (controls activity) in the CPU.

    B.   The ALU performs arithmetic computations and logical operations (comparisons).

C.   The primary storage unit (internal storage, memory, or main storage) holds all instructions and data necessary for processing.

II.   Instructions: Obtaining an overall perspective of the functions of each computer system component involves understanding the instruction and data flow through a computer system.

A.   Each computer instruction has two basic parts: (1) the OP code tells the control unit which operation to perform; and (2) the operand indicates the storage location of the data to be operated on.

B.   The next-sequential-instruction feature requires that the program instructions be placed in consecutive locations in memory.

C.   In the execution of a program, instructions and data are held in primary storage. The control unit reads each instruction to manipulate the particular data items specified.

III.   Stored-Program Concept: In order to increase processing speeds and efficiency, the stored program was developed; instructions were stored in the computer's main memory in electronic form.

A.   In early computers, instructions were:

1.   Wired on control panels and plugged into the computer at the beginning of a job, or
2.   Read into the computer from punched cards in discrete steps as the job progressed.

B.   The basic characteristic of memory, which allows instructions to be used over and over again, is non-destructive read/destructive write.

IV.   Storage: In order for the control unit to direct processing operations, it must be able to locate each program instruction and data item in storage.

A.   By assigning each location in storage a unique address, items can be located when needed by the stored-program instructions.

1.   Variables are meaningful names assigned by the programmer to keep track of data storage locations.

2.   While the variable name itself does not change, the data stored may.

B.   Primary storage is all storage considered part of the CPU (in contrast with secondary or auxiliary storage); it is composed of magnetic cores, semiconductors, or bubble memory.

   1.   Each magnetic core (tiny iron-alloy ring) can store one binary digit (bit) by being magnetized as an "on" or "off" state.

      a.   The combination of two half-currents at a core results in magnetization of that core but leaves others unaffected.
      b.   A sense wire reads the core to see whether it represents a 0 bit or a 1 bit.
      c.   Because sensing a core sets it to zero, an inhibit wire is used to return the core to its original state so that nondestructive read is possible.

   2.   A single semiconductor (circuitry on a silicon chip) may hold as much data as thousands of cores and processing is faster.

      a.   Semiconductor memory does not need to be restored after it has been read.
      b.   Two disadvantages of semiconductor memory are that it requires a constant power source and it is more expensive than cores.

   3.   Bubble memory consists of magnetized spots (magnetic domains) resting on a thin film of semi-conductor material.

      a.   Bubble memory retains its magnetism indefi-nitely; more data can be stored in a smaller space.
      b.   High costs and difficulty of production have been the factors limiting user acceptance.

C.   Read only memory (ROM) consists of complex calculation capabilities which are built into the computer hard-ware.

   1.   The only method of changing the contents of ROM is by altering the physical construction of the hard-ware circuits.

      2.   Microprograms are optional programs that a manufac-
           turer builds into a computer to meet the needs of
           the user.
      3.   Programmable read-only memory (PROM) can be
           programmed through conventional methods but then
           becomes unalterable.

  D. Registers are temporary storage areas in the CPU that
      facilitate the execution of programs.

      1.   They receive information, hold it, and transfer it
           quickly as directed by the control unit.
      2.   There are different types of registers, and they
           perform specific functions: accumulator, storage,
           instruction, address, and general-purpose.

V. Data Representation: In order to use computers, it is
    necessary to convert human symbols into a form the computer
    can "understand."

  A. Data is represented by the presence or absence of
      electrical signals in the circuitry of the machine.
      Only two states exist--a signal is either "on" or
      "off"; this is known as the binary system. The use of
      this system to represent data is called binary repre-
      sentation.

      1.   The binary system uses 1s and 0s in different com-
           binations to represent numbers.
      2.   Each digit in a binary number is called a bit
           (binary digit).
      3.   A bit is "on" if it contains a 1 and "off" if it
           contains a 0.

  B. The binary (base 2) number system operates in a manner
      similar to our decimal number system. Whereas each
      digit position in a decimal number represents a power
      of 10, each position in a binary number represents a
      power of 2.

  C. The octal number system in which each digit position
      represents a power of 8 is used by some computers.

  D. Some computers use hexadecimal representation (base 16)
      because:

      1.   The conversion from binary to hexadecimal is much
           easier and faster than conversion from binary to
           decimal.

2. Hexadecimal code is much easier to read than binary.
3. Significant savings of both paper and time are possible by printing the contents of storage (dump) in hexadecimal representation instead of binary.

E. There are numerous computer codes to represent numbers, letters, and special characters.

1. The 4-bit BCD (binary coded decimal) is used only for representing numbers.
2. The 6-bit BCD has zone bits and numeric bits and is used for representing letters, numbers, and special characters.
3. The 8-bit EBCDIC (Extended Binary Coded Decimal Interchange Code) has 256 different possible bit configurations to represent numbers, letters, and special characters.
4. ASCII (American Standard Code for Information Interchange) and ASCII-8 can be used to represent alphabetic, numeric, or special characters.
5. In the computers that use 8-bit codes (EBCDIC or ASCII-8), one alphabetic character or two numeric characters are represented by one byte.

   a. A fixed number of adjacent bits operated on as a unit is called a byte.
   b. Bytes then become the basic units of memory in these computers.

F. Computers have a self-checking technique to detect miscoding of characers in internal operations.

1. They use an extra bit (parity or check bit) for detecting lost data. Characters are written in either odd or even parity so that the internal circuitry can monitor whether or not a bit has been lost.
2. The use of a parity, or check, bit can only detect the miscoding of characters. It cannot detect the use of incorrect data.

VI. Classifications of Computer Systems

A. Digital and analog computers

1. The digital computer operates directly on decimal digits representing numbers, letters, and special characters.

2.   Analog computers measure continuous physical or electrical magnitudes such as pressure, tempera-ture, current, voltage, length, or shaft rotations.

B.   At the heart of a large-scale computer system is the mainframe.

1.   A mainframe processes very large amounts of data at very high speeds.
2.   Mainframes are used by corporations and organiza-tions that require extensive data processing capa-bility.
3.   Supercomputers, or maxicomputers, have been devel-oped for those corporations and organizations where the need for large data bases and complex calculation capabilities justify their relatively high cost.

C.   Minicomputers

1.   Initially minicomputers were generally less power-ful than mainframes.
2.   Advances in technology have moved minicomputers closer to mainframes in terms of capability, memory size, and overall processing power.
3.   Current minicomputers are more powerful than the mainframes of 10 years ago.

D.   Microcomputers

1.   They first appeared in 1975 and were used by hobby-oriented engineers and technical buffs.
2.   Today a microcomputer can be purchased for the home for $100 to $5,000.

ANSWERS TO REVIEW QUESTIONS

1.   See Figure 3-1 in text. The primary storage unit, also known as internal memory, holds instructions, data, and results during processing.

The control unit is the section of the CPU that directs the sequence of operations by electrical signals and governs the actions of the various units that make up the computer.

The arithmetic/logic unit is the section that handles arithmetic computations and logical operations.

2.   A stored program is a set of instructions needed to manipulate data that is stored or held in the internal memory of the computer. The same instructions can be executed over and over without human intervention, thereby increasing the speed of the operation.

3.   Semiconductor memory and bubble memory are technological developments in storage media. These developments decrease the amount of space needed while increasing the processing speed.

4.   ROM is a part of the hardware that allows items to be stored in a form that can be changed only by altering the circuits of the computer. Microprograms are sequences of instructions built into ROM to perform functions that would otherwise be performed by program instructions at a slower speed.

5.   Computer coding schemes are necessary to convert human symbols into a form that the computer can understand.

The 6-bit BCD code can be used to represent only upper-case letters of the alphabet and special characters allowing for 64 unique bit combinations. The EBCDIC code can be used to represent both upper- and lower-case letters plus additional special characters, allowing for 256 possible bit combinations.

6.   Data is represented in the computer by the presence or absence of electrical signals in the circuitry of the machine. Only two possible states exist, as is the case with the binary number system.

Hexadecimal notation can be used to represent binary data in concise form. Hexadecimal numbers are converted to decimal numbers in the same manner as binary numbers are converted.

The octal system is in base 8 whereas the hexadecimal system is in base 16. Both octal and hexadecimal systems are easily converted into a binary representation because 8 is equal to 2^3 and 16 is equal to 2^4.

7.   The next-sequential-instruction feature places instructions that make up a program in consecutive locations in memory because they have to be processes sequentially.

8.   The first four binary place values (from right to left) sum to 15, the highest single digit value in the hexadecimal number system. Four binary digits can be represented by one hexadecimal digit

9. binary to hexadecimal
00110111

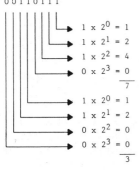

hexadecimal to decimal
3 7

binary	hexadecimal	decimal
00110111	37	55

10. binary to octal
1 01100101

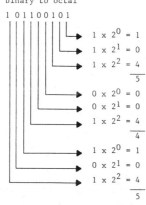

octal to decimal
5 4 5

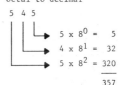

binary	octal	decimal
101100101	545	357

11.   Code check is used to detect where an error has occurred and to isolate the location of the error. Code check can only detect the miscoding of characters; it cannot detect the use of incorrect data.

12.   An analog computer measures continuous electrical or
physical magnitudes. (Examples: a gasoline pump or a car
speedometer). A digital computer operates on distinct data by
performing arithmetic and logical processes on the data.
(Examples include computers used in business, such as an IBM 360
or 370.)

ADDITIONAL REVIEW QUESTIONS

1.   What enables the CPU to locate each program instruction and
data item in storage?

2.   What is a register and where is it located?

3.   What is a bit? "Bit" is an abbreviation for what?

ANSWERS TO DISCUSSION POINTS

1.   Computers that are manufactured with similar characteristics, such as a common data format, a common instruction
set, and the capability of running the same high-level software,
are usually grouped as a family. The family members differ
from each other in terms of the range of available memory, the
number of input/output channels, the execution speed of the computer, and the types of devices that can be interfaced to it.

2.   Hardware considerations are:

- types and number of peripherals that can be used
- amount of internal memory
- execution speed
- software availability
- cost of hardware
- availability of maintenance repairs
- ROM
- registers present

These considerations will affect:

- forms of input and output
- amount of processing
- speed of processing
- cost justification
- reliability

ADDITIONAL DISCUSSION POINTS

1.   Discuss some features that will be available on the IBM 370 computer.

2.   What factors will influence the type of computers that IBM will market in the future?

ANSWER KEY TO STUDY GUIDE

True/False

2. T   4. T   6. F   8. F   10. T

Matching

2. d   4. f   6. i   8. a   10. b

Short Answer

2.   Once a copy of instructions have been stored they remain in
     storage until new ones are stored over them. It is
     possible to execute the same instructions over and over
     again until the instructions are changed.

4.   Even parity means an even number of 1-bits are used to
     represent each character. Odd parity means an odd number
     of 1-bits are used to represent each character.

6.   ASCII stands for American Standard Code for Information
     Interchange, and it is a 7-bit code developed to standard-
     ize code for all computers.

8.   The ALU performs arithmetic computations and logical opera-
     tions. Since the bulk of internal processing involves
     calculations or comparison, the capabilities of a computer
     often depend upon the design and capabilities of the ALU.

10. Primary storage comprises all storage considered part of
     the CPU. It may be supplemented by secondary storage which
     is separate from the CPU.

ENRICHMENT LECTURE

Supercomputers

The United States has led the world in developing computer technology. Each generation of computers surpassed the preceding generation in technological innovation, and the United States consistently remained ahead of all other countries in producing the newest, fastest, most powerful computers. The new machines were often called "supercomputers" and they were developed and built almost exclusively in the United States. But the days of the U.S. as a world leader in computer technology may be numbered. Other countries have entered the computer development business, and they are giving the United States stiff competition. The toughest competitor in the field of supercomputers is Japan, and the competition has created shock waves in the United States government.

The question, then, is why the concern over Japan's progress in supercomputer development? The answer is that while supercomputers account for a limited share of the total dollars spent in the computer market, they do represent the most advanced computer technology of our time. The computer industry changes very quickly, and new technology is rapidly absorbed into the mainstream of the computer industry. So, the country

that leads in supercomputer technology tends to have the most

powerful computers on other levels, too.

Supercomputers can also perform jobs that cannot be done by

other computers. The super machines can process millions of

operations in one second, and they are expected to soon reach a

performance level of one billion operations per second! This

lightning-fast operation speed makes it possible for supercom-

puters to run programs that are too complex for smaller com-

puters.

The rapid processing speed also makes the computers par-

ticularly well suited for use in nuclear weapons development,

weather forecasting, aerodynamic design, and scientific

research. All of these fields require the processing of massive

amounts of information. The country that has the fastest super-

computers has an edge over other countries in several signifi-

cant areas. Many people feel that if the United States falls

behind in supercomputer technology, it will fall behind as a

world leader in weapons development.

To prevent this situation from occurring, several things

are taking place. Government agencies are sponsoring renewed

efforts in supercomputer research. Universities are being

encouraged by the government to continue research in super tech-

nology. And the three manufacturers of supercomputers in the

United States, Cray, ETA Systems, and Denelcor, are planning new supercomputers that will surpass the power and speed of the current ones.

Despite these cooperative efforts, there are problems. Universities in the United States have not kept pace with universities in other countries in purchasing the powerful machines. As a result, research efforts have not kept pace with that of other countries, and students have not had many opportunities to work with supercomputers. Only three schools in the United States have purchased class VI machines. Class VI machines are the most advanced supercomputers available on the market today.

Because there are so few supercomputers on campuses, training in the operation of the machines has not kept pace with the demand. The United States is simply not producing enough professionals who know how to work with these machines. Even if the U.S. does pull forward in technological advances, there may not be enough people to staff the next generation of machines.

Another problem facing U.S. universities is money. The super machines are very expensive to buy and operate. Access charges to operate the computers may run as high as $2,000 to $3,000 an hour. Few universities have the funds to support operating costs that high.

In Japan, the government subsidizes access fees, so charges may be as low as $60 an hour. The National Science Foundation recommended that Congress appropriate $520 million to help ten universities purchase supercomputers and establish nationwide access networks. But for the time being, many researchers cannot afford to use the existing computers. Most university supercomputers are underused. The University of Colorado owns a supercomputer that runs only 20-30 percent of the time.

Without continued cooperative efforts by government, industry, and universities, the United States will surely lose the race for technological superiority.

Adapted from "SuperComputers: A Strange Imperative?" by Dwight B. Davis. <u>High Technology</u>, May 1984.

*Note: A transparency master is available for use with this lecture in your transparency packet that accompanies this textbook.

Suggestions For Discussion

1. Do you feel the United States is really threatened as a world leader if it falls behind in the race for supercomputer technology?

This calls for an opinion, but students should be able to support their answers.

2. Discuss ways other than government funding that might help ease the tremendous financial burden associated with purchasing and operating a supercomputer.

Some creative thinking is required here, but suggestions might include donations from industry and private foundations.

Input and Output

LEARNING OBJECTIVES

Students should be able to:

- Explain how data is represented on punched cards
- Describe key-to-tape and key-to-disk data-entry systems and their advantages
- Discuss how magnetic-ink character recognition is used
- Explain how different optical-character recognition equipment functions and for what each is used
- Describe the different types of remote terminals and their applications
- Describe the two major types of printers and the various methods used to produce hard copy
- Describe three types of special-purpose output devices

OUTLINE

I.   Data Input

    A.   Punched cards were one of the earliest forms of com-
        puter input. Data must first be punched on the cards,
        then converted by the computer into electrical
        impulses.

        1.   The standard card has 80 vertical columns and 12
            horizontal rows.
        2.   The horizontal rows are divided into three sec-
            tions:

       a.   The lower 10 rows, numbered 0 through 9, are
           digit rows.

       b.   The upper 3 rows, numbered 12, 11, and 0, are
           zone rows. Combined with digit punches, they
           can represent alphabetic and special charac-
           ters.

       c.   The print zone at the top of the card displays
           the represented characters in human-readable
           form.

   3.   Ideally, each card should be a complete record.

   4.   An IBM 96-column card uses a coding scheme similar
       to the 6-bit BCD system.

B.   Key-to-tape, key-to-disk, and key-to-diskette systems
are reusable, faster and more efficient than cards.

   1.   Key-to-tape magnetizes spots on tape in reels,
       cassettes, or cartridges. It uses hardware for
       verification and editing of input.

   2.   Key-to-disk uses a minicomputer to store and edit
       the input before it is transferred to disk.

   3.   Key-to-diskette uses a floppy disk and a keyboard
       with a screen.

   4.   These systems offer several advantages over tradi-
       tional punched-card input systems:

       a.   Errors are easily corrected.

       b.   Magnetic tapes, disks, and diskettes are
           reusable.

       c.   Since key-entry devices are electronic rather
           than mechanical, they are quieter and operators
           can transcribe data faster.

       d.   Record lengths are not limited to 80 columns.

       e.   Storage on tape or disk is more compact than
           card storage.

   5.   Their chief disadvantage is high cost.

C.   Source-data automation: The purpose of source-data
automation is to collect data about an event in
computer-readable form when and where the event takes
place; this greatly improves speed, accuracy, and efficiency of EDP.

   1.   Magnetic-ink characters, formed by using magnetized
       particles of iron oxide, are both human- and
       machine-readable.

a. Characters can be read and converted into machine code by magnetic-ink character recognition (MICR) devices.

b. The processing of bank checks is a typical application of MICR.

2. Optical-recognition devices read marks or symbols coded on paper and convert them into electrical impulses that can be transmitted directly to the CPU, or stored on tape or punched cards.

a. Optical-mark recognition (OMR) is often used in multiple-choice exams, surveys and question-naires, and order writing.

b. The bar-code reader can read special lines, or bars, representing data by the width of the bars and the distance between them; the most familiar is the universal product code (UPC) found on grocery items.

c. In optical-character recognition (OCR), electronic scanners read numbers, letters, and other characters and convert the images into machine code.

3. Remote terminals are used to collect data at their source and transmit them to a central computer for processing; usually transmission is by telecommunication equipment.

a. Remote terminals that perform the functions of a cash register and capture all sales data are point-of-sale (POS) terminals. They gather and provide both sales and inventory information.

b. Touch-tone devices are used with telephone lines for transferring data from remote locations.

D. Specialized Input Devices

1. Voice-recognition devices require a user to "train" the computer to understand his or her voice patterns. They are 99 percent accurate for low-volume, formal data entry.

2. Intelligent terminals have the same kinds of components as a full-size computer but have limited storage; there is a limited number of instructions they can perform. They can be programmed using stored-program instructions.

3. Touch-sensitive screens permit the screen itself to
    serve as input device; this eliminates a con-
    siderable amount of typing.
4. Electronic drawing pens and light pens contain a
    photoelectric cell; when the cell is placed on the
    terminal screen, the computer identifies the x and
    y coordinates.
5. Digitizers are used to transform two- or three-
    dimensional drawings into images on the display
    screen.

II. Information Output

A. Printers: Printers produce processed data in a form
    readable by the user--hard copy; there are two types of
    printers: impact and nonimpact.

1. Impact printers press printing elements against
    paper to produce an image. Printer-keyboards,
    wire-matrix, and daisy-wheel printers are
    character-at-a-time devices. Print-wheel, chain,
    and drum printers are line-at-a-time devices.

    a. A printer-keyboard is similar to an office
        typewriter except that a stored program, rather
        than a person, controls the character-at-a-time
        printing.
    b. A wire-matrix printing element is a rectangle
        composed of pins that can be activated in
        various combinations to print dots representing
        special characters, letters, and numbers, one
        at a time.
    c. A daisy-wheel printer also looks like an office
        typewriter. It has a flat disk with petal-
        like projections that produces high-quality,
        one-character-at-a-time print.
    d. A print-wheel printer contains 120 wheels, each
        containing 48 characters. Each wheel rotates
        until the desired character is in position,
        then an entire line is printed at once.
    e. A chain printer consists of a horizontally
        rotating chain of type characters. It prints
        when a hammer (one for each column on the
        paper) behind the paper forces it against an
        ink ribbon and the appropriate characters on
        the chain.

        f.   A drum printer consists of a metal cylinder that contains rows of characters engraved across its surface; one line of print is produced with each rotation of the drum.

  2. Nonimpact printers are generally faster, have a wide variety of type faces available, and produce cheaper copy than impact printers.

        a.   An electrostatic printer uses electromagnetic impulses and ink to form characters, then melts them onto the page.
        b.   An electrothermal printer uses heat sensitive paper and heated rods to form characters.
        c.   An ink-jet printer uses a stream of charged ink to form dot-matrix characters.
        d.   A laser printer uses laser beams and electrophotographic technology to create images on paper.
        e.   A xerographic printer uses printing methods similar to those used in common xerographic copying machines.

B. Visual display terminals: Visual display terminals use CRTs similar to TV screens to display soft-copy output for inquiry/response or verification. Graphic-display devices can also display drawings and charts. A light-pen can alter pictures on the screen.

C. Specialized output devices

  1. Plotters produce hard copies of graphs and drawings as directed by the CPU. A plotter consists of a pen, movable carriage, drum, and chart-paper holder.
  2. Computer output microfilm (COM) consists of photographed images produced in miniature and stored on microfilm. COM stores large amounts of data compactly and provides easy accessibility.
  3. Voice synthesizers constitute the output portion of a computerized voice-communication system.

ANSWERS TO REVIEW QUESTIONS

1.   A field is a group of related characters on a punch card treated as a single unit of information; it is composed of a group of consecutive columns. Social security numbers, phone numbers, and gross annual income are examples of fields.

2.   Input records do not have to be limited to 80 characters or less. However, because the Hollerith card has an 80-column limitation per card, multiple cards are needed if more than 80 columns are needed. This slows processing, since punch-card machines are designed to work on one card at a time.

3.   The unit-record concept implies that all the necessary data about a transaction or event is contained on a single punched card. In other words, each card is a complete record.

4.   Advantages of key-to-tape, key-to-disk, and key-to-diskette devices:

- Errors can be corrected by backspacing and rekeying (magnetic tape and disks are reusable).
- They are quieter and faster.
- Longer record lengths are possible.
- Storage is more compact.

Disadvantages:

- They are more expensive.
- Data cannot be read from a tape with the human eye.

5.   Source-data automation refers to the collection of data at the point where the transaction occurs. Techniques such as MICR and OCR, vastly increase speed, accuracy, and efficientcy of EDP.

6.
- optical-mark recognition: Marks are made with a lead pencil in a particular location on a paper. The marks are sensed by the optical-mark page reader as the documents are automatically passed under a light source. As the documents are read, the data are translated into machine language. OMR can be used for order writing, surveys, questionnaires, tests, etc.
- bar-code reader: Data is represented by a bar code in which the widths of the bars and the distances between them vary. A scanner, or wand reader, reads the bar codes, which are then translated. Bar codes can be used in POS systems, for credit-card verification, and for freight identification to facilitate warehouse operations.

- optical-character recognition: Similar to OMR except
  that data is represented by character shapes instead of
  positions of marks. OCR can be used for billings and
  inventory-control applications.

7.   Visual display terminals are faster and quieter than printers and can be connected to a printer in such a way that only
specified data is printed, reducing paper waste. In addition,
they can display graphs and drawings, and permit alterations
made with a light pen.

8.   An intelligent terminal contains an internal processor that
can be programmed to perform specified functions. These terminals can accept data at their origin, can process data, and
can extend the power of the central computer. They are used for
editing or manipulating data before they get to the central computer. An example is a remote job-entry system or a key-to-disk
system that permits programs to edit input data upon entry.

9.   An impact printer forms characters when a printing element
strikes a ribbon and paper. A nonimpact printer forms images by
using methods other than mechanical printing; the ink-jet
printer, laser printer, and electrostatic printer are examples.

   Impact printers are more common because they were developed
first and can produce carbon copies. However, nonimpact printers are continually being refined; they are faster, cheaper and
offer a wider variety of type faces. As their technology
improves, they will become more popular than impact printers.

10.   Character-at-a-time printers print one character at a time
(examples are printer-keyboards, wire-matrix printers, and
daisy-wheel printers).

   Line-at-a-time printers can print an entire line of characters at one time (examples are print-wheel printers, drum printers, and chain printers).

11.   A POS system is a remote terminal that performs the functions of a cash register and also captures sales data. It has a
keyboard for data entry, a panel to display the price, a cash
drawer, and a printer that provides a cash receipt. Supermarkets use POS systems.

12.   The Universal Produce Code (UPC) contains information as to
the identity of the item and the identity of the manufacturer,
but not the price; each retailer likes to reserve the right to
price items.

ADDITIONAL REVIEW QUESTIONS

1.   The use of punched cards restricts record length to 80 characters. Are record lengths limited when magnetic tape or disks are used?

2.   Key-to-disk and key-to-tape systems are best suited for use with which size computer systems? Explain.

3.   Discuss the advantages of using source-data automation.

4.   What is the difference between OCR and OMR?

5.   What is meant by the term "soft-copy output?" Give an example of a peripheral device that produces soft-copy output.

6.   What is a plotter? What is the major difference between a plotter and a graphic-display device?

7.   Give examples of applications that may employ computer output microfilm.

8.   What are two types of nonimpact printers? How do these printers operate?

ANSWERS TO DISCUSSION POINTS

1.   If an invoice cannot be read by the TRACE capture system, the data from the rejected invoices is manually keyed into a file which is merged with the file from the successfully scanned invoices. If there were no way to handle invoices that were rejected due to misregistered printing, smudged ink, and hand-written documents, the company would fail to invoice (and thus receive no payment for) 9 to 10 percent of their total invoices.

2.   Because of Gulf Oil's large volume of data transactions, speed and accuracy of data capture techniques are very important. If customer billings and customer applications for credit are not timely and accurate, Gulf Oil risks the loss of customers and possible dealer dissatisfaction.

ADDITIONAL DISCUSSION POINTS

1.   Gulf uses computers to read information on the front of invoices, then record it on the back, in bar-code represen-

tation.   Are there any other ways the information could be
recorded?

2.   What are the functions of TRACE?

ANSWER KEY TO STUDY GUIDE

True/False

2. T   4. T   6. T   8. F   10. T

Matching

2. c   4. b   6. i   8. e   10. d

Short Answer

2.   Punched cards must be processed sequentially, which often
      requires considerable time for preliminary sorting. This
      reduces the overall effectiveness and speed of data proc-
      essing. A second disadvantage is that cards, since they
      are handled extensively by humans, can be lost, torn, or
      mutiliated during use.

4.   • dot-matrix printer
      • wire-matrix printer
      • daisy-wheel printer
      • print-wheel printer
      • drum printer
      • chain printer

6.   Each magnetic-ink character is composed of a unique com-
      bination of 0-bits and 1-bits that are formed using magnet-
      ized particles of iron oxide. The magnetic-ink character
      reader translates the pattern of the 0 and 1 bits into the
      character represented.

8.   Optical marks are read by passing the document under a
      light source. The marks reflect the light and the reader
      translates the optical-mark data into machine language.

10.   A touch-tone device is a remote terminal used with ordinary
      telephone lines to transfer data from remote locations to a
      central computer.

ENRICHMENT LECTURE

Voice Input

The idea of talking to a computer seemed like a fantasy more appropriate to a space movie than to the work environment until just a few years ago. Although voice technology research has taken giant strides forward, the work continues. The ability of humans to recognize and understand speech is far ahead of even the most sophisticated capabilities of any computer.

Voice technology is generally divided into two areas: speech synthesis (computers "talking" to people) and voice recognition or input (computers listening to and understanding humans). This discussion is limited to voice recognition or voice input.

Today, voice input is playing an important role in the data-entry process in the manufacturing industry. While computers have only partially automated the data-entry process, voice input is increasing productivity and reducing errors in some areas of manufacturing. It frees workers' hands and eyes, allowing them to continue their work uninterrupted.

Voice input is growing in use. Quality control, product testing, and materials handling are all areas that require on-the-spot data collection and entry.

Manufacturers use a variety of techniques to enter and collect data. The methods may range from manually collecting data to computerizing collection methods using devices like punched cards and electronic scanners. Whatever the method used, workers must devote time to entering the data by hand. This slows down productivity and increases the opportunity for errors. Voice input allows workers to input data by speaking. Hands and eyes are free to remain involved in whatever task is before the worker. Productivity remains high and the margin for error is low.

Although many manufacturers are using voice input in factories, research to perfect the technique is ongoing. Research on voice recognition is divided into three categories: speaker independence, larger vocabulary recognition and interpretation, and continuous speech recognition and interpretation.

Speaker independence involves the computer's ability to recognize words when they are spoken by different voices. Each voice has its own distinctive pattern unlike any other voice, just as each fingerprint has its own unique pattern. The trick is getting a computer to understand the voice of whomever is speaking. Currently, all computers in operation are speaker-dependent. This means that before any voice recognition occurs, the computer must be programmed to understand the voice of the individual speaker.   A company called Voice Control Systems is working on speaker-independent technology, but has no product on the market yet.

Speaker independence is only part of the problem.   Computers must be programmed to recognize a specific vocabulary.   A friend would understand that you were upset if you expressed your feelings by using the word "mad," "angry," or "enraged," but chances are a computer programmed to recognize a specific vocabulary would understand only one of the three words.   Most products on the market today recognize between 50 and 200 words. While that may be an impressive vocabulary for a toddler, most adults would be severely restricted in their ability to communicate with only 200 available words!

The third area of research involves continuous speech recognition and interpretation.   This refers to programming a computer to understand what a speaker is saying while the speaker is using a normal flow of speech--no unnatural or artificial pauses while speaking.   One of the most sophisticated products on the market has been designed for use with the IBM PC.   The product is a voice card, the VPC 2000, developed by Votan.   The VPC 2000 will allow the speaker to speak in a normal voice and will enable the computer to understand 75 words.   It is compatible with many application programs.

Adapted from "The Voice of the Future" PC Magazine, June 26, 1984 and "Voice Data Entry" by Michael McCallig. Production Engineering, July, 1984.

*Note: A transparency master is available for use with this lecture in your transparency packet that accompanies this textbook.

Suggestions For Discussion

1.   Discuss ways other than in manufacturing that voice input might be useful.

Suggestions might include: with the handicapped, with executives that do not have keyboarding skills, and anywhere that conventional input devices are used.

2.   Discuss some of the problems that could arise if workers were forced to use an unnatural manner of speech with a voice input system.

Possible problems might include: worker annoyance with the system causing a decrease in productivity, or user rejection of the system, especially when forced to use the system for long periods of time.

Storage Devices

LEARNING OBJECTIVES

Students should be able to:

- Differentiate between primary and secondary storage
- Identify the characteristics, differences, and applications of sequential-access and direct-access storage
- Describe direct-access and sequential-access storage media and list advantages and disadvantages of each
- Discuss the capabilities of mass storage devices
- List some future trends in data storage

OUTLINE

I. Classification of Storage Media: A computer system contains two types of storage--primary and secondary.

    A. Primary storage, which is part of the CPU, stores both data and instructions.

    B. Secondary storage is not part of the CPU, but is used to store large amounts of data at a lower cost.

        1. The most common media are magnetic tapes and disks; media such as mass storage and magnetic drums are also used.
        2. Data in secondary storage can be accessed either directly or sequentially.

II. Sequential-Access Storage: Storage media such as magnetic
     tape and cassette tape must be read sequentially until the
     desired data is located.

     A. Magnetic tape stores data by magnetizing small spots of
         the iron oxide coating on the tape.

         1. A typical tape reel of 2,400 feet can store the
             equivalent of 400,000 punched cards.
         2. An electromagnetic head can detect or magnetize
             bits on the tape in order to read or write as
             required.
         3. Reading and writing on magnetic tape requires that
             it move past the read/write head at a constant
             speed; this is facilitated by interrecord gaps
             (IRGs) and interblock gaps (IBGs).

     B. Magnetic cartridges or cassettes provide a low-cost,
         convenient alternative to regular tape for systems
         requiring less storage.

     C. Advantages of magnetic tape and cassettes:

         ● Data transfer speeds are fast.
         ● Tapes can be erased and reused.
         ● It is perfectly suited for sequential processing.
         ● Tape can store large amounts of data at relatively
           low cost.

         Disadvantages:

         ● Since it is a sequential medium, the entire tape must
           be read to update--it cannot be used for instan-
           taneous retrieval.
         ● Data is not in human-readable form; tapes and reels
           must be labeled.
         ● It requires a carefully controlled environment--no
           dust, moisture, or static electricity.

III. Direct-Access Storage: Any location on this type of medium
     can be accessed almost instantaneously; preceding records
     do not have to be read.

     A. A magnetic disk has concentric circles (tracks) coated
         with magnetic recording material.

         1. Due to the direct-access nature of disks, they are
             typically used to store data against which frequent
             inquiries are made.

2. Several disks are assembled to form a disk pack. Read/write heads of the disk drive are located between each of the disks.
3. Data are accessed by locating the appropriate disk surface number, track number, and location of the data on the track; read speeds up to 850,000 characters per second are possible.

B. The flexible (floppy) disk is a new, low-cost, random-access storage medium (also called a diskette).

1. It is reusable, easy to store, and can be mailed; it is frequently used with POS terminals, minicomputers, and microcomputers.
2. Data are stored as magnetized spots in tracks as on conventional disks, and are addressed by track number and sector number.

C. Direct-access storage disks have several advantages over magnetic tape:

- They can be used for direct access and/or sequential access.
- Information can be updated immediately.
- Quick response can be made to inquiries.
- Coupled with special software, all files can be updated simulataneously.

Some disadvantages:

- It may cost as much as 10 times more than magnetic tape.
- There must be extra provisions for error checking, backup files, and security.
- It requires more sophisticated hardware, software security, and technical personnel to implement and maintain.

IV. Mass Storage: Mass storage devices are capable of storing large volumes of data; retrieval is relatively slow.

A. Large files, backup files, and infrequently used files can be placed in mass storage at a relatively low cost.

B. One approach to mass storage uses a high-density cartridge tape. Floppy-disk mass storage for minicomputers has also been introduced.

      C.   Most mass storage devices require extensive physical
movement because the needed files must be found and
mounted mechanically before data can be read or written.

V.   Future Trends in Data Storage: As technology continues to
advance, smaller, faster, and less expensive storage devices will become commonplace.

      A.   A recent innovation is the development of charge-
coupled devices (CCDs) which are similar to semiconductor memory.

      B.   In a laser storage system, data is recorded by the for-
mation of patterns by a laser beam on the surface of a
sheet of polyester material.

          1.   To read data, the laser reflects light off the sur-
face, reconstructing the data into a digital bit
stream.
          2.   Laser storage will not deteriorate over time, is
resistant to alteration, and does not lose data
during a power failure.

      C.   Another recent development is a laser system to be used
as a mass storage device for minicomputers.

      D.   Random-access memory (RAM) chips are a type of storage
device that approximates the speed of a microprocessor;
its retrieval rate is 50 times faster than a disk.

      E.   Josephson Junction is a form of storage that increases
the speed of primary storage by housing circuits in
liquid helium and thereby lessening the typical
resistance to the flow of electricity that exists in
semiconductors memory.

ANSWERS TO REVIEW QUESTIONS

1.   Primary storage is part of the CPU, unlike secondary
storage, which is external and operates at slower speeds.
Secondary storage media include magnetic tape, and magnetic
disks.

2.   Direct-access media are magnetic disks and floppy disks.
Sequential-access media include magnetic tape and cassette tapes.

Data records stored on a magnetic disk are recorded in
locations that are identified by addresses. Any record can be
accessed by giving the appropriate disk surface number, the
track number, and the location of the data on the track. The
read/write head can be positioned directly over the desired
track.

3.   Magnetic tape consists of a plastic base, coated with iron
oxide, which stores data by magnetizing areas on the tape. The
tape can be erased and reused. It is relatively inexpensive and
is suited for batch, or sequential, processing. Magnetic tape
is useful in situations where a large amount of data must be
stored and updated, such as state vehicle registration or a
customer billing file.

A magnetic disk is a metal platter that is coated on both
sides with a magnetic recording material. Direct-access processing is possible; however, disks are relatively expensive and
original records are destroyed when updating occurs. Airline
reservation systems use magnetic disk storage.

4.   The density of the data on the tape determines how fast it
can be transferred from the tape to the CPU. The density of
tape (how many characters per square inch) determines, along
with the speed of the tape, how fast the data is transferred.

5.   IRGs separate individual records and allow the tape to
regain the proper speed before the next record is read. If the
tape drive is very fast, longer gaps are needed, while slower
speeds require shorter gaps.

IBGs separate blocked records on magnetic tapes in order to
use the amount of storage available more efficiently and to
reduce the number of read/write (input/output) operations
required.

6.   Blocking is the grouping of records. Interblock gaps
separate records, allow enough space for the tape unit to reach
its operating speed, and allow enough space for the tape unit to
decelerate. Tape economy is realized by combining records into
blocks.

7.   The fast access time allows data files to be changed immediately; quick responses can be made to inquiries.

8.   Three reasons that removable disk packs may be preferred over permanently mounted disks.

- They provide added security for a computer system.
- There can be more disk files than disk drives.
- Disks files can be removed when data they contain are not needed.

Three reasons that permanently mounted disk packs may be preferred:

- Removability may not be necessary and/or appropriate in some instances.
- Disk packs that are permanently mounted cannot be lost or misplaced.
- Permanently mounted disks cannot be as easily damaged.

9.   Yes; if access time is a factor, it is best to store the data being accessed in the same cylinder rather than in adjacent cylinders because this will reduce the motion of the read/write heads and, hence, the access time.

10.   With the flexible (floppy) disk systems, the read/write head actually rides on the surface of the disk rather than being positioned slightly above it as with hard disk systems.

11.   Cartridge tape is a high-density tape, similar to cassette tape. A cartridge-oriented system controls the mounting of the tapes and can hold up to 8,000 tape reels.

Small floppy disks can provide mass storage for minicomputers.

Mass storage devices provide low-cost storage for a large amount of data; however, access time is slow and breakdowns are common because of the large number of mechanical parts involved.

12.   Floppy disks are inexpensive, reusable, easy to store and weigh less than two ounces. They are readily interchangeable, can be mailed, and can be removed from the location for security purposes.

They are typically used with minicomputer systems, microcomputers, and point-of-sale terminals.

ADDITIONAL REVIEW QUESTIONS

1.   What is meant by the densify of the tape? What other factor, besides density, determines how fast data can be transferred from the tape to the CPU?

2.   Is a tape drive an input device or an output device?
Explain.

3.   Compare an IRG to an IBG.

4.   Cassette tapes are suitable for what size computer systems?
Why?

5.   Floppy disks were developed to replace which form of data-
entry?

6.   What kind of storage is fastest when retrieving data? Why
is this so?

7.   List all the storage media discussed in the chapter. List
the least expensive first and the most expensive last.

ANSWERS TO DISCUSSION POINTS

1.   The purpose of back-up files is to provide security in case
anything should cause the destruction or erasure of a file.

     Republic Steel uses magnetic tape as a back-up storage
medium for magnetic tape files that are used periodically, for
archival storage, and also as a back-up for direct-access
storage devices.

2.   Republic Steel uses disk storage for its order-entry/billing
system because this activity is best facilitated by online processing. Direct-access storage media allow inquiries to be made
easily to customer and inventory files. All files can easily be
updated and are, therefore, always current when new orders come
in.

     If tape storage were used, orders would have to be held,
then processes periodically in batches. Files would not be
current by whatever activity that occurred since the last
update. Printouts from each update would be used by clerks to
answer questions from customers regarding inventory status of
desired items.

ADDITIONAL DISCUSSION POINTS

1.   What future trends in data processing does Republic Steel see for itself? Do you think this is similar to future trends of other large corporations? Why or why not?

ANSWER KEY TO STUDY GUIDE

True/False

2. T   4. T   6. F   8. F   10. T

Matching

2. h   4. c   6. j   8. b   10. f

Short Answer

2.   Sequential-access media require every record be read in order to find the desired record. Direct-access media go directly to the desired record without reading other records.

4.   The advantages of magnetic tape storage are:

   ● Data can be transferred at high speeds.
   ● Magnetic-tape records can be any length.
   ● Magnetic tape can be erased and reused.
   ● Magnetic tape is suited for sequential processing.

6.   When data are updated, the original data is erased and the new data is put in its place. If there are no provisions for a backup file, errors can go undetected and the data will be invalid.

8.   Characteristics of charged-coupled devices:

   ● made of silicon
   ● similar to semiconductor memory
   ● faster than magnetic bubbles
   ● stored data will be lost if a power failure occurs

10. Records can be accessed on a magnetic disk by disk surface number, track number, and record number.

ENRICHMENT LECTURE

Optical Disks

Laser technology has created new ways to store massive quantities of data for relatively low costs. One of the recent developments in laser technology is the optical disk. Optical disks use a laser beam to store digital information. Three of the most common methods of doing this will be discussed here.

Most optical disks are made of a thin layer of metal and a layer of special plastic, both placed inside a clear plastic disk. On disks that will be read only, or ROM disks, data has been stored by using a laser beam to burn extremely tiny pits into the metal layer. The metal layer is shiny and the microscopic pits are dull. The contrast between the two is detected by a laser that reads the data. This process of coding the data on the disk is done by the manufacturer.

Some optical disks permit users to create their own ROM disks. A write laser is directed through the clear layer of plastic. The shiny surface of the metal reflects the laser, and heat generated by the laser beam produces gas bubbles in the plastic. The gas bubbles create a dimple or pit in the surface of the metal. When the user wants to read back the information, a low-power laser reads the surface of the disk and locates the

dimples. Both this method and the first method of recording
data create a permanent record on the surface of the disk.

A new technique has been developed that allows data stored
on optical disks to be erased or edited. While the technology
for this process is still not perfected, it does exist. This
process is called "optically assisted magnetic recording." The
technique does not alter the physical surface of the disk.
Instead, lasers are used to change the magnetic field of the
disk.

The basis for the technique comes from the long known
scientific principle of magnetic polarization. When heated to a
certain temperature, magnets lose their magnetic properties. If
placed in the field of another magnet, the heated magnet will,
as it cools, conform to the polar field of the other magnet.

During manufacturing, optically assisted magnetic disks are
magnetized parallel to their surfaces. Sometimes a metal plate
is placed under the disk to increase the magnetic force. The
disk drive for these disks has a write head with both a laser
beam and a magnetic coil. When the user wants to write to the
disk, both the laser beam and magnetic coil are turned on. The
laser beam heats points on the surface of the disk. The heated
points lose their magnetic field. As the points cool, they conform to the magnetic field that surrounds the coil in the write
head. This change creates a vertical magnetic "bulge."

The process of reading the optical magnetic disks is complex. A low-powered laser beam is focused with all light waves going in a uniform direction. The beam penetrates the magnetic field of the disk. When the beam meets a bulge in the magnetic field, it rotates slightly. This tiny movement is detected by a complex series of prisms, beam splitters, and electronic circuits.

Erasing the contents of the disk is much simpler. The data areas are heated once again, and as the bulges cool, they conform to the magnetic field of the disk once again. Data stored on erasable disks can be erased either "bit by bit" or "track by track."

Adapted from "Seeing is Retrieving" by Rick Cook. PC World, July 1984.

*Note: A transparency master is available for use with this lecture in your transparency packet that accompanies this textbook.

Suggestions For Discussion

1. Discuss some ways that optical disks may be used.

Because of their large storage capabilities, optical disks may be well suited as a medium for distributing large amounts of information like large parts catalogs. In the publishing business they could be a low cost alternative for storing the contents of books and encyclopedias.

2.   Optical disks can store massive amounts of data and
information.   The Optimem 1000, an optical disk system, can
store one gigabyte.   A gigabyte is equal to 500,000 double-
spaced pages.   Do we really need that kind of storage capability?

      Perhaps not on the home computer level.   But banks,
      insurance companies, information services, and the govern-
      ment have growing information needs that could use gigabyte
      storage and optical disks.

Microcomputers

LEARNING OBJECTIVES

Students should be able to:

- Discuss the evolution and development of microcomputers
- Describe several microcomputer applications
- Define and describe the microprocessor
- Compare and contrast microcomputers and mainframes
- List and describe methods of data storage used with microcomputers
- Identify and discuss uses of microcomputers in the future

OUTLINE

I.   Microcomputers Today

    A.   Microcomputers were developed by entrepreneurs who risked their financial resources to develop their ideas. Their success is evidenced by the fact that since 1975 total sales of microcomputers have reached over five million units. Microcomputers gained acceptance much more rapidly than did mainframe computers; current and potential users include large corporations, small businesses, schools, and home owners.

    B.   Profitable applications of microcomputers are found in small businesses and the professions.

1. One-third of microcomputers are used in private business offices for accounting, inventory control, word processing, mailing labels, tax records, etc.
2. School teachers use microcomputers to devise exams and compute students' grades.
3. Doctors use microcomputers to keep patients' records.
4. Telecommuting enables businesses to employ persons to work in their homes using computer hookups between offices and homes.
5. Word processing, the manipulation of text data to achieve a desired output, is another area influenced by the introduction of low-cost microcomputers.

C. The microcomputer industry has recently switched from a predominatly mail-order business to one using retail computer stores to sell their computers.

II. Hardware

A. The microprocessor is a single integrated circuit that contains an arithmetic/logic unit as well as control capability for memory and input/output access; it is the heart of the microcomputer.

B. Key differences between microcomputers and mainframes include the following:

1. The microcomputer's microprocessor is composed of a single integrated circuit while a mainframe's CPU is composed of a series of integrated circuits and is much more sophisticated.
2. A microcomputer may take several processing steps to perform a function performed in one processing step by a mainframe computer. This is because a mainframe has a much larger and more powerful instruction set to choose from when performing its functions.
3. Microcomputers perform arithmetic computations with less precision because they have smaller register sizes for holding data.
4. Microcomputers are slower than mainframes when performing arithmetic computations because they have fewer registers.
5. Most microcomputers allow for only one user at a time, while mainframes allow for multiple users.

6. Current microcomputers are much more powerful and much less expensive than mainframe computers of 20 years ago.

C. Data storage in microcomputers: Peripheral methods of storing programs and data are necessary because the primary storage in a microcomputer is not large enough to store all of the applications that users might have.

1. Magnetic tape cassettes and cartridges are relatively low-cost method of storage; they are well suited for short programs and data that can be stored and retrieved sequentially.

2. Flexible (floppy) disks are the most widely used form of peripheral storage for microcomputers because they allow programs and data to be accessed directly and at many times the speed of tape cassettes or cartridges.

3. Hard magnetic disks come in two varieties, fixed and removable, and provide larger storage capacity as well as greater speed in accessing data.

   a. Fixed disk--a totally sealed unit with no user access; relatively low price and provides security from damage by untrained person.

   b. Removable disk--allows for a disk to be removed and another disk inserted; is relatively expensive but provides easier and quicker backup.

D. Microcomputer input/output devices

1. Monitors

   a. The most common input/output device
   b. Allows viewing of information before it is sent to the microprocessor for processing
   c. Allows viewing of the information sent from the microprocessor
   d. Information displayed in the form either of character or graphics
   e. Four types--color, RGB, monochrome, and combination TV/monitors

2. Joysticks and game paddles are used primarily with microcomputers that run game applications; they function as a means of positioning some object on the monitor screen.

3. The mouse fits into the palm of the hand and is used to position the cursor on the screen; it allows the user to make choices and initiate programs without using the keyboard.

III. Microcomputers in the Future: While microcomputers were initially envisioned as self-contained computer systems for home and small business use, they have begun to be used by large corporations in their management information systems.

A. Microcomputers are becoming a decision-making tool for managers because they help speed and increase the accuracy of everyday decision-making relative to financial planning, budgeting, and resource planning.

B. Some large corporations have used microcomputers in a system of distributed processing whereby microcomputers are integrated with minicomputers and mainframe computers in a computer hierarchy that shares the same data base. In this type of distributed processing system, managers are able to communicate with each other and also to pass information up and down the organizational structure.

C. In the future nearly everyone will have access to as much information as could be provided through the best of libraries; this will happen with the use of communication networks such as electronic mail systems and electronic bulletin boards.

ANSWERS TO REVIEW QUESTIONS

1.   The microcomputer was developed by businessmen and entrepreneurs using personal finances; the mainframe computer was developed by scientists and mathematicians with the financial support of the government and large corporations. Microcomputers received a more rapid public acceptance than did mainframes.

2.   The microprocessor performs the following functions:

- controls the sequence of operations
- controls arithmetic and logical operations
- stores data, instructions, and intermediate and final results

3.   The CPU of a mainframe computer is composed of a series of integrated circuits; a microprocessor is a single, integrated circuit. The CPU has a much larger and more powerful instruction set to choose from. A microprocessor takes several processing steps to perform a function that can be performed in one step by the CPU. CPUs have larger register sizes for holding data and more registers than microcomputers. Mainframes allow for more than one user at a time.

4.   A mainframe computer has an architectural design that permits a larger instructional set, access to more memory in a single step, and greater speed in processing large number arithmetic computations. Mainframe CPUs have more registers, those locations within the CPU that are used for temporary storage to facilitate the transfer of data and instructions; this facilitates the speed of arithmetic computations. CPUs also have larger registers; this facilitates the accuracy of arithmetic computations.

5.   Microcomputers are limited to one user because with microcomputers only one communication channel is used to communicate with peripheral devices. Mainframes can handle multiple uses because they are designed to accept a maximum number of communication channels with the ability to attach a maximum number of peripheral devices to each channel.

6.   Currently the most widely used form of external data storage on microcomputers is flexible (floppy) disks. It is the most popular because it allows data and programs to be accessed directly at many times the speed of tape cassettes or cartridges.

7.   The four formats of data storage for floppy disks are: single-sided/single density; single-sided/double-density; double-sided/single-density; and double-sided/double-density. It is important to realize that the four formats exist, because the format in which the data is stored on a floppy disk needs to be compatible with the way in which the disk drive unit reads the disk.

8.   Some of the popular input/output devices being used with microcomputers and their applications are as follows:

- monitor – allows viewing of information before sending it to the microprocessor for processing as well as viewing information sent from the microprocessor
- joysticks and game paddles – means of positioning objects on the screen for game applications

- the mouse - a means of positioning the cursor on a computer monitor that eliminates a considerable amount of keyboard typing

9.   In the future it is likely that microcomputers will be used significantly by large corporations both in the stand-alone (self-contained) mode as a manager's decision-making tool and as part of large integrated decentralized computer system that ties together supercomputers, minicomputers, and microcomputers using the same data base. Managers will be able to communicate among themselves and to pass information up and down the organizational hierarchy.

10.   Communication networks will greatly enhance our ability to have information, plus open up new learning opportunities. While the services of communication networks appear to be luxuries today, it is likely that the future generations will view them as necessities.

ADDITIONAL REVIEW QUESTIONS

1.   What is telecommuting and how has it influenced the world of work?

2.   Compare and contrast the uses of microcomputers by the Ford Motor Company, General Electrics, and North American Phillips. How are they similar and how are they different?

ANSWERS TO DISCUSSION POINTS

1.   Commodore had developed a widespread loyal dealer network in Europe because of the distribution of its calculators. Most other microcomputer manufacturers did not have this marketing opportunity in place. Commodore produces microcomputers "for the masses not the classes;" they attempt to sell more computers at lower prices than their competition. Thus, their computers have been among the first to be within the means of the large number of potential buyers for personal uses.

2.   Commodore's strategy for producing and marketing microcomputers used in business is similar to its strategy for marketing personal computers: market in volume and make the business computers attractive and "friendly," but with the professional in mind. This type of strategy is likely to help keep the costs of business microcomputers down to reasonable levels.

ADDITIONAL DISCUSSION POINTS

1.   What advantage does Commodore have by supplying its own microprocessor needs?

2.   Is Jack Tramiel's focus/emphasis on the present or the future? Explain.

ANSWER KEY TO STUDY GUIDE

True/False

2. T   4. F   6. T   8. F   10. F

Matching

2. f   4. d   6. e   8. c   10. g

Short Answer

2.   Some of the areas of application for microcomputers are:

- education
- home
- business

4.   The CPU of a mainframe computer has a more powerful instruction set and may take only one step to process something that may take a micro several steps. A mainframe may have a word size that can accomodate 64 bits, while a micro may handle only 8 or 16 bits. The mainframe can, therefore, access more memory in a single step. This gives them greater speed in processing.

6.   Microcomputers are very powerful in proportion to their size. The IBM 360 Model 30 computer could perform 33,000 additions per second at full speed. The IBM Personal

Computer can perform up to 700,000 additions per second. Many micros can produce similar results.

8.   Some of the features are:

- relatively low in price
- reliable
- secure from damage
- small in size
- large storage capacity

10.   Some of the applications are:

- financial analysis
- spreadsheets
- presentations
- plotting

ENRICHMENT LECTURE

LCD Breakthroughs

The cathode-ray tube (CRT) has been associated with micro-computers since their inception. Black and white and color monitors using CRT technology have provided personal computer users with a satisfactory means of viewing output. Portable computers brought a race for flat screen development and the use of liquid crystal display (LCD) technology. As the popularity of portable computers grows, however, LCD technology moves from infancy to adulthood in the form of color LCDs.

Traditional LCD screens produce images from molecules that align themselves in an ordered pattern when they are exposed to an electrical field. In LCDs, the liquid crystal is placed in a thin layer on a reflective background with glass over the top. The liquid crystal is divided into squares. Each square is connected to a voltage source. The connection is made by a transparent conductor often consisting of indium tin oxide. Individual cells of the transparent conductor change to opaque when voltage is applied to the cells. The opaque surface blocks the light reflected from the bright background, and a black dot appears on the screen. These dots are referred to as pixels. The greater the number of pixels on the screen, the better the resolution.

One problem that had to be overcome with this technology involved controlling the large number of pixels that were needed to produce images. To produce an image, each pixel must be controlled by a switch that is either "on" or "off." Even the smallest, most primitive display screens can have over 8,000 pixels, and each pixel needs a switch. A standard 24-line display screen may have as many as 96,000 pixels. That means 96,000 switches are required! The development of VLSI (very-large-scale integration) has helped overcome the switch problem because a single chip can now hold over 500,000 transistors.

The physical nature of liquid crystals presented another problem. To produce images, the layer of liquid crystal material must be precisely the correct thickness. If the layer is not exactly right, the crystals will not rotate and align themselves properly. When alignment problems occur, the screen image will have uneven dark areas. Changing temperatures and mechanically induced stress can affect the thickness of the crystals. This has hampered technological development.

Color LCD displays require three times more pixels than traditional displays. This complicates the pixel control problem mentioned earlier. Another complication in color LCDs stems from the thickness problem. The uneven rotation of crystals affects color saturation and purity.

Work to overcome these problems is ongoing. The compactness of LCD screens makes them highly valuable for many uses. Telephones may someday have color LCD screens that allow users to view each other while they speak. Home intercoms could have LCDs that monitor the arrival and departure of guests. And protable computers could display complex graphics software for people who travel for business.

Adapted from "Color LCDs On the Way" by Thom Hartmann. Popular Computing, January 1984.

*Note: A transparency master is available for use with this lecture in your transparency packet that accompanies this textbook.

Suggestions For Discussion

1. Discuss some of the possible advantages of LCDs over CRTs.

Possible advantages include: no screen flicker which causes eye strain, no radiation, and low power consumption.

2. Do you prefer LCD screens of the new portable computers or the traditional CRT screens? Why?

Answers will vary according to preference, but urge students to think about why they have a preference.

Telecom- munications

LEARNING OBJECTIVES

Students should be able to:

- Describe data-communication concepts, including modulation/demodulation, data transmission, and channels
- Explain the purposes of control units and channels
- Discuss how interactive/time-sharing systems operate
- List the major disadvantages and advantages of time-sharing
- Describe different types of multiple CPU configurations

OUTLINE

I.   Data Communication: Data communication is the electronic transmission of data from one location to another, usually over communication channels such as telephone/telegraph lines or microwaves. The combined use of communication facilities, such as a telephone system, and data-processing equipment is called telecommunication.

    A.   Message transmission: Data can be transmitted over communication lines in either analog or digital form.

        1.   Analog transmission sends data in continuous wave form.

a. Modulation converts data from computer-stored
    pulse form to wave form for transmission.
b. Demodulation converts data back to pulse form.

2. Digital transmission sends data just as it is
    stored, in pulse form. Therefore, it is faster and
    more accurate.

B. Input/output operations: Although I/O operations are
    very fast by human standards, CPU speeds are much
    faster; control units and channels have been developed
    to make EDP more efficient.

    1. The control unit is an electronic device, inter-
        mediate between a CPU and an I/O device, that per-
        forms standard functions such as code conversion
        and data buffering.

        a. Code conversion is transferring data into
            machine-executable code, such as ASCII or BCD.
        b. Data buffering is the temporary holding of data
            until the CPU is ready to process or transfer
            it to output; the transfer rate is, therefore,
            much faster.

    2. A channel is a limited-capacity computer that takes
        over the task of input and output from the CPU to
        free it to handle internal processing operations.

        a. When the CPU is slowed because of I/O opera-
            tions, the system is input/output bound.
        b. Selector channels are used with a high-speed
            I/O device such as a magnetic-tape or disk
            unit.
        c. A multiplexor channel can handle more than one
            I/O device at a time and is used with slow-
            speed devices such as terminals and card
            readers.

C. Communication channels: Telephone lines, coaxial
    cables, microwave links, communication satellites and
    laser beams are examples of communication channels that
    carry data from one location to another.

    1. The grade or bandwidth of a channel determines the
        range of frequencies it can transmit.

        a. A narrow bandwidth, such as a telegraph line,
            can transmit 45-90 bits per second.

        b.   A voice-grade channel, such as a telephone
            line, can transmit 300-9,600 bits per second.
        c.   Broad-band channels such as coaxial cables,
            microwave, laser beams and helical waveguides,
            are suitable for high-speed transmission of
            large volumes of data.

    2.   There are three basic modes of transmission:

        a.   A simplex channel can either send or receive
            data but it cannot do both.
        b.   A half-duplex channel can transmit data in
            either direction, but only one direction at a
            time.
        c.   A full-duplex channel can transmit in both
            directions simulataneously.

D.   Multiplexers and concentrators: These devices increase
     the number of input and output terminals that can use a
     communication channel.

    1.   A multiplexer receives input from several ter-
       minals, combines the input into a stream of data,
       and then transmits the stream over one com-
       munication channel.
    2.   A concentrator controls several terminals and
       transmits data from only one terminal at a time
       over the communication channel.

E.   A programmable communications processor is a device
     that relieves the CPU of handling many tasks typically
     involved in communication systems.

    1.   When a programmable communications processor is
       used for message-switching, its principal task is
       to receive messages and route them to the
       appropriate destinations.
    2.   A front-end communications processor performs
       message-switching and other operations such as data
       validation and preprocessing.

II. Communication Systems

    A.   Single CPU systems: When terminals and computers are
       in diverse locations and connected to the CPU by com-
       munication channels, it is a remote system.

1. Local vs. remote
2. Time-sharing permits several users to access the same central computer resources and receive what seem to be simultaneous results.

   a. These systems provide interactive computing, conversation between the user and the central computer, via the remote terminal.
   b. Users are allocated predetermined amounts of processing time through a technique called time-slicing.
   c. Two methods are used to establish time-sharing: in-house--within the organization; and service company--time-sharing capability is purchased.
   d. Major advantages of time-sharing systems are:
       • Greater versatility and economy for small users
       • Lower costs per unit
       • Quick response capabilities
   e. Some disadvantages are:
       • Communication costs can be prohibitive.
       • When speedy response is not needed, it may be needlessly expensive.
       • Additional equipment creates more opportunity for both mechanical and system-related problems.

B. Multiple CPU computer configurations: When the resources of a single CPU cannot provide adequate computing power for complex problems, several CPUs may be linked together to form a network.

   1. A star configuration uses a central controlling computer to facilitate workload distribution and resource sharing.
   2. A ring configuration uses a number of computers connected to a single transmission line.
   3. In a hierarchical network, different organizational levels receive different levels of computer support.
   4. Satellite-based networks extend their ranges to other continents but they are new and still very expensive.

C. Distributed data processing (DDP): When processing is completed, to some degree, at a site remote from but linked to the central computer, a DDP is in operation.

D. Local area network: This alternate form of distributed
    processing involves interconnecting computers in a
    single building or complex of buildings.

E. Electronic transmission of data: A communication
    system that has seen a recent dramatic increase in
    electronic funds transfer (EFT) including direct de-
    posit of paychecks and automatic teller machines
    (ATMs).

ANSWERS TO REVIEW QUESTIONS

1.   A modem, or data set, is a device that modulates and demod-
ulates signals transmitted over communication facilities.
Modems are used to handle the data stream from a peripheral
device to the central processor or vice versa through the common
carrier network. If a modem were not used and the computer or
peripheral were directly connected to a telephone channel, the
signal would be degraded and the data made unintelligible by the
electrical characteristics of the channel.

2.   The I/O control unit converts data into machine-readable
form and performs data buffering.

3.   Channels assume the tasks of input and output from the CPU
in order to free it to handle internal processing.

     A selector channel can accept input from only one device at
a time, while a multiplexor channel can handle input from more
than one I/O device at a time. Selectors are normally used with
high-speed devices and multiplexors are used with low-speed
devices.

4.   ● simplex - transmission is made in only one direction
     ● half-duplex - transmission can be in both directions, but
       not at the same time
     ● full-duplex - transmission can be made in both directions
       at the same time

     The bandwidth is important to the analyst because the width
of the frequency band provided is approximately proportionate to
the quantity of information that can be transmitted via the
channel.

     The transmission mode is important because it is directly
related to the equipment being used and the speed of the
transmission.

5.   Polling refers to the process whereby the concentrator checks with (polls) the communication terminals one at a time to see if they have any messages to send. The first terminal that is ready to send or receive data gains control of the communication channel that is free.

6.   A concentrator differs from a multiplexer in that it allows data to be transmitted from only one terminal at a time over a communication channel.

7.   A local system consists of any number of peripherals connected directly to a CPU, all in one location. A remote system allows terminals and even computers to be in separate locations from the main frame but connected via communication channels.

When the system uses one CPU as its mainframe, it is a single CPU system. As the complexity of business and scientific problems increases, several CPUs may be linked together to provide more efficient capabilities. A distributed system is a network of computers geographically dispersed, providing local processing capabilities.

8.   A time-sharing system is a good alternative for a firm that cannot cost-justify the purchase of a computer. However, time-sharing systems are susceptible to the following problems:

- A breakdown in telephone lines can affect service.
- Increases in communication costs can greatly affect users.
- Data can be easily accessed; therefore, appropriate security measures become more involved.
- This system could be needlessly expensive when speed is not important.
- System reliability may be lower than on-site systems.

9.   Star configuration has single-point vulnerability because it requires all transactions to go through a central computer before being routed to the appropriate network computer.

10. The concept of distributed data processing involves processing, which to some degree is done at a site independent of the central computer system.

11. The degree to which processing will be done at a distributed site depends on the structure and management philosophy of the company.

12.   Responses may refer to the idea that the corporation with a
centralized managerial philosophy may utilize their distributed
system mainly to communicate data to the central office computer
to be used for corporate-wide planning and control; the firm
with the philosophy of decentralization may utilize their
distributed system to process data in various functional areas
independent of the central computer on a regular basis.

ADDITIONAL REVIEW QUESTIONS

1.   Explain what is meant by data communication. How is data
communication accomplished?

2.   What is digital transmission? What is an analog
transmission?

3.   What is a communication channel? What is its purpose?

4.   Broad-band channels are suitable for which types of applications? Name two types of broad-band channels.

5.   What is time-slicing and how is it done?

6.   What are the two methods of establishing time-sharing capability?

7.   What are the advantages of distributed systems?

ANSWERS TO DISCUSSION POINTS

1.   Bank of America uses the Distributed Computing Facility to
keep up-to-the-minute account balances for its customers. A
group of minicomputers is connected to the mainframe computer
that runs the Versateller network. Six high-speed digital lines
pass customer account-transaction information between the host
computer and the distributed minicomputer system used by DCF.

        This operation prevents a branch from giving a customer
more money than is actually in his or her account.

2.   Today, many companies have offices throughout the world.
Any multinational corporation could make good use of the Money
Transfer Service.

ADDITIONAL DISCUSSION POINTS

1.   What is the Versateller Service and how does it work?

2.   What problems would Bank of America encounter if their systems were not online real-time?

ANSWER KEY TO STUDY GUIDE

True/False

2. T   4. F   6. T   8. T   10. T

Matching

2. c   4. e   6. i   8. f   10. b

Short Answer

2.   A buffer is a temporary holding area for data being trans-
     ferred to and from the CPU. The CPU can be processing
     other data while the buffer is holding data until a record
     is completely keyed in.

4.   The full-duplex channel is the most versatile channel,
     since it can transmit data in both directions simultane-
     ously.

6.   They provide an economical means for small users to use the
     resources of a large computer system. They allow each user
     to seem to be using a private computer. They provide quick
     response capabilities. Through resource polling, they pro-
     vide access to greater numbers of applications programs
     than would be available otherwise. The user does not have
     to worry about equipment obsolescence.

8.   A star configuration exposes a system to single-point
     vulnerability, while a ring configuration can bypass a
     malfunctioning unit without disrupting operations
     throughout the network.

10. Possible answers include:

     ● People might fear loss of control over the usual banking
       procedures.
     ● Transactions are more vulnerable to unauthorized changes.

- Although some people may believe a cashless, checkless society is going to be the way most transactions are handled, there will still be places where cash and checks must be used.
- It may be hard to keep track of everything as a result.
- Equipment for EFT may be very expensive for smaller banks to buy or use, so use of EFT would not be universal.

ENRICHMENT LECTURE

Around The World In 80 Seconds

A balloon trip in <u>Around the World in 80 Days</u> opened new,
wondrous, and exotic worlds for Phineus Fogg. With the marvels
of today's telecommunications, computer owners can travel around
the world; they can plug into a world of information, receiving
answers in a matter of seconds. They can do this without
leaving their homes.

Yet telecommunications is only in its infancy. The
April 9, 1984, issue of <u>U.S News and World Report</u> suggests many
possibilities for consumers by the 21st century. The standard
telephone console and a video screen will be all the computer
terminal most people will need, according to "What Next? A
World of Communications Wonders," by Stanley Wellborn. Data
will be delivered by electronically synthesized speech.

Automobiles will have telephones as standard equipment and
will be guided by satellite navigation devices. With laser
optics and computers, television will really seem "live" as
three-dimensional holographic images deliver the choreography of
football games and the theatrics of political debates into our

living rooms. Copper wires, radio signals, ground antennas, and
even electricity itself will be replaced by glass fibers,
microwaves, satellites, digital circuits, and laser beams.

Traditional analog transmission will give way to digital
transmission, which will increase accuracy of transmission while
reducing transmission costs. One example, ISDN, or integrated-
services digital network, is a global linkup using high-capacity
optical cables and sophisticated computers.

Optical fibers have great transmission capability: they
carry "tiny staccato pulses of light generated by lasers that
can turn on and off 90 million times a second." At that rate,
the 2,700-page Webster's Third New International Dictionary
could be sent over a single fiber in 6 seconds.

The optical fibers are difficult to wiretap and cheap to
produce. They are not affected by electrical interference. In
Los Angeles, a new fiber-optics system transmitted television
and phone links for the 1984 Summer Olympics. Soon light-wave
communications will bring television and radio entertainment,
computer programs and games, and messages into homes and offices. The new networks may become so advanced that you can be
reached anywhere--in a car, airplane, boat, or even walking on
the street with your nifty, superconvenient, hand-carried phone.
But wait--there's more. You may only have one phone number
throughout your entire life, no matter where you go or where you
live.

Satellite communications are becoming more common, too, as
businesses conduct job interviews, conferences, and phone calls
via satellite. With satellites, people in even the most remote
wilderness can have access to the outside world. And satellites
may even help track down a kidnap victim. Executives in
countries where frequent terrorist acts occur can have transmit-
ters implanted in their bodies. The transmitter can be
triggered to signal via satellite an executive's location in
case of kidnapping.

With technology advancing so fast, equipment can become
obsolete quickly. Bur Arno Penzias, an authority in telecommunications science, reminds us that "state-of-the-art equipment
should be flexible enough to work with any technology that has
preceded it." He says that consumers should be able to use
earlier technology if it suits their needs. Yet he believes
that information is the raw material of the economy's future,
just as petroleum and iron were for the 20th century. The only
question is, how fast will the new technologies appear?

Adapted from "What Next? A World of Communications Wonders"
by Stanley Wellborn and "The Telecommunications Revolution Has
Just Started." U.S. News And World Report, April 9, 1984.

*Note: A transparency master is available for use with
this lecture in your transparency packet that accompanies this
textbook.

Suggestions For Discussion

1.   Discuss the uses of telecommunications which people in the class might have taken advantage of already.

Electronic bulletin boards, electronic mail, television, airline reservations, information services like The Source, credit card checks (such as American Express Company's links around the world), and audio conferencing might be some ways people have already used telecommunication services.

2.   Discuss the advantages or disadvantages of having only one telephone number in your lifetime.

You'll never have to change your telephone number. You can be reached wherever you are with a minimum of fuss. Yet your privacy might be more easily intruded upon.

System Software

LEARNING OBJECTIVES

Students should be able to:

- Differentiate between system and application programming
- Describe an operating system, its functions, the different types, and the different components
- Explain the significance of multiprogramming and how it is accomplished
- Define virtual storage and explain how it is implemented
- Describe how multiprocessing systems are structured

OUTLINE

I. Programs: The term software is used to describe computer programs, a series of step-by-step instructions providing problem solutions; there are two types of programs--system and application.

    A. System programs facilitate the use of computer hardware and help the computer system run efficiently and quickly.

        1. They are machine-dependent.
        2. System programming is normally provided by the computer manufacturer or specialized software firm.
        3. Technically skilled system programmers tailor programs to meet specific organizational requirements.

B.   Application programs perform specific data processing
     or computational tasks to solve the organization's
     information needs.

     1.   They are usually developed in-house.
     2.   Application programs can be written without an in-
          depth knowledge of the computer.

II. Operating Systems: An operating system is a collection of
     programs designed to permit the computer to manage its own
     operations.

     A.   In the 1960s operating systems were developed to over-
          come the problems of time delays and errors caused by
          human operator intervention.

     B.   The operating system handles the allocation of computer
          resources to the users requesting them; it also keeps
          track of the resources for charging fees and for eval-
          uating the efficiency of CPU utilization.

     C.   There are two basic types of operating systems: batch
          (stacked-job) and real-time.

          1.   In a stacked-job processing environment, several
               user programs are grouped into a batch and proc-
               essed one after another in a stream.
          2.   A real-time system can respond to spontaneous
               requests for system resources.
          3.   Many operating systems can handle both types.

III. Components of Operating Systems: An operating system is an
     integrated system residence device; the operating system is
     composed of control and processing programs.

     A.   Control programs oversee system operations and perform
          tasks such as scheduling input and output, handling
          error interruptions, and communicating with operators
          or programmers.

          1.   The supervisor coordinates the activities of all
               parts of the operating system. It consists of
               resident routines which remain in main memory and
               transient routines which are brought in from secon-
               dary storage when needed.
          2.   The job-control program translates program instruc-
               tions into machine language. A job is an entire
               task to be completed by the computer.

3. The input/output management system controls and coordinates the CPU while receiving input from channels, processing instructions of programs in storage, and regulating output.

B. Processing programs simplify program preparation and execution, and are under the supervision of control programs.

   1. The language-translator program transforms the human-readable source program into a machine-executable program known as the object program.
   2. The linkage editor program "links" the object program from the system residence device to main storage.
   3. Library programs are user-written or manufacturer-supplied routines that are frequently used in other programs. They are stored in a system library.
   4. Utility programs perform specialized functions such as transferring data from one I/O device to another.
   5. Sort/merge programs sort records into a particular sequence to facilitate updating of files.

C. Additional software can be added to an existing system to improve it or add new capabilities.

IV. Multiprogramming: Multiprogramming is a technique that helps increase CPU active time; it allows for effective allocation of computer resources and aids in offsetting the slow I/O speeds by processing different programs concurrently.

A. In early computers, serial processing was used to execute programs one at a time. Overlapped processing was developed in order to utilize the CPU more efficiently. Now, multiprogramming permits a CPU to place several programs into partitions, then process them concurrently on a rotating basis.

B. The programs are kept separate in primary storage by partitions which are reserved areas, or regions, that are variable-sized areas that can contain one program.

C. Although multiprogramming increases the system's flexibility and efficiency, it also creates some problems.

1. There must be some way of keeping programs separate; this is accomplished by memory management or memory protection.
2. Another problem is the need to schedule programs to determine which will receive service first.

   a. Foreground partitions are loaded with the highest-priority programs (foreground programs).
   b. Programs of lowest priority (background programs) are loaded into background partitions; background programs are usually executed in batch mode.

V. Virtual Storage: An extension of multiprogramming, virtual storage has been developed on the principle that only a portion of a program has to be in primary memory at any given time, thereby giving the impression that memory size is unlimited.

   A. Virtual storage makes it possible for more programs to be executed within a given time period since portions of several programs can reside in primary storage simultaneously.

   B. Unused portions of programs remain in direct-access secondary storage (virtual storage). The process known as swapping transfers program instructions from virtual storage into primary storage (real storage) and back.

   C. There are two methods of implementing virtual storage:

      1. Segmentation--logical blocks (segments) or programs are kept in main memory; when a new segment is needed, it is exchanged (swapped) for one no longer being used.
      2. Paging--programs are separated into equal-size blocks (pages) and memory is divided in fixed-size areas called page frames.

   D. Virtual storage offers tremendous flexibility; the use of main memory is optimized since only needed portions of programs are in main storage at any one time.

   E. Its disadvantage is that it requires extensive online secondary storage capacity.

VI. Multiprocessing: Multiprocessing involves the use of two
     or more CPUs linked together for coordinated operation;
     stored-program instructions are executed simultaneously.

     A. Often a small CPU, called a front-end processor, is the
         interface between a large CPU and peripheral devices
         such as online terminals.

     B. An alternative is that a small CPU, or back-end proc-
         essor, could be solely responsible for maintaining a
         large data base.

     C. Many large multiprocessing systems have two or more
         large CPUs.

         1. The activities of each can be controlled by a com-
             mon supervisor program.
         2. Each CPU may be oriented toward a specific task, or
             both may be used together on the same task to pro-
             vide rapid response.

ANSWERS TO REVIEW QUESTIONS

1.   A system program is a sequence of instructions written to
coordinate the operation of all computer circuitry and to help
the computer run efficiently. These programs are generally provided by the computer manufacturer or by a software firm.
Application programs solve user problems and are usually developed internally. They perform specific data-processing tasks
or computational tasks to solve management problems.

     An example of a system program is one that allocates
storage for the data being entered. An example of an applications program is one that is used for inventory control.

2.   The major functions of an operating system are:

     ● allocation of the limited computer resources among
       multiple users
     ● recording all information required for accounting pur-
       poses
     ● establishing job priorities

The operating system for real-time processing would be more complex than the system for stacked-job processing. In stacked-job processing, user programs are processed in a continuous stream, one after the other. A real-time system must have the capabilities to respond to spontaneous requests for system resources.

3.   The major components of an operating system are:

- supervisor program - the major control component that coordinates the activities of all the other parts
- input/output management system - controls and coordinates the central processing unit while receiving input from channels, processing instructions of programs in storage, and regulating output. Also, assigns I/O devices to specific programs and saves data between them and specific memory locations
- job-control programs - translate job-control statements written by a programmer into machine-language instructions that can be executed by the computer
- library programs - programs and subroutines that are frequently linked with other programs to perform specific tasks
- utility programs - perform specialized functions such as transferring data from one I/O device to another or sorting and merging
- language translator - translates English-like programs into machine-language instructions

4.   The supervisor program coordinates the activities of all the other parts of the operating system.

5.   The JCL is the communication link between the programmer and the operating system. It translates job-control statements written by a programmer into machine-language instructions.

6.   A source program is an application program written by a programmer. Where this program is translated into machine language by a language translator program, it becomes an object program.

7.   A language translator is important because it enables the application programmer to write the source program in an English-like language. The language translator converts the program into machine language so that it can be executed.

8.   Since utility programs perform specialized functions such as transferring data from one I/O device to another, they are most commonly used by system operators.

9.   Multiprogramming is a technique in which several programs are placed in primary storage at the same time, giving the illusion that they are being executed simultaneously. It is used to increase the efficiency of CPU utilization.

Multiprocessing involves the use of two or more central processing units linked together for coordinated operation. Separate programs can be processed simultaneously by different CPUs.

Problems of multiprogramming are:

● There must be a way of keeping the programs separate.
● Programs must be scheduled according to which will receive service first.

10.   Being able to place programs in either foreground or background partitions of memory allows for establishing a higher priority for those programs that are required for online processing in a time-sharing system. Low priority programs are loaded into background partitions and are typically executed in batch mode.

11.   Virtual storage was developed because the physical limitations of primary storage become a critical constraint, and the productive use of memory becomes increasingly important. Virtual storage efficiently utilizes CPU space and makes it possible for more programs to be executed within a given time period.

Segmentation is a method of implementing virtual storage that involves dividing a program into variable-size blocks, depending upon program logic.

Paging refers to the process used in virtual storage where data or programs are broken into fixed-size blocks, or pages, and loaded into real storage when needed during processing without considering logical parts of the program.

12.   For this application, a front-end processor and a back-end processor should be used with the large CPU. The front-end processor would serve as the interface bewteen the large CPU and the peripheral devices such as online terminals. The back-end processor would be responsible for the data base.

ADDITIONAL REVIEW QUESTIONS

1.   What are the functions of job-control statements?

2.   Is the input/output management system part of the operating system processing programs or control programs?   Explain.

3.   What is meant by memory management?

4.   What is the difference between a partition and a region?

5.   What is the difference between real storage and virtual memory?

6.   Discuss the limitations of virtual storage.

ANSWERS TO DISCUSSION POINTS

1.   VRX is a group of software modules comprising an operating system that allows multiprogramming, virtual storage, and multiple virtual machine capabilities.   The virtual machine capabilities make it possible to tailor a system to operate on a specific programming language.   The language compiler translates the source code into an intermediate object-level code that is interpreted by firmware.   In most cases, one source-code instruction, which usually requires many object level commands, translates to one object-level command.

Advantages of a language-oriented computer system:

● One high-level language statement can accomplish the same results as a half-dozen or more machine-language instructions.
● Language-oriented computers are easier for users to understand.
● Less training is required for users.
● Programs in high-level languages are often transferrable from one computer to another with little change.   High-level languages allow the programmer to focus on problem solving rather than on computer operations.   Time and effort to write, correct, and modify a program is therefore reduced.

Some disadvantages are:

- A compiler program is necessary to translate a high-level source program into an object program.
- More sophisticated equipment is required to complete the necessary translations.

2.   Some advantages of purchasing an application package are:

- It is usually much less expensive to purchase than to develop the package.
- The organization does not have to wait while it is being developed.
- The vendor keeps the package updated and maintained.
- Most packages are already debugged.
- A purchased package may be more complete.

Some disadvantages are:

- The package is not specifically designed for the purchaser.
- Packages are designed for certain computers.
- The purchaser's programming personnel are not as familiar with the package as if they had written the program themselves.

ADDITIONAL DISCUSSION POINTS

1.   Name the operating system of MISSION and list its functions.

2.   NCR uses pages to implement virtual storage. How does this work? How else could they implement virtual storage?

ANSWER KEY TO STUDY GUIDE

True/False

2. F   4. T   6. T   8. T   10. F

Matching

2. h   4. g   6. i   8. f   10. e

Short Answer

2. One way the operating system maximizes efficiency is by
    eliminating the need for human intervention. Another way
    is that it allows several programs to share computer
    resources by allocating the resources (CPU time and
    peripheral time) among the programs.

4. Library programs are written by the user or can be obtained
    from the computer manufacturer. They are programs or
    subroutines that are used frequently in other programs.
    Librarian programs maintain a directory of library programs
    in the system library.

6. Multiprogramming increases system efficiency by utilizing
    CPU time while I/O operations are being performed. This is
    accomplished by executing the instructions from several
    programs concurrently. During the time one program's I/O
    operations are being performed, the CPU can execute the
    instructions from another program.

8. One limitation of virtual storage is that it requires large
    amounts of online secondary storage. It also requires
    significant amounts of internal storage. If virtual
    storage is not used wisely, thrashing can occur.

10. The front-end processor is usually a small CPU that acts as
    an interface between a large CPU and peripheral devices
    such as online terminals. It relieves the large CPU of I/O
    interrupts. The back-end processor is an interface between
    a large CPU and a large data base stored on direct-access
    storage devices. It relieves the large CPU of the task of
    maintaining the data base.

ENRICHMENT LECTURE

Should Operating Systems Software Be Given Copyright Protection?

Copyrights have long been protecting the works of com-
posers, authors, and artists of various media for years. It is
illegal to copy the original words of an author, the original
musical score of a composer, or the original trademark symbol
designed by a graphic artist. Should the computer program written by a programmer be given the same protection?

There is no doubt that the software for a computer video
game, for example, is the original, creative property of its
programmer. It is illegal to copy a software program except for
archival purposes. But the copying of object code (the instructions that actually run the computer, contained in the operating
system, application programs, or ROM) has only recently been
brought before the courts.

In the case of Apple vs. Franklin, Apple charged the
Franklin Computer Corporation with copyright infringement for
duplicating in its Ace 100 computer the operating system
programs contained in the Apple II. Apple sought an injunction
to prevent Franklin from selling the Ace 100. The U.S. Court
of Appeals for the Third Circuit became the first federal
appeals court to rule that object code is copyrightable. This

means that they are "original works of authorship fixed in . . . [a] tangible medium of expression."

So, based on the Third Circuit's interpretation, the Copyright Act of 1976, and the software amendments of 1980, all parts of computer programs, even those that are fixed in the computer and cannot be read by humans, are copyrightable. But when is the copying of software not a copyright infringement?

The purpose of software compatibility is to allow application programs designed for one computer to be run on another brand of computer. If all other computers require the copyrighted operating systems to run one computer's application programs, then software compatibility does not exist.

Just as paraphrasing of an author's copyrighted words is allowed, shouldn't programmers be able to "paraphrase" operating code instructions so that the application programs written for one computer would be compatible with another computer? Should only the exact reproduction of operating code be illegal?

The question at this time is how far does the computer industry want the courts to go in protecting against paraphrasing? Some people in the industry argue that everybody builds pretty closely on what the others in the industry have done. Making paraphrasing illegal would slow the expansion of computer knowledge. The bottom line is that the industry must find a compromise between protecting research and expanding the availability of computer knowledge.

Adapted from "A Watershed Case for Copyrighting" by Herbert Swartz. <u>Business</u> <u>Computer</u> <u>Systems</u>, January 1984.

*Note: A transparency master is available for use with this lecture in your transparency packet that accompanies this textbook.

Suggestions For Discussion

1. Do you agree that the operating code written for one computer should be protected by copyright law?

This calls for an opinion, but students should be able to support their answers.

2. If no paraphrasing of operating code is allowed, what would happen to the compatibility of software programs?

If no paraphrasing is allowed, software programs written for one computer will not be compatible with other computers. There would be no software compatibility.

Programming and Software Development

LEARNING OBJECTIVES

Students should be able to:

- Describe the five steps involved in computer problem solving
- Identify the four program logic patterns used in flowcharting
- Explain detailed and modular program flowcharting
- Describe the flowcharting symbols and their uses
- Develop and draw detailed and modular program flowcharts
- Differentiate between the various types of statements used in high-level programming languages
- Distinguish between machine, assembly, and high-level programming languages
- Describe the translation process necessary for programs to be understood by the computer
- Discuss the importance of documentation

OUTLINE

I. Computer Problem Solving: Programmers should use a struc-
    tured approach to problem solving and program development.
    The process consists of five steps:

    A. Defining the problem

    B   Designing a solution

C.   Writing the program

D.   Compiling, debugging, and testing the program

E.   Documenting the program

II.   Defining the Problem: A detailed description of the infor-
      mation needed or the task to be accomplished is determined
      at this time.   Sometimes systems analysts perform this
      function.

      A.   The analyst or programmer first determines the type of
           output users require from the computer.

      B.   Next, the input required to provide this output must be
           determined.

      C.   Input and output specifications help determine proc-
           essing requirements.

      D.   In the payroll example, the company's accounting
           department is overworked and outdated.

           1.   Output requirements include paychecks and reports
                such as payroll expenses, changes in employee
                salaries and positions, income taxes withheld, and
                union dues deducted.
           2.   Input requirements include employee time cards, pay
                scales, promotion data, tax tables, and union dues
                owed.
           3.   Processing requirements would therefore be to
                calculate gross pay, calculate and deduct taxes and
                union dues, figure net pay, print checks, and,
                finally generate reports.

III. Designing a Solution: The programmer breaks the problem
      into subunits (segments) and works out a tentative program
      flow.

      A.   Program flow, for all languages, follows four basic
           logic patterns:

           1.   Simple sequence pattern--one statement after
                another, executed in order as stored.
           2.   Selection pattern--requires a test, and, depending
                upon the result of the test, one of two paths is
                taken.

3. Loop pattern--a series of instructions that are executed repeatedly as long as specified conditons remain constant. Trailer values and counters control loop execution.

4. Branch pattern--makes the computer skip over certain statements. It can be confusing if used too often.

B. Pseudocode is an English-like description of the processing step in a program and is understandable even to those unfamiliar with the program logic.

C. A flowchart provides a visual frame of reference of the processing steps in a program.

1. Symbols are arranged in logical sequence corresponding to the program statements.

2. The symbols used include stop/start, input/output, processing, flowlines, decision, and connector.

3. A modular (macro) flowchart outlines the general flow and major segments of the program. The major segments are called modules.

4. A detailed (micro) flowchart lists the detailed processing required in each segment.

D. Problems are broken into manageable segments; then a solution and a flowchart can be designed for each segment.

E. Program loops must contain statements to accumulate totals. The accumulator must also print or store the total outside the loop once it has been executed the proper number of times.

IV. Writing a Program: This is the third step in the problem-solving process of program development. The program is written in a specific language.

A. Certain types of statements are common to most high-level programming languages:

1. Comments are inserted at key points to explain the purposes of program segments.

2. Declarations are definitional statements.

3. Input/output statements transfer data to and from main memory when appropriate.

4. Computational instructions perform all arithmetic operations.

> 5. Transfer of control instructions may cause loop or branch logic patterns to occur.
> 6. Comparison statements require a test and a decision as in the selection logic patterns.

B. Programs should be easy to follow, efficient, reliable, robust, and maintainable. Data names should **be** descriptive.

V. Compiling, Debugging and Testing the Program: This is the fourth step in program development. The source program is transformed into the object program, errors are resolved, and test runs are made.

A. There are three levels of programming languages:

> 1. Machine language is a code that designates the proper electrical states in the computer as combinations of 0s and 1s and is the only language the computer can execute directly.
> 2. Assembly language is an intermediate-level language that uses symbols and abbreviations instead of 0s and 1s.
> 3. High-level languages are English-like coding schemes that are procedure-, problem-, and user-oriented. One high-level language statement can accomplish the same result as a half-dozen or more machine-language instructions. The time and effort needed to write programs are reduced, and programs are easier to correct or modify.

B. Language translator programs convert English-like source programs into machine-executable object programs.

> 1. The translator program for an assembly language is called an assembler program; for a high-level language, it is called a compiler program.
> 2. During the translation process, the computer generates a listing of syntax (grammatical) errors that must be corrected before the instructions can be executed.

C. Errors in programs are "bugs" and the process of locating, isolating, and eliminating bugs is "debugging."

D.   When a compilation without errors is achieved, the
     program is run using input data that is either a repre-
     sentative sampling of actual data or a facsimile.

     1.   A complex program is frequently tested in separate
          units so that errors can be isolated to specific
          segments.
     2.   If exception-handling instructions are part of the
          program, the sample data should include items that
          test the program's ability to spot and reject
          improper data items.
     3.   "Desk-checking" is when the programmer reads
          through each instruction and simulates how the com-
          puter would process the data in order to catch
          flaws in logic.
     4.   A "dump" lists the contents of registers and pri-
          mary storage locations in hexadecimal notation.
     5.   A trace will list the steps followed during program
          exeuction in the order they occurred.

VI. Documenting the Program: This is the final step of program
     development. It consists of written descriptions and
     explanations of programs and other materials associated
     with an organization's data-processing systems.

     A.   The purposes of documentation are:

          1.   It serves as a reference guide for programmers and
               analysts who must modify or update existing
               programs and system procedures.
          2.   Documentation helps management evaluate the effec-
               tiveness of EDP applications.
          3.   It is essential for those who perform manual func-
               tions required by the system.

     B.   Program documentation should include:

          1.   Problem definition
          2.   Statement of objectives
          3.   Description of content and format of input, output,
               and files to be used
          4.   Hardware requirements
          5.   Software requirements

     C.   In the program planning phase, the most important docu-
          mentation is the flowchart.

   D. An operator's manual, or run book, should also be pre-
       pared with instructions necessary for running the
       programs.

   E. All documentation for a program or system can be com-
       bined to form a user's manual.

VII. Programming Case Study: The problem--to calculate the
     average numerical grade for each student in a course and to
     determine the final letter grade for each.

ANSWERS TO REVIEW QUESTIONS

1. Five Steps of Problem-Solving Process

	Performed by:	
	Systems Analyst	Programmer
Defining the problem	X	X
Designing a solution	X	X
Writing the program		X
Compiling, debugging, and and testing the program		X
Documenting the program		X

2.   An evaluation of desired output is most important at the
problem definition stage; it is important to determine if there
are any omissions or incorrect assumptions about the purpose of
the program as soon as possible.

3.   Pseudocode and flowcharting are two techniques of
illustrating a logical flow used in designing a solution to a
computer problem.

4.   Although definition and solution of a problem do not depend
on a particular programming language, the proposed solution may
limit the choices of languages that can be used. However,
knowing the processing requirements first helps the programmer
to select the language best suited to these requirements.

5.   Inputs-----Processing-----Outputs

      Inputs:

      • detailed listing of all vacant apartments in the city
      • range in which monthly rent payment must fall
      • number of bedrooms required
      • any other desired specifications (location, utilities
        included, swimming pool, etc.)

Processing:

- eliminate all apartments outside of specified price range
- eliminate all apartments without desired number of bedrooms
- eliminate all apartments that do not meet other specifications

Output:

- hard-copy list of apartments that fulfill all specified requirements

6.   Flowcharts provide a visual frame of reference using easily recognizable symbols to represent the processing steps in a program.   The symbols are placed in the same logical sequence in which corresponding program statements will appear in the program.

Pseudocode is the arrangement of narrative descriptions of the processing steps to be performed in a program.   The use of pseudocode allows the programmer to focus on the steps required to perform a particular process rather than on how they should be phrased in a computer language.

Both flowcharting and the use of pseudocode are very important in developing the logical sequence of computer program processing; however, flowcharting can provide the detail of each of the processing steps (micro flowcharts) or an overview of the major components (macro flowcharts).   It is also helpful in identifying omissions and providing program documentation.

7.

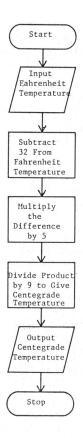

8.   Loop 1: repeat until end of data
              Read data (the dividend) into variable
              Set divisor equal to 2
                   Loop 2: repeat until remainder or divisor =
                       dividend
                            divide dividend by divisor
                            check for remainder
                            divisor equals divisor + 1
              End Loop 2
         If divisor = dividend then place number in array
      End Loop 1
      Sum values in array
      Output sum

9.   Types of statements:

      ● Comments have no effect on program execution; their pur-
        pose is documentation.
      ● Declarations are definitional statements.

- Input/output statements bring data to and from main storage as needed.
- Computational instructions perform all arithmetic operations.
- Transfer of control statements may conditionally or unconditionally alter the sequence of instruction execution.
- Comparison statements require a test of two items and based on the result, either I/O, computation, or transfer of control will occur.

10. Programs are of high quality when they are easy to read and follow and are understandable to users. They should also be reliable, efficient in their use of CPU time, maintainable, and they should be able to handle all conditions. Data names should be descriptive.

These qualities will result in a program that can be used without difficulty by persons other than the original programmer. Because the format will be easy to follow and understand, the program will be kept by the organization and modified as needed for changing requirements.

These qualities will also result in programs that are more economical, both in their use of computer time and personnel time.

11. A language-translator program translates the source program, the sequence of instructions written by the computer programmer into a machine-executable form known as an object program.

12. Language translators transform English-like programs into machine-language instructions. An assembler program is needed to translate a source program written in assembly language to an object program. A compiler program translates high-level-language source programs to computer-readable instructions.

13. Documentation consists of written descriptions and explanations of programs and of other materials associated with an organization's data-processing system. It should be included in each and every phase of system development and whenever any modifications, additions, or changes are made thereafter.

14. Up-to-date documentation is important because it is a reference guide for programmers and analysts who must modify or update existing programs and system procedures. It helps management evaluate the effectiveness of data-processing operations. Documentation is essential to those who perform manual functions required by the system, and it provides instructions to the computer operator about the requirements for running particular programs.

The computer operator requires a "run book", an operator's manual, the programmer and analyst require complete descriptions of all data inputs, outputs, and files to be used; they require a statement of hardware and software requirements; they require a flowchart; management requires all of these and a user's manual to help determine the program's effectiveness.

ADDITIONAL REVIEW QUESTIONS

1. Why is complete problem definition critical to successful program development?

2. Discuss the four basic logic patterns that can be used to solve any problem.

3. Distinguish between modular and detailed flowcharts, noting similarities and differences.

4. Explain the purpose of a trace. Distinguish it from a dump.

5. Why is documentation an ongoing process?

6. What are the reasons for not writing applications programs in machine language?

7. Distinguish between a software package and an application package.

ANSWERS TO DISCUSSION POINTS

1.   Users are heavily involved in the development of new applications because they know best what their needs are. Only by
working closely with users can programmers and analysts design
programs that will reduce operating expenses and provide users
with information that is relevant, accurate, timely, and
complete.

       Users participate in PLAD (Process for Lilly Application
Development) whenever a new application is required. In this
process they review and approve the system objectives as the
analysts have interpreted them. Then they receive further
reports so they can ascertain that the system, as planned by the
designer, will meet their specific needs. Next they participate
in the design of reports, screen formats, and inquiries. Later
they supply input data for test runs, review the system in
operation, and read the documentation to determine if their
needs have been satisfied. They can either document their
acceptance of suggest revisions.

2.   Debugging procedures:

   ● Live test data, sometimes supplied by users, is used for
     practice processing runs.
   ● Programmers submit trial runs with abnormal terminations
     that produce core dumps at the end of execution. Errors
     can often be uncovered by studying the contents of the
     dump.
   ● Trace programs can be used to indicate the execution flow
     through the entire sequence of instructions. In this way
     programmers can see if the flow has mistakenly entered a
     wrong section of the program.

ADDITIONAL DISCUSSION POINTS

1.   What is involved in the compilation process of PLAD? What
is the purpose of a compiler program?

2.   What is a program walkthrough?

3.   Outline the five phases of PLAD.

ANSWER KEY TO STUDY GUIDE

True/False

2. T   4. T   6. T   8. F   10. F

Matching

2. b   4. j   6. a   8. g   10. c

Short Answer

2.   The four basic logic patterns used by computers are:

- simple sequence
- selection
- loop
- branch

4.   A macro flowchart outlines the general flow and major segments of a program. It does not go into detail. A micro flowchart serves the opposite purpose. It lists every step necessary in a particular program.

6.   A robust program works under all conditions. It will work even if incorrect data are entered by the user. For example, if the user entered -75 for a person's height, the program might tell the user the data is invalid and allow the user to reenter the data.

8.   Two methods of controlling a loop are by using a trailer value and using a counter. A trailer value is placed at the end of the input data. When the program reads this value it will know that it is at the end of the input data. A counter is used to control how many times a loop will be executed. For example, a counter could be set to zero before a loop is executed and then increase by one every time the loop is executed. When the counter equals 20, the loop has been executed 20 times.

10.   A trace program causes all of the steps followed during program execution to be listed. This can help the prorammer to debug a program that isn't working correctly.

ENRICHMENT LECTURE

Is The Quality of Documentation What It Should Be?

Many people believe documentation accompanying computer hardware and software is in a sorry state. People who use software and hardware documentation regularly can list examples of situations where major steps were left out or not explained in the correct sequence. An extreme example of this is found in Apple's Profile Disk Drive manual: "Your Profile Drive is packed in a cardboard shipping carton. It is covered with polyethylene and is protected by thick foam material. After you open the carton, remove the top layer of foam and you will find a small cardboard box lying on top of the drive. The box contains this manual."

Another problem is that the writer may not use good writing style. Sentences may be incomplete. Often terms are not defined and there are no indexes for quick reference. All of this can lead to frustration on the part of the user.

A major reason these problems have occurred is that often documentation has been written by programmers who wrote for other programmers. More and more, however, experienced writers with little or no technical background are writing documentation for inexperienced users of computers and computer software.

It is important that the programmer who wrote the software is not the same person who writes the documentation for the layman. This programmer will probably not be able to write objective instructions about the product and may have no writing skills. Programmers often find it difficult to write in non-technical terms.

Often documentation is poor because it is done at the last minute when there is a big rush to get the product on the market. As Steward Brand, founder of <u>The Whole Earth Software Catalog</u> says, "Business operates at greed speed. The major technical procedural reason for bad documentation is that the software is being completed at the same time as the manual to explain it is."

Sometimes, expense keeps the quality of documentation poor. In small companies, all the money may go into developing the hardware or software, and documentation is an afterthought.

Documentation is gradually improving as experienced writers who are not involved in the product development begin doing more of the documentation. Companies are beginning to realize that good documentation is important to the user of their product and improves marketability.

Adapted from "Documentation's Sorry State" by Marguerite Zientara. <u>InfoWorld</u>, July 16, 1984.

*Note: A transparency master is available for use with this lecture in your transparency packet that accompanies this textbook.

Suggestions For Discussion

1. Ask the class to share experiences they have had with poorly written documentation. Do they have any ideas on how this documentation could have been written better?

The problems the students share will depend on their personal experiences. Probably, the most commonly heard complaints center around steps that have been completely left out of the documentation or presented in the incorrect order.

2. Discuss what qualifications a person writing hardware or software documentation should have. Should that person know how to program, or is it enough to be able to write clearly?

The general qualifications of a person writing documentation should be:

- the ability to write clearly and without using technical terms when writing for the layperson
- the ability to list the necessary steps in a task completely and in the proper order
- a thorough knowledge of the product being documented
- the ability to write objectively about the product

It is usually not necessary for the writer of the documentation to be a programmer. In fact, programmers are often poor writers and may lack objectivity. Generally, it is enough for the writer to be familiar with the product and its use.

Programming Languages

LEARNING OBJECTIVES

Students should be able to:

- Distinguish between batch- and interactive-programming languages and give examples of each
- Describe machine and assembly languages
- Differentiate between procedure-, and problem-oriented programming languages, and give examples of each
- Discuss the characteristics of COBOL, FORTRAN, PL/I, RPG, BASIC, APL, Pascal, Logo, and Ada
- Evaluate the different programming languages and describe their applications

OUTLINE

I.   Batch-Oriented vs. Interactive Programming Languages

    A.   Batch-oriented programming languages are normally used for solving problems of a recurring nature in which an immediate response is not required. There are three categories of batch programming languages: machine-, procedure-, and problem-oriented.

        1.   When using a machine-oriented language such as assembly, the programmer must pay close attention to the machine functions that take place during program execution.

2.   In a procedure-oriented language, the emphasis is
     on describing the computational and logical proce-
     dures for solving a problem.
3.   A problem-oriented language is one in which the
     problem is described without detailing the
     necessary computational procedures for solving it.
     RPG is an example.

B.   Interactive programming languages allow the programmer
     to communicate directly with the computer; three
     interactive programming languages are BASIC, APL, and
     Pascal.

II. Machine-Oriented Languages

A.   Machine language: The language of the computer is a
     combination of 0s and 1s; data addresses must be speci-
     fied; it is machine dependent.

1.   The OP code tells the computer what function to
     perform; the operand tells it what data to work on.
2.   Machine language is efficient in terms of storage
     area and execution speeds, but programming in it is
     tedious and time consuming.

B.   Assembly language: Mnemonics, or symbolic names and
     abbreviations, make assembly language once removed from
     machine language; but the programmer must still be
     conscious of the computer.

1.   In addition to an op-code and one or two operands,
     an assembly-language contains a label, which is a
     programmer-supplied name that represents the first
     storage location used for an instruction.
2.   Some advantages are:

     a.   It is highly efficient in terms of storage and
          processing time required.
     b.   It performs certain checking functions and
          generates error messages.
     c.   It is conducive to modular programming tech-
          niques.

3.   The disadvantages are:

     a.   The one-to-one relationship between assembly
          language and machine language instructions
          increases program preparation time.

      b.   It requires a high level of skill to use it effectively.

      c.   It is machine-dependent (a program written for one computer generally cannot be executed on a different computer).

III. High-Level Languages

   A.   Procedure-oriented versus problem-oriented languages

      1.   Procedure-oriented languages place programming emphasis on describing the computational and logical procedures required to solve a problem.

      2.   Problem-oriented languages describe problems and solutions without detailing the necessary computational procedures.

   B.   Scientific-oriented languages

      1.   FORTRAN (FORmula TRANslator) was the first commercially available high-level language.

          a.   It is a procedure-oriented language especially suited for scientific, mathematical, and engineering applications where numerous complex arithmetic calculations are necessary.

          b.   The basic element in a FORTRAN program is the statement, but the only statement that must appear in every program is "END."

          c.   There are four types of statements:

- Control statements determine the sequence in which operations are to be performed.
- Arithmetic statements direct the computer to perform calculations.
- I/O statements instruct the computer to read or write data.
- Specification statements describe the arrangement of the data being input or output.

          d.   Two kinds of variable names are used to designate storage locations for integers, real numbers, and alphanumeric characters.

          e.   Only four alphanumeric characters can be represented by one variable name.

          f.   Array variables represent groups of similar data items. The elements of the array are referred to by subscripts.

g. Advantages include:
- Extremely useful for scientific applications
- Can be used for quantitative analysis

h. Disadvantages include:
- FORTRAN is not well suited for programs involving file maintenance, editing of data, or production of documents.
- It does not bear much resemblance to English, so it requires good documentation.

2. APL (A Programming Language) is especially suited to handle tables of related numbers (arrays) via a terminal.

a. It can be used in two modes:
- Execution mode--the terminal can be used like a desk calculator (one instruction, one response).
- Definition mode--a series of instructions (program) can be executed on command of the programmer.

b. Advantages include:
- Different APL operators can be combined to perform very complex operations with a minimum of coding.
- It is free form, easily learned and powerful.

c. Disadvantages include:
- APL requires a special keyboard with its unique character set.
- It is difficult to read and may not be suitable for handling large data files.
- The compiler requires a large amount of primary storage. It is not widely supported.

C. Business-oriented languages

1. COBOL (COmmon Business Oriented Language) is the most frequently used business programming language.

a. This English-like language can be interpreted by even casual readers; the basic unit of a COBOL program is the sentence. Sentences are combined to form paragraphs, sections, and divisions.

    b. COBOL programs are divided into four divisions:

- IDENTIFICATION DIVISION provides documentation by giving the program a name, etc.
- ENVIRONMENT DIVISION states necessary hardware.
- DATA DIVISION describes data, files, and I/O
  formats.
- PROCEDURES DIVISION contains processing
  steps to be executed.

    c. Advantages include:

- Less documentation is needed; it tends to be
  self-explanatory.
- The programmer does not need to be concerned
  with detailed machine functions.
- Testing and debugging are simplified because
  the logic is easy to follow.
- It is standardized, and has strong file-handling capabilities.

    d. Disadvantages include:

- It requires a sophisticated, large compiler
  which may not be available on small computers.
- It has limited computational capabilities.
- It is wordy.

2. RPG (Report Program Generator) produces all kinds
of reports without need of skillful programmers.

    a. Advantages include:
- It is easy to learn and requires minimal
  programmer effort.
- Because it does not require large amounts of
  main storage, it is perfect for minicomputers.
- It efficiently produces simple reports.

    b. Disadvantages include:
- Its computational capabilities are limited.
- It is not standardized.

3. Ada is a relatively new programming language
derived from Pascal, another high-level language;
it was developed by the Department of Defense when
a 1974 study determined that no current high-level
programming language met their needs.

D. Education-oriented languages

   1. BASIC (Beginners All-Purpose Symbolic Instruction
       Code) is an easy-to-learn language designed for use
       in time-sharing systems.

       a. BASIC programs consist of a series of
           sequentially-numbered statements.
       b. There are three types of commands used:

           ● Programming language statements are used to
             write the program itself.
           ● System commands are used to communicate with
             the operating system.
           ● Editing commands are used to insert changes
             in, or to delete parts of source-program
             segments.
       c. Advantages include:

           ● It has both business and scientific applica-
             tions, and can be used for batch as well as
             interactive programming.
           ● It is easy to learn.
       d. Disadvantages include:

           ● It is not standardized.
           ● Programs written for one system may need
             substantial modification before being used on
             another.

   2. Logo is a procedure-oriented, interactive
       programming language developed by Seymour Papert at
       MIT in 1966.

       a. Logo's main attraction is that it allows
           children of all ages to begin to program and
           communicate with the computer in a very short
           period of time.
       b. Logo uses a "turtle" in an interactive program
           of graphics which allows the user to draw ima-
           ges, animate them, and color them.
       c. Advantages include:

           ● Logo's strength lies in helping the inex-
             perienced user to learn.
           ● Simplicity

    d.   Disadvantages include:

- Limited overall capability
- Few applications exist outside of the area of education.

E. Multi-purpose languages

    1.   PL/I (Programming Language One) was designed as an all-purpose, procedure-oriented language for both scientific and business applications. It combines the best features of COBOL and FORTRAN.

       a.   PL/I is free-form and can be constructed in modules.
       b.   The compiler has default features which reduce the number of statements needed in a program. Other built-in functions simplify the programmer's task and allow novices to write programs without difficulty.
       c.   Advantages include:

- It is concise and powerful.
- Its default and modularity features make is easy to learn.

       d.   Disadvantages include:

- A large amount of storage is required.
- It is used primarily with IBM computers. Therefore, there has been no government support to increase its use.

    2.   Pascal is suited for business and scientific applications, and can be used for batch as well as interactive programming.

       a.   Each program has two parts: a heading (in which definitions and declarations are made) and a body (in which input, processing, and output are accomplished).
       b.   Advantages include:
- It is easy to learn, English-like, and powerful.
- It has graphic capabilities.
- It is well suited for structured programming.
       c.   Disadvantages include:
- It is not standardized.
- It has poor input/output capabilities.

F. Natural languages

1. Natural languages, sometimes called query languages, are programming languages that use natural English-like sentences for the purpose of accessing information usually contained in the data base.
2. Natural languages have been designed primarily for the novice computer user; for use with a vocabulary of words and definitions that allow the processor to translate English-like sentences to machine executable form.
3. These languages are currently typed on a keyboard; however, in the future voice recognition may be used.
4. Natural language systems are expanding from mainframe use to minicomputer and microcomputer use as well.

IV. Programming Languages--A Comparison

A. The limited main-storage capacity of small computers usually prohibits the use of languages such as COBOL, FORTRAN, PL/I, and APL.

B. Business applications typically involve large data files but few calculations. The many I/O operations result in such applications becoming I/O bound. In such cases, COBOL and PL/I provide the necessary power for efficient operations.

C. Scientific applications may become process-bound because they require many complex calculations on relatively small amounts of data. FORTRAN, PL/I, and Pascal are suitable for such cases.

D. For interactive computing, BASIC, APL, and Pascal are appropriate.

E. In microcomputers and systems where main-storage capcity is a critical constraint and virtual storage capabilities are not available, programming may have to be done in assembly.

ANSWERS TO REVIEW QUESTIONS

1. Interactive programming allows the user to receive an immediate response from the computer whereas batch processing cannot. In batch processing, data is collected over a period of time and processed in a group. Programs submitted in a batch environment spend time in secondary storage until the CPU is

ready to execute them. Interactive programming, on the other
hand, compiles and executes programs and returns the results to
the user immediately. Typical interactive programs are one-time
requests for information and inquiries into data files. Batch
is regularly used for applications that require large volumes of
data to be processed on a periodic, recurring basis.

2.   Interactive programming is the key to online applications.
The results of such program applications as accounts receivable,
inventory, and billing must be translated, executed, and the
results returned to a remote terminal within a matter of
seconds. Most batch programs are used to solve specific
problems that occur according to some predetermined schedules.

3.   Machine language is a combination of 0s and 1s; assembly
language uses mnemonics which are converted to machine language
by an assembler. Machine language requires an op code and an
operand in each instruction. In addition to these, assembly
language may also use a label.

     Both are efficient in terms of storage and processing time
requirements. Both are machine-dependent and programming in
either one is tedious and time-consuming. Both require a high
level of skill to use them. In addition, assembly language performs certain checking functions, generates error messages, and
is conducive to modular programming techniques.

4.   Assembly language would be chosen because of its high
degree of efficiency in processing time.

5.   Procedure-oriented languages place programming emphasis on
describing the computational and logical procedures required to
solve a problem; problem-oriented languages describe problems
and solutions without detailing the necessary computational procedures.

     ● common procedure-oriented languages: COBOL, FORTRAN
     ● common problem-oriented languages: RPG, BASIC

6.   They are especially applicable where numerous complex
arithmetic calculations are necessary. Good business languages
require ability to process alphabetic data and files to format
printed reports.

7.   The CODASYL (Conference of Data Systems Languages)
Committee established the specifications for COBOL. One objective was to establish a language that was machine-independent;
another objective was to make the language look like English.

8.   COBOL advantages:

   ● Programs that use it require little additional documen-
     tation because of its English-like nature.
   ● It is much easier to learn than either machine language
     or assembly language.
   ● It has strong file-handling capabilities.
   ● COBOL's standardization allows firms to change computer
     equipment with little or no rewriting of existing
     programs.

9.   BASIC's uses have extended beyond the initial purpose of
university instruction with interactive time-sharing systems to
business, scientific, and batch-processing applications. Logo's
simplicity seems perfectly adapted to helping the inexperienced
user adjust to the programming environment; however, it is not
likely to expand in usage beyond this important educational
purpose.

10.   Pascal's suitability for structured programming, its relative ease of learning, and the fact that it is a powerful
language makes it a very good language for developing application systems.

11.   COBOL = COmmon Business-Oriented Language
      FORTRAN = FORmula TRANslator
      APL = A Programming Language
      BASIC = Beginners' All-Purpose Symbolic Instruction Code
      PL/I = Programming Language I

12.   Factors to be considered when choosing a programming
language:

   ● Size of system: Small computers may not have enough main
     storage to accommodate languages such as COBOL, FORTRAN,
     PL/I, and APL.
   ● Interactive vs. batch processing: BASIC is ideally
     suited for interactive processing. APL and Pascal can
     also be used.
   ● Will applications become I/O bound? COBOL and PL/I can
     provide the necessary power for efficient operations.
   ● Will application become process bound? FORTRAN, PL/I and
     Pascal can handle complex calculations.
   ● If there is very little main storage and virtual storage
     cannot be implemented, assembly language may be con-
     sidered.

ADDITIONAL REVIEW QUESTIONS

1.   Why was assembly language developed? What are the three basic parts of an assembly-language instruction?

2.   List and briefly describe the four types of statements used in FORTRAN.

3.   In PL/I, what is a default?

4.   Name the four divisions of a COBOL program and describe the function of each.

5.   What are some advantages of BASIC? For what type of applications is it suitable?

ANSWERS TO DISCUSSION POINTS

1.   Assembly language is highly efficient in terms of storage and processing time required. It is most appropriate when the amount of main storage is negligible and virtual storage cannot be implemented. Ohio Citizens Bank will continue to use it for teleprocessing monitors and MICR support. Also, some applications require I/O devices that can only be supported with assembly language provided by the equipment manufacturer. These programs and the operating systems will continue to be programmed in assembly.

2.   BASIC programs are very simple to change, and therefore, provide an excellent environment for manipulating alternative budget models. BASIC is easy to learn, is flexible, and is the ideal language for time-sharing systems. Management personnel using the budget models can easily learn to use BASIC, even if they have had little or no programming experience.

ADDITIONAL DISCUSSION POINTS

1.   What would be the advantage of using PL/I instead of COBOL at Ohio Citizens?

2.   What other language besides BASIC could Ohio Citizens use for their interactive programming applications?

ANSWER KEY TO STUDY GUIDE

True/False

2. T   4. T   6. F   8. F   10. F

Matching

2. a   4. b   6. e   8. c   10. g

Short Answer

2. Assembly language programs make efficient use of storage space and CPU time. But, the programs are difficult to write and to understand.

4. Execution mode causes the terminal to behave much like a calculator. Definition mode allows statements to be entered and the entire program to be executed on command.

6. Logo is a popular langauge used to teach children because it is easy to learn and it encourages the user to break a program down into steps. It allows the user to easily draw and animate figures.

8. If a programming application is input/output bound, this means it requires substantial file processing.

10. IDENTIFICATION DIVISION - Gives the name of the program and any program documentation.
    ENVIRONMENT DIVISION - Specifies the computer used to run the program; relates file information to input/outut devices.
    DATA DIVISION - Describes the variable names, records, and files to be used by the program.
    PROCEDURE DIVISION - Contains the processing instructions.

ENRICHMENT LECTURE

Will Computers Someday Speak English?

Computer scientists have always realized that computers can't achieve their full potential if only a few people know how to use them. Programmers have helped to make software "user friendly" by using menus and other devices to make the machines interact in human-like ways. But the need to know a programming language continues to be a barrier in computer use.

One way in which people's interaction with these machines could be greatly improved would be if data bases could be queried in plain English. Artificial intelligence research has been striving toward this goal for years. There are currently several natural-language processing systems that have reached the commercial stage. These systems merge computer science and linguistics so that the computer can "understand" natural language statements. Teaching a computer to recognize English words and sentences is enormously complex. The best of these systems have only a fraction of a person's capability to understand language. These systems use three fields of linguistics: syntax, semantics, and pragmatics.

Most systems use parsers to break sentences down into parts of speech. Parsers work in much the same way that an English student would when diagraming sentences. Yet, this syntactic analysis is not enough to enable the computer to understand statements. Most sentences can be parsed in several ways. Words may have different meanings in different contexts. This leads to the need for a great deal of sophistication in writing the program which will do the translating.

In many of these systems, semantic grammars are used which mix semantic constraints with the syntactic patterns of word order. Semantic grammars attempt to define words not only in terms of the word itself, but also in terms of the context in which the word has been used. For example, in determining a meaning for the word "head" it would be necessary to know if head was being used as a noun or a verb. The problem with this is that the grammars are closely tied to the application for which they are written. In some systems, algorithms have been developed that distribute information about the semantics into the syntactic grammar. This allows for the automatic production of grammars for specific data bases.

Pragmatics involves an interpretation of sentences that takes into account a variety of variables such as who wrote the sentence and why. This third area of natural language translation has barely been examined by language processing systems. This has been referred to as "situation semantics," that is, the meaning of a statement is very dependent upon the situation in which it is made. This is beyond the capability of present systems.

Although the development of natural language systems is continuing at a rapid pace, there is still a long way to go before they will be ready for real-life applications.

Adapted from "En·glish: The Newest Computer Language" by Dwight B. Davis. High Technology, February 1984.

*Note: A transparency master is available for use with this lecture in your transparency packet that accompanies this textbook.

Suggestions For Discussion

1. Discuss the three areas involved in translating English statements for use by the computer: syntax, semantics, and pragmatics. Which of these is the easiest to deal with? Which is the most difficult?

Syntax, although still difficult, is probably the easiest area to deal with. Programs have already been developed that can parse sentences to break them down into the various parts of speech. Pragmatics is the most difficult aspect of translating English into a form that can be used by the computer. This is because pragmatics involves taking into consideration who made a particular statement, when it was made, and why the person made it.

2. Discuss the development of programming languages (use the transparency). Programming languages have come a long way from the days of 0s and 1s. Each language level represents a significant improvement. Discuss the fact that assembly language still has important advantages, as mentioned in the chapter.

Early computers had to be programmed in machine language. This was very tedious and required a great deal of skill. Assembly language used mnemonics to make programs easier to write, but still was a complex process prone to error.

Assembly language does have the distinct advantage of using storage space and CPU time more efficiently than high-level languages. But, the development of high-level languages allowed the programmer to write programs that were much easier to follow and less error prone. The natural languages are theoretically the final step in this process. If developed fully, they will allow anyone to have the ability to program a computer.

Structured Design Concepts

LEARNING OBJECTIVES

Students should be able to:

- Discuss the features of the top-down design approach and its advantages
- Identify the tools and documentation techniques in top-down design
- Explain structured programming and reasons for its use
- Describe the methods used in the management of system projects

OUTLINE

I.   The Need for Structured Techniques: While structured techniques--structured design, structured programming and structured review--are not universally accepted in the data-processing community their use is increasing as business/corporation managers recognize their ability to improve the productivity of software development.

II. Structured-Design Methodology: Structured design methodology emphasizes the modular approach to problem solving. It is a standardized approach to program development in which a problem solution is defined in terms of functions to be performed.

    A. Top-down design is a method of defining a solution in terms of major functions to be performed, and further breaking down these major functions into subfunctions.

1. Structure charts are top-down design aides that
    graphically show (document) the relationships be-
    tween individual modules.

    a. The flow of control is from top to bottom.
    b. The higher-level modules are for both control
        and processing; the lower-level modules are
        only for processing.

2. Each module is independent of all others and has
    only one entry point and one exit point, and should
    be relatively small.
3. The complete solution is not established until the
    lowest level modules have been designed. To test
    and debug high-level modules early in the develop-
    ment cycle, dummy modules replace the lower-level
    modules.
4. Structure charts do not show the processing flow,
    the order of execution, or how control will
    actually be transferred to and from each module.

B. Documentation and design tools supplement structure
    charts in explaining system development.

    1. HIPO (Hierarchy plus Input-Process-Output) diagrams
        show inputs and outputs of each module. This type
        of documentation allows managers, analysts, and
        programmers to meet needs ranging from program
        maintenance to overhauling systems. HIPO consists
        of three types of diagrams describing a system from
        the general to the detailed level.

        a. The visual table of contents, similar to a
            structure chart, gives identification numbers
            to blocks in order to reference detailed
            modules.
        b. The overview diagram includes input, proc-
            essing, and outputs of a module.
        c. The specific functions performed and/or data
            items used in each module are described in a
            detail diagram.

    2. Pseudocode is an English-like description of the
        processing steps in a program and is understandable
        even to those unfamiliar with the program logic.

III. Structured Programming: Structured programming is a top-down modular approach that emphasizes dividing a program into logical sections to reduce testing time, increase programmer productivity, bring clarity to programming by reducing complexity, and decrease maintenance time and effort.

    A. A structured program uses only three basic control patterns: simple sequence, selection, and loop.

    B. A basic guideline of structured programming is that each module should have only one entry point and one exit point (a proper program).

    C. Structured programming logic flows from the beginning to the end of a program without backtracking or transferring control; therefore, it is called "GO-TO-less programming" (no branching).

    D. PL/I and ALGOL are especially suited to structured programming.

IV. Management of System Projects: Problems with system projects can be minimized through careful planning, coordination, and review.

    A. The goals of the chief programmer team (CPT) concept are to produce software that is easy to maintain and modify to improve programmer productivity, and to increase system reliability.

       1. The chief programmer coordinates the development of the programming project and supervises the activity of a small group of programmers.
       2. The backup programmer may help with system design, testing, and evaluation of alternative designs.
       3. The librarian maintains program descriptions, listings, coding, changes, test results, and up-to-date documentation.

    B. Structured review and evaluation are necessary if an error-free system is to be produced in the shortest possible time.

       1. Prior to coding of program modules, an informal design review is conducted in which the system design documentation is reviewed by management, analysts, and programmers.

2. A formal design review (structured walk-through)
    entails tracing through the program using valid and
    invalid data so that discrepancies will be noticed
    and problems corrected.

3. Egoless programming is another method of improving
    program quality; it involves establishing a program
    review process to determine if programs are being
    coded consistently and in adherence to predeter-
    mined coding standards.

Note: The Bethlehem Steel Corporation application appearing
later in this manual is appropriate to discuss after this
chapter has been studied.

ANSWERS TO REVIEW QUESTIONS

1.   There is a great need to increase the efficiency of software development; one of the ways in which the productivity of
software can be improved is through the use of structured techniques.

2.   The top-down approach is a method of defining a solution in
terms of major functions to be performed. A program is broken
down into functional modules. The highest-level module is the
main control module, which is further broken down into lower-
level modules. Modules are related to each other in a
heirarchical manner.

      Using this approach, a problem solution is defined in terms
of separate logical functions. The top-down approach is logical
and structured, and provides an organized method for system and
program design. Program development and maintenance costs are
reduced using this method.

3.   A module is a step in the solution process; it consists of
one or more logically related functions. A problem solution may
consist of several independent modules that perform the required
tasks together.

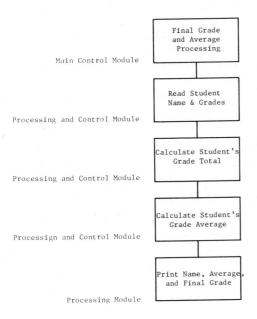

4.

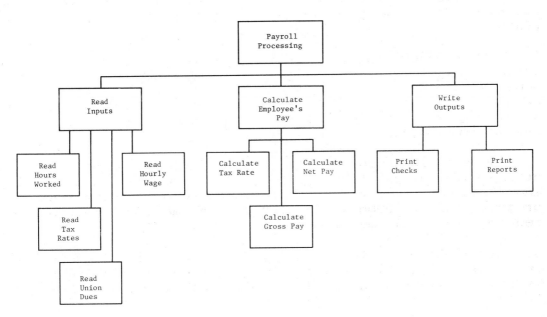

5.   HIPO and pseudocode are two methods of documentation. The
varying levels of detail incorporated in the different HIPO
charts allow them to be used by anyone associated with the
operations.

At times, flowcharts become too lengthy and difficult to read, or the logic or processing steps cannot be adequately expressed by ordinary flowchart symbols. In these situations, pseudocode is extremely useful.

6.   Visual table of contents for payroll example:

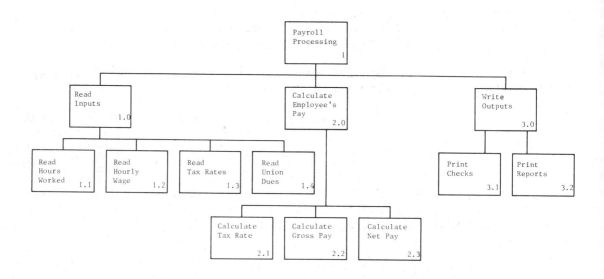

        Overview diagram for "calculate Employee's Pay" module of payroll example:

        Diagram ID : 2.0

Input	Process	Output
Hours worked	1. Calculate tax rate	Net pay
Hourly wages	2. Calculate gross pay	
Tax rates	3. Subtract tax	
Union dues	4. Subtract union dues	

Detail diagram for "calculate Employee's Pay" module of payroll example:

Input	Process	Output
Hours worked & Hourly rate	Multiply hours worked by hourly wages	Gross pay
Gross Pay	Is gross pay > 150 If yes multiply gross pay x .10 If no multiply gross pay x .06	tax
tax and union dues ($15)	Subtract tax and union dues ($15) from gross pay	net pay
net pay	Print amount on check	print check and repeat process until end of items

7.   The objectives of structured programming are: to reduce testing time, to increase programmer productivity, to increase clarity by reducing complexity, and to decrease maintenance time and effort.

8.   Languages such as FORTRAN and BASIC lack some features, making it difficult to avoid the use of "GO TO" statements. However, in other languages avoiding the use of "GO TO" statements does not reduce flexibility nor does it make coding more difficult.

9.   Structured programming divides a program into logical sections in order to reduce testing time, increase programmer productivity, and bring clarity to programming by reducing complexity. These objectives are reached by providing a standardized method for attacking a problem, emphasizing division of the program into logical sections using a top-down modular approach.

10.   All three of the basic structured control patterns (simple sequence, selection, and loop) are present in the flowchart.

11.   The CPT involves organizing a small number of programmers under the supervision of a chief programmer. This approach should produce a better software product that is easily maintained and modified. Also, CPT should improve programmer productivity and increase system realiability.

The librarian relieves the programmer of many clerical tasks such as:

- preparation of input from coding forms completed by programmers
- submission and pickup of inputs and outputs of runs
- maintaining up-to-date source program listings in archives for programmer use
- updating test data and implementing changes in programs and job-control statements
- maintaining up-to-date documentation

12.   Informal design review – the system design documentation is studied by selected personnel before the actual coding of the program modules; after a brief period each responds with suggestions for modifications of the system design.

Formal design review – this process, sometimes called a structured walk-through, involves distributing the documentation to a review team of two to four members; the team studies the documentation and then meets with the program designers to discuss the overall completeness, accuracy, and quality of the design.

ADDITIONAL REVIEW QUESTIONS

1.   Would there by any advantages to using a bottom-up approach to programming instead of using the top-down approach?

2.   What is a structure chart and why is it useful?

3.   Distinguish between an overview diagram and a detail diagram.

4.   Which languages are well suited to structured programming? Why are other languages not suitable for structured programming?

5.   In this chapter, a librarian is a person who aids programmers by performing clerical tasks; how was the term librarian used earlier in the text?

ANSWERS TO DISCUSSION POINTS

1.   The major benefit Armco receives from the structured approach is found in the area of preplanning and organization of the projects. This modular approach, with the weekly team reviews, has led to a tremendous reduction of errors. Also, the logic flow discussed between team members aids greatly in any follow-up and documentation.

The structured approach also reduced testing times, increases programmer productivity, and brings clarity to programming by reducing complexity.

2.   Armco uses the structured approach to programming extensively. They break each program into segments, or modules. "GOTO" statements are not used in the programs and the one entry/one exit guideline is used. This approach is not unique to Armco; however, it is not typical of many businesses.

ADDITIONAL DISCUSSION POINTS

1.   What is contained in Armco's Unit Development Plans?

2.   Which documentation and design tools could be beneficial to Armco?

3.   What goes on in the design phase of a project life cycle at Armco?

ANSWER KEY TO STUDY GUIDE

True/False

2. F   4. F   6. T   8. T   10. T

Matching

2. a   4. g   6. e   8. i   10. h

Short Answer

2.   Three useful structured techniques are

      ● structured design
      ● structured programming
      ● structured review

4.   HIPO stands for Hierarchy plus Input-Process-Output. Three
      types of diagrams are likely to be included in a HIPO
      package: a visual table of contents, an overview diagram,
      and a detail diagram.

6.   a. chief programmer   b. librarian   c. backup programmer

8.   Dummy modules are used in structured programs to test high-
      level modules before all of the low-level modules are writ-
      ten. Dummy modules may be inserted in place of these
      low-level modules and in this way, the program can be exe-
      cuted and the high-level modules can be tested for errors.
      This makes it easier to isolate the module in which an
      error is occurring.

10.   An informal review usually takes place in the early phases
      of development. It is used to determine if the system
      design effort is "on the right track." Later, after there
      is sufficient documentation such as flowcharts and pseudo-
      code, a formal design review often takes place to make sure
      the program design is complete and efficient.

ENRICHMENT LECTURE

Planning for the Worst

Data bases are extremely valuable to corporations. Some
people feel data bases are even more important than key executives. Donn B. Parker, a computer security expert, says "The computer is now the vault." So, what happens if a business loses
its entire data base?

Excessive heat, radiation, or humidity can destroy critical
data. Losses that occur from these excessive conditions happen
more often than most people realize. Most corporations attempt
to keep data losses a secret from the general public. The
companies fear a lessening of public confidence if data losses
became known. In spite of the damaging effects of data loss,
fewer than five percent of all businesses have a contingency
plan that can be implemented in the event of a data disaster.
The prevailing attitude seems to be one of hoping for the best!

If a company needs to cost-justify disaster planning, it
should consider the Securities Exchange Act of 1934 which was
amended by section 13(b) in 1977. Section 13(b) outlines a company's legal responsibility in preventing a data disaster.
According to lawyers representing Arthur Young, one of the
nation's largest accounting firms, "If a failure to comply with

section 13(b) is alleged to be either negligent of willful, a reporting company and members of its management may be defendants in an SEC injunctive action."

Several areas must be looked into as a part of disaster preparation. The current installation must be protected from power surges and environmental damage. Equipment maintenance must have a high priority. Valuable data should be duplicated and stored off site, preferably at an installation that specializes in this service. Planners should look into alternative facilities that can carry out critical applications during prolonged breakdowns. This is often referred to as a "hot site." "Cold site" backups should also be considered. A "cold site" is an empty shell which can quickly be changed into a working data processing facility in the event of an emergency. "Warm site" backups usually involve agreements between companies to help one another in the event of a disaster. Companies should look for other businesses that can meet their bare minimum needs as nearly as possible. A very expensive alternative is dual sites. This refers to keeping two (duplicate) data processing centers operating so, in the event of an emergency, all processing can be transferred to the site not affected. Although dual sites are the ideal solution, they are seldom a viable option because of the expense involved.

All of the above alternatives should be considered, but a disaster plan must be tailored to the exact needs of a par-

ticular corporation. To operate without a functional plan is
foolish and extremely hazardous to the well-being of a corporation. A structured disaster plan should be as much a part of a
company's planning as the other structured techniques covered in
this chapter.

Adapted from "Armed Against Calamity" by Dan W. Post.
Business Computer Systems, April 1984.

*Note: A transparency master is available for use with
this lecture in your transparency packet that accompanies this
textbook.

Suggestions For Discussion

1. Discuss the kinds of events that might happen that could
destroy an entire data base. What can companies do to attempt
to prevent this from happening?

The answers here will depend on the imagination of the
students and ideas they have gotten from reading. Some
possibilities include: flooding, earthquakes, tornadoes,
hurricanes, fire, terrorist activities, or sabotage from
alienated employees. Maintaining building and hardware
properly can go a long way in preventing many disasters.
Adequate security is also vital.

2. Could this kind of disaster planning be incorporated
into the other structured planning techniques discussed in this
chapter? Is there a necessity for structured disaster preparation?

Yes, structured disaster planning should be as much a part
of a corporation's structured planning as structured design
and review of projects undertaken. Not only is it vital
for the well-being of the corporation, but legally it is a
necessity.

Application Software

Students should be able to:

- Define word-processing software, data-management software, modeling software, graphics software, and integrated software
- Describe the uses and features of word-processing software
- Describe the uses and features of data-management software
- Describe the uses and features of modeling software
- Describe the uses and features of graphics software
- Describe the types and uses of integrated software

OUTLINE

I. Word Processing Software

    A. Definition – A word processor is an application software package designed to allow the user to enter, manipulate, format, print, store, and retrieve text.

    B. Word processing involves two steps: text editing and print formatting.

        1. Text editing allows the user to enter text into the computer where it can be stored until it is edited and the new version saved.

        a.   A line editor allows the user to operate on only one line at a time.

        b.   A screen editor can be used to edit the text shown at a given time on the entire screen.

    2.   Print formatting occurs when the word processor communicates with the printer, through the computer system, to tell it how to print the text.

C.   Common features offered by nearly all word processors fall into one of three categories: writing and editing, screen formatting, and print formatting.

    1.   Writing and editing features include cursor positioning, word wrap, scrolling, insertion, deletion, move, search, and undo.

    2.   Screen formatting features control the way that text is displayed on the screen as well as provide the user with status information concerning the document being entered or edited. Some of these features are display of upper- and lower-case letters, tab settings, and information as to the current page number and variable memory.

    3.   Print formatting features include: margin settings, line spacing, centering, automatic pagination, headers and footers, and character enhancements.

II.   Data-Management Software

A.   Definition - Data-management packages (or data managers) are application software packages that computerize the everyday tasks of recording and filing information.

B.   The two types of data managers used in data management are file handlers and data base packages.

    1.   File handlers were developed first and were designed to duplicate the traditional manual methods of filing. File handlers are popular with small businesses that can benefit from conversion of manual record keeping to computerized record keeping. They also can be used in the home for creating a computerized Christmas card list, creating a mailing list, and keeping track of books in a personal library.

2. Data bases consolidate various independent files into one integrated whole from which all users can have access to the information they need. Data bases are used by large companies that have large amounts of data stored which need to be accessible by many users.

C. Standard features found in data managers include: adding records, deleting records, searching for and/or updating records, sorting the data file, printing, and making some mathematical calculations.

III. Modeling Software

A. Definition - Modeling software is based on a mathematical model; a model is a mathematical representation of a real world situation.

1. Modeling software used with microcomputers is called an electronic spreadsheet.
2. Modeling software packages called planning packages are used with minicomputers and mainframes (to be discussed in Chapter 5).

B. Electronic spreadsheets, like word processors and data managers, are used in the home as well as in business.

1. In the home they are used for home budgeting and interest calculation.
2. In business they are used for simulation and decision making as well as for the traditional purposes in the areas of finance and accounting.

C. Features of electronic spreadsheets include the following: variable column width, automatic spillover, insert and delete, graphics, templates, locking cells, hiding cells, naming cells, windows, titles, copy, manual recalculations, and sort.

IV. Graphics Software

A. Definition - Graphics software packages are designed to allow the user to display images on a computer terminal or monitor or to print images on a printer.

B. Uses for graphics application software packages range from business to artistic uses.

1.   Business uses include producing pie charts and bar
     graphs as data summaries for presentations,
     creating slides and/or transparencies, and
     designing entire objects or parts (e.g. automo-
     biles).
2.   Computer artists can use this software to "paint"
     images or pictures on the display screen; these
     images can be readily changed if the artist is
     dissatisfied.
3.   The creation of computer games relies heavily on
     graphics packages.

C.   Features that are common to nearly all types of
     graphics software packages are as follows: two- and
     three-dimensional display, save, cursor positioning,
     high resolution graphics, color, and animation.

V.   Integrated Software

A.   Business oriented perspective

1.   Horizontal software integration refers to those
     application software packages that are general in
     nature and are capable of being used for a number
     of different types of applications.
2.   Vertical software integration indicates a specifi-
     city of purpose.

B.   Software design perspective

1.   Horizontal integration describes the combination of
     application packages (word processor, data manager,
     spreadsheet, and graphics) into one package that
     can share data.
2.   Vertical integration refers to the enhancement of a
     single package.

C.   Windows, or window environments, allow for a software
     design using horizontal integration and are enhance-
     ments to the normal operating system of a computer and
     allow more than one application software package to run
     concurrently.

ANSWERS TO REVIEW QUESTIONS

1.   A "word processor" is an application software package
designed to allow the user to enter, manipulate, format, print,
store, and retrieve text. "Word processing" is the term used to
describe the process of manipulating text using the word processor. "Word-processing system" is a term used to describe the
computer system, or a portion of the computer system, used for
the task of word processing.

2.   The two primary functions of a word-processor are text
editing and print formatting. In text editing a user enters
text into the computer via a word processor; there it can be
stored, edited, and the new version saved. Print formatting
occurs when the word processor communicates with the printer,
through the computer system, to tell it how to print the text.

3.   A line editor allows you to operate on only one line of
text at a time. A screen editor, on the other hand, can be used
to edit the text shown at a given time on the entire screen. A
page-oriented word processor treats a document as a series of
pages; the user can display and edit only one page at a time. A
document-oriented word processor treats a text file as one long
document, eliminating the need to work on pages separately.

4.   A cursor is usually a blinking line or box on the display
screen; it is used to identify the current position on the
display and indicates where the next character will be typed.
Common cursor positions include the following:

    a.   Home: upper left hand corner of the display screen.
    b.   Top of page: first character at top of current display
        screen.
    c.   End of page: last character at bottom of current
        display screen.
    d.   Tab: predefined positions from left margin of display
        screen.
    e.   Page up: displays top portion of current page and
        positions cursor to first character.

5.   A data manager (or a data management package) is an application software package that computerizes the everyday tasks of
recording and filing information. It is used to replace the
traditional manual filing system using pencil, paper, file
folders, and file cabinet.

6.   File handlers and data base packages differ in the way in which the data is stored and hence how it can be accessed. File handlers can access only one data file at a time; data bases consolidate various independent files into one integrated whole from which all users can have access to the information they need. A data base can be likened to a large, centrally located room with many file cabinets of information; all personnel have access to the information. A file handler can be likened to a single file cabinet kept in a particular department where only that department's employees have access to the data.

7.   Four of the more common features contained in data manage-ment software packages are as follows:

    a.   add/delete – the add feature allows the user to place a record or information in the file; the delete feature erases a record of information from the file.
    b.   search/update – the search feature allows the user to search an existing file for a record or records based on certain criteria; the update feature allows the user to change the value of a data field once it has been located.
    c.   sort – the sort feature provides the user with a way to alter the order of storage.
    d.   print – the print feature allows the user to have printing capabilities for purposes such as mailing lists, mailing labels, etc.

8.   Modeling is the mathematical representation of a real world situation. It can be beneficial to business managers by assisting them in decision-making.

9.   By developing a model, entering it into the computer via the modeling software, and then altering values of the variables within the model, a manager can see how changes in the variables will affect the outcome of the model.

10.   A cell is the point in a spreadsheet, a unique location, where a particular row and column meet. Cells can contain values, labels, and formulas.

11.   Pixels are individual dots on the video display screen; they create images. By controlling the pixels the computer user can create graphic images with various degrees of detail.

12.   Horizontally integrated software can offer the application software user the advantage of capability of combining a number of different types of application packages into one package that can share data; data can then be passed among the combined packages.

ADDITIONAL REVIEW QUESTIONS

1.   Describe the characteristics and functions of an electronic spreadsheet.

2.   List and describe six features of electronic spreadsheets.

3.   What is a window, or window environment?

ANSWERS TO DISCUSSION POINTS

1.   Microsoft considers the following three issues to be critical to software developers in the future: integration, user interface, and expanding the definition of what an operating system is.

     Integration is important because efficient use of various software applications requires finding ways to move data between separate applications without the need to go back in and reinput or redescribe the data.

     The user interface issue is the introduction of graphics; how we present data on the screen is a very important concern. Graphics technology in the future will allow users to put arbitrary images on the screen just as they would a piece of paper, and it will become a part of the definition of the machine itself, not just an add-on.

     Operating systems need to be expanded to include graphics capabilities, user interface capabilities, and networking; if application package developers can assume that these components are part of every machine and not just add-ons, these packages can be designed accordingly.

2.   Software developers are very concerned about the development of standards for user interface because there are certain expectations that users have, or should have, for their interface with computer applications. If software developers pay no attention to standards, users will be dissatisfied, and all software developers will suffer through the association.

Graphics are especially important to the issue of user interface because of the tremendous potential that graphics represent for software application packages. If, in the future, the screen can be used as a piece of paper on which to put arbitrary images, graphics are going to be used for a great deal more than simply drawing graphs.

ADDITIONAL DISCUSSION POINTS

1.   Why has Microsoft become such a large, successful company in such a relatively short time?

2.   What are some of the possible reasons behind the popular appeal of Microsoft's "Flight Simulator" software package?

ANSWER KEY TO STUDY GUIDE

True/False

2. T   4. F   6. T   8. T   10. T

Matching

2. b   4. j   6. e   8. a   10. i

Short Answer

2.   File handlers allow access to only one data file at a
      time, thereby causing the duplication of data between
      files. The problem of updating information consistently
      across files is much the same as that of a manual filing
      system. Data bases eliminate duplication of data by con-
      solidating independent files into one integrated file.
      When data is updated, it must only be done once and the
      changes are readily available to all users.

4.   The increased cost of developing application software and
      the rise in popularity of microcomptuers have contributed
      to the increased use of prewritten application software
      packages.

6.   List five common writing and editing features of word proc-
      essors.

      ● cursor positioning   ● insertion/deletion
      ● word wrap   ● search and find/replace
      ● scrolling   ● undo

8.   Modeling software can be used in a business setting for
      simulation, altering values of variables within a model in
      order to see how the changes will affect the outcome of the
      model. Another business application is the electronic
      spreadsheet which can be used to do financial calculations
      and record transactions. Both simulation and electronic
      spreadsheets help managers make decisions.

10.   Horizontal software integration refers to application
      packages that are general in nature while vertical software
      integration refers to packages designed for a specific pur-
      pose.

ENRICHMENT LECTURE

Can Software Replace Freud?

Application programs are available to help managers prepare accounting statements, develop concise reports, figure the tax implications of selling a subsidiary company, or design a new package for a product with lagging sales. Now managers can look to computer programs to help them handle their employees or even their bosses!

In the past, managers would turn to their personnel departments for advice when having problems with employees' attitudes, motivation, or work performance. But computer programs such as one called the Management Edge are changing traditional practices. The Management Edge asks a manager questions about the employee's personality and then gives advice ranging from how to get the employee to work more productively to whether or not to fire him or her.

Other programs offer simple, computerized management training courses, again replacing a function usually handled by the personnel department. One training program puts managers in charge of a hypothetical group discussion with employees to guide the manager in how to lead the discussion. Employees are represented on the screen by smiling faces if the manager is doing a good job and frowning faces if the manager is not.

Another program tries to teach managers about the importance of communicating effectively by putting its user in the positiion of an employee whose manager gives insufficient instructions and feedback. First, the program tries to explain how to play a computerized card game by giving minimal and somewhat confusing instructions. Then the program rushes the player with strict time limits. As the program progresses, it begins to give the player more feedback and less strict time limits. The purpose of the program is to show managers how frustrating it can be to receive unclear instructions and unreasonable deadlines.

It is no suprise that some management trainers, industrial psychologists, and others who stand to lose business to this type of software are skeptical. They say that the programs encourage simple-minded approaches to complex problems that could be better handled by humans.

Some managers, on the other hand, say that computers offer certain advantages over human-controlled management training. One is cost. Most of the programs are offered on floppy disks for between $200 and $500, which is much less than a typical management training course.

Not only are these computer programs being met with much success by managers seeking work-related advice, but they are

also being used to help them deal with personal problems. The
wife of one company president who used the Management Edge began
using the program to help her deal with family members such as
her stubborn three-year-old son. She told several friends
about the program and they enthusiastically began using it to
get advice on how to "handle" their husbands!

Adapted from "Managers Are Using Personal Computers to Help
Them Deal with Personnel Issues" by David Stipp. The Wall
Street Journal, July 25, 1984.

*Note: A transparency master is available for use with
this lecture in your transparency packet that accompanies this
textbook.

Suggestions For Discussion

1. How would you react to the knowledge that your boss had
used a computer program to analyze your personality?

Answers will be based on opinions.

2. Do you believe a computer program can be substituted
for the human interaction offered by regular management training
courses in learning to deal with other people?

Answers will be based on opinions.

System Analysis and Design

LEARNING OBJECTIVES

Students should be able to:

- Discuss system theory and the system approach to system analysis
- List the reasons system analysis may be conducted
- Name the sources the analyst may use in gathering data
- Describe some techniques used to analyze data
- Discuss what is included in a system analysis report
- Describe the steps involved in system design
- List the activities involved in implementation
- Identify the different methods of system conversion
- Discuss the importance of system audit and review

OUTLINE

I.   System Theory: A group of related elements that work together toward a common goal make up a system.

  A. A system consists of inputs, processes, outputs, and feedback.

  B. Every system interacts with other systems; every system is a part of a larger system.

  C. A business firm or organization can be viewed as a system (a group of related departments and employees) within a system (the world economy).

D.   The system approach models reality by viewing an orga-
     nization as a integrated whole; the system model high-
     lights important relationships, patterns, and flows of
     information.

E.   System methodology: These steps are involved in deve-
     loping or revising a system: analysis, design, imple-
     mentation, and an audit/review.

II. System Analysis: System analysis may be required because
     of a need to solve a problem, respond to new information
     requirements, incorporate new technology into a system, or
     make broad system improvements.

A.   When the proposal to conduct system analysis is
     accepted, the analyst begins to gather data.
     Information can be gathered internally and externally.

     1.   Internal sources include:

          a.   Interview
          b.   System flowcharts
          c.   Questionnaires
          d.   Formal reports

     2.   External reports include:

          a.   Books and periodicals
          b.   Brochures and manufacturer-produced specifica-
               tions
          c.   Customers, suppliers, and other companies

B.   After the data has been collected and documented, it
     must be analyzed.

     1.   The analyst should be very conscious of system
          theory when evaluating information.
     2.   Some techniques used to analyze data are:

          a.   Grid charts – show the relationships that exist
               between the components of a system or between
               the inputs and outputs.
          b.   System flowcharts – emphasize the flow of data
               through the entire data-processing system
               without describing details of internal computer
               operations.
               ● The symbols used to specify I/O and storage
                 devices are miniature outlines of the actual
                 media.

- System flowcharts representing the general information flow often represent many operations within one process symbol (contrast with program flowchart).

   c. Decision logic tables - represent the actions to be taken under different sets of conditions.

- The elements of the DLT are the condition stub, action stub, condition entries, and action entries.
- Because the DLTs present logic in a summarized form and are easy to understand, they are used to record facts collected on the old system, to summarize aspects of the new system being designed, and to aid programmers.

C. After the data has been collected and analyzed, the system analysis report should communicate the findings to management.

   1. This should include a statement of goals and objectives of the study and an explanation of the present system.

   2. A preliminary report of feasible alternatives and the resources and capital needed for a new system should be estimated.

III. System Design: The second state of the system methodology concentrates on how a system can be developed to meet the information requirements determined in the analysis. The steps in design follow.

A. The objectives of the new system must be carefully reviewed.

B. Design a system model, keeping the system approach in mind.

C. The organizational constraints must be evaluated so that available resources can be optimally utilized; typical constraints are budget, time requirements, staff, and hardware availability.

D. Technically feasible alternative designs must be created so management can choose from them.

   1. I/O requirements must be determined and evaluated so that priorities can be established and user needs met.

      2.   Programming specifications must be detailed for each alternative.

  E. A feasibility analysis must be done for each alternative. Technical, economical, legal, operational, and time constraints must be considered.

  F. The next phase involves evaluating each alternative to assess its benefits and the costs that will be incurred to realize these benefits.

      1.   Intangible benefits must be especially scrutinized, justified, and quantified.
      2.   Costs include both initial and ongoing expenses.
      3.   Selection of an alternative is often dependent upon which provides the best cost/benefit ratio.

  G. Finally, the design report is prepared to evaluate each alternative for management and to recommend the best alternative and suggest a plan for its implementation.

IV. System Programming

  A. Programming - an analyst or programmer may do this, or software packages may be purchased.

  B. Testing the system - before a system becomes operational, it must be tested and debugged.

  C. Documentation - clerical and computer procedures provide an easy frame of reference for system maintenance as information needs change.

  D. Special considerations include:

      1.   Input - the form of input to the program determines how the program should ask for data.
      2.   Processing - processing steps should verify the accuracy of the data and identify potential errors.
      3.   Output - the programs may be required to produce output that is not in hard-copy form.

V. System Implementation: The goal is to insure that the system is debugged, operational, and accepted by the users; it includes the following activities:

A. Personnel training - for the system to be successful,
    it is essential that all who are affected by the system
    know what can be expected from it and their respon-
    sibilities for insuring its smooth operation.

    1. Users include general management, staff personnel,
        line managers, operating personnel, customers, and
        suppliers.
    2. The personnel who will be operating the system must
        be trained in preparation of data input, storage-
        device operation, and the handling of problems that
        occur during processing.
    3. Training can be accomplished through large-group
        seminars, tutorial training, and on-the-job
        training.

B. System conversion - the switch from an old system to a
    new one is conversion.

    1. In parallel conversion, the new system is operated
        side-by-side with the old one for some period of
        time.
    2. When only a small part of the business is initially
        converted to the new system, it is called pilot
        conversion.
    3. During phased conversion, the old system is gra-
        dually replaced by the new one over a period of
        time.
    4. Crash, or direct, conversion takes place all at
        once.

VI. System Audit and Review: Feedback on system performance,
     which may take the form of an audit, involves analyzing
     system performance in terms of the initial ojbectives
     established for it.

    A. The audit should address the following questions:

        1. Does the system perform as planned and deliver the
            anticipated benefits?
        2. Was the system completed on schedule and with the
            resources estimated?
        3. Is all output used?
        4. Have the new procedures been implemented and are
            controls adequate?
        5. Has the system been accepted by the user?
        6. Is the processing turn-around time satisfactory or
            are delays frequent?

B. System maintenance detects and corrects errors, meets new information needs of management, and responds to changes in the environment.

C. The use of structured programming helps create a system that is easy to modify.

Note: The Kroger Company application appearing later in this manual is appropriate to discuss after this chapter has been studied.

ANSWERS TO REVIEW QUESTIONS

1.   Parts of organizations (departments, employees, etc.) have a degree of independence that influences the information system; and vice versa. An organization in which the decision-making was conducted by relatively few personnel in top executive positons would fit the central processing mode, whereas an organization in which the decision-making responsibilities were decentralized to a relatively large number of personnel would seem to fit the distributed processing information mode.

2.   A system is a group of related elements that work together toward a common goal. Our solar system is an example of a system. Its subsystems are the nine planets and their moons. Our solar system belongs to the Milky Way galaxy which is, in turn, a subsystem of the universe.

3.   The environment is anything outside the system that has an effect on or is affected by the system. The environment may supply inputs to the system and/or may receive outputs from the system.

4.   The proposal to conduct system analysis should provide management with the following:

- a clear and concise statement of the problem, or reason for system analysis
- a statement clearly defining the level of the system analysis and its objectives
- an identification of the information that must be collected and the potential sources of this information
- a preliminary schedule for conducting the analysis

The scope of the analysis determines the level of intensity of the data gathering and analyzing activities.

5.   System analysis is an evaluation of the current procedures and operations of an organization. The following are reasons why a firm might conduct a system analysis:

- The present system is not functioning properly.
- A new aspect has been added.
- A new development in computer technology has occurred.
- The organization wants to update the information system.

A firm may choose not to perform a system analysis if its present operations are efficient and functioning properly, or if the firm does not have adequate funds for the process.

6.   Four internal sources are interviews, system flowcharts, questionnaires, and formal reports. Interviews can be most effective when they are conducted properly.

7.   A decision logic table (DLT) is a tabular representation of the actions to be taken under various sets of circumstances. A DLT is used by a system analyst/programmer to summarize the logic required to make particular decisions in an understandable form.

8.   The system analysis report should contain:

- a restatement of the scope and objective of the analysis
- an explanation of the present system
- a statement of all constraints on the present system
- a preliminary report of feasible alternatives
- an estimate of the resources and capital required to either modify the present system or design a new one

9.   In the design phase the analyst changes focus and concentrates on how a system can be developed to meet the informational requirements; in the analysis phase the analyst focused on what the current system does or should be doing.

10.   It is difficult to design the "perfect" information system because what is considered "perfect" to one user may be considered useless by another. Every manager and every user has different needs, desires, and perceptions of what the system should do. It is impossible to provide exactly what everyone wants.

11.   The system design report should contain:

- explanations in general terms of how the various designs will satisfy the information requirements determined in the analysis phase

- reviews of the information requirements uncovered in the system analysis
- explain the proposed designs in both flowchart and narrative form
- detail the corporate resources required to implement each alternative
- make a recommendation

The report is presented to management personnel; it should avoid technical jargon and provide flowcharts of each alternative.

12.   Training can be provided by group seminars or tutorial training.   On-the-job training is also used.

Groups that must undergo training:

- those responsible for developing operating, and maintaining the system such as operators, system analyst, programmers, and data processing managers
- the user group, which includes general management, staff personnel, line managers, other operating personnel, customers, and suppliers

13.   System documentation provides a frame of reference for system maintenance as information needs change.   Program documentation includes explanations of major logical portions of the program; this is important, because the best designed systems can fail if users perform their functions incorrectly.

14.   • Parallel conversion – the new system is operated side by side with the old one for a period of time.
- Pilot conversion – involves converting only; a small portion of the organization to the new system.
- Phased conversion – the old system is gradually replaced by the new one over a period of time.
- Crash conversion – a direct conversion taking place all at once.

15.   A system audit acts as a strong incentive for insuring that a good system is designed and delivered on schedule.

An audit is an evaluation to ascertain that the system objectives have been met.   The audit is performed after implementation.   Maintenance is a process of surveillance of operations to determine what modifications are needed to meet changing demands.

ADDITIONAL REVIEW QUESTIONS

1.   Why must goals and objectives be reviewed in the design phase?

2.   What aspects besides economic ones does the feasibility analysis consider?

3.   What important factors should be considered when developing alternative system designs? Are processing requirements the same for each alternative?

4.   Why must every system be cost justified? On what factors is it difficult to put a price?

5.   What is involved in the implementation phase of system development?

6.   Distinguish between data collection and data analysis.

7.   What is the purpose of a decision logic table?

8.   Explain what is meant by system theory. Why would it help in system analysis?

9.   Describe the steps involved in system methodology.

ANSWERS TO DISCUSSION POINTS

1.   A detailed procedure such as PRIDE should be followed for large projects that cost a lot of money to develop. For small systems, or minor modifications to an existing system, PRIDE may not be necessary. Such a detailed methodology is very expensive and in some cases the investment in time, effort, and money may not be worth the payoff.

2.   In Phase I of PRIDE, a general flowchart of the proposed system is developed. It shows the flow of key documents and includes a narrative.

In Phase II the system design manual is generated. It contains thorough documentation of each subsystem: flowcharts, inputs, outputs, and files. A narrative is also included.

The documentation in Phase III makes up the subsystem design manual. Administrative and computer procedures are explained by flowcharts and narrative. Final formats for all output reports are generated.

The user's manual is generated in Phase IV.

In Phase V, the actual programs are produced. Documentation continues in each phase and is completed in Phase VII.

ADDITIONAL DISCUSSION POINTS

1.   In which phase of the PRIDE methodology is HIPO used? What do you remember about HIPO?

2.   What other departments at Marathon Oil may possibly help the Systems Development Division perform a cost/benefit analysis?

ANSWER KEY TO STUDY GUIDE

True/False

2. F   4. T   6. F   8. T   10. F

Matching

2. h   4. b   6. d   8. g   10. a

Short Answer

2.   System analysis, design, programming, implementation, and audit and review are the steps necessary in developing an information system.

4.   A DLT is helpful for analyzing data when multiple conditions are present that cause various actions to take place. If conditions are difficult to communicate and understand, using a DLT can make the logic clearer.

6.
   - financial limitations
   - personnel
   - organizational structure
   - time constraints
   - computer facilities available
   - technology

8.
   - Reasonableness check – looks at a data item to see if it is a possible value.
   - Range check – evaluates a data item to see if its value lies within an established range.
   - Type check – verififes that the data item is in the right form.
   - Correct code check – matches the data value to approved numbers used in the company.

10. A feasibility study determines whether or not a particular alternative is economically, legally, and technically feasible (possible). Also, users' backgrounds and education must be considered to see if they can understand and master the system. Finally, it must be possible to develop and implement the system design within a given time frame.

ENRICHMENT LECTURE

Use Care or Beware When Implementing a System

Getting your computer up and running can be a headache-less affair if you heed one warning: Always anticipate the worst that can happen and plan to avoid it. These words may sound a little pessimistic, but many computer systems have failed because the people in charge did not anticipate the problems that could arise.

One common mistake companies contemplating a new computer system make is placing 100 percent trust in the computer manufacturer. The following company did just that. Read on to find out what happened.

The president of a company called Widget Inc. (a fictitious name) realized his company needed a new accounting system because the manual system was no longer working. He called a computer manufacturer who quickly sent two salespeople to look at the situation at Widget Inc. They recommended a state of the art microcomputer to handle the company's information processing needs.

The only hitch was that the microcomputer required a custom program available only from a software vendor located 5,000 miles away.   But the salespeople assured the president that their company would provide local support if there were any problems.

When it came time to implement the system, the computer vendor realized that the microcomputer could not handle all of Widget's processing requirements.   But the salespeople talked the president into more equipment that would take care of everything.

After the hardware was installed, the software failed to work.   In the meantime, the software vendor went bankrupt and eventually Widget Inc. filed a lawsuit against the computer manufacturer.   The moral of the story is that the president of Widget Inc. believed everything the salespeople told him because he did not know enough about computers to make an informed decision.   He should have hired an expert to examine the proposed system to make sure it would do what it was supposed to.

The preceding story illustrates the problems that can arise with hardware and software.   Another aspect to consider when implementing a computer system is the people who will work with them.   The four tips that follow can help make you aware of some common "people" problems.

1.   Workers are afraid that daily exposure to computers could cause health problems.   A company should carefully review the possible health risks before purchasing equipment.

2.   Employees who will be working with the computer system feel left out if they have no say in selecting the system.   They should be allowed to attend vendor presentations before a system is purchased.

3.   Many workers worry about looking stupid in front of their co-workers.   The company should deal only with computer vendors with solid reputations for employee training.

4.   A good manager will discourage snobbery among those workers selected to be computer operators.   It is common for the computer operators to act superior to the secretaries who only use electric typewriters.   The manager should let everyone know that the computer is just another business tool.

To summarize, if you have a genuine concern for the person who will be staring at a computer screen all day and if you are not taken in by fast-talking salespeople, you will1 avoid some of the common problems of implementing a computer system.   Just use care when planning and your computer system can be a great asset to your company.

Adapted from "The Pains of Implementation" by Michael Tannenbaum and Larry McClain.   Popular Computing, March 1983.

*Note: A transparency master is available for use with this lecture in your transparency packet that accompanies this textbook.

Suggestions For Discussion

1.   Do you think hardware vendors be held responsible for computer systems they install that do not work as they should?

Answers will be based on opinions.   Legal consequences will be based on whether the statements made by the sales people are considered sales talk or contract liability.   When you acquire hardware and software from separate vendors, legal responsibility may be hard to place.

2.   If you were an employee selected to work as a computer operator, would you feel superior to the regular clerical workers?

Answers will be based on opinions.

File Organization and Data Design

LEARNING OBJECTIVES

Students should be able to:

- Distinguish between sequential, indexed-sequential, and direct-access processing and explain the characteristics and applications of each
- Explain how inquiries into each type of file organization are made
- Evaluate the advantages and disadvantages of each type of file organization
- Define the data base approach

OUTLINE

I.   File Processing: File processing is the operation of periodically updating permanent files to reflect the effects of changes in data.

A.   A field is a data item. A record is a collection of data items that relate to a single unit. A grouping of all related records is called a file, or data set.

B.   Three types of file arrangements are sequential organization, indexed-sequential, and direct-access design.

II.   Sequential Design: A unique identifier used to locate
individual records in a file is called a key. The records
ordered according to their key values form a sequential
file.

   A.   The basic file containing all existing records is
        called the master file. The file containing changes to
        be made to the master file is called the transaction
        file.

   B.   In batch processing, data items are collected and proc-
        essed periodically in a group by the computer. Before
        processing, items are sorted into sequential order
        (transaction file) to match the sequence of the records
        on the file to be updated (master file).

   C.   In order to interrogate sequential files, the entire
        master file must be read each time it is updated or
        accessed; there is no way of immediately accessing an
        individual record on the master file.

   D.   The advantages of batch processing and sequential file
        design include:

        1.   It is suitable for many types of applications in
             which it is not necessary to update records as
             transactions occur.
        2.   The method is economical when the number of records
             processed is high.
        3.   The design of sequential files is simple.
        4.   Magnetic tape, a low-cost medium, can be used to
             maximum advantage.
        5.   I/O speeds are faster than those achieved with
             direct input of transactions from keyboard ter-
             minals.

   E.   The disadvantages of this mode of processing include:

        1.   The entire file must be processed, even if only a
             few records need to be updated.
        2.   Transactions must be sorted into a particular
             sequence.
        3.   The master file is only as up-to-date as the last
             processing run.
        4.   The sequential nature of the file organization is a
             serious handicap when inquiries reference a field
             other than the one used as a key in the master
             file.

III. Direct-Access Design: Data grouping or sorting is not
necessary - data is submitted to the computer in the order
that it occurs. Direct-access storage devices make this
possible.

    A. The key to the record must be known in order to access
it. Two methods of direct-access addressing are:

        1. Using a directory that contains the reference num-
bers of records and their storage locations; during
processing the computer searches the directory to
locate a particular record.

        2. By performing a transformation process on the
record key (randomizing) so that no new identification key is required.

    B. Advantages:

        1. Transaction data can be used directly for updating
records via online terminals without first being
sorted.

        2. The master file is not read completely each time
updating occurs; this saves time and money.

        3. It takes only a fraction of a second to access any
record on a direct-access file.

        4. Direct-access files provide more flexibility in
handling inquiries.

        5. Several files can be updated concurrently.

        6. Random-access processing is suited to applications
involving files that have a low activity and a high
volatility.

            a. Activity refers to the proportion of records
processed during an updating run.

            b. Volatility refers to the changes in a file
during a specified time period.

    C. Disadvantages:

        1. During processing, the original record is destroyed
and replaced by the updated record; consequently,
to provide backup, a magnetic tape copy of the
master file must be made once a week, as well as
records of the weekly transactions.

        2. Because many users have access to records stored on
direct-access devices in online systems, the
chances of accidental destruction of data and
unauthorized access are greater.

3. Direct-access file organization leads to some
    unused file locations because of randomizing.
4. Implementation is more difficult because of the
    greater complexity and the high level of
    programming support needed.

IV. Indexed-Sequential File Organization: In this structure,
     the records are stored sequentially on a DASD and an index
     is established for selected record keys and their
     corresponding addresses.

     A. This type of file provides direct-access--a particular
         record can be accessed without processing all the
         records before it.

     B. Since all the records are ordered according to an iden-
         tification number, such a file can be processed
         sequentially.

     C. Advantages:

         1. This method is well suited for both inquiries and
             large processing runs.
         2. Access time is faster than in sequential organiza-
             tion.

     D. Disadvantages:

         1. More direct-access storage space is required for
             indices.
         2. Processing time is longer than in a direct-access
             system.

V.   Data Base Concepts: Data base organization is an
     integrated approach to file organization that eliminates
     duplicate data and uses one data base (collection of data)
     for all applications.

     A. Data organization

         1. Physical design refers to how the data is kept on
             storage devices and how it is accessed.
         2. Logical design refers to how data is viewed by
             application programmers or individual users.

     B. Manipulation, retrieval, and inquiry

         1. Simple structure is a sequential arrangement of
             data records.

2.   Linear structure is a list that has a specifically arranged (ordered) sequence of records.
3.   Hierarchical structure (or tree structure) is the term used to refer to the subdivision of a list into groups that contain "member" records and are headed by an "owner" record.
4.   Inverted structures contain indexes for selected attributes in a file similar to those used in indexed-sequential files, and addresses of records having those attributes.

C.   Data base management system is a set of programs that serves as the major interface between the data base and its three principal users: the programmer, the operating system, and the user. This system facilitates the use of a data base.

D.   Assessment of the data base approach

1.   Advantages include: data redundancy is minimized; updating involves only one copy of the data.
2.   Limitations include: errors may be propagated throughout the data base; highly skilled people are required to design data-base systems.

ANSWERS TO REVIEW QUESTIONS

1.   File processing is the operation of periodically updating permanent files to reflect the effects of changes in data. Updating involves two sets of files, the master file and the transaction file. The master file is the basic file containing all existing records; the transaction file contains the changes to be made. In updating, both the master file and the transaction file serve as input to the computer system.

2.   Records in a group are sorted into sequential order to match the sequence of the records on the file to be updated. The transaction file and the master file are both input to the computer system. When the computer finds matching keys on both files, a new master file is updated with the information from the transaction file. Unchanged records from the old master file are also written onto the new master file. The old master file and the transaction file may be retained for back-up.

3.   ● Master file--the basic file containing all existing
        records.
      ● Transaction file--the file containing changes to be made
        to the master file.

4.   Sequential processing is applicable when there is a high
volume of records and a large number of transactions that
undergo standard procedures at scheduled time intervals.

      This method is inefficient if only isolated data records
are processed, because the access time is too great. Along
with the time limitations, direct access is not possible with
batch processing. Also, the master file is only as up to date
as the last batch.

5.   In direct-access processing, a particular record or a
master file can be accessed directly and updated without all
preceeding records in the file being read.

6.   The two commonly used methods of addressing direct-access
files are:

      ● Using a directory that contains the reference numbers of
        records and their storage locations; during processing
        the computer searches the directory to locate a par-
        ticular record.
      ● Performing an arithmetic manipulation on the record key
        to create an address. There is no need to create a
        directory. This is referred to as randomizing or
        hashing.

7.   Direct-access processing is best suited for situations in
which the following apply:

      ● Only one file is processed at a time.
      ● The files must be current.
      ● The original record is not needed.
      ● The data must be retrieved and used without a time delay.

8.   In an indexed-sequential file organization, records are
placed in a file in sequence; a table of addresses is
established that equates the data record to selected keys or
codes.

      Indexed-sequential file organization allows both direct
access of files and the use of sequential processing.
Sequential files and direct-access files allow for only one or
the other.

9.   A data base structures data elements to fit the information
needs of an entire organization rather than to fit the needs of
one application or functional area.   An inverted structure can
be used to respond to a variety of unanticipated inquiries;
complex inquiries can be handled easily because indexes rather
than actual files are searched.

10.   Physical design refers to how the data is kept on storage
devices and how it is accessed.   These physical storage considerations are the responsibility of the data base administration team.   Logical design deals with how the data is viewed by
application programs or individual users.   The system analyst
and the data analyst attempt to model the actual logical, relationships that exist among data items.

11.

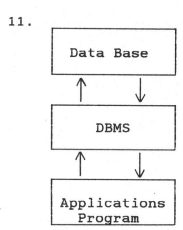

12.   No.   The systems analyst and data analyst attempt to develop a logical data design modeled an actual relationship that
exist among data items, not on all possible inquiries based on
all possible relationships.

ADDITIONAL REVIEW QUESTIONS

1.   Define the terms field, record, and file in relation to
each other.   Give an example of each.

2.   Explain the concept of a data base.   Were data bases in
existence before computers were developed?   Explain.

3.   What is a key?   How is a key significant to computer processing?

4.   Compare a master file to a transaction file. Which file is
of greater importance to an organization?

5.   Define activity and volatility.

6.   Which processing method permits transaction data to be used
for updating records without first being sorted?

7.   Applications involing files with a low activity and a high
volatility are best suited for which type of processing?

ANSWERS TO DISCUSSION POINTS

1.   Batch processing should be used if it is not necessary to
update records as transactions occur, if reports are needed only
periodically, and if the delays resulting from accumulating data
have no adverse impact. Batch processing is economical when
many records are processed. On the other hand, if the system
requires immediate update and the files have a low activity and
high volatility, online/direct-access processing should be
employed. Online/direct-access processing is used when immediate interrogation is necessary. However, the original record
is destroyed and the use of this method must be cost justified.

2.   An online/direct-access system is used for the sales order
entry application. This file organization method was chosen
because sales orders must be processed or updated immediately;
the sequential processing method is not practical for this
application. Also, the faster speed of online/direct-access
processing is required for the hundreds of inquiries made every
day concerning customer order status.

ADDITIONAL DISCUSSION POINTS

1.   Would online/direct-access processing better facilitate the
MRP system at Dana? Discuss.

2.   Give an example of a master file and a transaction file
that you might find at Dana.

ANSWER KEY TO STUDY GUIDE

True/False

2. T   4. T   6. T   8. T   10. T

Matching

2. j   4. d   6. b   8. h   10. i

Short Answer

2. A sequential file design is suitable for applications that require periodic updating of large numbers of records. They are not suitable when direct-access of records is needed.

4. The key is what is used by the program to locate a particular record. If two records have the same key, the program will not be able to determine when the correct one has been found.

6. Activity refers to the portion of records processed during a given run. Volatility means the frequency with which changes are made to a file.

8. They are complex to implement and maintain. An error in one input record may be spread throughout the data base.

10. Because it has indexes for selected attributes in a file, and the addresses of records having those attributes, these indexes can be searched, rather than the actual files. This can save considerable time.

ENRICHMENT LECTURE

Determining What Should Be Saved and What Should't

Our culture is sometimes referred to as an information society. While we are living in an information society during an information age, no one is yet certain of the implications of this new way of life.

Business people deal with large quantities of data but have only a vague concept of the dollar value of the information being stored in their data bases. Often, data that may have only minimal value are thrown into data bases. But this method quickly gets out of hand. It is expensive to save data. Therefore, it is becoming necessary to place a quantifiable value on various types of data. The problem is devising a method to do this. To determine what data is valuable enough to be stored, data must be treated as an asset. The value of data can be measured against:

1. Time

    a. obsolete

    b. retain

    c. current

2. Operations

    a. useless

    b. useful

    c. critical

3. Redundancy

    a. excessive

    b. modest

    c. nil

By creating value fields against which each data item can be evaluated, it becomes possible to measure the worth of each item. An item which is current, critical, and has nil redundance will receive high priority for being placed in the data base. On the other extreme, one that is obsolete, useless or redundant could be immediately eliminated. Of course, the relative importance of each of these areas will be dependent upon the particular situation.

Algorithms should be developed to determine how the value of data will be measured within a corporation. This allows corporations to develop cost-efficient data bases that will best meet their needs.

Adapted from "How Much Is Your Data Worth?" by Russell Lipton. Business Computer Systems, August 1984.

*Note: A transparency master is available for use with this lecture in your transparency packet that accompanies this textbook.

Suggestions For Discussion

1.   Discuss why company executives should be able to put a dollar value on their data. How reasonable is this? Discuss the fact that some businesses might lend themselves to this more easily than others.

By placing a dollar value on data, companies are able to quantify the worth of that data and determine what is valuable enough to be placed into the data base. This can be very difficult in an organization which is not able to determine accurately what will be needed in the future and what will not be needed.

2.   Have the class think of a type of business they are all reasonably familiar with, such as a savings and loan institution. Attempt to develop an algorithm that this institution might use to evaluate data. Categorize the different types of data the corporation would handle.

The responses given here will depend on the business chosen. The class should try to determine what records would be essential for the business to keep permanently, what records might only be kept for a limited time, and what information would probably not be worth saving.

Management Information and Decision Support Systems

LEARNING OBJECTIVES

Students should be able to:

- Define MIS
- Discuss the information needs of the different levels of management
- Discuss the problems in developing an effective MIS
- List the kinds of reports generated by an MIS
- Differentiate between alternative design structures

OUTLINE

I.   Elements of a Management Information System: An MIS is a formal information network using computer capabilities to provide management with information necessary for decision making.

A.   The goal of an MIS is to get the correct information to the appropriate manager at the right time.

1.   An MIS should provide:

a.   Decision-oriented reports
b.   Room for expansion and future growth
c.   Results that the user needs

B. Three levels of decision making in organizations are:

1. Top-level management – strategic decision making, future oriented, much uncertainty.
2. Middle-level management – tactical decision making, control and short-run planning.
3. Lower-level management – operational decision making, can be programmed, mostly control.

C. The information system must be tailored to provide appropriate information to each level of management.

1. The needs of first-level supervisors can be met by administrative data-processing activities such as preparation of financial statements.
2. Tactical decision making is characterized by a high use of internal information and dependence on rapid processing and retrieval of data.
3. It is extremely difficult to delineate top-level information needs; most problems are nonrepetitive, have great impact on the organization, and involve much uncertainty.

D. In analyzing its information needs, the firm should be conscious of itself as a system. It should consider its outputs, inputs, processes, and feedback mechanisms.

II. Decision-Oriented Reporting: An MIS can assist management, but it cannot guarantee decision-making success.

A. Typical reports generated by an MIS include:

1. Scheduled listings – these are produced at regular intervals and provide routine information.
2. Exception reports – performance is monitored and any deviation from expected results triggers an exception report.
3. Predictive reports – these are used for planning.
4. Demand reports – these provide quick responses to unanticipated inquiries.

B. The success of the system depends upon the attitudes of management and user involvement throughout the process.

III. Decision Support Systems (DSS): More effective decision-making in relatively unstructured situations is the goal of DSS; it aids top-level managers in strategic problem solving.

A.   The purpose of decision support systems is to enhance management information systems, not to replace them. A DSS emphasizes improving the effectiveness of semistructured or unstructured decisions.

B.   The use of decision models, mathematical representations of actual systems, is the heart of DSS.

C.   Commercial software packages are available to allow the manager to interactively probe a computerized model for results concerning various decision alternatives.

D.   Simulation, using a decision model to gain insight into the workings of an actual system, eliminates the need to experiment with a real world system.

    1.   Sensitivity analysis is a method of simulation that attempts to identify those sensitive, or key, variables that warrant management's attention.
    2.   "What if" analysis allows the manager to interactively process various decision alternatives quickly exploring the possible outcomes of these alternatives.
    3.   The goal-seeking method of simulation allows the manager to select one independent variable that can be altered to achieve a given output from the decision model.

E.   The future of DSS

    1.   Management is the key factor in the acceptance of decision support systems within business. If the full potential of DSS is to be recognized, it must overcome management resistance and lack of sophistication.
    2.   Many firms are attempting to develop simultaneous DSS which can coordinate the functional areas of a corporation as well as aid the organization's strategic and tactical planners.

IV.   Design Alternatives: This section covers four basic design structures – centralized, hierarchical, distributed, and decentralized.

A.   In centralized control, a separate department is set up to provide data-processing facilities for the entire organization. A common data base is set up.

    1.   It permits economies of scale, reduces redundancy and duplication of data.

    2.   Response to division needs is generally slow because priorities are assigned based on overall organizational needs.

B.   In hierarchical design, each management level is given the computer power necessary to support its objectives.

C.   In a distributed design the existence of independent units is recognized but central coordination and control is present.

D.   In a decentralized approach, the responsibility for computer support is placed in relatively autonomous organization operating units.

    1.   There is no central control.
    2.   Responsiveness to user needs is high.
    3.   This approach does not support the MIS concept.

ANSWERS TO REVIEW QUESTIONS

1.   Decision-oriented reports should provide information that is accurate, timely, complete, concise, and relevant; most importantly the information must meet the management user's requirements. Managers at all levels must be provided with decision-oriented information although the specific information needs of each level are different.

2.   There are three levels of management in most organizations:

- Top-level management – they require external, future oriented information. They deal in planning and strategies.
- Middle-management – they require internal, current performance information, historical and some predictive information. They deal in short-term planning and control. They must make tactical decisions.
- Low-level management – they require internal, historical, and current performance information. They make operational, control decisions.

It is difficult to supply the needed information to each level because they each have different requirements. A system that provides for the needs of middle- and lower-level management is unlikely to adequately support top-level management. Few information systems are able to provide the type of information top managers need. Their problems are unstructured, nonrepetitive and not programmable. They must make decisions in the face of a great deal of uncertainty. Computers are not yet adept at predicting the future because there are so many unknown variables involved.

3.   Strategic decisions are made by top-level managers; they are future-oriented decisions that involve a great deal of uncertainty such as goal setting. In contrast, tactical deci- sion making emphasizes the decision activities required to implement the strategies and goals determined at the top level. Operational decisions are those that ensure the completion of specific jobs. Most of these decisions are based on pre- determined decision patterns established at higher levels of management.

4.   Simulation, in all of its various methods, allows the manager to gain insight as to the effects any changes in varia- bles will have by altering the values of the model. Simulation could help a top-level manager cope with the uncertainty and newness of the decisions he/she has to make.

5.   The following reports are generated by an MIS:

- Scheduled listings - provide routine information on a regular basis. Examples include sales reports by sales representative, product, or geographical area.
- Exception reports - are triggered by deviations from a predefined standard. Examples include variance reports for labor, material, and factory overhead.
- Predictive reports - are produced by models that simulate actual events. Top managers may use such techniques to choose between several potential capital investment plans or to decide on a new plant location.
- Demand reports - are produced in response to inquiries. For instance, management might request a listing of all employees who have a specific background that might qualify them for a vacant position.

6.   Management is the most important group in developing an MIS. Management should be brought into the MIS development at an early stage so that the manager can tell the systems analyst what their information requirements are.

7.   A decision support system is geared to aid top-level man- agement in strategic problem solving. An MIS actually performs many routine tasks found in lower levels of the organization. An MIS is geared toward middle and lower levels of management where information needs are more specific, more repetitive. A DSS supplements an MIS by providing support for the level of

management which was least helped by MIS. A DSS serves as an
analytical aid to top managers, but it does not make decisions
for them.

8.   The purpose of a DSS is to assist managers who make relatively unstructured decisions. A DSS does not automate the
manager's decision making or impose solutions; it uses a computer as an analytical aid.

9.   A decision model is a mathematical representation of an
actual system. The model represents the manager's perception of
the real world and is based on his or her judgment of how the
system works. Thus, it may not be all inclusive (not an exact
replica), but it contains the inputs (independent variables)
that determine the value of the output (dependent variable).

10.   The major disadvantage with commercial planning packages is
the fact that a manager's specific input in model development is
not possible since the model has already been incorporated
within the system's package. Planning packages developed in-
house involve the manager's perception of how the system operates as input, but they are more expensive to produce.

     However, the Interactive Financial Planning System (IFPS)
is a commercially prepared package that is interactive and is
based on the manager's perceptions of the real world since it
does not incorporate a specific model.

11.   Simulation types discussed in this chapter are: sensitivity analysis, "what if" analysis, and goal seeking.
Sensitivity analysis is used to help the manager identify the
key, sensitive, variables that warrant his or her attention.
Goal seeking simulation helps the manager to select an independent variable that can be altered to achieve a desired, pre-
selected output from the decision model. A "what if" analysis
allows the manager to explore possible alternative outcomes
which may come about because of decision alternatives.

12.   A distributed system is a design alternative in which each
activity center has its own computer power, but with the
existence of total organization-wide control.

     In a centralized system, computer power is located within
one group, including a common central data base. A separate
department is set up in the organization to provide data-
processing facilities for the entire organization.

A distributed system would probably be more responsive to user needs since the organization is divided into small activity centers with adequate computer power to support them. This system is oriented to the individual users while a centralized system employs standard regulations and procedures with respect to the entire organization. With a centralized system, managers do not have control over their data-processing needs and some divisions can be neglected if they are assigned a low priority.

ADDITIONAL REVIEW QUESTIONS

1.   Differentiate physical design from logical design.

2.   Discuss the statement, "Too much information is just as bad, if not worse, than not enough information."

3.   Do you think decision support systems will ever automate any of top management's activities? Support your answer.

ANSWERS TO DISCUSSION POINTS

1.   The parts-ordering system is used as a management tool for corporate decision making by allowing dealers to order and receive parts in the most timely manner and at the same time providing corporate management with the necessary information to effectively and economically control inventory.

2.   Originally, the system was intended to help dealers order exceptional parts. Now it is used for normal stock reorders. The dealers have three different ordering alternatives to use in different situations. In general, the system makes the ordering process faster and easier while giving more control.

ADDITIONAL DISCUSSION POINTS

1.   Which specific design alternative does Ford use for its computer operations?

2.   Which level of management is the parts-ordering system designed to benefit?

ANSWER KEY TO STUDY GUIDE

True/False

2. F   4. T   6. T   8. T   10. F

Matching

2. e   4. h   6. g   8. a   10. b

Short Answer

2.   Advantages of a centralized design approach are that it permits economies of scale, reduces redundancy and duplication of data, and results in better utilization of data-processing capability.

4.   • Scheduled listings - provide routine information for a wide variety of users at regular intervals.
      • Exception reports - generated only when abnormal conditions occur.
      • Predictive reports - used to aid in the projection of future outcomes.
      • Demand reports - provides answers to a random variety of inquiries by management.

6.   Instead of each functional unit of an organization having its own DSS, corporate planning models attempt to combine into one system the various functional areas which affect the performance and output of other functional areas of an organization.

8.   Managers may feel that the computer is taking over their jobs or that they are losing control of routine decisions.

10.   Simulation is using a decision model to gain insight into the workings of an actual system. Simulation can eliminate the need to experiment with a real-world system by identifying key variables, analyzing the effects of changing key variables, and identifying the optimal solutions for a decision.

ENRICHMENT LECTURE

The Emergence of Decision Support Systems

Decision support systems, or the use of computer-generated information to help business managers make better, faster decisions, have become a hot topic. Just how did the DSS evolve? Computers were first used to automate routine, repetitive tasks such as payroll and accounts receivable. Then data processing emerged to improve an organization's operations and data flow while MIS (management information systems) evolved from data processing to provide managers with the information they request.

But with an MIS, the computer is limited to predictable functions. Managers, on the other hand, need to overcome the unpredictable--to act spontaneously. They often change their minds before coming to a final decision. Computers never do. Computers think and act alike while managers have unique approaches to problems. Managers have to work with many different people, communicate with them all, and lead them effectively. In short, managers deal with qualitative information. Computers handle quantitative data.

In the mid-1970s, Peter G. Keen began relating the computer to the mind of a manager. He coined the term "decision support

system" (DSS). But he was using established programming languages. Meanwhile, Dr. Gerald Wagner was developing a new
modeling language that was easy for managers to relate to. It
expressed the decision support idea. His approach was to make
DSS an extension of the executive mind. Dr. Wagner called the
software the interactive financial planning system (IFPS). Dr.
Wagner's IFPS became a workable, successful DSS package. This
DSS made sense to managers and executives and they used it
wholeheartedly.

The key component that really distinguishes DSS from other
computer software is its ability to model. Its strength lies in
its ability to express relationships among variables. DSS needs
a good data base to support modeling. But the data base merely
supplies the facts. Putting it all together is done in the
executive's mind.

A manager must understand how different factors affect each
other and how they are related. A computer just supplying data
is not decision support. Only when it helps the manager make
the interconnections does it become DSS.

When certain variables change, what happens to the others?
For example, if sales increase ten percent and costs decrease
three percent, what happens to profit? If the computer is given
a model that relates sales and costs to profit, it can supply
the manager with information to aid decision-making.

DSS provides a model that is easy to build, easy to understand, and easy to change. The use of "non-procedural" languages lets the manager use his or her own language to enter commands. Finally, DSS software should work on both mainframes and personal computers so that the varied demands of different departments and individuals can be met.

Adapted from "Plugging into the Computer" by Michael J. Major. Modern Office Technology, November 1983.

*Note: A transparency master is available for use with this lecture in your transparency packet that accompanies this textbook.

Suggestions For Discussion

1.   Do you think computers will someday replace executives for making crucial decisions?

Answers will be based on opinion.

2.   Explain the differences between MIS and DSS.

DSS help managers make interconnections between variables; emphasize unstructured, unpredictable decisions; allow managers to use their imaginations.

MIS supplies information needed; emphasizes structured, predictable decisions; limits managers' imagination.

16

The Impact of Computers on People and Organizations

LEARNING OBJECTIVES

Students should be able to:

- List and describe several human behavioral aspects of the impact of computers on people and organizations
- Describe office uses of computers including word processing, electronic mail, teleconferencing, telecommuting, telecomputing, and local area networks
- Identify and describe points of computer impact within business including accounting, finance, management, marketing, and sales
- Discuss the impact of computers on industry including CAD/CAM and robotics
- Describe the impact of computers on government including simulation, modeling, and data bases

OUTLINE

I.   Behavioral Aspects

    A.   Computer anxiety or computerphobia describes the degree to which people are afraid of or intimidated by computers.

        1.   Some people fear that if they make a mistake and punch a wrong button, the computer will be damaged.

2. Some people fear the loss of jobs because of computerization.
3. Computer anxiety can also be caused by the overwhelming amount of unfamiliar jargon used.
4. Women have tended to be anxious about computer related jobs even though some studies have shown that they are better programmers than men.
5. High-tech anxiety is more predominant among older people who have had limited contact with computers, in general.
6. Many people have developed negative attitudes toward computers because of their role in depersonalization of society.

B. Computer literacy courses prepare students for a highly technical society.

1. Students need a knowledge of basic programming techniques and the functions of various hardware components.
2. Knowing the history of computers, its current uses, and projected trends are important for understanding how computers effect our lives.

C. The effects of computers on job displacement and retraining have been the topics of several studies which have generally concluded that:

1. Since the computer can take over many routine clerical jobs, a certain amount of job displacement is to be expected.
2. Job displacement is related to the following factors:

a. The goals that are sought from the use of the computer.
b. The growth rate of the organization.
c. The planning that has gone into the acquisition and use of the computer.

3. Some of the popular forms of retraining include robotics maintenance, word processing, and computer programming.

D. Changes in the workplace for farmers, secretaries, and business managers alike have been influenced by computers.

1. Farmers are using computers to store animal health records and to assist with feed selection and book-keeping.
2. Office workers have reported complaints of eyestrain and backstrain.
3. A new science, ergonomics, (studying the design of computer hardware and software to enhance employee productivity and comfort) promises to improve the different elements of the work station.

II. Office automation refers to all processes that integrate computer and communication technology with the traditional manual processes.

A. Word processing, the manipulation of written text to achieve a desired output, is the most widely adopted office automation technology.

1. Word processors offer many functions to increase efficiency in the text manipulation process including: automatic centering, pagination, and alphabetizing.
2. Word processing can be used for a variety of tasks including editing lengthy documents and producing original form letters.
3. A typical word processing system consists of a keyboard for data input, a display screen, a secondary storage unit, and a printer.
4. Major advantages of word processing are increased productivity and reduction in preparation time of the document.
5. Disadvantages include the cost of word processing systems and the increasing number of times that a document is revised.

B. Computerized communication capabilities allow the electronic exchange of information between employees.

1. Electronic mail, the transmission of messages at high speeds over telecommunication facilities, is used primarily for routine, internal com-munications.
2. Teleconferencing, when two or more remote locations communicate via electronic and image-producing facilities, has five forms: audio conferencing, augmented audio conferencing, computer confer-encing, video seminars, and video conferencing.

3. Telecommuting, using a computer connected to the office from home via leased phone lines, is already being tried by some companies on an experimental basis.

4. Telecomputing permits workers to access online data bases thus receiving additional information and saving considerable research time.

C. A local area network (a network is a linking of CPUs and terminals by a communication system) operates in a well-defined area with the stations being linked by cable.

1. LANs are best suited where there is a great deal of information to be shared.

2. Three types of physical layouts (star networks, bus network, and ring network) may be employed by a LAN.

3. The four types of cable, communication media, used with LANs are twisted pair, base-band, broadband, and fiber optic.

4. The two methods of traffic management used to ensure uninterrupted transmission of data across the line are collision detecting and token access.

III. Computers in Business and Industry

A. Impact on business: The greatest impact of computers in American society has been in business and industry because computers speed operations, reduce mistakes in calculations, and give companies efficient cost-effective analysis.

1. The most common uses of general accounting software are in preparing checks, reports, and forms; the most common use of the computer in financial analysis is the electronic spreadsheet.

2. Managers use computers to produce graphs that keep them informed and current on company sales records and other statistics; computer graphics are the most cost-effective means of presenting the manager with the 20 percent core data needed to run their businesses.

3. Marketing and sales operations use computers to facilitate sales, record sales, update inventories after sales, and make projections based on expected sales.

B. Impact on industry

1. Computer-aided design (CAD) allows the engineer to design, draft, and analyze a prospective product using computer graphics on a video terminal.
2. Computer-aided manufacturing (CAM) allows the engineer to analyze the manufacturing process.
3. Robotics is the science that deals with robots, their construction, capabilities, and applications; currently American factories have over 6,000 robots hard at work.

C. Impact on government: The federal government is the single largest user of computers in the United States.

1. Government agencies use computer simulation and modeling in a wide variety of ways from teaching military tactics to forecasting weather.
2. Large data bases, including those in the Library of Congress, the FBI, and the IRS, are most prevalent within the government; much of the data comes from census returns and income tax returns.

Note: The Office of Personnel Management application later in this manual is appropriate to discuss after this chapter has been studied.

ANSWERS TO REVIEW QUESTIONS

1.   Computer anxiety is the feeling of fear and/or intimidation that some people have when dealing with computers or computer-related activities. People who design, implement, and maintain computer applications need to be aware of the presence of computer anxiety and to account for this phenomenom in their design and implementation. Even the best designed applications will not be successful if the user is handicapped by computer anxiety.

2.   Ergonomics is the science that studies the design of computer hardware/software in order to enhance employee productivity and comfort. Resultant recommendations include: a maximum of two hours a day of continuous screenwork, periodic rest breaks, and the transfer of pregnant women upon request.

3.   The major advantages of office automation are increased productivity and reduction in communication time.

4.   The four types of word processors are as follows:

- electronic typewriters – office with a minimum of word processing needs

- dedicated word processors – offices where word processing is the major activity

- dedicated data processors – office where other applications besides word processing are predominant, but some word processing is needed

- small business computers – in a distributed environment where many personnel need word processors and in the home

5.   The five forms of teleconferencing are audio conferencing, augmented audio conferencing, computer conferencing, video seminar, and video conferencing. Audio conferencing is simply a conference call linking three or more people. Augmented audio conferencing combines graphics with audio conferencing and is frequently used for technical discussions that require supplemental graphics to explain concepts. In computer conferencing information is exchanged at the participant's convenience using computer terminals. Video seminars (employing one-way, full-motion video with two-way audio) are used for formal presentations that involve a question-and-answer session. Video conferencing provides the most effective simulation of face-to-face communication by providing two-way full motion video plus two-way audio.

6.   Telecommuting is the use of a computer connected to an office from home via leased phone lines; telecomputing permits workers to access online data bases.

7.   Telecommuting may cut down on office space needed and can help where there are problems with mass transit or parking. Also, it can permit the handicapped, and others who cannot work outside of their home, to be employed.

8.   A local area network is a communication system that links CPUs and terminals that operate in a well-defined area with the stations linked by cable.

9.   Graphically displayed data makes the manager's task of dealing with pages and pages of data in order to make decisions much more manageable.

10.   Computer technology has enabled the federal government to gather and analyze large amounts of information in large data bases.   Thus, important tasks such as census taking and tax collecting can be completed more efficiently and effectively.

11.   Responses will vary; they may include quicker access to larger amounts of data, more efficient and effective decision-making, job displacement, depersonalization of the workplace and society in general, etc.

12.   As humans, we will probably permit one society to become as automated as possible without limits. Placing limits on the expansion of knowledge, except in the short term, is not congruent with the history of the human condition. Hopefully the expanded use of computers will include the enhancement of our self-understanding, so that the current trend in the direction of self-destruction may be reversed.

ADDITIONAL REVIEW QUESTIONS

1.   What is the difference between first- and second-generation robots?

2.   What are CAD and CAM? How can they be used together?

3.   How do businesses use computers in the area of marketing and sales?

ANSWERS TO DISCUSSION POINTS

1.   When microcomputers were first introduced at PRUPAC the employees' response developed in three stages. First, after the initial exposure to the microcomputers, PRUPAC employees were very anxious; they felt that the machines were too complicated, and they were afraid that they might break something. The second stage was marked by anger, confusion, and frustration as they blamed the computers for their own mistakes which they made during their learning process. The third and final stage was characterized by positive acceptance of the microcomputers as an important part of their job.

      The reaction to microcomputers witnessed at PRUPAC is probably a fairly typical reaction when computers are introduced in similar situations.

2.   The hand-held computer has enabled PRUPAC's agents to concentrate on selling insurance; it has enabled them to present

a more professional image to their clients and to try several "what if" possibilities that would be of interest for consideration by the customer. The client is kept involved in the process.

In the future it is probable that remote data links will be used to make it possible for information gathered by the agent to be fed directly into the company's central computer. It may also be possible to sell insurance without the step of the agent visiting the client/customer in his or her home. The client may be able to contact the data bank directly from his or her home using a personal computer.

ADDITIONAL DISCUSSION POINTS

1.   Describe the evolution of The Prudential Life Insurance Company of America's use of computers. Do you think that the current applications represent maximum usage? Explain why or why not.

2.   Is it possible that the PRUAC agent's use of the hand-held computer may meet some resistance in the future from customers? Why or Why not? Explain.

ANSWER KEY TO STUDY GUIDE

True/False

2. F   4. T   6. T   8. F   10. F

Matching

2. b   4. f   6. d   8. e   10. i

Short Answer

2.   Many people realize there is no turning back in the increasing use of computers in jobs, entertainment, and home life. They realize that knowing about computers can make the difference in promotions and job security.

4.   Farmers might use microcomputers to store animal records and to assist with financial records.

6.   Word processing eliminates the need for retyping documents
      for new uses, error correction, or changes. It reduces
      the amount of time in preparing documents by relieving
      workers of time-consuming and routine tasks.

8.   Augmented audio conferencing allows sending graphics by
      facsimile, electronic blackboards, or freeze-frame slide
      shows that help when a company relays a lot of technical
      information that can be better explained with the help of
      graphics. It can be more cost effective than videocon-
      ferences for companies that do not have major offices
      throughout the country or for companies that do much
      information exchanging with other companies.

10.   Three major agencies of the federal government that use
      data bases are: the Library of Congress, the FBI, and the
      IRS. The Library of Congress now can store more compactly
      its library cards. The FBI makes it's five million index
      cards more useful by providing access to the data base for
      its 500 offices. The IRS processes the millions of tax
      returns and audits by computer which would take years to do
      manually.

ENRICHMENT LECTURE

Commute By Auto or Computer?

Maybe you are getting tired of traveling 25 miles from a suburban home to your job in the city. Or maybe the hour it takes to drive eight miles bumper-to-bumper on the expressway is finally wearing you down. Perhaps you have children at home, but want to continue a career, too. Maybe a physical handicap places certain restrictions on your activity.

Wouldn't it be nice to work at home?

The computer age has made working at home a viable option. Using a computer and some type of telecommunications equipment-- telephone hookup or satellite dish antenna--you can work at home. Of course, one must have the type of job that lends itself to telecommuting. Likely candidates are researchers, accountants, writers, programmers, or data-entry operators. People who work at home are those who don't need face-to-face contact in their work.

Working at home allows people to work at the time of day when they are most productive. It also permits the handling of appointments or emergencies in a more convenient way. Tele- commuting helps control travel costs in time and expense for the

employee. It may also help a business limit the costs of maintaining office space.

The advantages to handicapped people or parents with
preschool children are obvious. These people have the opportunity for employment that they often would not otherwise have.
Traveling salespeople might use the computer and telecommunications to report to the office or enter specific sales
data.

But before you jump on the telecommuting bandwagon, you'll
want to examine the disadvantages as well as the advantages of
working away from the office.

Some workers find it difficult to discipline themselves to
do work at home. They also miss the social contact that occurs
in an office. Sometimes this contact can translate into a pro-
motion or raise when the employee sees the boss on frequent and
regular basis. "Out of sight, out of mind" can apply to telecommuting as well as to romance.

Other people in a firm might not be able to deal with telecommuters adequately. A manager may feel a loss of control over
telecommuting employees and their work. Peers may even think
the people who work at home are not really working.

Despite the problems, telecommuting is becoming more and
more a trend of the future. Alvin Toffler in his book, The
Third Wave, claims that the work place as we know it today will
be replaced by the "electronic cottage"--people working on com-

puters in homes and neighborhood centers linked to employer's computers. Toffler reminds us that only in the last 300 years has out-of-home work been the rule rather than the exception. And futurist Jack Nilles predicts that by 1990 as many as 10 million people will telecommute. While the Industrial Revolution brought people out of their homes to work in factories, the computer age may send people back to their homes to work, as it was during the first 10,000 years of human existence.

Information taken from various sources.

*Note: A transparency master is available for use with this lecture in your transparency packet that accompanies this textbook.

Suggestions For Discussion

1.   Discuss any ethical problems that telecommuting might present.

Ethical problems might include the ability to roam at leisure through any company files a worker might accidentally gain access to, using company computer equipment to do other tasks that one might do with a home computer, and reporting more time at work than actually was spent.

2.   Discuss some ways that might help telecommuters overcome the lack of social contact and fears about their work.

Some telecommuters might work at home two days per week and at the office three days, or vice versa. Even regularly scheduled visits of two or three hours to report progress, attend meetings, or do research can alleviate the stagnation that might come with working at home alone.

Computer Security, Crime, Ethics, and the Law

LEARNING OBJECTIVES

Students should be able to:

- Define computer crime
- Describe the types of computer crime
- Discuss the methods of computer security and computer crime prevention
- List and discuss several issues related to ethics and privacy with computer usage
- Describe and discuss the legal issues surrounding warranties and copyrights

OUTLINE

I. Computer Crime and Security: The first known computer crime occurred just a few years after the marketing of the first line of business computers in 1958; in the mid-1970s yearly losses were estimated at $300 million.

    A. Computer crime is definded as a criminal act that poses a greater threat to a computer user than it would to a non-computer user, or a criminal act that is accomplished through the use of a computer.

    B. Computer crimes can be classified into four broad categories.

   1. Sabotage of computers results in destruction or
      damage of computer hardware.
   2. Theft of services can occur in a variety of ways
      due to inadequate or nonexistent security pre-
      cautions.
   3. Theft of property is not limited to actual hardware
      or merchandise but may also extend to software.
   4. Financial crimes are not the most common type, but
      they are the most serious in terms of monetary
      loss.

C. Computers can be used to prevent and detect crime;
   because of their ability to analyze large amounts of
   data they can become computerized crime predictors.

D. Computer security involves the technical and administrative safeguards required to protect a computer-
   based system (hardware, personnel, data).

   1. Physical threats to security include fire, natural
      disasters, environmental problems, and sabotage.
   2. Data security measures include the following:
      storing backup copies of data outside the organiza-
      tion's location; giving special passwords to
      authorized users; giving access to specific por-
      tions of the data base only to those whose job
      necessitates it; installing internal security
      guards; translating data into a secret code; and
      using fingerprints and voice patterns as
      identification.
   3. Computer security can be established using the
      following principles: computer users must
      recognize their role in security, recognization of
      the need to have a well-trained security force,
      careful screening and selection of people who have
      access to computers, and discharging of employees
      who stray beyond legal and ethical boundaries.

II. Ethics and Privacy

A. Ethics: Computer ethics is a term used to refer to the
   standard of moral conduct in computer use.

   1. Hacking is a computer term used to describe the
      activity of computer enthusiasts who are challenged
      by the practice of breaking computer security
      measures designed to prevent unauthorized access to
      a particular computer system; hacking is the same
      as intentionally committing a crime.

2. Employee loyalty is a particularly relevant issue in computer businesses because of the many job opportunities and considerable amount of job changing among data-processing employees.

3. Software copying or piracy refers to the unauthorized copying of a computer program that has been written by someone else; whether done for personal use or to sell for profit, software piracy is a crime.

B. Privacy: The issue of privacy is becoming a matter of great importance because computers are being used as the main means of personal information storage.

1. Data bases have become more and more popular as a means of storing information on individuals because of the ease of computer storage and retrieval.

2. Because personal information related to credit, employment, taxes, etc. is being collected, there have been many concerns raised relative to the individual's right to privacy and data bases.

3. Privacy legislation has been enacted to protect one's privacy. The Privacy Act of 1974 makes several provisions for federal agencies including the following:

a. There must be no secret data banks of personal information.

b. A way must be provided for individuals to correct wrong information.

III. Computers and the Law

A. Warranties: The Uniform Commercial Code (UCC) is a set of provisions proposed by legal experts to promote uniformity among state courts in their legal treatment of commercial transactions. For UCC to apply to computer acquisitions the contract must be for goods not services and second, the contract must be for the sale of goods.

1. An express warranty is created when the seller makes any promise or statement of fact concerning the goods being sold which the purchaser uses as a basis for purchasing the goods.

2.   Implied warranties provide that a contract for the
     sale of goods automatically contains certain
     warranties that exist by law; it need not be ver-
     bally made nor included in the written warranties
     of a contract to be effective.

B.   Copyright law has applied to computer software or com-
     puter programs since 1964; in order for a program to be
     protected under copyright law it must contain a notice
     of copyright that is visible to the user.

ANSWERS TO REVIEW QUESTIONS

1.   Computer crime is a criminal act that poses a greater
threat to a computer user than it would to a non-computer user,
or is a criminal act that is accomplished through the use of a
computer. Computer crime is a serious problem in our society,
for, as the number of applications continues to grow, so will
the possible opportunities for computer crime. It is likely
that in the future most aspects of our daily lives will be
integrated with computer usage; therefore, the opportunity for
computer crime to affect our lives is likely to be quite great.

2.   The computer's ability to make complex statistical analyses
with large amounts of data enables the development of computerized crime predictors which have been used to predict probable targets to arson and variables related to criminal suspects
such as the Atlanta child killer. Also, data bases can be used
to collect information on criminals from a large variety of law
enforcement agencies.

3.   Data security measures include the following:

   ● storing backup copies of data outside the organization's
     location
   ● use of special passwords for authorized uses
   ● giving access to specific portions of the data base only
     to those whose jobs necessitate it
   ● use of internal security guards
   ● translating data into a secret code
   ● use of fingerprints and voice patterns as legitimate user
     identification devices

4.   Computer ethics refers to the standard of moral conduct in computer use. Computer ethics would always be required. Responses/examples should refer to instances where specific laws have not been passed or the spirit of the law lends itself to differing interpretations.

5.   Whether or not computer ethics within an organization are described in a formal document, computer ethics remain a personal issue which, by definition, is left to the discretion of each employee. For example, while a company policy document may specifically state the condition of what is and what isn't a problem of employee loyalty, an employee may believe that loyalty is an either/or issue, not subject to conditions. Thus, no matter what the company has accepted and written as official ethical behavior, the beliefs of employees with regard to ethical behavior are personal in nature.

6.   The issue of privacy is becoming a matter of great importance, because computers are being used as the main means of storage of personal information relating to credit, employment, taxes, and other aspects of person's lives. Organizations should be required to disclose the information in their records to the people to which the information pertains in order to verify their records because inaccurate records are of little use to organizations and they may be harmful to the individual. In cases where allowing individuals to see the information may be harmful to others, the decision as to whether or not to disclose the record should de decided by a court of law.

7.   Express warranties are created when the seller makes a statement or promise of fact concerning the goods being sold which the purchaser uses as the basis for purchasing the goods; implied warranties need not be verbally made nor included in the written warranties. The term indicates that a contract for a sale of goods automatically contains certain warranties that exist by law. Two major types of implied warranties are: (1) implied warranty of merchantability, and (2) implied warranty of fitness for a particular purpose.

8.   Copyright law is important to computer software vendors; if software is not protected by copyright, it may be copied indiscriminately, thus, losing its value as goods available for sale/purchase. Registration is not required since copyright protection exists from the moment of creation; registration is required only to obtain the right to sue for copyright infringement.

ADDITIONAL REVIEW QUESTIONS

1.   Describe the computer crime referred to as the "round off fraud."

2.   What is encrypting as applied to computers? How does it differ from decrypting?

3.   What is meant by the implied warranty referred to as "implied warranty of fitness?"

ANSWERS TO DISCUSSION POINTS

1.   The GAO thinks that federal information systems are subject to threats of natural hazards, unintentional actions, and intentional actions.

Advances in microcomputers and telecommunication technology pose the following types of problems to federal information systems:
● Larger systems store more sensitive information in electronic form.
● Expanded use of remote terminals provides more isolated points of access and makes it difficult to pinpoint errors or attacks.
● More individuals now have the potential capability to access, create, and manipulate data bases by bypassing central controls.
● Linking computers and terminals through telecommunications networks provides potential penetration with more opportunities, techniques, and devices to access systems, to insert communications, and to intercept and interpret communications.

2.   The key factors that support federal efforts to provide security are legislation, policy, management by central and executive government agencies, and auditing.

Legislation serves to define information security goals and objectives and to assign overall management responsibilities for security.

Information security policy should provide government agencies with a clear and concise blueprint for implementation of relevant legislation.

Four central agencies (OMB, GSA, Dept. of Commerce, and OPM) have management responsibilities to issue policies, guidelines, and regulations that are consistent and coordinated with each other and contain "how to" specifics where applicable to assist executive agencies in meeting legislative and executive office requirements.

Systematic internal audits provide management with periodic reports on the level of protection actually provided over automated systems and particularly their sensitive applications.

ADDITIONAL DISCUSSION POINTS

1.   What is the potential impact of the GAO's involvement in the federal governmental use of computers and telecommunications networks?

2.   What is the greatest threat to federal government information systems involving microcomputers and telecommunications networks? Provide a rationale for your response.

ANSWER KEY TO STUDY GUIDE

True/False

2. F   4. T   6. T   8. F   10. F

Matching

2. c   4. f   6. b   8. d   10. g

Short Answer

2.   Some "property" is stolen that really doesn't exist because of computer record manipulation. Checks can be made to vendors for receipt of merchandise that never existed, for instance. Or programs or data can be stolen, and electronic data can be hard to define as property.

4.   Be sure computer equipment is away from sources of water or if that is impossible, that all protective measures are taken against any leaks, pipe bursts, etc. Be sure that data is secure from magnetic fields created by any electric motors in the area, by removing those motors if possible. Arrange for backup power in case of brownouts or blackouts. If a very severe problem exists with external radiation, consider a shield for computer equipment and software.

6.   Make sure employees realize the seriousness of security of
     information and are aware of the security measures. Have a
     well-trained security force knowledgeable about data
     security, system audits, and questions to ask. Carefully
     select people who will have access to the systems.
     Discharge employees who commit ethical and legal infrac-
     tions.

8.   It basically abolishes the concept of "buyer beware".
     Under common law, buyer protection is not presumed or
     implied and must be negotiated in the final agreement.

10. When a seller makes any promise or statement of fact con-
     cerning the goods being sold which the purchaser uses as a
     basis for purchasing them, he or she must make good on the
     promises. The seller guarantees that the goods are those
     that meet the needs of the consumer. The one problem is
     that the purchaser must keep the goods, and will only get a
     reduction in price.

ENRICHMENT LECTURE

Does It Take One to Know One?

You have probably heard about cat burglars who start consulting services for home security. They know which homes lend
themselves to breaking and entering and which homes burglars
avoid. And they sell their knowledge. Once homeowners realize
the danger points--large bushes around windows, darkened cor-
ners, the accumulation of daily newspapers that say the owner is
out of town--they can begin to protect themselves.

The same has happened in the area of computer crime. Once
caught, the criminals decide they would be further ahead
starting their own consulting firms to advise corporations
about computer and data security. The basis for the decision is
that companies can protect themselves better if they are aware
of the kinds of computer crime now being committed.

Computer crimes can be divided into three types: the input
scam, the output scam, and the "thruput" scam. The most common,
according to the June 1984 issue of INC magazine, is the input
scam.

Input scams involve changing data which is entered into the
computer system. Sometimes this is called "data diddling."

Data diddlers change grades in university computer systems or
make up fictitious vendors that require payment for nonexistent
equipment sold to corporations. Data diddling can even be done
without a computer. One man simply placed MICR-coded bank
deposit tickets printed with his account number on a bank table
with the "generic" deposit slips customers used when they forgot
to bring their own. Sixty-seven thousand dollars went into his
account that day.

Output scams involve any item that a computer produces.
Lists of customers, a hard copy of a program, disks or magnetic
tapes--all can be output items stolen to benefit the thief.
Sometimes a disgruntled employee will leave a company to start
his own business--only he has a head start with a list of
clients or a raft of computer programs from his previous
employer.

Output scams can also include information gained from
wiretapping computer systems. Some transmission methods, such
as satellites, are more easily accessed. Intercepting devices
such as satellite dishes can be easily set up. Other transmission types such as fiber optic cable are much more difficult
to tap.

The type of crime in which the computer itself is made to
"commit" the crime is called "thruput" scam. In this scam, a
program is modified to benefit the perpetrator.

A well-known thruput scam is the Trojan Horse. Additional
lines are planted within an existing program to instruct the
computer to perform certain tasks. For instance, a programmer
could alter a program so that any withdrawals from his account
are never recorded. He feeds the account with funds from sup-
posedly dormant accounts.

Bank programs can be altered to slice off amounts of
interest or bank charges in the "salami technique." This method
siphons off amounts so trivial that no one notices what's happening. The salami scam is usually accomplished by planting a
Trojan Horse in the program to round off interest so a few cents
are left. The extra pennies are placed in a special account.
Miniscule amounts from thousands of accounts can add up to a
substantial savings in the criminal's account.

Logic bombs can be inserted in programs to go off at a
designated time. In one case, a programmer inserted a logic
bomb in his company's personnel file. The "bomb" would delete
the entire personnel staff file if it ever "went off." Many of
the crimes are not discovered because of the same kind of care-
lessness that a homeowner can exhibit about protecting his home
from burglars. Passwords are tacked to bulletin boards or taped
to desk drawers. Floppy disks are left out in the open.
Transition periods from manual to computerized systems are
undertaken carelessly. Audits are conducted infrequently enough
to guarantee some measure of success with data diddling.

In smaller companies, protection amounts to a kind of "Catch-22." They may not be able to afford security measures-- without which they may go bankrupt. Yet, calling in an expert-- a person who knows practical yet inexpensive precautions--can make the difference between losing a bundle and successfully operating a business by computer.

Main source: "Of Trojan Horses, Data Diddling, and Logic Bombs" by Vin McLellen. <u>INC.</u>, June 1984.

*Note: A transparency master is available for use with this lecture in your transparency packet that accompanies this textbook.

Suggestions For Discussion

1. Use this material as a starting point for out-of-class reports on protection methods for computer systems. Magazine articles, computer books, system analysis books, and others may provide material for students to compile a list of things to watch for and ways to secure a system.

Suggestions might include screening employees carefully, changing passwords frequently, separating employee func- tions so that overlapping functions cannot provide a way to change data, encoding data, and conducting regular audits. Even physical protection--such as guards, patches or badges for computer users, and written logs--may be needed for some sensitive information.

2. In research, a number of case studies could be found so that students can use "hindsight" and tell what could have been done to make a certain crime less apt to occur.

Cases might include the Assassins, the three boys who stole data, hardware, and software from some 30 organizations in 1983, or the National Bonded Money Co. case in which a Trojan Horse was planted by a programmer.

Computers in Our Lives: Today and Tomorrow

LEARNING OBJECTIVES

Students should be able to:

- Describe the uses of computers in homes
- Discuss the impact of computers within the field of education
- List and discuss several current uses of computers in medicine and science
- Identify and describe examples of the use of computers in the arts, recreation, and entertainment
- Discuss the use of computers in the future including artificial intelligence

OUTLINE

I. Computers at Home: Most people who have used or have been affected by computers either love computers or they hate them.

    A. Home computer services have been proven successful but have grown somewhat slowly because of expense and consumer resistance.

        1. Home-based shopping allows consumers to insert a keyed charge card into their home terminal and, by pressing a button, to have the order placed for home delivery or pickup.

2.   In-home, 24-hour banking allows bank customers to
     pay bills automatically, to transfer funds from one
     account to another, and to receive instant updated
     information which has traditionally been available
     only in monthly statements.
3.   Home information services can provide the user
     video versions of stock market reports, major
     newspapers, movie reviews, an encyclopedia, etc.
     through telecommunication networks.

B.   Automated homes use microcomputers to control automated
     systems such as environmental control (heating;
     cooling, opening-shutting of doors and windows),
     security (intruders and fire warnings), electrical
     switching system, energy management system, and infor-
     mation storage and retrieval system.

C.   Home robots have seen limited use so far; they perform
     tasks such as welcoming guests, acting as sentinels,
     and retrieving objects. They will undoubtedly see more
     use in the homes of the future.

II. The Impact on Education

A.   Computer-assisted instruction (CAI) is a process in
     which a student interacts directly with a computer that
     serves as an instructor to guide the student through
     the learning material.

     1.   CAI rarely teaches new skills and seldom presents
          learning material in an unusual manner.
     2.   Most students learn material more quickly with CAI
          than through traditional classroom learning.
     3.   Students who use CAI frequently are not really
          becoming computer literate because of the
          experience.

B.   Computer camps where people of all ages can learn about
     computing along with traditional recreational activites
     are now available.

C.   Innovative educational uses of computers include pupil
     development of learning games using graphics and a
     speech synthesizer, and videodisc technology to teach
     dance skills and architectural skills.

III. Computers in Medicine and Science

A.   Medicine: Most medical computer applications are found
     in hospitals.

     1.   Computer-assisted diagnosis is reached by evalu-
          ating numerical data and comparing them with nor-
          mal or standard values.

          a.   Multiphasic health testing uses a patients'
               answers to questions about their health and the
               results of several medical tests. The computer
               then makes the comparison between the patients'
               results and normal limits.
          b.   Computerized tomographcy (CAT) scanning is a
               method which combines x-ray techniques and a
               computer for quick and accurate physical
               diagnosis.

     2.   Computerized life-support systems have replaced the
          need for around-the-clock nurses for critically ill
          patients; computers monitor physiological variables
          such as heart rate, temperature, and blood
          pressure.

B.   Science

     1.   Three-dimensional electron microscopy has been de-
          veloped by scientists at Oak Ridge National
          Laboratory; it will be used to determine the three-
          dimensional structure of biological specimens.
     2.   The use of computer models of human and animal
          bodily functions as replacements of animals in
          laboratory testing of drugs and chemicals is in its
          early stages of development.

IV. Computers in Arts, Recreation, and Entertainment

A.   The arts

     1.   Computer art--the computer artist uses knowledge of
          programming as the conventional artist uses
          knowledge of brushes, brush strokes, and paints.
     2.   Computerized music--sounds, of specific musical
          instruments as well as for special sound effects,
          can be stored on floppy disks and modified to imi-
          tate various moods.

B. Recreation and entertainment: Computer uses in sports, recreation, and entertainment have expanded beyond calculating statistics to athletic shoe construction.

  1. Computerized sports research is highlighted by the science of biomechanics which uses high-speed cameras, digitizer pens, computers, and computer software in the process of analyzing human movement.
  2. EPCOT Center at Walt Disney World represents computerization at its finest as it puts visitors in touch with the future world through the use of an array of computer-fed, interactive video screens and high-technology electronic libraries.

V. Future Technology

A. Brain-wave interface is an input method now being developed. To control a computer with this technology a person gazes at a particular flashing light while wearing electrodes like those used for an electro-encephalogram.

B. Artificial intelligence is a computer's ability to think and reason as humans do.

  1. Expert systems use what is known of the human thought process to build computer programs that mimic the decision-making process of human experts.
  2. Nonmonotonic logic theory is being proposed as a way of getting the computer to allow for unusual situations not covered by monotonic logic, which allows conclusions to be drawn from assumptions.
  3. Script theory says that in any particular situation humans have an idea of how the thinking or dialogue would go; some researchers are attempting to give the computer a way to make inferences based upon the situation at hand.

ANSWERS TO REVIEW QUESTIONS

1.   Types of services currently available to personal computer owners through networks include banking, shopping, video versions of major newspapers, stock market reports, magazine subscriptions, and library research. There are many valuable services that may be available in the future including at-home diagnoses of medical and/or psychological problems.

2.   Practical applications of home robots include home security and the retrieval of objects, such as beverages from the refrigerator.

3.   The growth of computer technology has been rapid and will likely continue to expand; there are some serious concerns that education has not, and may not in the future, keep up with this growth by developing effective computer literacy programs. When children are exposed to computers at a young age they learn to be at ease with them and overcome computer anxiety more readily. The danger in exposing children to computers at a young age is the same as for any other early learning experience. If the child has a poor experience it is likely to carry-over into future years and make learning about computers as a teen-ager or adult even more difficult.

4.   CAI rarely teaches skills that are new and it seldom presents learning material in an unusual manner. CAI allows students to progress at their individual paces; it provides an unintimidating relationship (it is always patient and good natured); and it is more efficient (the majority of students cover the required material in less time than it would have been covered in the traditional classroom setting).

5.   By attending a computer class or a computer camp, adults have the added benefit of interacting with others like themselves who are learning about computers. The reinforcement of the presence of others can be very helpful in new learning experiences.

6.   Actually, the use of computers in medicine may, in the long run, add to renewed personalization in the field. Computerization covers the necessary, but very time-consuming tasks required of physicians and nurses in the areas of diagnosis and intervention monitoring, allowing them more time to consult with patients.

7.   The use of computer models in place of laboratory animals could save millions of dollars in the cost of purchasing laboratory animals. Also, it cuts down on the killing of research animals. Computer modeling could also be a great asset in determining the effects of certain environmental contaminants on the human body without having to expose humans, or animals, to the contaminants.

8.   The use of computers in the various areas of art is not likely to limit human creativity. On the contrary, the use of computers in this field is likely to stimulate interest and creativity in some people who would have otherwise never real- ized they had artistic ability or were interested in art as a form of personal expression.

9.   A film of an athlete in motion is used, along with a digi- tizer pen, to enter the athlete's motions into the computer. Software is then used to analyze the motions and to provide data concerning the distance the body moves, the speed at which it moves, and the forces acting on the body. The athlete can use this data to correct his or her motion so that it is the best possible for a given sport. This science is called bio- mechanics.

10. EPCOT Center certainly has benefit beyond being a tourist attraction. The CommuniCore and the World Key Information exhibits not only make vistors aware of the uses and benefits of computers in our daily lives, they also help visitors to gain confidence in their ability to use them.

11. The introduction of artificial intelligence into computer technology may be a threat to human existence or it may be a boon to human life. Like the introduction of any other new technology, the consequences of the existence of artificial intelligence depends on the users, human beings. To the degree that human beings tend to use technology in threatening ways, it will be a threat to us.

ADDITIONAL REVIEW QUESTIONS

1.   Which of the systems of artificial intelligence is the closest to being realized in our current world?

2.   Why is it appropriate for the EPCOT Center to provide a strong emphasis on computers?

3.   Describe the benefits of a computerized life-support system.

ANSWERS TO DISCUSSION POINTS

1.   The modern-day NASA and its supporting industries would not exist without digital computers; none of the major accomplishments of NASA could have been possible without the modern digital computer. The cost of providing computer systems for space operations is far less than the cost of providing the facilities needed to support the engineering, development, and delivery of those computer operational systems to be used in space. The evolution of the computer may not have progressed to its present state without the impetus of the space effort; it is difficult to identify which technology advancement drives which.

2.   Some of the applications in which NASA uses computers are: engineering support, spacecraft systems, ground-based systems, research and training facilities, business support, office automation, and mission reconfiguration.

     Engineering support: By using the experience base available in NASA and computer processes developed from data obtained from previous space missions, new components, space vehicles, or even complete missions can be conceived through computer simulations to meet new requirements.

     Spacecraft systems: Guidance, navigation, and control of spacecraft as well as other functional spacecraft systems are interfaced with onboard digital systems for instrumentation, communications, and systems management roles.

     Ground-based systems: This data-handling involves world-wide communication complexes, large data-processing and storage centers, and complex data-display systems, all of which are based on digital computers.

     Research and training facilities: Simulations involving large tunnels, space environment, life science, and training facilities can be controlled and operated accurately, efficiently, safely, and profitably with real-time digital control systems.

     Business support: All of the traditional day-to-day business areas are supported by digital processing in NASA.

     Office automation: Distributed word-processing systems allow the office staff to provide a high level of inter- and intra-office correspondence, both formal and informal.

Mission reconfiguration: A large complex of digital computers, processors, procedures, and data distribution mechanisms is being developed. These support the processing of information about past space shuttle flights to give the necessary information required to reconfigure future space shuttle systems.

ADDITIONAL DISCUSSION POINTS

1.   Which is the most important NASA application of computers? Explain.

2.   Did the development of the digital computers stimulate the growth of NASA's space effort or did the impetus of the space effort stimulate the development of computers? Explain.

ANSWER KEY TO STUDY GUIDE

True/False

2. T   4. T   6. T   8. F   10. F

Matching

2. a   4. i   6. f   8. h   10. g

Short Answer

2.   A home computer could control home environment and manage energy use, monitor security, monitor for fire, adjust lights, and provide information storage and retrieval.

4.   The time used for routine tests and comparisons is done by computer, saving the physician for evaluating and making recommendations to the patient. (Other reasonable answers would be acceptable.)

6.   A musician can use a computer to alter and transform musical sounds produced by instrumentalists, to edit during recording, and to reproduce sounds of specific instruments and add colorful sound effects to a composition.

8.   ● microelectronics
       ● computer software
       ● laser videodisc
       ● television
       ● touch-sensitive screens
       ● fiber-optic transmission systems

10.   Expert systems are computer programs that try to mimic the
       decision-making processes of human experts.

ENRICHMENT LECTURE

Tomorrow Is Here!

There you were--watching <u>Star Wars</u> or reading Isacc Asimov. Or maybe you were watching the oldies-but-goodies on television and a sit-com featuring a beeping, metal robot vacuuming the living room.   Or perhaps the <u>Star Trek</u> reruns were showing, and you noticed the climate-controlled rooms, entered through doors that sensed a man's presence and opened automatically for him. And you thought to yourself, "Nah, that's bunk."

But the future is here.   The September 1984 issue of <u>Popular Computing</u> magazine features a "Buyer's Guide to Home Control Devices."   You may want a few electronic brains here and there to control temperature and sense intruders.   Perhaps you will want a pet robot that says comforting things to you and listens when you talk.   And when you visit Grandma, you might be surprised to see that her life is made much safer by electronic devices.

Grandma's electronic system is equipped with 24-hour biofeedback monitors and a radio-controlled household robot who is companion and butler.   Since Grandma can no longer read the newspaper, the robot plays out the morning news, minus the sports and ads.   If Grandma decides to take a leisurely stroll down the lane, the robot stays at home--but carefully monitors Grandma's location. Grandma could talk to the robot from a remote location or even place a phone call, if necessary.

The robot knows Grandma pretty well. It monitors her blood pressure and pulse, notes changes in voice and muscle tension, and records when she laughs or grows silent. From a personality profile, the robot can predict the subjects Grandma might be interested in hearing about.

To be sure, Grandma has many human visitors, and she tele-communicates with family and friends all over the world. But she can live independently, knowing she has her robot and her house computer to help her.

If you read the Buyer's Guide, you will find products that do some of the things you might have noticed in Grandma's house. Some devices are master systems that sense emergencies such as break-ins, floods, or fire, and can dial preset telephone num-bers. A few offer accessories to control lawn sprinklers, garage door openers, heating appliances, or lighting.

The guide also mentions controllers that work with personal computers. Some can be trained to recognize commands and distinguish voice patterns. Most control appliances, lights, temperature and humidity, and sense intruders, fire, and flooding. Some can be programmed in BASIC.

But there's more. Robots such as Comro's Tot Robot, Hubotic's Hubot, and Personal Robotics Corporation's RoPet-HR will do light household chores such as vacuuming. The robots

can be programmed with joysticks or BASIC commands.

Perhaps the imaginary tale about Grandma isn't so unreal

after all. Wouldn't you be more comfortable knowing that

Grandma was well-cared for in your absence?

Adapted from a trio of articles by Tan A. Summers, Norman
Spinrad, Roy Mason, and Lane Jennings. Popular Computing,
September 1984.

*Note: A transparency master is available for use with
this lecture in your transparency packet that accompanies this
textbook.

Suggestions For Discussion

1. Discuss the kinds of things in "The House of the
Future" that people have already had experience with. Discuss
how the optimists may look at the electronic future and how the
pessimists may look at it.

People may have personal computers at home that they have
rigged up to control lights or a security system. Others
may have appliances that are computer-controlled. Some may
have visited Epcot Center or other places where electronic
homes are on display. Some may have taken advantage of
computer learning through networks or software packages.

Some may feel that all people will benefit gloriously from
computers--learning to their full potential in school,
spending a greater amount of leisure time together, and
participating in many new art forms. Others may see functional illiterates watching television and being watched by
BIG BROTHER, being waited on hand and foot by sneaky little
robots, and avoiding social interaction with other humans.

2. Plan a house with electronic controllers, personal computers, and robots. Explain what tasks should be done by which
equipment.

Answers will vary according to research performed.

Bethlehem
Steel Corporation

BETHLEHEM, PA--Bethlehem Steel Corporation was incorporated on December 10, 1904, but its history can be traced to the Saucona Iron Company, a small iron works established in 1857 in Bethlehem, Pa. The business initially was oriented to building blast furnaces and producing iron rails for America's rapidly expanding railroad system.

The firm entered the steel industry in 1882 when the U.S. Government decided to rebuild the Navy with steel. By the turn of the century, the discovery of high-speed tool steels at Bethlehem had ushered in the age of mass production. Thus, even in its infancy, the small steel company at Bethlehem, Pa., made signigicant contributions to America's economic growth.

During each World War, Bethlehem expanded capacity to keep the allies supplied with submarines, naval vessels, guns, and munitions. In World War II alone, the firm repaired nearly 38,000 ships. Some of the national landmarks built by Bethlehem between the two wars are San Francisco's Golden Gate Bridge, the Waldorf-Astoria Hotel, and the George Washington Bridge in New York City.

Today, in addition to being the third largest steel producer in the U.S., Bethlehem is prominent in supplying raw materials and mining, in shipbuilding, in manufacturing steel products, and in producing plastics. The shipyards build huge, mobile off-shore drilling platforms which are used to seek out new oil reserves.

Despite Bethlehem's 1983 loss of $164 million, the corpora-
tion took a number of important steps to implement its strategic
plan to become a leaner, more profitable producer of high-
quality steel products. It completed the restructuring of the
Lackawanna, N.Y., and Johnstown, Pa., plants and continued to
decentralize and dispose of assets which were unprofitable or
did not fit the strategic plan. In addition, the corporation
made further progress in reducing and controlling employment
costs and it moved ahead on key elements of a modernization
program. Bethlehem improved its financial position through new
equity financings and increased its emphasis on quality and
technology in all aspects of its business. This is one area of
progress that is particularly important to Bethlehem's future.

Bethlehem is changing what has often been an adversarial
relationship between management and labor to a more realistic
and cooperative one. Interests are mutual and the corporation
needs the ideas and contributions of every employee to find ways
to improve efficiency, avoid waste, and improve working conditions.

The substantial progress Bethlehem is making in these
areas, however, will not make it adequately profitable for the
longer term if a solution to the massive and growing problem of
unfairly traded steel imports is not found.

The Information Services Department within Bethlehem Steel
is composed of three corporate staff divisions and four regions.
The staff divisions provide centralized technical direction,
systems consulting, and administrative planning and control.
The four regions each support a data center and one or more
application development groups. The regional data centers and
development groups are housed in or nearby the company's major
plants. Distributed through these sites are 13 major computers
with associated tapes and printers, over 250 billion characters
of disk storage, and a mass storage system. In addition, an
extensive communications network, based on IBM's SNA concepts,
ties together all the major computers, many minicomputers and
personal computers, and nearly 6,000 terminals. The facilities
are available 24 hours a day. Numerous software applications,
many of which come from IBM, aid in meeting information
requirements.

The Bethlehem Region provides data-processing support for
the Bethlehem Plant and all departments at the corporate
headquarters. Among the varied applications developed and
supported are sales marketing control by product, manifesting,
pricing and invoicing, accounting, payroll, personnel, employee
benefits, legal, medical, transportation, finance, cost,
engineering, and inventory systems. The other Regions support

local production planning and control systems for their respective manufacturing and administrative systems.

Due to variances in size, requirements, and complexities, and to the differences in approaches for developing all the systems necessary to perform Bethlehem Steel's operations, a standard methodology to develop systems was implemented. The methodology is a project-development cycle consisting of six separate and distinct phases. The six phases are diagnostic study, external design, internal design, programming, testing, and installation. All phases are not always applied to all projects, due to the circumstances surrounding each project. However, all external system specifications are completely agreed to prior to the start of internal-system design. Also, the internal-system design phase of the project-development cycle must be completed before the start of programming. The concepts of structured design generally are applied during the internal-design phase of the project-development cycle.

The internal-design phase begins with preparation of data-flow graphs for an entire application. These graphs illustrate the flow of data through the system and the transformation of data within the system. They provide the means for identifying and defining the system's major functions. The data-flow graphs may be further refined as the major functions are assembled into the subsystems required by the application.

Structure charts are developed by factoring the data-flow graph functions into subfunctions and then each subfunction into its parts. The structure chart represents all the functions included in the system and the data communication necessary. Because individual modules will be programmed to accomplish the functions, the structure chart depicts the relationship of the modules as they comprise the system. Packaging is the technique used to provide an efficient and practical process of logically grouping functions. These groupings then become implementable pieces which can be defined as subsystems, programs, or subroutines.

Module specifications are developed after packaging, and HIPOs (hierarchy plus input, processing, and output) are used as the documentation standard for translating the specifications from the structure chart for the programmer. The HIPOs, combined with a narrative, document the inputs, processes, and outputs for each module. In addition to the narrative and HIPO, the programmer receives all the information necessary to code and unit test the module.

The programming phase follows a prescribed procedure during which all code is reviewed by more than one team member using code reading and code walk-through techniques. The following steps are adhered to during the programming and testing phases:

(1) The project or team leader reviews the module specifications with the programmer.

(2) The programmer develops the logic charts for the module.

(3) Three project members conduct a walk-through to formally review the module's logic.

(4) The programmer codes the modules following structured-code guidelines.

(5) The code is read and reviewed by another team member.

(6) The librarian keys and compiles the module into the project libraries.

(7) The test case for the code walk-through and unit test is developed.

(8) Three project members conduct a code walk-through formally reviewing the module's code.

(9) The librarian moves the module to a test library, and the programmer conducts the unit test.

(10) The librarian moves the module to an integration library after unit testing. The project leader, team leader, or lead programmer integrates the module with other modules and tests the program.

(11) Program documentation is completed.

(12) The librarian moves the program modules to the master library and compiles the program.

(13) The program is then integrated with other programs and the subsystem is tested.

To support the project-development cycle, Bethlehem developed the Bethlehem Interactive Time-Sharing System (BITS) by integrating several IBM application development tools. Procedures were developed to compile, link, and test modules through the use of project libraries.

The Sheet & Tin Marketing Control System (STMCS) is a prime example of the application and success of structured design within the project-development cycle. The main objective of this particular system is to process a customer order and provide the producing facility with complete order specifications as rapidly as possible after receipt of an order from the customer. STMCS is an online system operating in an IMS environment.

The STMCS team consisted of a project leader, team leader, two analysts, and a librarian during the internal design phase. The team reviewed and revised data-flow graphs, structure

charts, and programming specifications. During the programming
and testing phases, two lead programmers and four other programmers were added to the project.

The STMCS consists of four major subsystems: Order Entry
and Changes, Retrieval (output reports and documents), Plant
Interface (production data transmitted to the plants), and
Tables (data necessary for table look-ups). The system contains
72 programs comprised of 2,037 modules; each module contains
approximately 100 lines of Procedure Division code. The
internal design started January, 1977, and the system was
implemented in July, 1979. Approximately 31,200 man-hours were
expended for internal design, programming, and installation; and
each module required nearly 17 hours from HIPO to integration.
Because manageable functions were identified through the use of
structured design, overlapping development of different portions
of the system was possible with a minimum of risk. The staffing
of the project team peaked at a maximum of 10 members during the
programming phase. Programming, data-field naming, linkage, and
processing standards were established by the team. "GO TO-less"
code was strictly enforced with the exception of allowing a "GO
TO" to an exit line within a performed routine.

The benefits realized using structured design techniques
for the development of STMCS and other systems were many. The
approach yields ease of change and enhancement. There are
practically no maintenance requirements due to error in the
interpretation of the designer's logic. Though more time is
spent in the design and specification process than traditionally
was spent in the past, the payback during programming, testing,
and installation is immeasurable. The review process and
walk-through produce a sharing of knowledge and advancing of
skills for the junior members of the team. Progress is more
visible, and corrective action for errors or omissions is more
timely and less costly. System documentation occurs prior to
and during development instead of after installation (or not at
all). The entire project becomes more manageable from the
viewpoint of planning, scheduling, and control. The system can
be installed in pieces, offering earlier payback and higher
savings. Projects are installed on time without last-minute
delays or misinterpreted requirements. The modular design makes
it easy to reuse significant portions of the code on subsequent
applications, either directly or with minor modification.

DISCUSSION POINTS

1.   Describe the standard methodology used by Bethlehem Steel
to develop systems.   What are some of the benefits of employing
a standard methodology?

2.   Discuss some of the benefits realized by Bethlehem Steel by
using structured design techniques for the development of STMCS
and other systems.

Office of Personnel Management

One of the ways that computers are affecting our lives is through the career opportunities they provide. In addition to the opportunities available in private industry, the federal government, through the Office of Personnel Management (OPM), offers a virtually unlimited range of career opportunities in computer-realted fields. Previously known as the Civil Service Commission, the Office of Personnel Management presently offers application in the analysis of air traffic patterns, the structure of chemical compounds, foreign policy determination, and missile design. In nearly every instance in which the government touches the lives of United States citizens, a computer is providing support. Consider the difficulty of issuing retirement checks or income tax refunds, tabulating election results, or monitoring drivers' license applications without the assistance of computers.

The federal government obviously needs people to support these various activities. These individuals are broadly classified in four major groups: computer system administrators, computer specialists, computer operators, and computer aides and technicians. Table 1 indicates the total number of people employed in each classification, the corresponding average salary, and the federal agencies that hire the most significant numbers. The Department of Defense employs nearly 60 percent of these individuals, but a substantial number of computer-related jobs exist in civilian agencies also.

The computer-specialist classification includes programmers, system analysts, equipment analysts, and computer specialists. More people are employed in this category than in the other three combined. A programmer plans and develops the machine logic necessary to perform the data manipulations required by applications programs, as specified by the system analyst. The analyst must possess the ability to logically relate activities involved in the flow of data through a system, as well as an extensive knowledge of hardware. Equipment analysts are more technically oriented; they are often responsible for evaluating equipment before a purchase decision. A computer specialist is a person with outstanding abilities in more than one of the areas described above. He or she usually is involved in a broad range of activities.

JOB TITLE	AVERAGE SALARY	Defense	Treasury	DEPARTMENT HEW	Agriculture	Other	TOTAL
Computer System Administrator	$34,399	764	134	198	34	483	1,613
Computer Specialist	$26,841	15,452	1,462	2,203	1,060	7,327	27,504
Computer Operator	$16,058	6,796	958	802	195	2,304	11,055
Computer Aides and Technicians	$14,311	4,027	521	443	347	1,649	6,987

Table 1
EDP EMPLOYMENT BY
FEDERAL AGENCIES

Computer system operators and peripheral-equipment operators are grouped under the computer-operator category. The system operator is concerned with the computer control console and devices to which it is connected. A peripheral-equipment operator works with card readers, card punches, printers, optical scanners, and related equipment.

Aides and technicians do support work associated with computer operations. Typical tasks performed by a technician include translating program routines and detailed logic steps designed by others into machine-readable instructions and code, developing charts showing the flow of documents and data through specified areas, and revising programs.

Of benefit to federal data-processing employees are the educational development programs available through the OPM's Workforce Effectiveness and Development Group. This Group is

divided into many functional areas, one of which offers training
and educational programs in automatic data processing (ADP).

The OPM segments the entire country into ten regions which
serve as a basis for distributed operations. The Workforce
Effectiveness and Development Group has established ADP
Management Training Institutes in these regions. The courses
offered fall into four broad categories--user education,
upward-mobility training, computer-specialist training, and
office automation training.

User education programs are designed for people whose jobs
are affected by the computer, but who are not directly involved
in its operation. Courses offered include Management Introduction to ADP, Executive Seminar in ADP, and Introduction to
ADP Systems Analysis. The purpose of these courses is not to
help an individual develop extensive technical competence but to
familiarize him or her with the capabilities of an ADP system.

The upward-mobility curriculum is designed to provide ADP
technical training for government personnel who want to upgrade
their skills. These people usually are working in dead-end jobs
and have had no previous training in data processing. Beginning
courses in this sequence include Introduction to Computer
Operation, Introduction to Computer Programming, and Basic Card-
Punch Operator Training.

The most technically involved courses are offered in the
area of computer-specialist training. These courses are
designed to provide further training to those integrally
involved in the everyday operation of a computer facility. As
new and better technologies evolve, these specialists must keep
abreast of the latest advancements.

The office automation training is designed for managers and
employees whose offices are being automated. This includes
members of the implementation project teams. The purpose of
these courses is to familiarize them with office automation, its
potential, and successful ways of implementing it.

The largest of the ADP Management Training Institutes is
the Center for Information Management and Automation (CIMA) in
Washington, D.C. Participants in the CIMA courses have direct
access to a third-generation, medium-scale, batch-processing
computer which provides opportunities for "hands-on" experience.
In addition, time-sharing systems are available to participants
for further acutal practice with programming theory.

The CIMA offers training in each of the four categories described above. Courses offered at this center are more in-depth and more comprehensive than those offered at the regional centers. Figure 2 indicates the variety of educational opportunities available to computer specialists. From basic courses, such as those covering COBOL, FORTRAN, and BASIC programming, the trainee can progress to the study of advanced programming techniques, system analysis, and eventually, complex telecommunication and data-base concepts.

Courses of General Interest

Seminar in ADP Management and Administration	Computer/Microfilm Information Systems
Seminar in Advanced Computer Systems Technology	Auditing Automated Systems: Tools and Techniques*
Seminar in Computer Systems Evaluation and Procurement*	Auditing On-Line Systems*
Decision Logic Table Workshop	Automated Accounting Systems*
Security and Privacy of Computer Systems	Automated Budgeting Systems*
Seminar on Minicomputers	Integrating Office Operations with Information Technology*
Tape/Disk Librarian Functions	

Systems Analysis and Design Courses

Data Entry/Source Data Automation and Computer Output Devices*	Systems Workshop for Computer Specialists	Design of Computerized Management Information Systems*
Systems Analysis for Computer Programmers	ADP Systems Analysis Seminar*	**Data Base/Data Communication Series**

Workshop/Seminar Series in ADP Systems Analysis Techniques (WASAT)

I. Data Gathering Techniques*	V. Statistical Approaches to Data Analysis	I. Introduction to Computer File Structures and Data Base Design
II. Computer Forms Design*	VI. Data Processing Project Management	II. Fundamentals of Data Communications
III. Documentation and Flowcharting Techniques	VII. ADP Performance Management*	III. Data Base Management Systems
IV. Structured Design	VIII. Distributed Data Processing*	IV. Systems Design Considerations in an On-Line Environment
		V. Data Base/Data Communications Systems Design (An Advanced Course)

Programming Courses

Fundamentals of ANS COBOL	Fundamentals of ADP for Computer Specialist Trainees
COBOL Programming Techniques	Programming in BASIC
Fundamentals of FORTRAN IV	Fundamentals of PL/I
FORTRAN Programming Techniques	

Office Automation Courses

Introduction to OA	Implementing OA Systems
OA Technologies	Microcomputers and Microcomputer Software

*Agencies are encouraged to send teams of user personnel and computer specialists.

Fundamentals of ANS COBOL is an example of a programming course offered. It is structured to help participants develop a working knowledge of the COBOL programming language. The two-week workshop covers such topics as computer fundamentals, the program-development process, a description of the four divisions in a COBOL program, and the actual writing and testing of the programs. The knowledge gained from this course serves as a foundation for COBOL Programming Techniques, a course dealing with file storage, input/output control, sorting, and file-processing methods as executed in the COBOL programming language.

The individual who is already proficient in programming can select among various advanced courses, such as Structured Design. This course aims to help participants understand design techniques which support structured programming, team organization, top-down approach, and HIPO. Such techniques become

more important as the government obtains the massive online
storage required for data bases. A course called Data Base
Management Systems ties the structured-design fundamentals
together with complex data-base concepts and functions. Topics
covered include data-base software, evaluation, and various DBMS
packages currently available.

People who are automating their offices can take courses in
the office automation implementation process: Introduction to
OA, Requirements Analysis, Design, and Implementation, as well
as in management skills once the office is automated. OA
technology courses include Electronic Mail, Teleconferencing,
Micrographics, and Microcomputers and Microcomputer Software.

The goal of the CIMA is to develop competent personnel to
staff federal agencies. By training those already familiar with
agency operations, a higher level of efficiency can be readily
achieved. The federal government strives not only to provide
jobs for many people in data processing and related fields but
also to enable them to upgrade their job skills. This opportunity makes government employment extremely attractive.

DISCUSSION POINTS

1. What are the benefits associated with training government
employees through the ADP Management Training Institutes rather
than through typical colleges and universities?

2. As an entry-level programmer, what course might you select at
the CIMA to enhance your professional development?

The Kroger Company

In 1883, twenty-five-year-old Bernard H. (Barney) Kroger and his friend B.A. Branagan opened a small store in Cincinnati, Ohio, with $722 in capital. It was named "The Great Western Tea Company" and sold coffees, teas, sausages, staples, and china-ware. At the end of the first year, with assets amounting to $2,620, Kroger bought out the store and ran it by himself. One hundred years later, in 1983, the Kroger Company was the fourth largest retailing company in the United States as ranked by total sales; and Kroger Food Stores was the country's second largest supermarket chain, with 1,428 stores in nineteen states. Most Kroger stores are "superstores" with sizes ranging from 25,000 to 45,000 square feet. These stores offer specialty and personal service departments such as delicatessens, bakeries, cheese shops, and floral departments.

Kroger also manufactures and processes food for sale by these supermarkets, a tradition that began before the turn of the century. The company operates regional bakeries and dairies in addition to two cheese plants, a peanut butter plant, and a general processing plant.

The Kroger Company headquarters are in Cincinnati, Ohio, as are the data-processing facilities that serve and support the corporate activities. The data-processing operation is concen-trated in two mainframe computers at headquarters. Most transactions are transmitted to them by private leased lines connecting fifteen other marketing-area locations. Thirteen of these locations consist of an area headquarters, an area warehouse, and fifty to a hundred supermarkets. Each marketing-area location also has a data-processing staff. This configu-ration is illustrated in Figure 1.

FIGURE 1

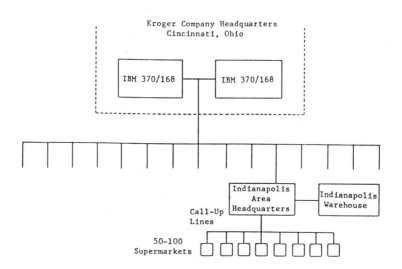

The MIS Department at the Cincinnati headquarters provides
services to most departments in the company, including merchan-
dising and buying, warehousing, transportation, store operations, finance and accounting, manufacturing, personnel, and
market research. Current applications in these departments
include order-entry and billing, inventory control, payroll,
accounts payable, and accounting. The MIS Department has a
staff of about 185 employees, 136 of them involved in system
analysis and programming, the remaining 49 in operations,
communications, and data entry.

Kroger has been an industry leader in the development and
implementation of the electronic scanning operations that have
flourished since the introduction of the Universal Product Code;
544 Kroger supermarkets have fully operational point-of-sale
terminals, and their number is expected to reach 600 by the end
of 1984.

DEVELOPMENT OF THE UNIVERSAL PRODUCT CODE SYSTEM

The idea of using product codes to facilitate automatic
checkout counters has been around since the 1930s, but technology did not advance sufficiently to make it feasible until
the 1960s. During that decade, there was much discussion
throughout the food industry concerning the need for a nation-
ally standardized unique identifier for each product. The
question was how to get producers, packagers, distributors, and

retailers to agree on a uniform coded symbol and how to integrate the code with electronic data processing. An initial
system study was conducted on an industry-wide scale for three
basic reasons:

1. To solve the problem,
2. To take advantage of new technology, and
3. To respond to new information-processing requirements that
resulted from the rapid growth and increasing complexity of the
industry.

What is remarkable about this particular system study is
that competitors from all levels of the task environment
combined their efforts to study a common problem and succeeded
in formulating a common objective to solve it. At this level,
the system study was very broad; but it illustrates some notable
points: Kroger, a system in itself, is only one small subsystem
within a larger system, the food industry. And all of the
business firms in the food industry system interact with one
another in their pursuit of common goals--profit and growth.

Around 1968, John L. Strubbe of Kroger, one of the task
force members for the study, began teaching electronics firms
about the information-processing requirements of the grocery
business so they could design scanning equipment to read a
standard code. RCA pioneered in the development of an electronic scanning device, which was tested in a Kenwood, Ohio,
Kroger store for fifteen months in 1971 and 1972. The Universal
Product Code was chosen by the task force in 1971, and a council
consisting of a broad spectrum of industry leaders was set up to
govern policy. The consulting firm of McKinsey & Co. was hired
to do the feasibility study, and their investigation concluded
that the proposal was economically sound.

KROGER'S SYSTEM ANALYSIS

Kroger had started individual system analysis around 1970.
Specifically, its goals were to improve speed and accuracy at
the customer input and to advance its inventory control capabilities. The analysis was conducted by the MIS Department in
conjunction with Store Operating Services and Accounting Policy
Methods and supported by all other departments. This was a
pioneer effort for Kroger--never before had an MIS project
included and affected every single working element in the entire
organization.

The UPC council, a primary external source of information,
provided written descriptions, flowcharts, and other documentation of how the system would function and what data it would
need. Internal surveys, matrices, and existing documentation

helped the Kroger group to determine general design requirements. It also monitored competitors' activities for further
ideas.

In doing its feasibility study, Kroger concentrated on
quantifiable benefits such as more customer traffic, increased
accuracy, lower inventory costs, and higher sales. Many of the
projected figures were based on the experiences of Kroger's
pilot electronic scanning operations, which were launched in
1974. In computing the predicted return on investment, Kroger
ignored intangible benefits, which were difficult, if not
impossible, to quantify. Still, it was able to justify the
system even without considering the "soft savings."

The first pilot store utilized IBM scanning equipment; and
the second, which opened six months later, was equipped with
Univac computers. Major phase-in operations began in 1978; and
by the end of 1984, almost half of all Kroger stores should be
equipped with electronic scanning equipment. These stores
communicate directly with their area headquarters, which in turn
communicate with corporate headquarters.

DISCUSSION POINTS

1. System theory implies that elements of a system interact.
Describe how a transaction at a new Kroger checkout will affect
files within different departments in the organization.

2. Discuss some of the intangible costs and benefits Kroger
chose not to analyze in its feasibility study.

SCRIPT FOR SLIDE PRESENTATION

Narrative to Accompany

A Tour of A Computer Facility

Slide #	Narrative
1	A receptionist area permits monitoring of all individuals seeking to enter the computer facility. The computer room should be nondescript and located with security in mind.
2	A receptionist checks for proper authorization before permitting entry. It is imperative that only essential personnel obtain access to the computer area.
3	Only authorized individuals may approach the locked computer facility. The combination of human surveillance coupled with mechanical devices assures optimum security.

4   Only specially coded cards will unlock the doors.
There are also other more sophisticated entry-
protection devices that require passwords or combinations. The critical aspect is in protecting the key
that unlocks the door.

5   CRT consoles directly interconnected to the central
processing units. This is the principal method that
permits the operator to communicate with the computer.
Switches are not thrown and dials are not turned
contrary to many science fiction movies.

6   Operators communicating with the operating system.
Modern computer operations require individuals more
highly trained than previous sytems. The operating
system programs form the interface between the human
operator and the computer hardware.

7   Magnetic tape drive units. These drives permit data to
be stored and retrieved at high speeds in a sequential
manner. Similar to a home stereo tape deck, multiple
read/write heads pass in parallel over the tape
creating channels to store the data. However, due to
the speeds involved, a vacuum environment is required.

8   One of the central processing units interconnected in a multiprocessing system. There are three computers in this system capable of sharing the load. If any one central processing unit experiences a failure, the remaining units can take over the load at a reduced speed. Each unit is color coded for operator ease: red, blue, white.

9   A library storage facility for magnetic tapes. Since many organizations store great quantities of data, an effective storage facility for the physical media is essential. The vulnerability of the tapes to heat and moisture in the event of fire or flood must be con-sidered in the design.

10 Computerized inventory control for the tape library. An important aspect of processing the appropriate data is determining the physical device upon which it is located. Because of the volume of tapes required by some corporate operations, computer control of the tapes becomes a necessary solution.

11   Magnetic disk drives. The most popular method of storing data in modern computer systems. Since data can be processed in a direct/random manner rather than sequentially, it is required for any application requiring rapid retrieval. Each surface of the disk can be viewed similarly to a standard record. The disk units themselves are removable.

12   Magnetic disk units that resemble pizza ovens. The advantage of magnetic disk over other forms of data storage have inspired manufacturers to develop larger, more cost effective units. The cost of such storage is continuing to decline at such a rapid rate than many authorities predict a future with only direct access storage.

13   High speed line printer. Most output today is still in the form of printed paper. This typical impact printer is quite capable of producing multiple carbon copies.

14   Front-end processor for controlling the communication
system. The requirements of a large telecommunication
system would utilize large resources of the central
processing unit. In order to free up these resources
for production, smaller computers are placed in between
the communication system and the central processing
unit to act as an interface sharing the load.

15   Patch panel and monitoring equipment for a telecommunication system. Each communication line entering
the system must be physically interconnected to
establish the data link.

16   A line tester to monitor the communication system. The
transmission inconsistencies associated with telephone
lines require constant monitoring and testing. This
often becomes the critical aspect in a telecommunications system.

17   Modems for the telecommunication system. Since data in
a computer system is stored in digital form while
transmission along phone lines can only occur in analog
form, a device is needed to accomplish the conversion
for each active line at both the computer port and the
user terminal. Direct digital transmission often by
microwave eliminates the need for modems but is rarely
employed.

18 | Air conditioning unit controls. The modern large-scale computer is still highly sensitive to temperature and humidity. In fact, some large systems require a water cooling system to augment the air conditioning. Through the use of heat exchangers, these computers can then provide heat for the rest of the building. Most minicomputer and microcomputer systems do not require environmental controls.

19 | Controller for magnetic disk units. Similar to front end processors, these controllers are computers capable of reducing the resource requirements on the central processor and shifting the work to these interface units. The lights seen are fire warning devices to alert computer room personnel.

20 | Fire control panels. The largest common security hazard faced by all computer facilities is the risk of fire. This sophisticated fire-control system integrates sensor devices with halon gas. Computer room fires are extremely difficult to control with water or carbon dioxide. However, halon gas is expensive and the system must be recharged after being activated.

Introduction to Data Processing

MULTIPLE CHOICE

BACKGROUND

1-1.   Which statement about computers is false?
    a.   Computers cannot perform any task that a person has not predetermined.
    b.   Computers have no intelligence of their own.
    c.   Computers can only perform very simple addition without relying on human intelligence.
    d.   Computers need humans.

1-2.   Which of the following is a function that computers cannot perform?
    a.   arithmetic operations
    b.   storage operations
    c.   comparison operations
    d.   all above are computer functions

1-3.   The instruction set of the computer
    a.   typically consists of thousands of unique instructions
    b.   can be easily changed by the user
    c.   is manipulated to create computer programs
    d.   controls only logical operations

1-4.   Most computers are referred to as
    a.   general-purpose machines
    b.   dedicated machines
    c.   special-purpose machines
    d.   dedicated-purpose machines

1-5.   The switching speed of the computer's electronic circuits
and the distances that electric currents have to flow are
important factors most closely related to a computer's
a. accuracy   c. memory
b. speed   d. accuracy and speed

1-6.   Which of the following units of time represents one-
billionth of a second?
a. nanosecond   c. mallosecond
b. microsecond   d. picosecond

1-7.   Traditionally the computer time required to perform one
addition ranged from
a. 6 microseconds to 600 picoseconds
b. 4 microseconds to 200 nanoseconds
c. 5 milliseconds to 500 picoseconds
d. 4 microseconds to 100 nanoseconds

1-8.   Garbage in-garbage out (GIGO) refers to the fact that
a. if input collected for use by the computer is
incorrect, it is impossible for the computer to produce meaningful output
b. if input collected for use by the computer is irrelevant, it is not impossible for the computer to produce meaningful output
c. if programs used to manipulate data are not correct,
it is impossible for the computer to produce meaningful output
d. if processing instructions are incorrect, it is
impossible for the computer to produce meaningful
output

1-9.   The primary memory capacity of many large computers can
store up to _____ characters.
a. 16,000   c. 500,000
b. 100,000   d. 1,000,000

1-10.   External storage devices are referred to as
a. primary memory   c. secondary storage
b. output   d. input

1-11.   External storage devices can be utilized to increase the
computer's memory, in some cases up to _____ times.
a. 40   c. 500
b. 100   d. 1,000

1-12.   The primary memory of some small computers stores as few
        as _____ characters.
        a.   16,000   c.   64,000
        b.   32,000   d.   128,000

1-13.   The amount of storage available in today's computers
        _____ according to user requirements.
        a.   can be increased
        b.   can be decreased
        c.   can be increased or decreased
        d.   cannot be tailored

DATA PROCESSING

1-14.   Using the electronic computer to collect, manipulate, and
        distribute data to achieve certain objectives is referred
        to as
        a.   automatic data processing (ADP)
        b.   binary data processing (BDP)
        c.   electronic data processing (EDP)
        d.   electronic information processing (EIP)

1-15.   The difference between "information" and "data" is that
        a.   information is processed data
        b.   information is organized data
        c.   information can be used to make meaningful decisions
        d.   all of the above

1-16.   Which of the following is not a required characteristic
        of information which is useful to decision makers?
        a.   accurate   c.   redundant
        b.   relevant   d.   timely

1-17.   In the data processing flow, the step of the input stage
        which refers to the elimination of garbage in-garbage out
        is
        a.   collecting   c.   coding
        b.   verification   d.   sorting

1-18.   In the data processing flow, the steps in the processing
        stage referring to the reduction of large amounts of data
        to concise, usable form is called
        a.   calculating   c.   summarizing
        b.   sorting   d.   classifying

1-19.   The three steps involved in the output stage of the data
        processing flow are
        a. conversion, summarizing, communicating
        b. retrieval, conversion, communication
        c. conversion, calculation, communication
        d. retrieval, sorting, summarizing

1-20.   In data processing, the term which has the broadest con-
        notations is
        a. data base   c. record
        b. field   d. file

1-21.   All data processing follows the same basic flow pattern
        involving _____ stages.
        a. 2   c. 4
        b. 3   d. 5

1-22.   The "input" stage involves _____ steps.
        a. 2   c. 4
        b. 3   d. 5

1-23.   The "output" phase involves _____ steps.
        a. 2   c. 4
        b. 3   d. 5

1-24.   Categorizing data according to certain characteristics is
        part of
        a. input   c. processing
        b. verifying   d. output

1-25.   Coding data is part of the _____ phase of data proc-
        essing.
        a. input   c. collection
        b. processing   d. output

1-26.   Verification is part of the _____ phase of data proc-
        essing.
        a. input   c. collection
        b. processing   d. output

1-27.   Calculation is part of the _____ phase of data proc-
        essing.
        a. input   c. collection
        b. processing   d. output

1-28.   Conversion is part of the _____ phase of data proc-
        essing.
        a. input   c. collection
        b. processing   d. output

1-29.   Making sure that information reaches the proper users at
        the proper time in intelligible form is part of the
        _____ phase of data processing.
        a.   input   c.   collection
        b.   processing   d.   output

1-30.   Verifying the accuracy and completeness of data is part
        of the _____ phase of data processing.
        a.   input   c.   collection
        b.   processing   d.   output

1-31.   Which of the following terms does not belong with the
        others?
        a.   classify   c.   calculate
        b.   verify   d.   summarize

1-32.   Which of the following terms does not belong with the
        others?
        a.   retrieve   c.   sort
        b.   convert   d.   communicate

1-33.   Which of the following terms does not belong with the
        others?
        a.   classify   c.   code
        b.   collect   d.   verify

1-34.   A single data item, such as a social security number, is
        known as a
        a.   field   c.   file
        b.   record   d.   data base

DATA PROCESSING APPLICATION

1-35.   Payroll preparation is suitable for electronic data proc-
        essing because of the following characteristics:
        a.   well-defined, simple to understand, small numbers of
             records
        b.   repetitive and complex
        c.   repetitive and difficult to define
        d.   large number of records, repetitive, well-defined

1-36.   Which of the following procedures in payroll preparation
        can a computer not complete?
        a.   read total hours worked from time card
        b.   calculate withholding and social security tax
        c.   compute gross pay
        d.   all can be completed by a computer

IMPACT OF COMPUTERS

1-37.   By utilizing computers to monitor intensive care
        patients, critical factors like body temperature, pulse,
        and breathing can be checked as often as
        a. several times per second
        b. several times per minute
        c. several times per hour
        d. once a minute

1-38.   Which of the following is not true concerning the impact
        of computers on our society? Computers have
        a. enhanced our problem-solving capability
        b. not found much use in government
        c. increased our capacity to handle complex rela-
            tionships
        d. not replaced human decision making

1-39.   CAI is used most frequently in _____ settings.
        a. business   c. educational
        b. health care   d. industrial

APPLICATION

1-40.   FlightSafety International Inc. has _____ learning
        centers in the United States, Canada, and France.
        a. 10   c. 50
        b. 30   d. ,24

1-41.   Advantages of simulated flight training include all but
        a. insurance company encouragement
        b. conservation of high fuel costs
        c. ability to practice emergency procedures too
            dangerous to try in the air
        d. all the above are advantages

1-42.   What is the main benefit of FlightSafety's simulator
        training of emergency procedures?
        a. It saves time.
        b. It allows procedures too dangerous to try in the air
            to be practiced.
        c. It saves money.
        d. Less equipment is needed.

1-43.   In which programming language is the simulation software
        written that is used by FlightSafety?
        a. COBOL   c. Pascal
        b. PL/I   d. FORTRAN

1-44.   What kind of input do the systems that position the cock-
        pit instruments and control the motion base on the flight
        simulator require?
        a. analog   c. digital
        b. numeric   d. alphabetical

1-45.   In order to simulate a real-time environment, the I/O
        process in the flight simulator needs to be is repeated
        a. at very high speeds   c. at very low speeds
        b. at moderate speeds   d. at the speed of light

ANSWER KEY

1-1.	c	1-16.	c	1-31.	b
1-2.	d	1-17.	b	1-32.	c
1-3.	c	1-18.	c	1-33.	a
1-4.	a	1-19.	b	1-34.	a
1-5.	b	1-20.	a	1-35.	d
1-6.	a	1-21.	b	1-36.	d
1-7.	b	1-22.	b	1-37.	a
1-8.	a	1-23.	b	1-38.	b
1-9.	d	1-24.	c	1-39.	c
1-10.	c	1-25.	a	1-40.	d
1-11.	a	1-26.	a	1-41.	d
1-12.	a	1-27.	b	1-42.	b
1-13.	c	1-28.	d	1-43.	d
1-14.	c	1-29.	d	1-44.	a
1-15.	d	1-30.	a	1-45.	a

2

The Evolution of Computers

MULTIPLE CHOICE

EARLY DEVELOPMENT

2-1.   The slide rule was directly adapted from which of the following early calculating devices?
a. difference engine   c. Napier's bones
b. abacus   d. shepherd's knots

2-2.   Who translated Napier's invention into the slide rule around 1650?
a. Blaise Pascal   c. Robert Bissaker
b. Gottfried von Leibnitz d. Charles Babbage

2-3.   To whom is the development of the first real mechanical calculator attributed?
a. Leibnitz   c. Babbage
b. Jacquard   d. Pascal

2-4.   Blasie Pascal is credited with the development of the first real
a. mechanical calculator c. digital computer
b. slide ruler   d. computer language

2-5.   The mathematician who developed a machine that could multiply, divide, and calculate as well as add and subtract was
a. Blaise Pascal   c. Robert Bissaker
b. Gottfried von Leibnitz d. Charles Babbage

2-6.   One of the first real developments in programmable
        instructions for machines came from the
        a. French government   c. printing industry
        b. weaving industry   d. ship building industry

2-7.   The punched card was a concept first used in the _____
        industry.
        a. mining   c. steel
        b. weaving   d. farming

2-8.   Which of the following are true about Babbage's
        Difference Engine?
        a. It could avoid the printing errors that were common
            in its day.
        b. It was designed to calculate logarithm tables and
            print the results.
        c. When he tried to make a larger version, parts could
            not be manufactured to the tolerances required by the
            machine.
        d. All of the above.

2-9.   Babbage's vision of using punched cards for inputting
        data and instructions went relatively unnoticed until
        a. about 1850   c. the early 1900s
        b. the late 1800s   d. about 1950

2-10.   A model of Babbage's analytical engine based on his
        drawings and notes was put together in 1871 by
        a. his son   c. Blaise Pascal
        b. Dr. Herman Hollerith   d. Robert Bissaker

2-11.   The person with the reputation for being the "father of
        computers" was
        a. Herman Hollerith   c. Charles Babbage
        b. Howard Aiken   d. William Burroughs

2-12.   Hollerith's Tabulating Machine Company evolved into the
        present-day corporation know as
        a. Burroughs Corporation
        b. IBM
        c. UNIVAC
        d. Hollerith Code Corporation

2-13.   Hollerith's machines reduced the time required to process
        the census data to _____ despite an increase of three
        million in population.
        a. 1 year   c. 2½ years
        b. 2 years   d. 3 years

2-14.   Babbage's vision of an automatic calculator was realized
        in the machine known as the
        a.   Mark I
        b.   IBM 200
        c.   Electronic Numerical Integrator and Calculator
        d.   ABC

2-15.   In 1974 a federal court declared _____ to be the true
        inventor of the first electronic computer.
        a.   Babbage   c.   Berry
        b.   Atanasoff   d.   Eckert

2-16.   The first real step toward the development of the com-
        puter as we know it was made in
        a.   1925   c.   1944
        b.   1934   d.   1954

2-17.   The chief competitors for the honor of developing the
        first electronic compter were
        a.   Eckert and Mauchly   c.   Eckert and Presper
        b.   Presper and Johns   d.   Mauchly and Johns

2-18.   The ENIAC could perform a multiplication in three-
        thousandths of a second, compared with about _____
        seconds required by the Mark I.
        a.   15   c.   5
        b.   10   d.   3

2-19.   The first stored program was spurred by principles pro-
        posed by
        a.   Mauchly   c.   Neumann
        b.   Eckert   d.   Hollerith

2-20.   The _____ was the first stored-program computer.
        a.   ENIAC   c.   EDVAC
        b.   EDSAC   d.   ENVAC

2-21.   EDSAC was the first computer to perform
        a.   addition, subtraction, multiplication, division, and
             square roots
        b.   arithmetic operations
        c.   arithmetic and logical operations without human
             intervention
        d.   logical operations

2-22.   The first stored-program computer could perform a com-
        putation in
        a.   three milliseconds
        b.   twenty-five milliseconds
        c.   ten milliseconds
        d.   fifty milliseconds

FIRST GENERATION: 1951-1958

2-23.   The beginning of the first-generation computers was
        marked by which event?
        a.   the purchase of the UNIVAC I by the U.S. Census
             Bureau
        b.   the invention of the UNIVAC II by Mauchly and Eckert
        c.   the invention of the UNIVAC I as a one-of-a-kind spe-
             cialized scientific purpose computer
        d.   the purchase of the first one-of-a-kind computing
             machine by the U.S. government for military purposes

2-24.   In first-generation computers, cylinders coated with
        magnetized material stored as tiny magnetized spots were
        called
        a.   magnetic disks   c.   magnetic cylinders
        b.   magnetic drums   d.   magnetic cores

2-25.   Which of the following was not true of first-generation
        computers?
        a.   huge in size
        b.   special air-conditioning equipment required
        c.   optional internal storage capacity
        d.   considerable maintenance required

2-26.   Most of the first-generation computers used in business
        were used to process payroll and billing because
        a.   they were the only applications the computer could
             perform
        b.   they were the only use businesses had for a computer
        c.   the computers were not very accurate
        d.   the computers were easy to program and cost justify

2-27.   Which of the following is a mnemonic?
        a.   symbolic code
        b.   binary code
        c.   machine-language instruction
        d.   series of 0s and 1s

2-28.   The first set of programs to tell the computer how to
        translate symbolic languages into binary codes was devel-
        oped by
        a.   Mauchly   c.   Eckert
        b.   Hopper   d.   Von Neumann

SECOND GENERATION: 1959-1964

2-29.   Which of the following characteristics did not apply to
        second-generation computers when compared with the first
        generation?
        a.   larger in size
        b.   required less power to operate
        c.   increased storage capacity
        d.   faster

2-30.   Direct or random access to records on file is supplied by
        a.   magnetic tape   c.   punch cards
        b.   magnetic disks   d.   paper tapes

2-31.   The modular hardware concept can be characterized by all
        of the following except
        a.   a building-block approach to electronic circuit
             design
        b.   a great reduction in down time due to malfunction
        c.   difficult and time consuming replacement of complete
             modules called breadboards
        d.   flexibility

2-32.   Which of the following does not apply to high-level
        languages?
        a.   application oriented
        b.   machine oriented
        c.   problem oriented
        d.   resemble English more than earlier languages

2-33.   The principal storage medium associated with batch proc-
        essing was
        a.   punch cards   c.   magnetic disks
        b.   magnetic tape   d.   diskettes

2-34.   The substitution of magnetic tapes for punched cards
        increased input/output processing speeds by a factor of
        at least
        a.   20   c.   40
        b.   30   d.   50

2-35.   The first high-level language to achieve widespread
        acceptance was
        a. FORTRAN   c. PL/I
        b. COBOL   d. BASIC

THIRD GENERATION: 1965-1971

2-36.   Which of the following is not true when third-generation
        computers are compared with those of the second genera-
        tion?
        a. third-generation computers were faster
        b. third-generation computers were smaller
        c. third-generation computers were less expensive
        d. third-generation computers used similar internal
            design

2-37.   Which of the following was not an important improvement
        in third-generation equipment?
        a. greater storage capacity
        b. ability to perform several operations simultaneously
        c. use of large-scale integrated circuits
        d. automation of many tasks previously handled by human
            operators

2-38.   The use of remote terminals and the development of time
        sharing environments is associated with which computer
        generation?
        a. first   c. third
        b. second   d. fourth

2-39.   The first silicon integrated circuit was developed by
        a. Hopper   c. Mauchly
        b. Kilby   d. Eckert

2-40.   The transition from the second to the third generation
        occurred when _____ introduced the System/360 computers
        in 1965.
        a. DEC   c. IBM
        b. Xerox   d. Burroughs

2-41.   The first commercially accepted minicomputer was intro-
        duced by _____ in 1965.
        a. DEC   c. IBM
        b. Xerox   d. Burroughs

2-42.   Which of the following is not an important improvement of
        the third-generation computers?
        a.   greater storage capacity
        b.   ability to perform several operations simultaneously
        c.   modular design and compatibility between equipment
        d.   capability to handle both business and scientific
             applications in the same machines

FOURTH GENERATION: 1971-?

2-43.   LSI stands for
        a.   large-sized industrial computers
        b.   large-scale integrated circuits
        c.   large-sized integrated computers
        d.   large-scale integrated computers

2-44.   Which of the following is not a reason that the computers
        since 1971 are referred to as fourth generation?
        a.   significant performance improvement over third-
             generation computers
        b.   significant price reductions over third-generation
             computers
        c.   emergence of minicomputers
        d.   LSI replaced by VLSI

2-45.   Common examples of data-recording equipment to capture
        data at its point of origin include all except
        a.   MICRs   c.   mainframes
        b.   OCR devices   d.   a and b

2-46.   Which generation is marked by the beginning of growth in
        the home computer market?
        a.   first   c.   third
        b.   second   d.   fourth

2-47.   The first microprocessor was invented in
        a.   1965   c.   1975
        b.   1969   d.   1979

2-48.   Although there is some debate on the topic, it is usually
        recognized that _____ invented the microprocessor when
        he worked for _____.
        a.   Hof, Datapoint Corp.   c.   Hof, Intel Corp.
        b.   Poor, Datapoint Corp.   d.   Poor, Intel Corp.

2-49.   The use of vacuum tubes in electronic circuits and mag-
        netic drums as a primary internal storage medium typifies
        the _____ generation of computers.
        a. first   c. third
        b. second   d. fourth

2-50.   The use of integrated circuits and magnetic core, solid
        state main storage typifies the _____ generation of
        computers.
        a. first   c. third
        b. second   d. fourth

2-51.   The use of large-scale integrated circuits and an
        increased storage capacity and speed typifies the _____
        generation of computers.
        a. first   c. third
        b. second   d. fourth

2-52.   The use of transistors for internal operation typifies
        the _____ generation of computers.
        a. first   c. third
        b. second   d. fourth

A HISTORICAL REVIEW OF THE COMPUTER INDUSTRY

2-53.   Major competitors in the mainframe market of the computer
        industry include all of the following except
        a. IBM   c. Burroughs
        b. Apple   d. CDC

2-54.   The oldest sector of the computer industry is the
        a. mainframe sector   c. microcomputer sector
        b. minicomputer sector   d. supercomputer sector

2-55.   The high end of the computer market is becoming saturated
        because
        a. only a few users are finding it more economical to
            purchase small computer systems
        b. purchases of new mainframes are only made when the
            company needs expanded capability
        c. more corporations are learning to complete their own
            maintenance
        d. consumers have been slow to purchase microcomputers

2-56. Important advantages of minicomputer systems include all
       of the following except
       a. They do not require special air conditioning and
           water cooling systems.
       b. They can be enlarged to meet the needs of growing
           corporations.
       c. They can be utilized in an unlimited number of con-
           figurations.
       d. The rate of growth of the minicomputer industry is
           rapidly increasing.

2-57. Minicomputers are typically used in all of the following
       applications except
       a. processing of large amounts of complex data
       b. word processing
       c. industrial automation
       d. time sharing

2-58. The microcomputer associated with the initial concept of
       a person being able to walk into a retail store and
       purchase a low-priced computer was the
       a. Apple   c. TRS-80
       b. Commodore PET   d. Osborne I

2-59. Who is associated with the initial use of the 6502
       microprocessor and the later selling of it to other
       microcomputer manufacturers?
       a. Steven Jobs   c. Adam Osborne
       b. Stephen Wozniak   d. Jack Tramiel

2-60. Who invented the scientific calculator that later led to
       the development of the Apple Computer Company?
       a. Steven Jobs   c. Adam Osborne
       b. Stephen Wozniak   d. Jack Tramiel

2-61. Why do analysts think that the large computer companies
       are most likely to succeed in the microcomputer market?
       a. Consumers are influenced by "brand name" recognition.
       b. They have the greatest marketing strength.
       c. They have the lowest cost manufacturing.
       d. They have the lowest cost manufacturing and the
           greatest marketing strength.

268   COMPUTERS AND DATA PROCESSING

APPLICATION

2-62.   Which major military force supported the development of
        the Mark I?
        a. Army   c. Air Force
        b. Marines   d. Navy

2-63.   Early calculations were performed on the Mark I to build
        what?
        a. air craft carrier   c. machine gun
        b. atomic bomb   d. submarine

2-64.   In 1953, J.W. Forrester developed _____ memory that
        became standard for all digital computers.
        a. silicon chip   c. bubble
        b. magnetic drum   d. magnetic core

2-65.   Who directed the Electronic Computer Project of the
        Institute for Advanced Study in 1946?
        a. J.W. Forrester   c. Howard Aiken
        b. John von Neumann   d. J. Presper Eckert, Jr.

ANSWER KEY

2-1.	c	2-21.	c	2-41.	a	2-61.	d
2-2.	c	2-22.	a	2-42.	c	2-62.	d
2-3.	d	2-23.	a	2-43.	b	2-63.	b
2-4.	a	2-24.	b	2-44.	c	2-64.	d
2-5.	b	2-25.	c	2-45.	c	2-65.	b
2-6.	b	2-26.	d	2-46.	d		
2-7.	b	2-27.	a	2-47.	b		
2-8.	d	2-28.	b	2-48.	c		
2-9.	b	2-29.	a	2-49.	a		
2-10.	a	2-30.	b	2-50.	c		
2-11.	c	2-31.	c	2-51.	d		
2-12.	b	2-32.	b	2-52.	c		
2-13.	c	2-33.	b	2-53.	b		
2-14.	a	2-34.	d	2-54.	a		
2-15.	b	2-35.	a	2-55.	b		
2-16.	c	2-36.	d	2-56.	d		
2-17.	a	2-37.	c	2-57.	a		
2-18.	d	2-38.	c	2-58.	c		
2-19.	c	2-39.	b	2-59.	d		
2-20.	b	2-40.	c	2-60.	b		

Hardware

MULTIPLE CHOICE

CENTRAL PROCESSING UNIT

3-1.   Which of the following components is not part of the computer's central processing unit (CPU)?
a.   control unit   c.   arithmetic/logic unit
b.   secondary storage unit   d.   primary storage unit

3-2.   The heart of the computer system, also known as the mainframe of a large system, is
a.   the control unit   c.   primary storage
b.   the CPU   d.   the ALU

3-3.   The function of the CPU control unit includes all of the following except
a.   interpreting the instructions of a program in storage and signaling circuits to execute instructions
b.   communicating with an output device to initiate transfer of results from storage
c.   transferring data into storage by signaling the ALU to perform arithmetic computations and logical operations
d.   none are functions of the CPU

3-4.   The CPU is composed of _____ units.
a.   2   c.   4
b.   3   d.   5

270

3-5.   The CPU unit that maintains order is the _____ unit.
      a.   control   c.   logic
      b.   secondary storage   d.   primary storage

3-6.   The CPU unit that holds data and intermediate and final
      results is the _____ unit.
      a.   control   c.   arithmetic/logic
      b.   secondary storage   d.   primary storage

3-7.   The CPU unit that performs arithmetic computations is the
      _____ unit.
      a.   control   c.   arithmetic/logic
      b.   secondary storage   d.   primary storage

3-8.   Printers, visual-display units, tape drives, and disk
      drives are all examples of _____ devices.
      a.   control
      b.   input
      c.   output
      d.   secondary storage

INSTRUCTIONS

3-9.   Each computer instruction has _____ basic parts.
      a.   2   c.   4
      b.   3   d.   5

3-10.   Which term does not belong in the following grouping?
      a.   op code   c.   ADD
      b.   operand   d.   COMPARE

3-11.   What is the name of the feature in a computer that proc-
      esses instructions sequentially unless otherwise
      instructed?
      a.   the sequential operation feature
      b.   the programmed sequential feature
      c.   the next-sequential-instruction feature
      d.   the next-operational-instruction feature

3-12.   Computers can execute _____ at a time.
      a.   over 1,000,000 instructions
      b.   over 1,000 instructions
      c.   from 10 - 50 instructions
      d.   only 1 instruction

STORED PROGRAM CONCEPT

3-13.   The basic characteristic of memory is known as
        a. nondestructive read/destructive write
        b. destructive read/nondestructive write
        c. nondestructive write/destructive read
        d. destructive write/nondestructive read

3-14.   A series of instructions placed into a computer's
        memory is called
        a. an instructional set   c. a stored program
        b. an optional program   d. a nondestructive program

STORAGE

3-15.   Each storage location is assigned an address
        a. so that the CPU's arithmetic/logic unit can locate
            data items in storage
        b. so that the CPU's control unit can maintain the
            operation of the arithmetic/logic unit
        c. so that the CPU's control unit can locate each
            instruction
        d. so that the storage units of the ALU can locate units
            stored in the control unit

3-16.   Meaningful names assigned to storage locations within a
        program are called
        a. variables   c. addresses
        b. secondary storage   d. bits

3-17.   Information is transferred between primary and secondary
        storage through
        a. magnetic lines   c. electrical lines
        b. magnetic cores   d. electrical tapes

3-18.   The most common secondary storage devices are
        a. magnetic tape and magnetic disk units
        b. magnetic tape units
        c. magnetic disk units
        d. magnetic cores

3-19.   Semiconductor memory
        a. does not store data magnetically
        b. is composed of circuitry on silicon chips
        c. does not require a constant power source
        d. can be written to but not read from

3-20. Magnetization of a core in a clockwise direction
       indicates
       a. an "off" (0) condition   c. an "on" (0) condition
       b. an "off" (1) condition   d. an "on" (1) condition

3-21. One silicon chip may hold as much as _____ of cores
       can.
       a. tens   c. thousands
       b. hundreds   d. millions

3-22. Which of the following is not true about the comparisons
       of magnetic domains (bubbles) and magnetic cores?
       a. Bubbles and cores are not similar in size.
       b. Bubbles and cores cannot retain their magnetism
           indefinitely.
       c. Bubbles can store more data in a smaller area.
       d. Bubbles and cores can store similar types of data.

3-23. Which of the following is a reason why widespread
       industry and user acceptance of bubble memory has not
       been forthcoming?
       a. high cost only
       b. difficulty in production only
       c. high cost and difficulty in production
       d. use is limited to input/output devices

3-24. Which of the following statements is not true of biochip
       technology?
       a. It uses groupings of molecules to create an electric
           circuit.
       b. It is currently being manufactured for use by the
           computer industry.
       c. It has great potential for the future.
       d. It has received major financial commitments from uni-
           versities and corporations.

3-25. An alternative method of producing primary storage
       currently in the development phase and not yet on the
       market is
       a. bubble memory   c. read-only memory
       b. biochips   d. hard-wired memory

3-26. Which of the following is not true about ROM?
       a. Instructions cannot be changed.
       b. Instructions are hardwired.
       c. Instructions can be deleted entirely, but they cannot
           be changed.
       d. All are true.

3-27.   Microprograms are
    a.   slower speed stored-program instructions
    b.   faster speed stored-program instructions
    c.   sequences of instructions built into ROM which can be
          altered by users
    d.   sequences of instructions built into ROM which cannot
          be altered by users

3-28.   Which of the following is not true about read-only
         memory?
    a.   ROM instructions are hard-wired.
    b.   Read-only memory can be changed by other stored
          programs.
    c.   Items can be read repeatedly without loss of infor-
          mation.
    d.   The contents of memory can be changed by altering the
          physical construction of the circuits.

3-29.   The type of memory that can be erased after being sub-
         mitted to a special process, such as being bathed in
         ultraviolet light, is called
    a.   RAM   c.   ROM
    b.   PROM   d.   EPROM

3-30.   Which of the following is not true of registers?
    a.   Registers can receive information.
    b.   Registers are not considered part of primary storage.
    c.   Registers are located in the CPU.
    d.   Registers are not controlled by the CPU's control
          unit.

3-31.   Which of the following is true of the comparison between
         cache memory and primary storage?
    a.   Use of cache memory is less expensive than primary
          storage.
    b.   Use of cache memory without primary memory eliminates
          the need to access secondary storage.
    c.   Use of cache memory increases processing speed.
    d.   Cache memory use is less expensive and its use elimi-
          nates the need to access secondary storage.

3-32.   A bubble memory module only slightly larger than a
         quarter can store _____ characters of data.
    a.   10,000   c.   40,000
    b.   20,000   d.   80,000

3-33.   Which of the following is not true of PROM?
        a.   It can be programmed by the manufacturer.
        b.   It can be programmed by the user.
        c.   Mistakes programmed into it can be corrected.
        d.   It cannot be erased.

3-34.   Which term in the following group does not belong?
        a.   cache memory   c.   permanent
        b.   speed   d.   buffer

DATA REPRESENTATION

3-35.   Data are represented in core storage by
        a.   bubble positions   c.   electric currents
        b.   magnetic states   d.   magnetic bubbles

3-36.   The "on" and "off" two-state system used to represent
        data in a computer is known as
        a.   the decimal number system
        b.   the octal number system
        c.   the binary number system or binary representation
        d.   the bilateral number system or bilateral represen-
             tation

3-37.   The storage locations in primary memory known as "words"
        are typically measured in all of the following units ex-
        cept
        a.   16 bits   c.   36 bits
        b.   24 bits   d.   8 bits

3-38.   A programmer sometimes prints out the contents of certain
        memory locations in order to discover what went wrong;
        this procedure is called
        a.   a byte generation   c.   a bit generation
        b.   a dump   d.   a storage review

3-39.   A base 16 number system is also known as
        a.   the hexadecimal number system
        b.   the double octal number system
        c.   the binary number system
        d.   none of the above

3-40.   One of the most basic coding schemes, called 4-bit binary
        coded decimal (BCD), represents each decimal digit in a
        number by using
        a.   four bits   c.   one bit
        d.   eight bits   d.   four bytes

3-41.   The 6-bit BCD can be used to represent all of the
        following except
        a.   decimal digits 0 through 9
        b.   letters A through Z
        c.   twenty-eight characters in addition to the digits 0
             through 9 and the letters A through Z
        d.   it can represent all of the above

3-42.   An 8-bit code can be used to represent
        a.   only lower-case letters
        b.   only upper-case letters
        c.   only upper- and lower-case letters
        d.   upper- and lower-case letters and additional special
             characters

3-43.   In EBCDIC the _____ are zone bits.
        a.   four rightmost bit positions
        b.   four leftmost bit positions
        c.   six rightmost bit positions
        d.   six leftmost bit positions

3-44.   The key difference between ASCII-8 and EBCDIC is
        a.   the machines on which they each will work
        b.   EBCDEC is only a 7-bit code
        c.   ASCII-8 cannot represent any special characters
        d.   the bit patterns used to represent certain characters

3-45.   The basic units of memory are
        a.   8-bit groupings   c.   6-bit groupings
        b.   4-bit groupings   d.   16-bit groupings

3-46.   A computer that has 256K bytes of storage can store
        a.   132,072 characters   c.   262,144 characters
        b.   66,036 characters   d.   524,288 characters

3-47.   The bit used to detect when an error has occurred and to
        isolate the location of the error is called a(n)
        a.   isolation bit   c.   check or parity bit
        b.   error bit   d.   review bit

3-48.   If an odd number of 1-bits is used to represent each
        character, the characters are said to be written in
        a.   even parity   c.   ASCII-8
        b.   odd parity   d.   no parity

3-49.   Code checking is necessary, because a bit may be lost due
        to
        a.   dust   c.   magnetic fields
        b.   moisture   d.   all of the above

3-50.   One K generally equals
        a.   512   c.   2,048
        b.   1,024   d.   4,096

3-51.   The octal number system uses digits
        a.   0 to 7   c.   1 to 8
        b.   0 to 8   d.   1 to 7

3-52.   The hexidecimal number system uses digits
        a.   0 to 16   c.   1 to 16
        b.   0 to 15   d.   1 to 15

CLASSIFICATIONS OF COMPUTER SYSTEMS

3-53.   Analog computers operate by measuring all of the
        following except
        a.   continuous physical magnitudes
        b   continuous electrical magnitudes
        c.   "on" and "off" states represented by binary digits
        d.   they can measure all of the above

3-54.   Computers that have been designed to meet the faster
        processing needs of science are
        a.   microcomputers   c.   minicomputers
        b.   supercomputers   d.   all of the above

3-55.   Analog computers are _____ digital computers.
        a.   more accurate than   c.   about as accurate as
        b.   less accurate than   d.   exactly as accurate as

3-56.   Which of the following components is not directly related
        to the others?
        a.   CPU   c.   ALU
        b.   secondary storage device d.   control unit

3-57.   Which of the following is not true about minicomputers?
        a.   contain smaller memories than mainframes
        b.   are more powerful than mainframes manufactured 10
             years ago
        c.   have a price range of $15,000 to $250,000
        d.   are less powerful than mainframes manufactured 10
             years ago

3-58.   The personal computing market began when the _____ was
        introduced.
        a.   TRS-80   c.   Apple II
        b.   Commodore PET   d.   Altair 8800

3-59.   The CRAY-2 is an example of a
         a.   microcomputer   c.   mainframe
         b.   minicomputer   d.   supercomputer

3-60.   The minicomputers of today are more powerful than the
         mainframes manufactured _____ years ago.
         a.   5   c.   15
         b.   10   d.   20

3-61.   Minicomputers sell for prices in the _____ range.
         a. $5,000 to $10,000   c. $15,000 to $250,000
         b. $10,000 to $15,000   d. $500,000 and up

3-62.   A microcomputer for the home can be purchased in the
         _____ price range.
         a. $250 to $1,000   c. $300 to $10,000
         b. $100 to $5,000   d. $50 to $2,000

APPLICATION

3-63.   What is IBM's major business?
         a.   electronic typewriters
         b.   educational and testing materials
         c.   mainframe computers
         d.   information handling

3-64.   How are computers with similar characteristics grouped?
         a.   system or series   c.   by company brand names
         b.   network   d.   by cost

3-65.   What is a modular computer?
         a.   one that can be transported in parts
         b.   one onto which the user can build to get as much or
               as little processing power as needed
         c.   one that different people can operate at the same
               time
         d.   one that can run only part of a program rather than
               the entire program

ANSWER KEY

3-1.	b	3-21.	c	3-41.	d	3-61.	c
3-2.	b	3-22.	b	3-42.	d	3-62.	b
3-3.	c	3-23.	c	3-43.	b	3-63.	d
3-4.	b	3-24.	b	3-44.	d	3-64.	a
3-5.	a	3-25.	b	3-45.	a	3-65.	b
3-6.	d	3-26.	d	3-46.	c		
3-7.	c	3-27.	d	3-47.	c		
3-8.	c	3-28.	b	3-48.	b		
3-9.	a	3-29.	d	3-49.	d		
3-10.	b	3-30.	d	3-50.	b		
3-11.	c	3-31.	c	3-51.	a		
3-12.	d	3-32.	b	3-52.	b		
3-13.	a	3-33.	c	3-53.	c		
3-14.	c	3-34.	c	3-54.	b		
3-15.	c	3-35.	b	3-55.	b		
3-16.	a	3-36.	c	3-56.	b		
3-17.	c	3-37.	c	3-57.	d		
3-18.	a	3-38.	b	3-58.	d		
3-19.	b	3-39.	a	3-59.	d		
3-20.	d	3-40.	a	3-60.	b		

Input and Output

MULTIPLE CHOICE

DATA INPUT

4-1.   Which of the following is not considered to be an example
        of punched cards as user-oriented documents?
        a.   bills
        b.   checks
        c.   time cards
        d.   all are examples of punched cards as user-oriented
             documents

4-2.   Punched card processing involves _____ steps.
        a.   5   c.   3
        b.   4   d.   2

4-3.   The standard punched card has _____ vertical columns.
        a.   40   c.   80
        b.   60   d.   100

4-4.   The standard punched card has _____ horizontal rows.
        a.   12   c.   16
        b.   14   d.   18

4-5.   The standard punched card is called a _____ card.
        a.   key   c.   Hollerith
        b.   diskette   d.   unit

4-6. The standard punched card is divided horizontally into
      _____ sections.
      a. 2   c. 4
      b. 3   d. 5

4-7. The lower ten rows of a standard punched card are called
      _____ rows.
      a. zone   c. digit
      b. print   d. field

4-8. The upper three rows of a standard punched card are
      called _____ rows.
      a. zone   c. digit
      b. print   d. field

4-9. The section of the standard punched card which displays
      the actual character punched into a card column is called
      the _____ section.
      a. zone   c. digit
      b. print   d. field

4-10. To represent a number on the standard punched card, a
      hole is punched in the appropriate _____ row.
      a. zone   c. digit
      b. print   d. field

4-11. To represent letters on a standard punched card, one
      _____ punch is used in combination with one or two
      numeric punches.
      a. zone   c. digit
      b. print   d. field

4-12. On a standard punched card, a group of related characters
      treated as a single unit of information is called a
      a. unit   c. zone
      b. field   d. row

4-13. If a punched card contained all the data pertaining to
      the sale of an automobile it would be called a
      a. field record   c. unit record
      b. column record   d. zone record

4-14. Which of the following is not considered to be a major
       disadvantage of the punched card?
       a. Two or more cards must be used if records are
           extensive.
       b. Punched cards are used with machines that can only
           handle two cards at a time.
       c. If less than an entire card is needed for a record,
           the remainder of the card is wasted.
       d. Mutilation during handling may hinder processing.

4-15. Which of the following operations is not done automati-
       cally by the key punch?
       a. keys the cards   c. stacks the cards
       b. feeds the cards   d. positions the cards

4-16. Which of the following cannot be used to replace data
       with new data?
       a. tape   c. disk
       b. punched cards   d. all cannot replace data

4-17. As many as 1,600 characters are commonly stored on
       _____ of magnetic tape.
       a. one inch   c. one-half inch
       b. two inches   d. one and one-half inches

4-18. Data stored on tape or on disk can be read into the CPU
       _____ times faster than data on cards.
       a. 10   c. 50
       b. 25   d. 100

4-19. The television-like screen in a key-to-tape system is
       used to
       a. hold data while they are being checked for accuracy
       b. enter data
       c. write data on tape
       d. verify and correct data

4-20. The configuration where several keyboards are linked to
       one or two magnetic-tape units which combine data as
       keying takes place is called a _____ device.
       a. clustered key-to-tape
       b. self-contained key-to-tape
       c. stand-alone key-to-tape
       d. none of the above

4-21. The fact that data can be checked for accuracy and corrected, if necessary, prior to processing is an advantage of which configuration?
a. clustered key-to-tape
b. self-contained key-to-tape
c. stand-alone key-to-tape
d. a and c

4-22. Which of the following is not an advantage of key-to-disk data entry system over traditional punched-card input?
a. disks are reusable
b. errors can be corrected by re-keying correct data over incorrect data
c. disk entry costs less
d. operators can transcribe data faster

4-23. Which of the following operations is completed before computer processing in a key-to-diskette data entry system?
a. collection and pooling of data
b. editing of data
c. displaying of data on a screen
d. all are completed before computer processing

4-24. The method whereby data are collected about an event in computer readable form, where and when the event takes place, is called
a. clustered configuration automation
b. source-data automation
c. stand-alone key-to-tape automation
d. stand-alone key-to-disk automation

4-25. The approach to source-data automation which was originally introduced by the banking industry to facilitate check processing is called
a. magnetic ink character recognition
b. optical recognition
c. optical-mark recognition
d. touch-tone recognition

4-26. When using magnetic-ink characters, no special data conversion step is needed because
a. magnetic-ink characters are formed with magnetized particles
b. magnetic-ink characters can be read by both humans and machines
c. each character is composed of certain sections of a large matrix
d. a binary notation is utilized

4-27.   Each magnetic-ink character is composed of certain sec-
        tions of a _____-section matrix.
        a. twenty   c. seventy
        b. fifty   d. ninety

4-28.   Magnetic-ink characters are formed of magnetized par-
        ticles of
        a. iron alloy   c. chromium
        b. iron oxide   d. silicon

4-29.   When using an MICR device the presence of a magnetic
        field in a section of the area represents
        a. a 1 bit   c. a 1 or a 0 bit
        b. a 0 bit   d. neither a 1 nor a 0 bit

4-30.   All magnetic characters on checks are formed with the
        standard _____ character set.
        a. ten   c. thirteen
        b. twelve   d. fourteen

4-31.   An MICR device can read and sort between _____ checks
        per minute.
        a. 250 - 500   c. 750 - 1,500
        b. 500 - 750   d. 1,500 or more

4-32.   The simplest approach to optical recognition is
        a. bar-code reading   c. wand reading
        b. mark sensing   d. point-of-sale reading

4-33.   When an optical-mark page reader is directly connected to
        a computer, up to _____ forms of the same type can be
        read and processed in an hour.
        a. 500   c. 1,500
        b. 1,000   d. 2,000

4-34.   Which of the following is typically used with a POS
        system?
        a. bar-code reader   c. mark-sensing reader
        b. optical-mark page reader   d. machine language reader

4-35.   Which of the following pieces of information is not
        directly identified through the UPC?
        a. brand name   c. price
        b. manufacturer   d. product identification

4-36.   Both OCR and OMR devices rely on _____ to translate
        written data into machine-readable form.
        a. shapes of characters   c. positions of marks
        b. reflected light   d. shapes of marks

4-37. Which of the following OCR input can only be utilized with the most advanced optical-character reader?
a. computer printouts
b. cash register tapes
c. adding machine tapes
d. handwritten mail envelopes

4-38. Which of the following is not considered a remote data collection terminal?
a. POS terminal
b. touch-tone devices
c. OMR terminal
d. intelligent terminals

4-39. When using a touch-tone device, generally _____ modifications must have been made to the telephone connection to allow data to be transferred over the line.
a. major
b. slight
c. no
d. quite a few

4-40. VRMs are available that can recognize a predetermined set of words and phrases with up to _____ accuracy.
a. 60%
b. 75%
c. 90%
d. 99%

4-41. Which of the following is not true of intelligent terminals?
a. They can be programmed by use of stored instructions.
b. They have the same kinds of components as full-sized computers.
c. They have almost unlimited storage capability.
d. They are useful for editing data prior to transmission.

4-42. Touch-sensitive screen applications are particularly helpful in
a. saving time
b. reducing costs
c. increasing accuracy
d. none of the above

4-43. Once an object is drawn on the screen using a light pen changes
a. are limited to 3 to 5 per minute
b. can be made until the user is satisfied
c. cannot be made
d. are not possible unless the pen is equipped with a spatial digitizer

INFORMATION OUTPUT

4-44.   Impact printers were developed _____ nonimpact prin-
        ters.
        a. before   c. at about the same time
        b. after   d. at exactly the same time

4-45.   The permanent, readable copy of computer output is often
        referred to as
        a. soft copy   c. hard copy
        b. impact copy   d. print element

4-46.   Character-at-a-time printing typically prints at speeds
        of _____ characters per minute.
        a. 100 to 300   c. 600 to 900
        b. 300 to 600   d. 900 to 1200

4-47.   Line-at-a-time printers can print at speeds of up to
        _____ lines per minute.
        a. 500   c. 2000
        b. 50   d. 10,000

4-48.   The usual speed of a printer-keyboard is about _____
        characters per minute.
        a. 300   c. 900
        b. 600   d. 1200

4-49.   Which of the following is not a principal character-at-a-
        time printing device?
        a. dot-matrix printer   c. printer-keyboard
        b. daisy-wheel printer   d. drum printer

4-50.   Which of the following is considered to be slow and
        therefore is typically used for small amounts of output?
        a. dot-matrix   c. drum printer
        b. printer-keyboard   d. daisy-wheel printer

4-51.   Dot-matrix printers can typically print up to _____
        characters per minute.
        a. 900   c. 1500
        b. 1200   d. 1750

4-52.   Which of the following is based on a design that is simi-
        lar to that of a football or basketball scoreboard?
        a. dot-matrix   c. drum printer
        b. printer-keyboard   d. daisy-wheel printer

4-53. Which of the following is often used in conjunction with
       word processors to give high quality type output with a
       professional appearance?
       a. dot-matrix   c. drum printer
       b. printer-keyboard   d. daisy-wheel printer

4-54. Which of the following is not a line-at-a-time impact
       printer?
       a. print-wheel printer   c. chain printer
       b. printer-keyboard   d. drum printer

4-55. A print-wheel printer typically contains _____ print
       wheels.
       a. 48   c. 120
       b. 64   d. 150

5-56. Each print wheel on a print-wheel printer contains
       _____ characters.
       a. 48   c. 120
       b. 64   d. 150

4-57. Print-wheel printers can produce about _____ lines per
       minute.
       a. 48   c. 120
       b. 64   d. 150

4-58. Which of the following assembles characters in a train
       that revolves horizontally past all print positions?
       a. print-wheel printer   c. chain printer
       b. printer-keyboard   d. drum printer

4-59. Which of the following line-at-a-time printers prints the
       fewest lines per minute?
       a. print-wheel printer   c. chain printer
       b. printer-keyboard   d. drum printer

4-60. Which of the following line-at-a-time printers prints the
       most lines per minute?
       a. print-wheel printer   c. chain printer
       b. printer-keyboard   d. drum printer

4-61. With which of the following line-at-a-time printers can
       type fonts be changed easily, allowing a variety of fonts
       to be used?
       a. print-wheel printer   c. chain printer
       b. printer-keyboard   d. drum printer

4-62.   When a drum printer operates, _____ printed for each
         revolution of the drum.
         a.   1 line is   c.   3 lines are
         b.   2 lines are   d.   4 lines are

4-63.   Which of the following is not a nonimpact printer?
         a.   electrostatic printer   c.   train printer
         b.   electrothermal printer   d.   ink-jet printer

4-64.   Which of the following nonimpact printers has the fastest
         printing capability?
         a.   ink-jet printer   c.   electrostatic printer
         b.   xerographic printer   d.   laser printer

4-65.   Which of the following nonimpact printers has the slowest
         printing capability?
         a.   ink-jet printer   c.   electrostatic printer
         b.   xerographic printer   d.   laser printer

4-66.   The printing capability of electrothermal nonimpact prin-
         ters is the same as
         a.   ink-jet printers   c.   electrostatic printers
         b.   xerographic printers   d.   laser printers

4-67.   The predominant means of producing hard-copy output in
         the future is likely to be
         a.   impact printers   c.   daisy-wheel printers
         b.   nonimpact printers   d.   drum printers

4-68.   Which of the following is not an advantage of nonimpact
         printers over impact printers?
         a.   They are generally much faster.
         b.   They offer a wider choice of face types.
         c.   They produce high quality carbon copies.
         d.   They offer better speed-to-price ratios.

4-69.   Which of the following nonimpact printers forms an image
         of a character on special paper using a dot matrix of
         charged wires?
         a.   electrostatic printer   c.   xerographic printer
         b.   electrothermal printer   d.   laser printer

4-70.   Which of the following nonimpact printers is often used
         in applications where noise may be a problem?
         a.   drum printer   c.   xerographic printer
         b.   electrothermal printer   d.   laser printer

4-71. Which of the following nonimpact printers uses printing
       methods much like those used in common xerographic
       copying machines?
       a.   electrostatic printer   c.   xerographic printer
       b.   electrothermal printer   d.   laser printer

4-72. Which of the following nonimpact printers projects
       character images onto a piece of film which is developed
       and fixed in a manner similar to that used for photo-
       graphs?
       a.   electrostatic printer   c.   xerographic printer
       b.   electrothermal printer   d.   laser printer

4-73. Which of the following nonimpact printers produces high
       quality, letter-perfect images?
       a.   electrostatic printer   c.   xerographic printer
       b.   electrothermal printer   d.   laser printer

4-74. A typical visual display screen can hold _____ lines.
       a.   12   c.   36
       b.   24   d.   48

4-75. Each line of a typical visual display screen contains
       _____ characters.
       a.   20   c.   60
       b.   40   d.   80

4-76. Visual display terminals supply output which is known as
       a.   hard copy   c.   soft copy
       b.   permanent record copy   d.   printed copy

4-77. Visual display terminals are well suited for applications
       involving
       a.   inquiry and response   c.   response and recall
       b.   memory and recall   d.   none of the above

4-78. Visual display terminals display data on _____ which
       are similar to television screens.
       a.   CTRs   c.   RCTs
       b.   CRTs   d.   TCRs

4-79. The type of visual display terminal used heavily in CAD
       and CAM applications is called a
       a.   graph and chart device   c.   curves and shapes device
       b.   technical display device d.   graphic display device

4-80.   Which of the following is not true relative to a com-
        parison of visual display terminals to printers?
        a.   They display output much faster than printers.
        b.   They cannot produce hard copy as printers do.
        c.   They are much quieter than impact printers.
        d.   All are true.

4-81.   The pen used with a plotter can be positioned at up to
        _____ points in each square inch of paper.
        a.   20,000   c.   40,000
        b.   25,000   d.   45,000

4-82.   Some plotters can produce drawings in up to _____
        colors.
        a.   8   c.   12
        b.   10   d.   16

4-83.   The major difference between a plotter and a graphic
        display device is the plotter produces
        a.   hard copy output
        b.   soft copy output
        c.   images faster
        d.   both soft and hard copy outputs

4-84.   Which of the following is not a component of a plotter?
        a.   pen
        b.   movable carriage
        c.   drum
        d.   all are components of plotters

4-85.   A computer output microfilm system can be _____ times
        faster than traditional printing.
        a.   10 to 20   c.   25 to 50
        b.   20 to 25   d.   50 to 100

4-86.   The primary advantage of COM is
        a.   data can be stored quickly
        b.   data can be stored compactly
        c.   data can be stored confidentially
        d.   data can be stored accurately

4-87.   Which of the following specialized output devices has
        seen limited use to date?
        a.   COMs   c.   CRTs
        b.   plotters   d.   voice synthesizer

APPLICATION

4-88.   The information services division personnel of Gulf Oil
        in the United States are based in _____ major loca-
        tions.
        a.   two   c.   four
        b.   three   d.   five

4-89.   The information services division staff based in the
        U.S.A. is composed of approximately _____ employees.
        a.   250   c.   900
        b.   500   d.   1,500

4-90.   The TRACE capture system used by Gulf Oil in their credit
        card center reads data at the rate of _____ documents
        per minute.
        a.   400   c.   1,400
        b.   1,000   d.   2,400

4-91.   The Gulf Oil customer billing statements are printed by a
        _____ printer at approximately 13,000 lines per minute.
        a.   laser   c.   drum
        b.   electrothermal   d.   daisy-wheel

4-92.   The Gulf Oil POS system can handle over _____ authori-
        zation call from dealers per day.
        a.   1,000   c.   5,000
        b.   2,000   d.   10,000

ANSWER KEY

4-1.	d	4-26.	b	4-51.	a	4-76.	c
4-2.	d	4-27.	c	4-52.	a	4-77.	a
4-3.	c	4-28.	b	4-53.	d	4-78.	b
4-4.	a	4-29.	a	4-54.	b	4-79.	d
4-5.	c	4-30.	d	4-55.	c	4-80.	d
4-6.	b	4-31.	c	4-56.	a	4-81.	d
4-7.	c	4-32.	b	4-57.	d	4-82.	a
4-8.	a	4-33.	d	4-58.	c	4-83.	a
4-9.	b	4-34.	a	4-59.	a	4-84.	d
4-10.	c	4-35.	c	4-60.	d	4-85.	c
4-11.	a	4-36.	b	4-61.	c	4-86.	b
4-12.	b	4-37.	d	4-62.	a	4-87.	d
4-13.	c	4-38.	c	4-63.	c	4-88.	b
4-14.	b	4-39.	b	4-64.	d	4-89.	c
4-15.	a	4-40.	d	4-65.	a	4-90.	d
4-16.	b	4-41.	c	4-66.	c	4-91.	a
4-17.	a	4-42.	a	4-67.	b	4-92.	d
4-18.	b	4-43.	b	4-68.	c		
4-19.	d	4-44.	a	4-69.	a		
4-20.	a	4-45.	c	4-70.	b		
4-21.	d	4-46.	c	4-71.	c		
4-22.	c	4-47.	c	4-72.	d		
4-23.	d	4-48.	c	4-73.	d		
4-24.	b	4-49.	d	4-74.	b		
4-25.	a	4-50.	b	4-75.	d		

Storage Devices

MULTIPLE CHOICE

CLASSIFICATION OF STORAGE MEDIA

5-1.   Currently the most widely used form of primary memory is
            _____ memory.
        a. bubble   c. magnetic tape
        b. semiconductor   d. magnetic disk

5-2.   Which of the following is not a type of secondary
        storage?
        a. magnetic tapes   c. magnetic drums
        b. magnetic disks   d. magnetic bubbles

5-3.   The type of storage which is part of the CPU is
        a. sometimes primary storage
        b. sometimes secondary storage
        c. always primary storage
        d. always secondary storage

5-4.   Storage of large volumes of data is made economically
        feasible because of
        a. secondary storage
        b. primary storage
        c. primary and secondary storage
        d. industry-wide price reductions for large volume users

5-5.   Which of the following is not true concerning magnetic
        tape?
        a. data are stored by magnetizing small spots of iron
            oxide coating on the tape
        b. not suitable for storing large volumes of information
        c. used for sequential access storage
        d. typically 1/2 inch wide and wound in lengths from
            400 to 3,200 feet

SEQUENTIAL-ACCESS STORAGE

5-6.   The most common method of representing data on tape uses
        a _____-track coding scheme.
        a. two   c. nine
        b. five   d. twelve

5-7.   The most common method of coding data for magnetic tape
        is _____ the Extended Binary Coded Decimal Interchange
        Code (EBCDIC).
        a. similar to   c. the opposite of
        b. identical to   d. more difficult than

5-8.   Which of the following is not a typical packaging for
        magnetic tape?
        a. drum   c. cartridge
        b. reel   d. cassette

5-9.   Magnetic tapes are typically _____ wide.
        a. 1/4 inch   c. 3/4 inch
        b. 1/2 inch   d. 1 inch

5-10.   Magnetic tape is typically found in lengths of approxi-
        mately _____ feet.
        a. 1,000   c. 20,000
        b. 2,000   d. 40,000

5-11.   Densities of about _____ characters per inch are
        common on magnetic tape.
        a. 1,000   c. 4,000
        b. 1,600   d. 2,500

5-12.   Some magnetic tapes are capable of storing over _____
        characters per inch.
        a. 6,000   c. 100,000
        b. 500,000   d. 70,000

5-13.   How many bits (and tracks) are used to represent each
        character using the typical method of coding data on
        magnetic tape?
        a.   two   c.   eight
        b.   five   d.   nine

5-14.   Typical magnetic tape drives move tapes at speeds ranging
        from 25 to _____ inches per second.
        a.   75   c.   150
        b.   100   d.   200

5-15.   The process whereby the read/write head magnetizes the
        appropriate spots on the tape, erasing previously stored
        data, is called
        a.   writing   c.   nondestructive writing
        b.   reading   d.   nondestructive reading

5-16.   The process whereby the read/write head detects the
        magnetized spots and converts them to electrical pulses
        is called
        a.   writing   c.   destructive writing
        b.   reading   d.   destructive reading

5-17.   The _____ of the data determines how fast they can be
        transferred from the tape to the CPU.
        a.   complexity   c.   density
        b.   diversity   d.   none of the above

5-18.   The length of the interrecord gap (IRG) depends on
        a.   the size of the tape drive
        b.   the size of the tape drive's read/write head
        c.   the size of the tape
        d.   the speed of the tape drive

5-19.   The IRG allows the tape _____ before the next record is
        read.
        a.   to regain the proper speed
        b.   to adjust to a lower speed
        c.   to stop
        d.   to maintain a gradual deceleration

5-20.   Which of the following statements is not true of IBGs?
        a.   They make computer resources more efficient.
        b.   They allow the amount of storage on the tape to be
             used more efficiently.
        c.   They provide for a significant reduction in the
             number of read/write operations.
        d.   They provide for an increase in the number of
             input/output operations that can be accomplished.

5-21.   Which of the following is not an advantage of magnetic
         tape as a storage device?
         a.   Data can be transferred at high speeds.
         b.   It can be erased and reused.
         c.   It makes instantaneous retrieval of data possible.
         d.   It provides high-capacity storage at relatively low
              costs.

5-22.   Which of the following is not true of magnetic tape as a
         storage device?
         a.   Environmental factors can distort data.
         b.   It requires a relatively large amount of space for a
              relatively small amount of data.
         c.   Humans cannot read the data.
         d.   All tapes and reel containers must be properly
              labeled.

5-23.   Magnetic tape cassettes have recording densities ranging
         from _____ characters per inch.
         a.   50 to 125   c.   200 to 250
         b.   125 to 200   d.   200 to 500

5-24.   Magnetic tape cartridges have recording densities ranging
         from _____ characters per inch.
         a.   50 to 125   c.   400 to 500
         b.   125 to 200   d.   200 to 800

5-25.   The common length of tape in a magnetic tape cassette is
         between _____ feet.
         a.   150 and 200   c.   350 and 500
         b.   200 and 350   d.   500 and 750

5-26.   Magnetic tape in cartridges comes in lengths up to
         _____ feet.
         a.   200   c.   400
         b.   300   d.   500

5-27.   Which of the following environmental factors can distort
         data stored on magnetic tape?
         a.   dust   c.   moisture
         b.   static electricity   d.   all of the above

5-28.   Magnetic tape, which is 2,400 feet in length, usually
         costs
         a.   from $10 to $20   c.   from $30 to $40
         b.   from $20 to $30   d.   from $40 to $50

5-29.   The most common storage medium in systems using
        sequential processing is
        a.   magnetic tape   c.   magnetic disk
        b.   magnetic drum   d.   magnetic diskettes

DIRECT-ACCESS STORAGE

5-30.   Which of the following is false in regard to magnetic
        disks?
        a.   coated with a magnetizable material
        b.   data are recorded in spiraling grooves
        c.   data are recorded in concentric circles on the disk
        d.   doesn't have grooves

5-31.   A conventional magnetic disk is _____ inches in
        diameter.
        a.   14   c.   18
        b.   16   d.   20

5-32.   A typical magnetic disk has from _____ tracks per
        surface.
        a.   100 to 200   c.   200 to 500
        b.   200 to 300   d.   100 to 500

5-33.   A disk pack may contain anywhere from _____ disks.
        a.   5 to 50   c.   5 to 250
        b.   5 to 100   d.   5 to 500

5-34.   A disk pack with ten disks provides _____ usable
        recording surfaces.
        a.   20   c.   16
        b.   18   d.   14

5-35.   Users of removable disk packs typically have _____ disk
        packs than disk drives.
        a.   many more   c.   several less
        b.   a few more   d.   a few less

5-36.   Disk drives rotate all disks in unison at speeds ranging
        from _____ revolutions per second.
        a.   40 to 3,600   c.   40 to 4,800
        b.   80 to 3,600   d.   40 to 1,600

5-37.   Most disk units have _____ for each disk recording
        surface.
        a.   one read/write head   c.   three read/write heads
        b.   two read/write heads   d.   four read/write heads

5-38.   The number of cylinders per disk pack _____ the number
         of tracks per surface.
         a.   is much greater than   c.   equals
         b.   is less than   d.   is one greater than

5-39.   Disk units that have one read/write head per track
         a.   have a lower cost than other models
         b.   require the mechanism to move from track to track
         c.   are popular and frequently used
         d.   have a much faster access time

5-40.   Tracks on the outside of a disk store _____ tracks
         toward the center of the disk.
         a.   much more data than
         b.   slightly more data than
         c.   the same amount of data as
         d.   slightly less data than

5-41.   Which of the following components is not part of a disk
         address?
         a.   surface number   c.   track number
         b.   disk number   d.   record number

5-42.   Disk records are separated by gaps _____ the
         interrecord gaps on magnetic tape.
         a.   exactly the same as   c.   quite different than
         b.   similar to   d.   the opposite of

5-43.   Disks may attain read speeds of up to _____ characters
         per second.
         a.   100,000   c.   500,000
         b.   250,000   d.   850,000

5-44.   Diskettes are not very popular for use in
         a.   mainframe computers   c.   microcomputers
         b.   minicomputers   d.   POS terminals

5-45.   Which of the following terms is not synonymous?
         a.   flexible disk   c.   diskette
         b.   hard disk   d.   floppy disk

5-46.   The flexible disk was introduced
         a.   in the mid-1960s   c.   in the late 1970s
         b.   in the early 1970s   d.   in the early 1980s

5-47.   Flexible disks are made of
         a.   plastic   c.   metal
         b.   fiberglass   d.   heavy cardboard

5-48. A typical flexible disk can store as much data as _____ punched cards.

      a. 6,000   c. 18,000
      b. 12,000   d. 24,000

5-49. Flexible disks often sell for as little as

      a. $10   c. $2
      b. $50   d. $100

5-50. Which of the following is not true about flexible disks?

      a. They are easy to store, are readily interchangeable, and can be mailed.
      b. They weigh less than two ounces.
      c. They are not reusable.
      d. Security may be a problem because of the ease in gaining access to data on disks.

5-51. Flexible disks come in two standard sizes:

      a. 5 inches and 7 inches   c. 6¼ inches and 8 inches
      b. 8 inches and 5¼ inches   d. 8¼ inches and 5¼ inches

5-52. A standard 8-inch flexible disk has _____ tracks and _____ sectors.

      a. 66, 27   c. 44, 62
      b. 55, 72   d. 77, 26

5-53. A flexible disk rotates at _____ revolutions per second.

      a. 120   c. 360
      b. 240   d. 480

5-54. The read/write head on a flexible disk system _____ the surface of the disk.

      a. rides slightly above   c. rides ¼ inch above
      b. rides on   d. rides ½ inch above

5-55. Which of the following is not an advantage of magnetic disks over magnetic tapes?

      a. Files can be changed immediately.
      b. Files can be organized sequentially or for direct-access processing.
      c. Quick response can be made to inquiries.
      d. Backup files are provided even though original data are erased.

5-56. Which of the following is not a disadvantage of magnetic
       disks?
       a. They are a relatively expensive storage medium.
       b. When existing disk data are altered, the original
           data are erased.
       c. They can be organized for direct-access processing or
           for sequential-access processing.
       d. Security may be a problem.

5-57. Storage requires more complicated programming for gaining
       access to records and updating files; skilled technicians
       are required to maintain the highly complicated hardware.
       These statements are true of
       a. magnetic disks   c. magnetic tape cartridges
       b. magnetic tape cassettes   d. all of the above

MASS STORAGE

5-58. Which of the following is not a reason that mass storage
       devices were developed?
       a. Primary storage is very expensive.
       b. Disk storage can be very expensive.
       c. Primary storage requires physical movement.
       d. None of the above.

5-59. Which of the following is not true of mass storage
       devices?
       a. They allow rapid access to data.
       b. Their access times are faster than those of magnetic
           disk.
       c. Large files and back-up files can be placed at
           relatively low cost.
       d. Infrequently used files can be placed at relatively
           low cost.

5-60. High-density tape used in cartridges requires _____
       percent less storage space than common magnetic tape.
       a. 90   c. 50
       b. 75   d. 25

5-61. A mass storage system using cartridge tapes can hold the
       equivalent of over _____ tape reels.
       a. 1,000   c. 5,000
       b. 2,500   d. 7,500

5-62.   In a mass storage system, the mounting of tapes is under
         the control of
         a.   the system   c.   the primary storage
         b.   the operator   d.   none of the above

5-63.   Which of the following storage media is not typically
         used in a mass storage system?
         a.   magnetic tape   c.   hard disks
         b.   flexible disks   d.   magnetic cartridges

FUTURE TRENDS IN DATA STORAGE

5-64.   Future technological advances in data storage devices are
         likely to be described with all of the following except
         a.   smaller   c.   simpler
         b.   faster   d.   less expensive

5-65.   Which of the following statements is not true of
         charge-coupled devices (CCDs)?
         a.   made of plastic coated with iron oxide
         b.   similar to semiconductor memory
         c.   much faster than magnetic bubbles
         d.   somewhat slower than semiconductor memory

5-66.   Which of the following statements is not true about laser
         storage systems?
         a.   Laser storage doesn't deteriorate over time.
         b.   Laser data can be lost because of power failures.
         c.   Laser data resist alteration.
         d.   Laser storage provides a secure storage system.

5-67.   A laser storage system can store nearly 128 billion
         characters of data at about _____ the cost of standard
         magnetic media.
         a.   one-half   c.   one-quarter
         b.   one-third   d.   one-tenth

5-68.   The laser disk used in a minicomputer laser system can
         store _____ bits on its 40,000 tracks.
         a.   10 billion   c.   10 thousand
         b.   10 million   d.   100 billion

5-69.   The speed of optical laser disks is _____ that of hard
         disks.
         a.   much faster than   c.   about the same as
         b.   somewhat faster than   d.   somewhat slower than

5-70.   An optical laser disk the size of a 12-inch record can
        hold text equivalent to over _____ books per side.
        a. 100   c. 1,000
        b. 500   d. 1,500

5-71.   A line on a laser optical disk one inch long contains
        about _____ pits, or bits, of data.
        a. 50   c. 5,000
        b. 500   d. 10,000

5-72.   Accessing data on disks is _____ when compared with the
        speed at which a microprocessor can manipulate data.
        a. relatively slow   c. relatively fast
        b. extremely slow   d. extremely fast

5-73.   To the computer, a RAM chip is indistinguishable from
        a. a printer   c. a communications channel
        b. a disk drive   d. primary memory

5-74.   A RAM chip for use with a microcomputer has a data
        retrieval rate _____ times faster than a disk.
        a. 100   c. 25
        b. 50   d. 10

5-75.   It is estimated that when the technology of the Josephson
        Junction is perfected, the speed at which primary storage
        operates will be increased _____-fold.
        a. ten   c. thirty
        b. twenty   d. one hundred

5-76.   The Josephson Junction is a form of primary storage that
        houses semiconductor circuits in _____, thereby
        eliminating, to a large extent, the typical resistance to
        the flow of electricity that exists in semiconductor
        memory.
        a. liquid oxygen   c. liquid helium
        b. liquid hydrogen   d. liquid nitrogen

APPLICATION

5-77.   Republic Steel maintains its data processing activities
        in _____ large data centers and _____ satellite
        processing centers, which transfer data to the company
        by remote job entry.
        a. 4, 3   c. 5, 2
        b. 3, 4   d. 2, 5

5-78.   Republic Steel uses extensive data communication tech-
        niques connecting about _____ terminals to the large
        data center.
        a.   500   c.   1,500
        b.   1,000   d.   2,000

5-79.   The trend of Republic Steel's data-processing operation
        has been toward utilization of
        a.   microcomputers   c.   laser technology
        b.   telecommunications   d.   new large data centers

ANSWER KEY

5-1.	b	5-21.	c	5-41.	b	5-61.	d
5-2.	d	5-22.	b	5-42.	b	5-62.	a
5-3.	c	5-23.	b	5-43.	d	5-63.	c
5-4.	a	5-24.	d	5-44.	a	5-64.	c
5-5.	b	5-25.	a	5-45.	b	5-65.	a
5-6.	c	5-26.	d	5-46.	b	5-66.	b
5-7.	b	5-27.	d	5-47.	a	5-67.	d
5-8.	a	5-28.	b	5-48.	b	5-68.	a
5-9.	b	5-29.	a	5-49.	c	5-69.	a
5-10.	b	5-30.	b	5-50.	c	5-70.	d
5-11.	b	5-31.	a	5-51.	b	5-71.	c
5-12.	a	5-32.	c	5-52.	d	5-72.	a
5-13.	c	5-33.	b	5-53.	c	5-73.	b
5-14.	d	5-34.	b	5-54.	b	5-74.	b
5-15.	a	5-35.	a	5-55.	d	5-75.	a
5-16.	b	5-36.	a	5-56.	c	5-76.	c
5-17.	c	5-37.	a	5-57.	a	5-77.	a
5-18.	d	5-38.	c	5-58.	c	5-78.	c
5-19.	a	5-39.	d	5-59.	b	5-79.	b
5-20.	d	5-40.	c	5-60.	a		

Microcomputers

MULTIPLE CHOICE

MICROCOMPUTERS TODAY

6-1.   The first microcomputers were developed
        a.   at Harvard University
        b.   by the U.S. War Department
        c.   by individuals or small companies
        d.   by IBM

6-2.   The evolution of microcomputers
        a.   has paralleled that of mainframes
        b.   has differed greatly from that of mainframes
        c.   has paralleled that of minicomputers
        d.   none of the above

6-3.   The evolution of the microcomputer _____ that of the
        mainframe computer.
        a.   differs greatly from   c.   is similar to
        b.   differs from   d.   is exactly the same as

6-4.   The first microcomputers were developed by
        a.   the military   c.   large corporations
        b.   the government   d.   small businesses

6-5.   The key figures in the development of microcomputers were
        a. scientists
        b. entrepreneurs
        c. mathematicians
        d. computer science specialists

6-6.   The microcomputer was introduced in
        a. 1965   c. 1975
        b. 1970   d. 1980

6-7.   Since the introduction of the microcomputer, total sales
        have surpassed the figure of _____ units.
        a. 2 million   c. 4 million
        b. 2.5 million   d. 5 million

6-8.   Mainframe computers gained widespread acceptance
        a. almost immediately upon introduction to the
            marketplace
        b. only after the introduction of microcomputers
        c. almost 15 years after introduction to the marketplace
        d. almost 20 years after introduction to the marketplace

6-9.   Which of the following is not a way in which micro-
        computers can be valuable assets to business managers?
        a. help in managing businesses more effectively and
            efficiently
        b. act as links to minicomputers and/or mainframes in a
            distributed-processing system
        c. completely take over the decision-making process
        d. help reduce operating cost

6-10.   An estimated _____ of all microcomputers are located
        in private offices.
        a. one-third   c. one-half
        b. one-fourth   d. three-fourths

6-11.   Which of the following statements is not true about tele-
        commuting?
        a. It has helped many companies to reduce their employee
            turnover.
        b. It has helped people who find the rising cost of
            gasoline to be a problem.
        c. Its use has enabled 50% of the handicapped adults to
            be gainfully employed.
        d. Its use has helped women to remain in the kind of
            work they did before they began to raise a family.

6-12.   The concept of computer hookups between offices and homes
        that allows employees to work at home is called
        a. telecommuting   c. telecommunication
        b. teleconferencing   d. teletraveling

6-13.   The leading manufacturer of word-processing equipment is
        a. IBM   c. Control Data Corporation
        b. Hewlett Packard   d. Wang Laboratories

6-14.   The new microfloppy disk is encased in a _____ enclo-
        sure.
        a. flexible   c. metal
        b. rigid   d. transluscent

6-15.   Until recently personal computing was
        a. a business found only in the big cities
        b. a door-to-door sales business
        c. a mail-order business
        d. a small retail store business

6-16.   Until recently, personal computer buying was
        a. nonexistent
        b. primarily a mail-order business
        c. limited to lower-income families
        d. limited to purchases made from computer stores

6-17.   Computer stores as businesses are structured to appeal to
        a. corporate managers
        b. computer professionals
        c. personal users and owners of small businesses
        d. scientific users

HARDWARE

6-18.   A microprocessor is to a microcomputer as a _____ is to
        a mainframe computer.
        a. CPU   c. secondary storage device
        b. primary memory device   d. logic/arithmetic unit

6-19.   The prefix "micro" should be interpreted in terms of
        a. cost and capability
        b. size and capability
        c. size and cost
        d. capability, cost, and size

6-20.   The heart of a microcomputer is the
        a. arithmetic/logic unit   c. memory unit
        b. microprocessor   d. input/output devices

6-21.   The manner in which the microprocessor and the main-
        frame's CPU carry out their functions
        a. is the same   c. differs greatly
        b. differs slightly   d. is completely opposite

6-22.   The design of a mainframe computer, as compared to a
        microcomputer, permits all of the following except
        a. equally precise arithmetic computations
        b. access to more memory in a single step
        c. a larger instructional set
        d. greater speed in processing arithmetic computations

6-23.   Microcomputers are slower than mainframe computers when
        performing arithmetic computations because they have
        a. less secondary storage
        b. larger word sizes
        c. fewer registers
        d. more down time due to circuitry gaps

6-24.   Microcomputers are limited to one user because only one
        _____ is used to communicate with the computer's
        _____.
        a. peripheral device, communication network
        b. communication channel, user
        c. communication channel, peripheral devices
        d. peripheral channel, communication device

6-25.   Simultaneous data movement through a number of com-
        munication channels is known as
        a. peripheral movement   c. channel overload
        b. parallelism   d. communication feedback

6-26.   The computer listed below with the largest word size is
        the
        a. Apple IIe   c. VIC-20
        b. IBM Personal Computer   d. IBM 370/3033

6-27.   As the word size increases, the number of instructions in
        the instructional set
        a. increases
        b. decreases
        c. stays about the same
        d. decreases proportionately

6-28.   The software used to run a microcomputer is much less
        complex than that used to run a mainframe because
        a.   only two or three communication channels are used
        b.   only one communication channel is used
        c.   the operating system is less complex
        d.   word size is larger

6-29.   Which of the following statements about microcomputers is
        not true?
        a.   They are very powerful in proportion to their size.
        b.   In some cases their power is equal to that of early
             mainframes.
        c.   They require air conditioning for cooling purposes.
        d.   Primary storage is typically not capable of storing
             all the applications required.

6-30.   Which of the following is not true of the comparison be-
        tween the current IBM Personal Computer and the IBM 360,
        Model 30 of the early 1960s?
        a.   the 1960s IBM cost more
        b.   the current IBM PC does not require air conditioning
        c.   the 1960s IBM was much larger
        d.   the current IBM PC can perform almost as many
             additions per second

6-31.   Which of the following statements about microcomputer
        data storage in the form of magnetic-tape cassettes and
        cartridges is not true?
        a.   it provides relatively quick access to data
        b.   it is relatively low in cost
        c.   it follows a sequential format
        d.   it is suited for the storage of short programs

6-32.   The most widely used form of peripheral storage for
        microcomputers is
        a.   magnetic tape   c.   magnetic cassettes
        b.   floppy disk   d.   magnetic tape cartridges

6-33.   The amount of data storage on floppy disks varies
        according to the
        a.   speed at which the data were recorded
        b.   type of disk drive used
        c.   size of the disk and the number of grooves on the
             surface
        d.   size of the disk being used for storage and the den-
             sity of the storage

6-34.   Which of the formats below is not a format for data
        storage on a floppy disk?
        a.   single-sided/single-density
        b.   double-sided/double-density
        c.   double-sided/triple-density
        d.   all are formats used on floppy disks

6-35.   Which of the following statements about disk storage for
        microcomputers is not true?
        a.   Data storage on floppy disks varies according to the
             density of the surface of the disk.
        b.   The format for data storage on a floppy disk never
             varies.
        c.   Double-sided storage allows data to be stored on both
             of the floppy disk surfaces.
        d.   The format in which data are stored on a floppy disk
             may not be compatible with the way all disk drives
             read disks.

6-36.   A double-density format allows _____ data to be stored
        on the disk's surface.
        a.   the same amount of   c.   eight times as much
        b.   two times as much   d.   four times as much

6-37.   Which of the following statements is not true with
        reference to the issue of floppy disk storage format and
        disk drive unit compatibility?
        a.   Double-sided disks cannot be used by single-sided
             disk drives.
        b.   Double-density disks cannot be used by single-density
             disk drives.
        c.   Reversible disks cannot be used on single-
             sided/single or double density disk drives.
        d.   Disks designed for one disk drive may not operate
             properly on another.

6-38.   All of the following statements are true about hard disks
        except
        a.   they are magnetic
        b.   they have a larger storage capacity than floppies
        c.   they are available only as fixed disks in totally
             sealed units
        d.   they provide for greater speed in access

6-39. The issue of spill-over capability within the software
       to allow copying partial files from one disk to another
       is of special concern when working with
       a. fixed hard disks
       b. removable hard disks
       c. floppy disks
       d. removable and fixed hard disks

6-40. Currently the use of fixed hard disks predominates over
       the use of removeable disks because
       a. they are easier to use than removable disks
       b. they cost less
       c. they are less likely to become damaged
       d. they provide for better backup capability

6-41. Which of the following is not a feature of a fixed disk?
       a. relatively low price   c. large storage capacity
       b. slow access to data   d. reliability

6-42. Which of the following is not a feature of the removable
       disk?
       a. easy backup
       b. quicker backup
       c. security from damage by untrained persons
       d. physical detachability

6-43. The most common type of input/output device is
       a. the monitor   c. the game paddle
       b. the joystick   d. the mouse

6-44. Monitors allow users to do all of the following except
       a. to view the information before sending it to the
           microprocessor
       b. to view the information while it is in the microproc-
           essor
       c. to view the information sent from the microprocessor
       d. to view the information in some type of graphic
           display

6-45. Which of the following is not a category of monitors?
       a. RGB   c. color
       b. monochrome   d. LSI

6-46. What does RGB stand for in reference to monitors?
       a. red, green, blue
       b. red, green, brown
       c. rust, green, brown
       d. none of the above

6-47.   The monitor that displays the sharpest images and is most
        commonly used for high quality graphic displays is the
        a. RGB monitor   c. color monitor
        b. monochrome monitor   d. LSI monitor

6-48.   Joysticks and game paddles both function as means to
        _____ objects on the screen.
        a. identify   c. position
        b. intensify   d. stimulate

6-49.   The most significant characteristic of the mouse is that
        a. it fits in the palm of your hand
        b. it eliminates much keyboarding
        c. it positions the cursor
        d. it helps the computer user make choices

6-50.   A device that eliminates considerable keyboarding and
        fits in the palm of your hand is a
        a. game paddle   c. light pen
        b. joystick   d. mouse

MICROCOMPUTERS IN THE FUTURE

6-51.   In the last few years the number of microcomputers being
        introduced in large corporations
        a. has stayed about the same each year
        b. has dropped slightly
        c. has risen slightly
        d. has risen significantly

6-52.   When introduced, microcomputers were generally envisioned
        for use
        a. in the home as stand-alone systems
        b. in small businesses as part of information networks
        c. in large corporations as stand-alone systems
        d. in large corporations as part of information networks

6-53.   Which of the following is not a major mainframe and mini-
        computer vendor which has recently become interested in
        microcomputers?
        a. IBM   c. Commodore
        b. DEC   d. Xerox Corporation

6-54.   In which of the following corporations are managers using
        their personal computers in the stand-alone mode only?
        a. General Electric   c. North American Philips
        b. Ford Motor Company   d. Radio Shack, Tandy Corp.

6-55.   Which of the following is using personal computers in a
        stand-alone mode as well as providing limited access to a
        remote computer?
        a.   General Electric   c.   North American Philips
        b.   Ford Motor Company   d.   Radio Shack, Tandy Corp.

6-56.   Which of the following corporations uses microcomputers
        in an integrated decentralized distributed data proc-
        essing approach along with minicomputers and mainframes?
        a.   General Electric   c.   North American Philips
        b.   Ford Motor Company   d.   Radio Shack, Tandy Corp.

6-57.   In a distributed-processing system the manipulation of
        large data files is the responsibility of
        a.   microcomputers
        b.   minicomputers
        c.   microcomputers and mainframes
        d.   mainframes

6-58.   CompuServe, Inc. is a communication network that
        a.   specializes in stocks/bonds and financial information
        b.   provides information on a variety of topics
        c.   specializes in travel information
        d.   specializes in weather

6-59.   Which of the following is not a statement of prediction
        relative to the future of microcomputers?
        a.   By the year 2000 a personal computer will be as
             necessary as a car is now.
        b.   Nearly everyone will have as much information as can
             be provided by the best of libraries.
        c.   The cost associated with information transmission may
             be prohibitive.
        d.   Location will no longer keep people from access to
             information.

APPLICATION

6-60.   Commodore's research expenditures comprise over _____
        percent of sales.
        a.   5   c.   15
        b.   10   d.   25

6-61.   An existing communication network that is used to send
        messages to various user groups is called
        a.   an electronic bulletin board
        b.   an electronic network
        c.   a distributed system
        d.   a distributed network

6-62.   Commodore began as a _____ and marketing organization
        for electromechanical office equipment.
        a.   financial consultation
        b.   business enhancement
        c.   typewriter repair store
        d.   none of the above

6-63.   Commodore sells more computer units _____ than any
        other computer company.
        a.   in the U.S.A   c.   in North American
        b.   world-wide   d.   in the U.S. and Canada

6-64.   Commodore is able to supply its own microprocessor needs
        and give itself a significant lead time in new product
        development by utilizing a _____ organization.
        a.   vertically integrated   c.   vertically autonomous
        b.   horizontally integrated d.   horizontally autonomous

6-65.   The _____ was Commodore's first personal computer.
        a.   Commodore 64   c.   VIC-20
        b.   TRS-80   d.   PET

ANSWER KEY

6-1.	c	6-21.	c	6-41.	b	6-61.	a
6-2.	b	6-22.	a	6-42.	c	6-62.	c
6-3.	a	6-23.	c	6-43.	a	6-63.	b
6-4.	d	6-24.	c	6-44.	b	6-64.	a
6-5.	b	6-25.	b	6-45.	d	6-65.	d
6-6.	c	6-26.	d	6-46.	a		
6-7.	d	6-27.	a	6-47.	a		
6-8.	c	6-28.	b	6-48.	c		
6-9.	c	6-29.	c	6-49.	b		
6-10.	a	6-30.	d	6-50.	d		
6-11.	c	6-31.	a	6-51.	d		
6-12.	a	6-32.	b	6-52.	a		
6-13.	d	6-33.	d	6-53.	c		
6-14.	b	6-34.	c	6-54.	b		
6-15.	c	6-35.	b	6-55.	a		
6-16.	b	6-36.	b	6-56.	c		
6-17.	c	6-37.	c	6-57.	d		
6-18.	a	6-38.	c	6-58.	b		
6-19.	c	6-39.	a	6-59.	c		
6-20.	b	6-40.	b	6-60.	a		

Telecom-
munications

MULTIPLE CHOICE

DATA COMMUNICATION

7-1.   Data can be transmitted over communication lines in one
       of _____ forms.
       a. 2   c. 6
       b. 4   d. 8

7-2.   The faster form of communications transmission is
       a. pulsar   c. analog
       b. digital   d. modular

7-3.   Sending continuous waves down a wire is likened to
       _____ communications transmission.
       a. pulsar   c. analog
       b. digital   d. modular

7-4.   Sending distinct "on" and "off" pulses is likened to
       _____ communications transmission.
       a. pulsar   c. analog
       b. digital   d. modular

7-5.   The major means of relaying messages over long distances
       in the past was _____ transmissions.
       a. pulsar   c. analog
       b. digital   d. modular

7-6.   AT&T traditionally provided the type of communication
       lines that provided for _____ transmissions.
       a.   pulsar   c.   analog
       b.   digital   d.   modular

7-7.   The most accurate form of communications transmission is
       a.   pulsar   c.   analog
       b.   digital   d.   modular

7-8.   Data communication is
       a.   mechanical transmission of data from one location to
            another
       b.   another term for demodulation
       c.   electronic transmission of data from one location to
            another
       d.   not possible over long distances

7-9.   Terminals refer to
       a.   input devices only   c.   input and output devices
       b.   ouput devices only   d.   communication channels

7-10. Which of the following is not an example of communication
       channels?
       a.   telegraph lines   c.   telephone lines
       b.   microwaves   d.   modems

7-11. Telecommunications is the combined use of communications
       facilities and
       a.   telephone lines
       b.   data processing equipment
       c.   telegraph lines
       d.   terminals

7-12. Which of the following is false in regard to a communi-
       cation network?
       a.   provides communication between input devices and com-
            puters
       b.   provides communication between output devices
       c.   can involve multiple computers
       d.   does not allow communication between input and output
            devices

7-13. Transmission of data in continuous wave form is referred
       to as _____ transmission.
       a.   pulsar   c.   analog
       b.   digital   d.   modular

7-14. The process of converting data from pulse form to wave form is called
a. pulsar transmission
b. modulation
c. demodulation
d. modular transmission

7-15. The process of converting data from wave form to pulse form is called
a. pulsar transmission
b. modulation
c. demodulation
d. modular transmission

7-16. The purpose of a modem is
a. data transmission
b. data interpretation
c. data reception
d. data conversion

7-17. Another name/term for modem is
a. data set
b. terminal
c. channel
d. input terminal

7-18. The computer stores data in _____ form.
a. pulse
b. digital
c. analog
d. modular

7-19. The transmission form with the lowest error rate is
a. pulsar
b. digital
c. analog
d. modular

7-20. The error rate of the digital transmission mode is _____ times lower than the analog transmission method.
a. 10
b. the error rate is higher
c. 50
d. 100

7-21. An I/O control unit is _____ the control unit of the CPU.
a. similar to
b. different from
c. the opposite of
d. exactly the same as

7-22. An I/O control unit
a. performs code conversion
b. performs data buffering
c. is different from the control unit of the CPU
d. all of the above

7-23. Data from punched cards need to be converted from _____ to _____.
a. Hollerith code – machine code
b. machine code – ASCII
c. BCD – ASCII
d. machine code – Hollerith code

7-24.   A(n) _____ is a separate storage unit used as a tempo-
        rary holding area for data being transferred to or from
        the CPU.
        a. I/O control unit   c. buffer
        b. modem   d. network

7-25.   A buffer allows a large quantity of data to be trans-
        ferred _____ if the data were transferred individually,
        item by item.
        a. slightly faster than
        b. much faster than
        c. at about the same speed as
        d. slightly slower than

7-26.   The CPU can execute _____ at one time.
        a. one instruction
        b. two instructions
        c. one to six instructions
        d. three instructions

7-27.   Compared with CPU's internal processing speeds, I/O
        speeds are
        a. very fast   c. slightly slower
        b. about the same   d. very slow

7-28.   The term input/output-bound refers to
        a. the slowing down of the CPU due to power failure
        b. the stoppage of the CPU due to large amounts of data
        c. the slowing down of the CPU because of I/O operations
        d. the stoppage of the CPU because of I/O device stop-
            page

7-29.   The CPU sits idle
        a. only when input occurs
        b. only when output occurs
        c. when input or output occurs
        d. only when the power is off

7-30.   Which of the following statements is not true about
        channels?
        a. They are computers.
        b. They are located only within the CPU.
        c. They serve as data roadways.
        d. They receive instructions from the CPU.

7-31.   The relationship of a channel to a CPU is similar to the
         relationship of
         a.   an assistant manager to a manager
         b.   a manager to an assistant manager
         c.   two managers working collaboratively
         d.   the company president to a manager

7-32.   The type of channel that can accept input from only one
         device at a time is called a _____ channel.
         a.   magnetic   c.   multiplexer
         b.   selector   d.   printex

7-33.   There are _____ types of channels used in communication
         networks.
         a.   2   c.   4
         b.   3   d.   5

7-34.   The type of channel that can accept more than one input
         at a time is called a _____ channel.
         a.   magnetic   c.   multiplexer
         b.   selector   d.   printex

7-35.   The type of channel usually associated with slow-speed
         devices is a _____ channel.
         a.   block multiplexer   c.   bit multiplexer
         b.   byte multiplexer   d.   I/O multiplexer

7-36.   The type of channel associated with high-speed devices is
         a _____ channel.
         a.   block multiplexer   c.   bit multiplexer
         b.   byte multiplexer   d.   I/O multiplexer

7-37.   Which of the following is not a type of communication
         channel?
         a.   communication satellites
         b.   telephone lines
         c.   laser beams
         d.   low-speed helium waveguides

7-38.   The range of frequencies that a channel can transmit is
         determined by
         a.   the grade   c.   the intensity
         b.   the volume   d.   the size

7-39.   The rate at which data can be transmitted across the
         channel is _____ proportional to the _____ of the
         frequency band.
         a.   indirectly – size   c.   directly – width
         b.   indirectly – width   d.   directly – volume

7-40.   Narrow bandwidth channels can transmit data at a rate of
        _____ bits per second.
        a.   45 to 90   c.   50 to 150
        b.   25 to 50   d.   120 to 175

7-41.   A typical narrow bandwidth channel is a _____ channel.
        a.   satellite   c.   telephone
        b.   microwave   d.   telegraph

7-42.   Voice-grade channels can transmit at rates of from
        _____ bits per second.
        a.   100 to 1,000   c.   1,000 to 10,000
        b.   300 to 9,600   d.   500 to 8,000

7-43.   Which of the following is not an example of a broad-band
        channel?
        a.   microwave   c.   laser beam
        b.   telegraph   d.   coaxial cable

7-44.   Telpak is a broad-band service capable of transmitting
        data a rate of up to _____ bits per second.
        a.   120,000   c.   50,000
        b.   75,000   d.   25,000

7-45.   Channels operate in one of _____ basic transmission
        modes.
        a.   two   c.   four
        b.   three   d.   five

7-46.   A _____ channel can either send or receive; it cannot
        do both.
        a.   simplex   c.   half-duplex
        b.   duplex   d.   full-duplex

7-47.   A _____ channel can send or receive, but in only one
        direction at a time.
        a.   simplex   c.   half-duplex
        b.   duplex   d.   full-duplex

7-48.   A _____ channel can send data in both directions
        simultaneously.
        a.   simplex   c.   half-duplex
        b.   duplex   d.   full-duplex

7-49.   The type of channel most commonly used in telephone net-
        works is
        a.   simplex   c.   half-duplex
        b.   duplex   d.   full-duplex

7-50.   The type of channel that is the most versatile is the
        a.   simplex   c.   half-duplex
        b.   duplex   d.   full-duplex

7-51.   I/O devices operate at a _____ speed than do com-
        munication channels.
        a.   much slower   c.   much faster
        b.   slightly slower   d.   slightly faster

7-52.   A _____ allows data to be transmitted from only one
        terminal at a time over a communication channel.
        a.   multiplexer   c.   concentrator
        b.   polling device   d.   I/O device

7-53.   Which of the following allows for a single communication
        channel to substitute for many slower channels?
        a.   multiplexer   c.   concentrator
        b.   polling device   d.   I/O device

7-54.   Which of the following polls the terminals one at a time
        to see if they have messages to send?
        a.   multiplexer   c.   concentrator
        b.   polling device   d.   I/O device

7-55.   Which of the following relies on the assumption that not
        all terminals will be ready to send or receive data at a
        single given time?
        a.   multiplexer   c.   concentrator
        b.   polling device   d.   I/O device

7-56.   A programmable communications processor is a device that
        relieves the _____ of many of the tasks usually
        required in a communications system.
        a.   I/O device   c.   channel
        b.   CPU   d.   terminal

7-57.   The process where by a programmable communcations pro-
        cessor validates transmitted data before it is
        transmitted to the central computer is called
        a.   message switching   c.   front-end switching
        b.   front-end processing   d.   message processing

COMMUNICATION SYSTEMS

7-58.   A local communication system must
        a.   be located within the same room
        b.   be connected directly to the CPU
        c.   be connected to the mainframe by a communication
             channel
        d.   be connected to a remote system

7-59.   In a time-sharing system,
        a.   users have total control of the computer
        b.   users must be directly connected to the system
        c.   users have one computer's time divided among them
        d.   one user can monopolize the computer's time

7-60.   The switching of programs in time-sharing is very rapid,
        and users are usually unaware of it; this technique is
        called
        a.   time-slicing   c.   time-splicing
        b.   time-sampling   d.   time-testing

7-61.   The competition in the business of providing time-sharing
        service can be described as
        a.   just beginning   c.   moderate
        b.   mild   d.   intense

7-62.   Comshare, Tymshare and ADP are examples of
        a.   time-sharing services   c.   channels
        b.   mainframe manufacturers d.   none of the above

7-63.   Which of the following is not an advantage of time-
        sharing systems?
        a.   Each user seems to possess a private computer.
        b.   Security of software applications is enhanced.
        c.   Quick response capability is provided.
        d.   There is no worry about equipment obsolescence.

7-64.   Which of the following is not a problem of time-sharing?
        a.   uneconomical for small users
        b.   system reliability may be lowered
        c.   telephone lines breaking down
        d.   increased telephone/communication costs

7-65.   Which of the following is not a characteristic of a
         distributed system?
         a.   reduced organizational input
         b.   lessened ability to withstand failure
         c.   greater flexibility
         d.   greater responsiveness

7-66.   The distributed-processing configuration in which all
         transactions must go through a central computer is called
         _____ configuration.
         a.   ring   c.   basic
         b.   star   d.   hierarchical

7-67.   The distributed processing configuration in which a
         number of computers are connected to a single
         transmission line is called a _____ configuration.
         a.   ring   c.   basic
         b.   star   d.   hierarchical

7-68.   The _____ configuration exposes the distributed proc-
         essing system to single point vulnerability.
         a.   ring   c.   basic
         b.   star   d.   hierarchical

7-69.   The _____ configuration allows a malfunctioning unit to
         be bypassed without disrupting the total network.
         a.   ring   c.   basic
         b.   star   d.   hierarchical

7-70.   The distributed processing system in which one company's
         needs are divided into multiple levels, controlled by a
         single computer, is called a _____ configuration.
         a.   ring   c.   basic
         b.   star   d.   hierarchical

7-71.   A distributed processing system which consists of a net-
         work of small computers tied into a large central com-
         puting complex is a _____ configuration.
         a.   ring   c.   basic
         b.   star   d.   hierarchical

7-72.   Satellite-based networks use small dish-like antennas to
         a.   send messages only   c.   send or receive messages
         b.   receive messages only   d.   decode transmissions

7-73.   Which of the following types of computers has recently
         gained acceptance as part of the concept of distributed-
         data processing?
         a.   mainframes   c.   microcomputers
         b.   minicomputers   d.   supercomputers

7-74.   In recent years the use of microcomputers by managers for
        planning and control in a distributed system has
        a.   increased   c.   remained about the same
        b.   increased dramatically d.   decreased somewhat

7-75.   A company with _____ managerial philosophy will do a
        large amount of processing at distributed sites.
        a.   a centralized
        b.   a decentralized
        c.   either a centralized or decentralized
        d.   a democratic

7-76.   Local area networking involves inter-connecting computers
        a.   without sharing information
        b.   remote communication channels
        c.   single building only
        d.   in a single building or a complex of buildings

7-77.   Which of the following characteristics does not apply to
        local area networks?
        a.   overall cost reduction
        b.   information has greater data integrity
        c.   more timely updates of information
        d.   information accessed more readily

7-78.   When using electronic mail, if the member receiving the
        mail is not connected to the network
        a.   the message will be returned to the sender
        b.   the sender will be notified
        c.   the message will be saved until the member connects
        d.   the message will be saved for ten days

APPLICATION

7-79.   In the Bank of America's ATM service network a single
        programmable control unit can support up to _____
        Versateller machines.
        a.   10   c.   14
        b.   12   d.   18

7-80.   The two host mainframes in the Bank of America's
        Versateller service are tied together by a communication
        link that uses
        a.   telephone facilities   c.   earth satellites
        b.   microwave receivers   d.   multiplexers

7-81.   In the early 1980s the Bank of America decided to utilize
         IBM's Information Management System (IMS) in order to add
         new on-line services from its DCF branch to the host;
         this strategy required integration of the bank's massive
         retail customer data bases into
         a. 6 - 8 segmented files   c. one segmented file
         b. 2 segmented files   d. 12 - 20 segmented files

7-82.   Which of the following is not one of Bank of America's
         three major communication networks?
         a. Money Transfer Service
         b. Automated Teller Service
         c. San Francisco Data Center
         d. Distributed Computing Facility

7-83.   Which of the following pairs of Bank of America's com-
         munication channel links between San Francisco and London
         does not represent a consecutive step?
         a. earth satellite station San Francisco to earth
             satellite station New York
         b. San Francisco data center microcomputer to earth
             satellite station San Francisco
         c. undersea cable to London Data Center
         d. earth satellite station to undersea cable

ANSWER KEY

7-1.	a	7-26.	a	7-51.	a	7-76.	d
7-2.	b	7-27.	d	7-52.	c	7-77.	a
7-3.	c	7-28.	c	7-53.	a	7-78.	c
7-4.	b	7-29.	c	7-54.	c	7-79.	d
7-5.	c	7-30.	b	7-55.	c	7-80.	a
7-6.	c	7-31.	a	7-56.	b	7-81.	c
7-7.	b	7-32.	b	7-57.	b	7-82.	c
7-8.	c	7-33.	a	7-58.	b	7-83.	b
7-9.	c	7-34.	c	7-59.	c		
7-10.	d	7-35.	b	7-60.	a		
7-11.	b	7-36.	a	7-61.	d		
7-12.	d	7-37.	d	7-62.	a		
7-13.	c	7-38.	a	7-63.	b		
7-14.	b	7-39.	c	7-64.	a		
7-15.	c	7-40.	a	7-65.	b		
7-16	d	7-41.	d	7-66.	b		
7-17.	a	7-42.	b	7-67.	a		
7-18.	b	7-43.	b	7-68.	b		
7-19.	b	7-44.	a	7-69.	a		
7-20.	d	7-45.	b	7-70.	d		
7-21.	b	7-46.	a	7-71.	d		
7-22.	d	7-47.	c	7-72.	c		
7-23.	a	7-48.	d	7-73.	c		
7-24.	c	7-49.	c	7-74.	b		
7-25.	b	7-50.	d	7-75.	b		

System Software

MULTIPLE CHOICE

PROGRAMS

8-1.   System programmers
        a.   maintain the system's programs in good running order
        b.   do not need a technical background
        c.   design solutions to problems such as inventory con-
             trol and accounting
        d.   use the capabilities of the computer to solve spe-
             cific problems

8-2.   System programming is usually provided by
        a.   application programmers
        b.   the organization or company utilizing the system
        c.   the computer manufacturer or a specialized
             programming firm
        d.   none of the above

8-3.   System programs are initially written in a general
        fashion in order to
        a.   be used on different computers without modifications
        b.   facilitate tailoring to particular user specifica-
             tions
        c.   account for the weak technical background of organi-
             zational users
        d.   meet as many user requirements as possible

8-4.   System programs are written specifically for a particular
       type of computer because
       a.   computers differ in primary storage capacity
       b.   the methods used to code and store data are different
            with different computers
       c.   computers differ in the number of instructions they
            can perform
       d.   all of the above

8-5.   System programs
       a.   coordinate the operations of the computer
       b.   can be either control programs or application
            programs
       c.   perform specific computational tasks
       d.   include programs for inventory control and accounting

8-6.   Which of the following is not an example of application
       programs?
       a.   inventory control
       b.   accounting
       c.   updating of checking and savings account balances
       d.   control programs   .

8-7.   Application programs concentrate on a particular problem
       to be solved such as
       a.   simplifying program preparation for the computer
            system
       b.   allocating storage for data being entered into the
            system
       c.   updating savings account balances
       d.   transferring data from file to file

8-8.   Application programs are designed to do all of the
       following except
       a.   perform specific data processing tasks
       b.   perform specific computational tasks
       c.   solve organizations' information needs
       d.   solve computer operations problems

8-9.   The application programmer's job includes all but which
       of the following?
       a.   knowing the computer's technical operations
       b.   using the capabilities of the computer to solve spe-
            cific problems
       c.   understanding the particular user problem very well
       d.   explaining the computer's design to system analysts

OPERATING SYSTEMS

8-10.   Operating systems were developed to overcome the problem
        of
        a.   time delays and errors caused by human operators
        b.   slow input/output devices compared to the CPU
        c.   limited primary storage capacity
        d.   faulty computer equipment

8-11.   An operating system performs all of the following func-
        tions except
        a.   managing the resources of the CPU
        b.   directing the CPU's handling of batch processing
        c.   directing the CPU's handling of online processing
        d.   scheduling jobs on a first come, first serve basis

8-12.   Current mainframe and minicomputer operating systems can
        handle
        a.   either batch or online applications, but not both
        b.   both batch and online applications sequentially
        c.   both batch and online applications simultaneously
        d.   online applications only

8-13.   Operating systems are an improvement over human operators
        for all except which one of the following reasons?
        a.   the computer's ability to manage its own operations
             more quickly
        b.   the computer's ability to efficiently prepare I/O
             devices to be used with each program
        c.   the human's ability to manage computer resource allo-
             cation more efficiently
        d.   the computer's ability to load programs into storage
             quickly and correctly

8-14.   In order to maximize efficiency in processing operations,
        an operating system
        a.   requires human intervention
        b.   does not allow programs to share computer resources
        c.   schedules jobs on a first come, first serve basis
        d.   eliminates human intervention and shares the com-
             puter's resources among several programs

8-15.   The primary difference between batch and online operating
        systems is that
        a.   batch processing allows several jobs to be processed
             one after the other in a continuous stream
        b.   the online operating system frees the operator to
             perform other tasks
        c.   online systems cannot process without interruption
             until all jobs are complete
        d.   batch systems can respond to inquiries from online
             terminals

8-16.   Operating systems that have only online application capa-
        bilities
        a.   can process several jobs in a continuous stream
        b.   can respond to interrupts
        c.   can free the operator to perform other tasks
        d.   cannot respond to spontaneous requests for system
             resources

8-17.   Operating systems were developed in the
        a.   1950s   c.   1970s
        b.   1960s   d.   1980s

8-18.   There are _____ basic types of operating systems.
        a.   2   c.   4
        b.   3   d.   5

8-19.   The type of operating system that groups several user
        programs together and processes them one after the other
        in a continuous stream is called a(n) _____ operating
        system.
        a.   CPU   c.   batch
        b.   online   d.   online or batch

8-20.   The type of operating system that can respond to spon-
        taneous requests for system resources is a(n) _____
        operating system.
        a.   CPU   c.   batch
        b.   online   d.   online or batch

8-21.   Operating systems currently in use on _____ can handle
        _____ applications simultaneously.
        a.   microcomputers--batch and online
        b.   minicomputers and mainframes--batch and online
        c.   mainframes--online and offline
        d.   microcomputers, minicomputers, and mainframes--online
             and batch

COMPONENTS OF OPERATING SYSTEMS

8-22.   The operation system programs that oversee system opera-
        tions and perform tasks such as input/output, scheduling,
        and communicating with the computer operator are
        a. processing programs
        b. foreground programs
        c. control programs
        d. processing programs and control programs

8-23.   Once the language-translator program converts the
        English-like program into machine language, the result is
        called the
        a. source program   c. library program
        b. object program   d. application program

8-24.   Which of the following programs is not a processing
        program contained in the operating system?
        a. supervisor program   c. language translator
        b. utility program   d. linkage editor

8-25.   The secondary storage device where operating system
        programs are stored is the
        a. operating system device
        b. system residence device
        c. input/output management system
        d. system library

8-26.   The major component of the operating system is the
        a. resident routine
        b. job-control program
        c. input/output management system
        d. supervisor program

8-27.   Library programs
        a. are often called librarian programs
        b. are usually used once or twice by an organization
        c. are stored in primary storage
        d. are frequently used in other programs

8-28.   The purpose of job-control statements is to
        a.   translate English-like programs written by program-
             mers into machine-language instructions
        b.   convert machine-language instructions into 1s and 0s
             the computer can understand
        c.   coordinate a directory of programs contained in the
             system library
        d.   identify for the operating system which operations
             are to be performed and which devices are needed to
             perform them

8-29.   All but which one of the following are utility programs
        that can be included in the operating system?
        a.   sort/merge programs
        b.   programs that transfer data from tape to disk
        c.   programs that contain the appropriate procedures for
             adding and deleting programs
        d.   programs that transfer data from file to file

8-30.   Processing programs are used by the programmer to
        a.   perform input/output tasks and scheduling
        b.   communicate with the operating system
        c.   load nonresident system programs into primary storage
        d.   simplify program preparation for the computer system

8-31.   Control programs are designed to:
        a.   communicate with the computer programmer
        b.   communicate with the computer operator
        c.   handle interrupts
        d.   all of the above

8-32.   Which of the following is not an example of a processing
        program stored on a magnetic disk?
        a.   a language translator   c.   linkage editor
        b.   job-control program   d.   library program

8-33.   Job control language (JCL) is used to do all of the
        following except:
        a.   identify the beginning of a job
        b.   oversee system operations
        c.   indicate the required I/O devices
        d.   describe the work to be done

8-34.   The supervisor program is also called the
        a.   monitor   c.   resident
        b.   controller   d.   reviewer

8-35.   The processing program that assigns appropriate primary
        storage addresses to each byte of the translated applica-
        tion program is called the
        a.   object program   c.   library program
        b.   linkage editor   d.   utility program

8-36.   Sort/merge programs are
        a.   control programs
        b.   referred to as non-utility programs
        c.   used to put file records into a particular sequence
        d.   library programs

8-37.   There are _____ major types of processing programs con-
        tained in operating systems.
        a.   2   c.   4
        b.   3   d.   5

8-38.   A program that transfers data from file to file or from
        one I/O device to another is called a
        a.   librarian program   c.   linkage editor
        b.   utility program   d.   object program

MULTIPROGRAMMING

8-39.   When a computer system is said to be efficient, it means
        that
        a.   the CPU remains very active
        b.   the CPU and I/O devices are active at all times
        c.   the CPU must never wait for I/O operations
        d.   serial processing is being used to execute programs

8-40.   When programs are executed concurrently, it means they
        are
        a.   processed at the same time
        b.   processed simultaneously
        c.   processed over the same period of time
        d.   executed serially

8-41.   When two programs of the same priority request CPU
        resources at the same time
        a.   they are both processeed simultaneously
        b.   both programs are rejected
        c.   the decision as to which gets control first may be
             arbitrary
        d.   the program that has been in primary storage longer
             always receives control first

8-42.   Which of the following is true in regard to foreground
        programs and background programs?
        a.   Background programs are usually executed in a batch
             mode.
        b.   Foreground programs are high priority programs.
        c.   Programs used for online processing in a time-sharing
             system are considered foreground programs.
        d.   All of the above.

8-43.   In multiprogramming, the CPU executes instructions from a
        program until
        a.   a specified time limit is reached
        b.   the program is finished
        c.   another program is added to primary storage
        d.   an interrupt for input or output is generated

8-44.   Overlapped processing refers to the process whereby the
        CPU
        a.   executes programs serially
        b.   executes programs simultaneously
        c.   executes programs concurrently
        d.   executes programs sequentially

8-45.   In the earliest computer operating systems most programs
        were executed using
        a.   serial processing
        b.   simultaneous processing
        c.   concurrent processing
        d.   sequential processing

8-46.   Applications requiring the use of light pens with display
        terminals require
        a.   library programs
        b.   subsystems to be added to the operating system
        c.   utility programs
        d.   language-translator programs

VIRTUAL STORAGE

8-47.   One reason virtual storage alleviates the problem of
        limited primary storage capacity is that
        a.   programs are smaller and take up less space
        b.   the computer's real storage is expanded
        c.   only one program at a time is kept in primary storage
        d.   only the part of the program being used is kept in
             primary storage

8-48. Which of the following is not a characteristic of virtual storage?
       a. It offers tremendous flexibility to programmers.
       b. It gives system analysts more time to devote to solving the problem at hand rather than spending too much time fitting programs into storage.
       c. It increases the amount of primary storage.
       d. It decreases the need for extensive online secondary storage.

8-49. Segments are
       a. logical parts of a program
       b. equal-sized blocks of programs
       c. portions of primary memory
       d. the same as pages

8-50. Pages are
       a. equal-sized blocks of programs
       b. capable of being swapped into or out of memory as needed
       c. not based on logical portions of programs
       d. all of the above

8-51. The difference between pages and segments is that
       a. pages vary in size while segments are fixed in size
       b. segments vary in size while pages are fixed in size
       c. pages are logical parts of the program and segments are entire programs
       d. pages are used in multiprogramming while segments are used in virtual storage

8-52. When more time is spent locating and exchanging program pages/segments than is spent in actual program processing, the following condition is occurring:
       a. swapping   c. paging
       b. thrashing   d. segmenting

8-53. Limitations of multiprogramming include all but which one of the following?
       a. Each partition must be large enough to hold an entire program.
       b. All program instructions are kept in primary storage throughout the program execution whether they are needed or not.
       c. There is inefficient memory usage.
       d. Much time must be spent locating and exchanging program segments or pages.

8-54.   The process of moving data or instructions from real
        storage to virtual storage is called
        a.   swapping   c.   paging
        b.   thrashing   d.   segmenting

8-55.   Virtual storage
        a.   refers to indirect access storage
        b.   requires that only the portion of a program being
             used needs to be in primary storage at any given
             time
        c.   allows for two to four programs to be executed within
             any given time
        d.   allows primary storage to become unlimited

8-56.   Virtual storage is the same as
        a.   virtual memory   c.   primary storage
        b.   real storage   d.   CPU storage

8-57.   Segmentation is to paging as segments are to
        a.   pages   c.   page frame segments
        b.   page frames   d.   page segments

8-58.   Which of the following is not a major limitation of vir-
        tual storage?
        a.   It requires extensive online secondary storage.
        b.   It requires significant amounts of internal storage.
        c.   Primary storage usage is inefficient.
        d.   It may result in too much time spent "swapping."

MULTIPROCESSING

8-59.   Multiprocessing systems that utilize several large CPUs
        require
        a.   careful planning
        b.   sophisticated software
        c.   services of outside consultants in many cases
        d.   all of the above

8-60.   In multiprocessing, a front-end processor acts as
        a.   an interface between a large CPU and a large data
             base
        b.   the backup CPU if the main CPU malfunctions
        c.   an interface between a large CPU and peripheral
             devices
        d.   the CPU responsible for updating specific data fields

8-61.   A back-end processor
        a.   is a large CPU
        b.   is an interface between a large CPU and peripheral
             devices
        c.   is responsible for maintaining I/O operations
        d.   is a small CPU that is responsible for maintaining a
             data base

8-62.   Which of the following is false in regard to multiproc-
        essing systems ?
        a.   allow a large CPU to engage in complex processing
             without interruption
        b.   relieve a large CPU of routine tasks such as sche-
             duling and maintaining files
        c.   allow instructions to be executed simultaneously
        d.   do not allow for efficient use of CPU time

8-63.   Multiprocessing involves the use of _____ linked
        together for coordinated operation.
        a.   two CPUs   c.   three or more CPUs
        b.   two or more CPUs   d.   at least five CPUs

APPLICATION

8-64.   The system that NCR developed for customer use had to go
        through a series of tests. Which one was not in this
        test series?
        a.   Beta test
        b.   Custom Verification Test (CVT)
        c.   Gamma test
        d.   Alpha test

8-65.   VRX is a group of software modules that make up an
        operating system. Which of the following does the group
        not allow for?
        a.   multiprogramming
        b.   virtual storage
        c.   multiprocessing
        d.   multiple virtual machine capabilities

ANSWER KEY

8-1.	a	8-21.	b	8 41.	c	8-61.	d
8-2.	c	8-22.	c	8-42.	d	8-62.	d
8-3.	d	8-23.	b	8-43.	d	8-63.	b
8-4.	d	8-24.	a	8-44.	c	8-64.	d
8-5.	a	8-25.	b	8-45.	a	8-65.	c
8-6.	d	8-26.	d	8-46.	b		
8-7.	c	8-27.	d	8-47.	d		
8-8.	d	8-28.	d	8-48.	c		
8-9.	a	8-29.	c	8-49.	a		
8-10.	a	8-30.	d	8-50.	d		
8-11.	d	8-31.	d	8-51.	b		
8-12.	c	8-32.	b	8-52.	b		
8-13.	c	8-33.	b	8-53.	d		
8-14.	d	8-34.	a	8-54.	a		
8-15.	a	8-35.	b	8-55.	b		
8-16.	b	8-36.	c	8-56.	a		
8-17.	b	8-37.	c	8-57.	a		
8-18.	a	8-38.	b	8-58.	c		
8-19.	c	8-39.	a	8-59.	d		
8-20.	b	8-40.	c	8-60.	c		

9

Programming
and Software
Development

MULTIPLE CHOICE

COMPUTER PROBLEM SOLVING

9-1.   Which of the following is not one of the five stages
       involved in the structured approach to problem-solving
       and program development?
       a. defining the problem   c. writing the program
       b. designing a solution   d. reviewing the program

9-2.   Which of the following sequences accurately describes the
       evolution of the computer?
       a. development of higher level languages/instructions
           coded in machine language/translation of English-like
           commands into computer language
       b. instructions coded in machine language/translation of
           English-like commands into computer
           language/development of higher level languages
       c. translation of English-like commands into computer
           language/development of higher level languages
       d. development of higher level languages/translation of
           English-like commands into computer
           language/instructions coded in machine language

9-3.   Which of the following conditions could cause a program
       to be executed incorrectly or not at all?
       a. illogical sequential order of instructions
       b. unanticipated condition arising
       c. failure to analyze logical conditions in detail
       d. all of the above

340

9-4.   Which of the following sequences correctly identifies the
       structured approach to problem solving and program deve-
       lopment?
       a.   defining the problem/designing a solution/writing a
            program/compiling, debugging, and testing the
            program/documenting the program
       b.   documenting the program/defining the
            problem/designing a solution/writing a
            program/compiling, debugging and testing the program
       c.   defining the problem/writing a program/compiling,
            testing, and debugging the program/designing a
            solution/documenting the program
       d.   defining the problem/documenting the
            program/designing a solution/writing a
            program/compiling, debugging and testing the program

9-5.   A good understanding of the advantages and limitations of
       the language used is required for completing the
       following steps in problem solving and program develop-
       ment.
       a.   writing the problem/defining the problem
       b.   documenting the problem/writing the problem
       c.   compiling, testing, and debugging/designing a solu-
            tion
       d.   defining the problem/compiling, testing, and
            debugging

9-6.   The structured approach to problem solving and program
       development utilizes _____ steps.
       a.   3   c.   5
       b.   4   d.   6

9-7.   Which of the following steps in considered to be the
       first step in the structured approach to problem solving
       and program development?
       a.   writing the program
       b.   designing a solution
       c.   documenting the program
       d.   defining the problem

9-8.   Which of the following steps is considerd to be the last
       step in the structured approach to problem solving and
       program development?
       a.   writing the program
       b.   designing a solution
       c.   documenting the program
       d.   defining the problem

9-9.   Which of the following steps can be followed regardless
        of the programming language used?
        a. designing a solution
        b. writing the program
        c. documenting the program
        d. debugging and testing the program

9-10.   Which of the following steps does not involve translating
        the solution into one of several computer programming
        languages?
        a. writing a program
        b. debugging and testing the program
        c. defining the problem
        d. documenting the program

9-11.   Which of the following steps is considered to be the
        second step in the structured approach to problem solving
        and program development?
        a. writing the program
        b. designing a solution
        c. documenting the program
        d. defining the problem

9-12.   When programs were first written, there were _____ for
        programmers to follow.
        a. many programs   c. few rules
        b. a wealth of rules   d. few programs

DEFINING THE PROBLEM

9-13.   When designing the solution to problems the solution must
        be
        a. able to express required output in terms of the
            user's information requirements
        b. stated in clear objectives
        c. stated in concise terms
        d. all of the above

9-14.   In order to determine the appropriate _____ , the sys-
        tem analyst reviews the current systems to see what data
        may be available and to determine what new data must be
        captured.
        a. output   c. processing
        b. input   d. time frame

9-15.   The system analyst determines _____ requirements by
        reviewing output specifications and the required input
        established by careful evaluation of current systems.
        a. input-output   c. output-processing
        b. input-processing   d. processing

9-16.   The system analyst determines _____ from the infor-
        mation requirements of users and management.
        a. output   c. processing
        b. input   d. input/output

9-17.   Which of the following tasks/steps is sometimes completed
        by a system analyst who is not part of the company's
        programming staff?
        a. documenting the program
        b. writing and compiling the program
        c. designing a solution
        d. debugging the program

9-18.   There are _____ basic steps in the task of defining the
        problem in the problem solving process.
        a. 2   c. 4
        b. 3   d. 5

9-19.   Which of the following is least likely to work directly
        with the others on a team in the problem solving process?
        a. system analyst   c. programmer
        b. manager   d. board chairman

9-20.   A "company's payroll section" is to "paychecks" as the
        task of "defining the problem" is to
        a. input   c. processing
        b. output   d. reprocessing

DESIGNING A SOLUTION

9-21.   Which of the following is not a basic logic pattern used
        in writing computer programs?
        a. simple sequence   c. loop
        b. flow   d. branch

9-22.   Unless it is told otherwise, the computer assumes that
        all statements entered by the programmer are to be exe-
        cuted in the _____ pattern.
        a. simple sequence   c. loop
        b. selection   d. branch

9-23.   The basic logic pattern that is especially useful if the
        same sequence of statements is to be executed over and
        over is the _____ pattern.
        a.   branch   c.   loop
        b.   simple sequence   d.   flow

9-24.   The logic pattern that requires the computer to compare
        one memory location with another is called the _____
        pattern.
        a.   branch   c.   simple sequence
        b.   selection   d.   flow

9-25.   In order to "design a solution" the programmer needs to
        know the _____ basic logic patterns used by the com-
        puter.
        a.   2   c.   4
        b.   3   d.   5

9-26.   The computer can understand and execute only the basic
        logic patterns; however, _____ may have more compli-
        cated statements.
        a.   machine languge   c.   token language
        b.   asssembly language   d.   high-level language

9-27.   A trailer value should be a value that is not part of the
        input data because
        a.   a counter cannot then be used
        b.   more data will be entered after the trailer value is
             encountered
        c.   it causes the computer to exit from the loop
        d.   a counter cannot recognize the signal

9-28.   Which of the following ways can "counters" be used?
        a.   entered at the time of program execution
        b.   as a value in an instruction in the program
        c.   computed within the program
        d.   all of the above

9-29.   Which logic pattern allows programmers to skip past
        statements in a program, leaving them unexecuted?
        a.   branch   c.   flow
        b.   loop   d.   simple sequence

9-30.   Which of the following is not a reason that branching is
        considered to be the most controversial logic pattern?
        a.   It is efficient.
        b.   When a program uses it frequently, the computer runs
             inefficiently because it must jump from one part of
             the program to another too often.
        c.   It can be difficult for other programmers to follow
             the logical flow of the pattern.
        d.   It can be time-consuming to maintain.

9-31.   Which of the following is true in regards to pseudocode?
        a.   sometimes called a block diagram
        b.   uses symbols to represent the type of processing per-
             formed
        c.   arranges narrative descriptions of the processing
             steps to be performed in the program
        d.   sometimes called a logic diagram

9-32.   Pseudocode statements can be translated into _____
        program statement(s).
        a.   only one   c.   two
        b.   one or more   d.   one to six

9-33.   Which of the following statements about flowcharts is not
        true?
        a.   provide an excellent documentation of a program
        b.   used to guide programmers in determining needed
             changes
        c.   used to guide programmers in deciding where state-
             ments should be located when making changes
        d.   provide a narrative description of the processing
             steps to be performed in a program

9-34.   In a flowchart, a process step such as addition or
        subtraction uses the following symbol:
        a.   ▭   c.   ⬭

        b.   ◇   d.   ▱

9-35.   In a flowchart the _____ symbol indicates that the
        program requires either input or output.
        a.   ▭   c.   ⬭

        b.   ▱   d.   ◇

9-36.   In a flowchart, comparing values is indicated by:

a. ▱   c. ▢

b. ⬭   d. ◇

9-37.   The symbol appearing at the beginning or the end of a program flowchart is

a. ▢   c. ⬭

b. ◇   d. ▱

9-38.   The flowchart symbol ◇ is most closely related to which logical pattern?

a.   branch   c.   flow
b.   selection   d.   sequence

9-39.   A flowchart that outlines the general flow and major segments of a program is called a _____ flowchart.

a.   detail   c.   micro
b.   flowline   d.   macro

9-40.   In order to accumulate totals in a program that uses a loop, the programmer must

a.   include provisions for printing and storing the total outside the loop
b.   include statements within the loop to accumulate the desired totals
c.   insure that the necessary statements appear at the correct logical points of the loop
d.   all of the above

9-41.   If correctly written, each pseudocode statement

a.   must be translated into more than one program statement
b.   cannot be translated into more than one program statement
c.   can be translated into one or more program statements
d.   cannot be translated without further revision

9-42.   Which of the following terms does not belong in the group?

a.   block diagram   c.   pseudocode
b.   flowchart   d.   logic diagram

9-43.   Which of the following characteristics has little to do
        with the value of a flowchart?
        a.   up-to-date   c.   complete
        b.   easy to read   d.   inexpensive

9-44.   In a flowchart, which logic pattern would be represented
        by a flowline pointing away from the normal flow to a
        circle with a number in it?
        a.   branch   c.   flow
        b.   loop   d.   selection

9-45.   In a flowchart, a flow line from the last symbol included
        in the loop up to the first block to be reexecuted would
        represent a _____ logic pattern.
        a.   branch   c.   flow
        b.   loop   d.   selection

9-46.   In a flowchart accumulators are positioned within a
        a.   branch   c.   flow
        b.   loop   d.   selection

9-47.   How many things must a programmer do in a flowchart in
        order to accumulate totals in a program?
        a.   2   c.   4
        b.   3   d.   5

WRITING THE PROGRAM

9-48.   A remark (or comment)
        a.   is used to define items used in a program
        b.   has no effect on program execution
        c.   brings data into primary storage
        d.   compares two items in a program

9-49.   Which of the following is not a type of programming
        statement common to most high-level programming
        languages?
        a.   declaration   c.   computation
        b.   input/output statement d.   accumulator

9-50.   Which of the following types of programming statements
        is used to define items?
        a.   input/output   c.   declaration
        b.   computation   d.   transfer of control

9-51.   Which of the following is not a desirable program
        quality?
        a.   easy to read and understand
        b.   use of short data names
        c.   efficiency and maintainability
        d.   reliability

9-52.   Which is not an important reason why programs should be
        efficient?
        a.   CPU time is a valuable resource.
        b.   Computers are very expensive.
        c.   Efficient programs guarantee a successful program.
        d.   Users may save thousands of dollars per year if pro-
             grams run efficiently.

9-53.   Exponentiation is an example of a type of statement used
        in writing programs called
        a.   comments   c.   computations
        b.   declarations   d.   transfers of control

9-54.   The type of statement used in writing a program that
        alters the sequence only when a certain condition can be
        met is called
        a.   comments   c.   computations
        b.   declarations   d.   transfers of control

9-55.   The type of statement used in writing a program that
        defines items used in the program is called
        a.   comments   c.   computations
        b.   declarations   d.   transfers of control

9-56.   The type of statement used in writing a program that has
        no effect on program execution is called
        a.   comments   c.   computations
        b.   declarations   d.   transfers of control

9-57.   Input/output statements _____ from one programming
        language to another.
        a.   differ slightly in form and function
        b.   differ considerably in form and function
        c.   differ considerably in form but not so much in func-
             tion
        d.   differ slightly in form but not so much in function

9-58.   When a program is said to be robust it means the program
        a.   is maintainable
        b.   will work under all conditions
        c.   is efficient
        d.   is easy to read and understand

COMPILING, DEBUGGING, AND TESTING THE PROGRAM

9-59.   The computer programming language levels include all of
        the following except
        a.   high-level language   c.   machine language
        b.   pseudocode   d.   assembly language

9-60.   One high-level language statement can do the same thing
        as six or more machine language instructions principally
        because
        a.   the addresses for required storage locations are
             handled automatically
        b.   no language translator is needed
        c.   a computer can understand high-level languages
        d.   high-level languages are more complex

9-61.   The machine-executable form of a program is known as the
        a.   source program
        b.   object program
        c.   language-translator program
        d.   assembler program

9-62.   With an interpreter program a statement must be entered
        correctly by the programmer before the next statement can
        be entered because
        a.   the interpreter is designed to process a program
             statement by statement
        b.   too many error messages will not allow the program to
             continue
        c.   program statements are used and evaluated over and
             over again
        d.   the interpreter translates the entire program at one
             time

9-63.   Which of the following types of errors cannot be detected
        by a language translator?
        a.   syntax errors   c.   spelling errors
        b.   grammatical errors   d.   logical errors

9-64.   Two commonly used diagnostic procedures available to
        programmers when errors prove especially difficult to
        locate are
        a.   refine programs and search programs
        b.   check programs and review programs
        c.   dump programs and trace programs
        d.   review programs and refine programs

9-65.   The code that directly represents the proper electrical
         states in the computer is
         a.   machine language   c.   assembly language
         b.   low-level language   d.   high-level language

9-66.   The computer language that uses mnemonics is called
         a.   machine language   c.   assembly language
         b.   low-level language   d.   high-level language

9-67.   The computer language that is furthest removed from the
         hardware is called
         a.   machine language   c.   assembly language
         b.   low-level language   d.   high-level language

DOCUMENTING THE PROGRAM

9-68.   Which statement is not true about the role of program
         documentation?
         a.   It is not essential to those who must perform manual
               functions required by the system.
         b.   It provides instructions to the computer operator
               about the requirements for running particular
               programs.
         c.   It helps management to determine what changes are
               necessary.
         d.   It helps to keep pace with program modifications and
               changing needs.

9-69.   The process of documentation begins
         a.   during the program definition stage
         b.   with the initial request for information
         c.   with the problem solution phase
         d.   with the compiling and debugging stage

9-70.   The most important documentation in the planning phase
         is
         a.   flowcharting   c.   flowlines
         b.   pseudocodes   d.   case studies

PROGRAMMING CASE STUDY

9-71.   Which of the following sequences is accurate?
   a.   review logic/construct flowchart/enter the source
        program into the computer/express the solution in
        programming language
   b.   enter the source program into the computer/review
        logic/construct flowchart/express the solution in
        programming language
   c.   construct flowchart/review logic/express solution in
        programming langauge/enter the source program into
        the computer
   d.   none of the above are accurate

APPLICATION

9-72.   At Eli Lilly and Company, which area handles the firm's
        business data processing needs?
   a.   Scientific Information Systems Division
   b.   Corporate Information Systems and Services
   c.   Corporate Computer Center
   d.   Information Systems Development Division

9-73.   Which one is not a phase in the multiphase process, PLAD
        (Process for Lilly Application Development)?
   a.   documentation of the objectives and requirements of
        the requested system
   b.   coding and unit-test phase
   c.   external design phase
   d.   implementation phase

9-74.   At Eli Lilly and Company, which area handles the firm's
        activities related to research and development?
   a.   Information Systems Development Division
   b.   Corporate Computer Center
   c.   Scientific Information Systems Division
   d.   Corporate Information Systems and Services

ANSWER KEY

9-1.	d	9-21.	b	9-41.	c	9-61.	b
9-2.	b	9-22.	a	9-42.	c	9-62.	a
9-3.	d	9-23.	c	9-43.	d	9-63.	d
9-4.	a	9-24.	b	9-44.	a	9-64.	c
9-5.	b	9-25.	c	9-45.	b	9-65.	a
9-6.	c	9-26.	d	9-46.	b	9-66.	c
9-7.	d	9-27.	c	9-47.	a	9-67.	d
9-8.	c	9-28.	d	9-48.	b	9-68.	a
9-9.	a	9-29.	a	9-49.	d	9-69.	b
9-10.	c	9-30.	a	9-50.	c	9-70.	a
9-11.	b	9-31.	c	9-51.	b	9-71.	c
9-12.	c	9-32.	b	9-52.	c	9-72.	b
9-13.	d	9-33.	d	9-53.	c	9-73.	d
9-14.	b	9-34.	a	9-54.	d	9-74.	c
9-15.	d	9-35.	b	9-55.	b		
9-16.	a	9-36.	d	9-56.	a		
9-17.	c	9-37.	c	9-57.	c		
9-18.	b	9-38.	b	9-58.	b		
9-19.	d	9-39.	d	9-59.	b		
9-20.	b	9-40.	d	9-60.	a		

10

Programming
Languages

MULTIPLE CHOICE

BATCH PROGRAMMING VERSUS INTERACTIVE PROGRAMMING

10-1.   "The programs are translated and executed, and the
        results are returned to the remote terminal within a
        matter of minutes"--Which of the following is most
        directly characterized by this statement?
        a.   batch programming
        b.   interactive programming
        c.   either batch or interactive programming
        d.   neither batch nor interactive programming

10-2.   "Has increased because of the increased demand for online
        systems"--Which of the following is most directly charac-
        terized by this statement?
        a.   batch programming
        b.   interactive programming
        c.   either batch or interactive programming
        d.   neither batch nor interactive programming

10-3.   "These programs are used to solve specific problems that
        occur according to some predetermined schedule "--Which
        of the following is most directly characterized by this
        statement?
        a.   batch programming
        b.   interactive programming
        c.   either batch or interactive programming
        d.   neither batch nor interactive programming

10-4.   "Applications such as accounts receivable, inventory
        control, and billing"--Which of the following is most
        directly characterized by these applications?
        a.   batch programming
        b.   interactive programming
        c.   either batch or interactive programming
        d.   neither batch nor interactive programming

10-5.   "The generation of monthly reports and the generation of
        unscheduled reports that are not needed immediately"
        --Which of the following is most directly characterized
        by these uses?
        a.   batch programming
        b.   interactive programming
        c.   either batch or interactive programming
        d.   neither batch nor interactive programming

MACHINE-ORIENTED LANGUAGES

10-6.   Some of the earliest computers were programmed
        a.   using the stored-program concept
        b.   using high-level languages
        c.   by arranging various wires within the components
        d.   using assembly language

10-7.   The first stored-program computer was the
        a.   ENIAC   c.   IBM 360
        b.   EDSAC   d.   EAINC

10-8.   Which of the following is true in regard to machine
        language?
        a.   uses mnemonics
        b.   takes the form of 1s and 0s
        c.   makes inefficient use of storage areas
        d.   must be translated before the computer can understand
             it

10-9.   Which of the following is false about machine language?
        a.   It uses mnemonics.
        b.   It takes the form of 1s and 0s.
        c.   It is the only language that computers directly
             understand.
        d.   It functions as the object language for higher level
             languages.

10-10. When a programmer uses machine language,
  a. a thorough understanding of how the computer operates internally is needed
  b. only a general understanding of how the computer operates internally is needed
  c. no knowledge of how the computer operates internally is needed
  d. execution speed is sacrificed

10-11. Each machine language instruction must have _____ parts.
  a. 2   c. 4
  b. 3   d. 5

10-12. The _____ tells the computer which function to perform.
  a. label   c. assembly code
  b. op code   d. operand

10-13. The _____ tells the computer what data to use when performing a function.
  a. label   c. assembly code
  b. op code   d. operand

10-14. Which of the following characteristics is not true with regard to machine language?
  a. It is very efficient in terms of storage.
  b. It is very efficient in terms of execution speed.
  c. It can be transferred from one computer to another.
  d. Programming with it can be very tedious.

10-15. Which of the following is false in regards to mnemonics?
  a. replaces coding in 1s and 0s
  b. are English-like abbreviations
  c. is symbolic
  d. is used with machine language

10-16. Which of the following is not true in regards to machine language and assembly language?
  a. Assembly languages were developed to alleviate many of the disadvantages of machine-language programming.
  b. Programming in assembly language utilizes symbols, not 1s and 0s.
  c. Assembly-language programs written for one type of computer can be executed on other types of computers with modification.
  d. There are more basic parts to an assembly language instruction than there are for a machine language instruction.

10-17. Mnemonic codes for assembly-language instructions
    a.   are abbreviations for operands
    b.   differ depending on the type and model of a computer
    c.   are abbreviations for labels
    d.   do not eliminate the need to code in 1s and 0s

10-18. Assembly-language instructions have _____ basic parts.
    a.   two   c.   four
    b.   three   d.   six

10-19. A label represents the first storage location to be used
    for an instruction and is supplied by
    a.   the computer company
    b.   an analysis of the machine-language code
    c.   the programmer
    d.   an analysis of previously used labels with regard to
          former storage locations

10-20. Which of the following is false concerning assembly lan-
    guage?
    a.   It can be used to develop programs which are highly
          efficient in terms of storage space use.
    b.   The assembler program performs certain checking func-
          tions and generates error messages.
    c.   It doesn't require a high level of skill to use it
          effectively.
    d.   Assembly language encourages module programming tech-
          niques.

10-21. Which of the following is the main disadvantage of
    assembly language?
    a.   Program preparation time is long.
    b.   It is cumbersome to use.
    c.   The programmer must know the computer to be used.
    d.   It is machine-dependent.

10-22. Each instruction in assembly language can contain
    _____ operands.
    a.   one or two   c.   one to six
    b.   one, two, or three   d.   one to twelve

10-23. Which of the following is not true about assembly
language?
a. It is machine dependent.
b. It is well-suited for operating-system programming.
c. The assembly language programmer needs no knowledge
of binary or hexidecimal numbers.
d. The most difficult phase of the problem resolution
with assembly language is writing the solution to the
problem.

HIGH-LEVEL LANGUAGES

10-24. There are _____ basic categories of higher-level
languages.
a. 2   c. 4
b. 3   d. 6

10-25. The type of high-level language that places programming
emphasis on describing the computational and logical procedures required to solve a problem is called
a. procedure-oriented   c. problem-oriented
b. scientific-oriented   d. computational-oriented

10-26. The type of high-level language that places programming
emphasis on the problem and solution without detailing
the necessary computational procedures is called
a. procedure-oriented   c. problem-oriented
b. scientific-oriented   d. solution-oriented

10-27. Which of the following high-level languages is not
included in the same category as the others?
a. COBOL   c. FORTRAN
b. RPG   d. PL/1

10-28. The oldest high-level programming language is
a. COBOL   c. FORTRAN
b. RPG   d. PL/1

10-29. The first commmercially available high-level language
originated in the
a. mid-1950s   c. mid-1960s
b. early 1940s   d. early 1960s

10-30. The effort to produce the first commercially available
high-level language was backed by
a. Hewlett Packard   b. Burroughs
c. IBM   d. DEC

10-31. The version of FORTRAN which was developed specifically
for beginning or student programmers is
a. Basic FORTRAN   c. FORTRAN IV
b. FORTRAN II   d. FORTRAN--WATFOR

10-32. Which of the following groups was not a primary user when
FORTRAN was first released?
a. engineer   c. scientists
b. business managers   d. mathematicians

10-33. FORTRAN is best suited for programs involving
a. editing data
b. file maintainance
c. complex arithmetic calculations
d. production of documents

10-34. The one statement that must appear in every FORTRAN program is
a. BEGIN   c. START
b. END   d. STOP

10-35. In FORTRAN the type of statements that determine the
sequence in which operations will be performed is a(n)
_____ statement.
a. control   c. input/output
b. arithmetic   d. specification

10-36. In FORTRAN the type of statement that directs the computer to perform computations is a(n) _____ statement.
a. control   c. input/output
b. arithmetic   d. specification

10-37. In FORTRAN the type of statement that tell FORTRAN how
to interpret data read from an input device is a(n)
_____ statement.
a. control   c. input/output
b. arithmetic   d. specification

10-38. In FORTRAN the type of statements that instruct the
computer to read data from, or write data to, an I/O
device is called a(n) _____ statement.
a. control   c. input/output
b. arithmetic   d. specification

10-39. In FORTRAN numbers are represented by _____ kinds of
variables.
a. 2   c. 6
b. 4   d. 8

10-40. In FORTRAN a variable name is usually limited to a length
of _____ characters.
a. 2   c. 6
b. 4   d. 8

10-41. In FORTRAN alphanumeric characters include _____ characters.
a. numeric, alphabetic, and special
b. only alphabetic and numeric
c. only numeric and special
d. only special and alphabetic

10-42. In FORTRAN a string of alphanumeric characters must be
divided in groups of _____ characters each.
a. 2   c. 6
b. 4   d. 8

10-43. In FORTRAN elements of the array variables are referred
to by
a. elements   c. data items
b. subscripts   d. types

10-44. APL became available to the public in
a. the early 1960s   c. the early 1970s
b. the late 1960s   d. the mid-1970s

10-45. A programmer can use APL in _____ modes.
a. 2   c. 6
b. 4   d. 8

10-46. In APL, when the terminal is used much like a desk calculator, the _____ mode is being used.
a. definition   c. execution
b. statement   d. command

10-47. In APL, when a series of instructions is entered into
memory and the entire program is executed on command from
the programmer, the _____ mode is being used.
a. definition   c. execution
b. statement   d. command

10-48. Which of the following statements about APL is false?
a. APL is easy to read.
b. APL is a very powerful language.
c. APL can be learned quickly by programmers.
d. APL is available through time-sharing networks.

10-49. The basic unit of COBOL is
    a. a word   c. a section
    b. a sentence   d. a division

10-50. No computer programming language suitable for business application existed before
    a. 1960   c. 1970
    b. 1965   d. 1975

10-51. The specifications for COBOL were developed by
    a. the CODASYL committee
    b. IBM
    c. the U.S. Department of Defense
    d. Burroughs

10-52. Which of the following is not a division of COBOL?
    a. identification   c. context
    b. data   d. procedure

10-53. The division of COBOL that provides documentation of the program is called
    a. identification   c. context
    b. data   d. procedure

10-54. The division of COBOL that describes the variable names, records, and files to be used by the program is called
    a. identification   c. context
    b. data   d. procedure

10-55. The _____ division of COBOL contains the actual processing instructions.
    a. identification   c. context
    b. data   d. procedure

10-56. Approximately _____ words are contained in COBOL's reserved word list.
    a. 250   c. 1,000
    b. 500   d. 1,500

10-57. Which of the following statements about COBOL is false?
    a. COBOL has string file handling capabilities.
    b. COBOL is well standardized.
    c. COBOL is much easier to learn than machine or assembly language.
    d. COBOL is ideally suited for scientifc applications.

10-58. Which of the following statements about COBOL is false?
   a. A large, sophisticated compiler program is needed to translate a COBOL source program into machine language.
   b. COBOL tends to be "wordy."
   c. COBOL programs require extensive rewriting if computer equipment is switched.
   d. COBOL's computational abilities are limited.

10-59. Survey polls indicate that over _____ percent of business application programs are written in COBOL.
   a. 20   c. 60
   b. 40   d. 80

10-60. There are currently _____ versions of RPG.
   a. 2   c. 4
   b. 3   d. 5

10-61. RPG II, introduced in _____, has essentially replaced the original version of RPG.
   a. the late 1960s   c. the early 1960s
   b. the early 1970s   d. the late 1970s

10-62. _____ programming skill is required to use RPG.
   a. an unusually high level of
   b. a great deal of
   c. little
   d. no

10-63. RPG is used primarily with _____ computer systems.
   a. small   c. large
   b. medium   d. extra large

10-64. Which of the following statements about RPG is false?
   a. RPG is easy to learn and to use.
   b. RPG is a well-standardized language.
   c. RPG provides an efficient means for generating reports.
   d. RPG is commonly used to process files for general ledgers and inventory.

10-65. Because of the involvement and influence of _____, it is believed that Ada will someday replace COBOL as the most widely used programming language in business.
   a. Charles Babbage
   b. The U.S. Department of Defense
   c. IBM
   d. Burroughs

10-66. BASIC was developed for use by students at Dartmouth
College in
a. the mid-1950s   c. the late 1970s
b. the mid-1960s   d. the early 1970s

10-67. Which of the following statements about BASIC is false?
a. easy to learn
b. used for scientific and business applications
c. supported by most microcomputers
d. easily transported between different systems

10-68. BASIC is the language most often supported by
a. microcomputers   c. mainframe computers
b. minicomputers   d. supercomputers

10-69. Writing a BASIC program involves typing _____ types of
entries from the terminal.
a. 2   c. 4
b. 3   d. 5

10-70. In BASIC _____ are used to communicate with the
operating system.
a. programming-language statements
b. auxiliary commands
c. editing commands
d. system commands

10-71. In BASIC, GOTO, and PRINT are examples of
a. programming-language statements
b. auxiliary commands
c. editing commands
d. system commands

10-72. Which of the following statements about BASIC is false?
a. It is simple and flexible.
b. It is easy to learn.
c. It is used solely as an interactive programming
language.
d. Many manufacturers offer different versions of the
BASIC.

10-73. Logo is a procedure-oriented programming language developed by Seymour Papert _____ in 1966.
a. at the U.S. Department of Defense
b. at Harvard
c. at MIT
d. at Yale

10-74. Logo accomplishes its program of graphics by using an object called a
    a. triangle   c. fish
    b. ball   d. turtle

10-75. Which of the following statements about Logo is false?
    a. Its main advantage is simplicity.
    b. It helps the user learn to communicate with the computer.
    c. It has been developed as an education- and business-oriented language.
    d. It helps the user to learn the procedure to solve problems with a computer.

10-76. PL/I was designed to be a _____ language.
    a. procedure-oriented   c. problem-oriented
    b. scientific-oriented   d. computational-oriented

10-77. PL/I is sponsored primarily by
    a. Burroughs
    b. colleges and universities
    c. the U.S. Department of Defense
    d. IBM

10-78. PL/I combines the best features of
    a. FORTRAN and COBOL
    b. FORTRAN and BASIC
    c. COBOL and BASIC
    d. BASIC and FORTRAN

10-79. Various subsets for PL/I have been developed especially for _____ use.
    a. scientific   b. business
    c. educational   d. mathematical

10-80. PL/I was designed to be used by
    a. novice programmers only
    b. expert programmers only
    c. both novice and expert programmers
    d. programmers who know BASIC well

10-81. Which of the following statements about PL/I is false?
    a. PL/I's greatest strength is its power.
    b. PL/I is compatible with small computers.
    c. PL/I allows the use of structured programming.
    d. PL/I is well-suited for short programming projects.

10-82. Each Pascal program has _____ basic parts.
    a. 2   c. 4
    b. 3   d. 5

10-83. Pascal was originally developed in
    a. the early 1960s   c. the early 1970s
    b. the late 1960s   d. the late 1970s

10-84. Pascal seems to be a good alternative to _____ for use with microcomputers.
    a. FORTRAN   c. COBOL
    b. BASIC   d. PL/1

10-85. Which of the following statements about Pascal is false?
    a. It is suitable for structured programming.
    b. It can be used in batch and interactive modes.
    c. It is well standardized.
    d. It is relatively easy to learn.

PROGRAMMING LANGUAGES--A COMPARISON

10-86. Which of the following high-level languages has very good graphics capabilities?
    a. FORTRAN   c. COBOL
    b. PL/1   d. Pascal

10-87. Which of these phrases does not belong in the following group?
    a. Pascal   c. query language
    b. natural language   d. English-like sentences

10-88. Which of the following languages does not require significant amounts of primary storage and sophisticated hardware?
    a. COBOL   c. BASIC
    b. FORTRAN   d. APL

10-89. Which of the following languages should be selected if interactive processing is desired?
    a. APL   c. RPG
    b. Pascal   d. PL/1

10-90. Which of the following langauges should not be chosen for scientific applications?
    a. FORTRAN   c. PL/1
    b. Pascal   d. COBOL

10-91. In systems where primary storage capacity is a critical
       constraint and virtual storage capacities are not
       available, _____ the most appropriate.
       a.   assembly languages is
       b.   machine languages is
       c.   FORTRAN is
       d.   COBOL is

APPLICATION

10-92. Ohio Citizens Bank's data processing facilities utilize
       _____ mainframe computers.
       a.   2   c.   4
       b.   3   d.   5

10-93. Which of the following languages is not used by Ohio
       Citizens Bank's data processing applications?
       a.   COBOL   c.   PL/1
       b.   BASIC   d.   assembly language

ANSWER KEY

10-1.	b	10-26.	c	10-51.	a	10-76.	a
10-2.	b	10-27.	b	10-52.	c	10-77.	d
10-3.	a	10-28.	c	10-53.	a	10-78.	a
10-4.	c	10-29.	a	10-54.	b	10-79.	c
10-5.	a	10-30.	c	10-55.	d	10-80.	c
10-6.	c	10-31.	d	10-56.	a	10-81.	b
10-7.	b	10-32.	b	10-57.	d	10-82.	a
10-8.	b	10-33.	c	10-58.	c	10-83.	b
10-9.	a	10-34.	b	10-59.	d	10-84.	b
10-10.	a	10-35.	a	10-60.	b	10-85.	c
10-11.	a	10-36.	b	10-61.	b	10-86.	d
10-12.	b	10-37.	d	10-62.	c	10-87.	a
10-13.	d	10-38.	c	10-63.	a	10-88.	c
10-14.	c	10-39.	a	10-64.	b	10-89.	b
10-15.	d	10-40.	c	10-65.	b	10-90.	d
10-16.	c	10-41.	a	10-66.	b	10-91.	a
10-17.	b	10-42.	b	10-67.	d	10-92.	a
10-18.	b	10-43.	b	10-68.	a	10-93.	c
10-19.	c	10-44.	b	10-69.	b		
10-20.	c	10-45.	a	10-70.	d		
10-21.	b	10-46.	c	10-71.	a		
10-22.	a	10-47.	a	10-72.	c		
10-23.	c	10-48.	a	10-73.	c		
10-24.	a	10-49.	b	10-74.	d		
10-25.	a	10-50.	a	10-75.	c		

Structured
Design
Concepts

MULTIPLE CHOICE

THE NEED FOR STRUCTURED TECHNIQUES

11-1. In relation to hardware costs, the costs of system design
       and maintenance
       a. continue to rise dramatically
       b. remain relatively constant
       c. are beginning to drop
       d. are rising slightly

11-2. Software development
       a. is as good as it humanly can be
       b. is not an important consideration for companies
       c. lags far behind existing technology
       d. is far ahead of existing technology

11-3. In the days of UNIVAC I, the leading scientists of that
       period predicted that the world would need only _____
       computers like the UNIVAC I for the rest of time.
       a. 10   c. 30
       b. 20   d. 50

11-4. In the first generation of computers, hardware accounted
       for _____ percent of computer costs and software
       accounted for _____ percent.
       a. 60, 40   c. 80, 20
       b. 40, 60   d. 20, 80

11-5.   Today, hardware accounts for _____ percent of computer
        costs, and software accounts for _____ percent.
        a. 60, 40   c. 80, 20
        b. 40, 60   d. 20, 80

11-6.   Which of the following terms does not describe
        programming in its early days?
        a. creative   c. artistic
        b. structured   d. minimal standards

11-7.   Which of the structured techniques discussed in this
        chapter deals with the way in which the actual program is
        written?
        a. structured design   c. structured review
        b. strucuted programming   d. structured walk-through

11-8.   The data-processing community began to see an expansion
        of structured programming techniques in
        a. the late 1960s   c. the early 1980s
        b. the early 1970s   d. the late 1970s

11-9.   The structured techniques discussed in this chapter do
        not include
        a. structured review   c. structured design
        b. structured programming   d. structured processing

11-10. Which of the following will not increase the efficiency
        of a data processing department?
        a. automating the software development process
        b. requiring employees to work longer and/or harder
        c. changing software development methodologies
        d. using unstructured programming languages

11-11. Which is generally considered to be the most efficient
        way to increase software production?
        a. hire more programmers
        b. increase the hours programmers work
        c. improve software development methodology
        d. automate software development

STRUCTURED DESIGN METHODOLOGY

11-12. Which of the following is not part of a modular approach
to problem solving?
a. analyzing the problem as a whole
b. defining the problem in terms of functions to be performed
c. simplifying problems by breaking into segments, or
subunits
d. developing modules consisting of one or more logically related functions

11-13. A module is
a. a program
b. a step in a solution process
c. the entire solution to a programming problem
d. another name for a flowchart

11-14. In a top-down design, the _____ level modules contain
the greatest amount of detail.
a. lowest   c. highest and lowest
b. middle   d. highest

11-15. In top-down design, modules at the _____ level(s) contain only broad descriptions.
a. lowest   c. middle and lowest
b. middle   d. highest

11-16. What is the direction of flow in a structure chart?
a. from left to right
b. from specific to general
c. from top to bottom
d. from bottom to top

11-17. In a structure chart, each module has control of the
modules
a. directly above it
b. directly below it
c. on the same level as it is
d. of similar content

11-18. At the _____ level(s) in a top-down design, the modules
involve only processing.
a. lowest   c. middle and highest
b. middle   d. highest

11-19. Which of the following is not a rule in using top-down design?
   a. Each module should be independent of all other modules.
   b. Each module should have only two exit points.
   c. Each module should be relatively small.
   d. Each module should have only one entrance point.

11-20. A program module may
   a. be executed any number of times in a program
   b. never be over 50 lines in length
   c. be executed only once in a program
   d. be executed up to three times in a program

11-21. When a top-down design is used, a complete solution is not established until the _____ modules have been designed.
   a. lowest level   c. highest level
   b. main control   d. dummy

11-22. The use of dummy modules in top-down design permits the testing and debugging of all other modules before the _____ modules have been coded.
   a. lowest level   c. highest
   b. main control   d. processing

11-23. Which of the following is shown on a structure chart?
   a. processing flow
   b. relationship of functions
   c. order of execution
   d. how control will be transferred

11-24. Which of the following is not a typical supplement to a structure chart?
   a. record layouts   c. record flow program
   b. program flowcharts   d. system charts

11-25. Which of the following is part of a HIPO but not emphasized in a structure chart?
   a. structure   c. function
   b. modules   d. input

11-26. Which of the following is not part of typical HIPO package?
   a. detail diagram
   b. visual table of contents
   c. pseudocode
   d. overview diagram

11-27. Which type of HIPO diagram is almost identical to a
structure chart but includes some additional information?
a. detail diagram
b. visual table of contents
c. pseudocode
d. overview diagram

11-28. HIPO stands for
a. Hypothetical Input-Process-Output
b. Hierarchical Programming Output
c. Hierarchical Input-Process-Output
d. Hierarchy plus Input-Process-Output

11-29. Which type of HIPO diagram includes the modules' inputs,
processing and outputs?
a. detail diagram
b. visual table of contents
c. pseudocode
d. overview diagram

11-30. Which type of HIPO diagram describes the specific
functions performed and data items used in each module?
a. detail diagram
b. visual table of contents
c. pseudocode
d. overview diagram

11-31. Which of the following people would be the least likely
to use HIPOs?
a. analysts   c. board chairmen
b. managers   d. programmers

11-32. Which of the following statements about pseudocode is
false?
a. It is understandable even to those unfamiliar with
    program logic.
b. It does not follow rigid rules.
c. It follows a top-down design.
d. It uses symbols to represent processing steps.

11-33. In an overview diagram, the location of a particular
module within the system is indicated by
a. a certain shape   c. a color coding scheme
b. an arrow or arrows   d. a reference number

11-34. The amount of detail used in a detail diagram depends on
the _____ the problem.
a. length of   c. cost of solving
b. complexity of   d. seriousness of

11-35. A method that is becoming increasingly popular to express
program logic is
a. flowcharting   c. design review
b. diagramming   d. pseudocode

STRUCTURED PROGRAMMING

11-36. Which of the following is not an objective of structured
programming?
a. reducing testing time
b. increasing personnel
c. increasing productivity
d. decreasing maintenance time and effort

11-37. Which of the following comments would usually not apply
to structured programming?
a. well thought-out program logic
b. logic understood only by the original programmer
c. standardized model
d. benefits productivity

11-38. Structured programming increases programmer productivity
because
a. it advocates the use of branching structures
b. programs are developed in a logical, efficient way
c. it makes programming an art
d. it can only be used with structured programming
languages

11-39. Which of the following is not a basic control pattern
used in structured programming?
a. simple sequence   c. branch
b. selection   d. loop

11-40. There are _____ basic control patterns used in
structured programming.
a. 2   c. 4
b. 3   d. 5

11-41. In structured programming, program modules should not have more than one exit because
a. they take longer to write
b. they make program logic difficult to follow
c. they take longer to execute
d. the computer finds this confusing

11-42. If the number of entrances and exits of a "proper program" are added together, the total is
a. 2
b. 3
c. 4
d. 5

11-43. GOTOs are discouraged in structured programming mainly because
a. they lead to programs that are long
b. they make it difficult to follow program logic
c. they use more computer time
d. they must follow rigid programming rules

11-44. Structured programs should have _____ GOTO statements.
a. many
b. some
c. very few
d. no

11-45. Which of the following programming languages is not as well suited to structured programming as the others?
a. Pascal
b. PL/I
c. ALGOL
d. BASIC

11-46. Which of the following statements would be more true of unstructured programming than structured programming?
a. It terminates a program in a processing module.
b. Management has had difficulty in accepting its implementation.
c. Represents potential cost savings.
d. Has consistency in the passing of control.

MANAGEMENT OF SYSTEM PROJECTS

11-47. A CPT is _____ programmers under the supervision of a chief programmer.
a. two
b. twelve
c. a small number of
d. a large number of

11-48. The initials CPT stand for
a.   controlled programming team
b.   chief programmer team
c.   controlled processing team
d.   chief processing team

11-49. Which of the following goals is not a goal of the CPT
approach?
a.   to produce software that is easy to maintain
b.   to improve management productivity
c.   to produce software that is easy to modify
d.   to increase system reliability

11-50. A CPT typically consists of all the following except
a.   manager from user department
b.   librarian
c.   chief programmer
d.   lead analyst

11-51. The CPT member who is responsible for the overall success
of the project is the
a.   technical development analyst
b.   librarian
c.   lead analyst
d.   assistant to the chief programmer

11-52. The CPT member who is responsible for coding the most
critical parts of the program and helping in system
testing and evaluation is the
a.   technical development analyst
b.   librarian
c.   chief programmer
d.   assistant to the chief programmer

11-53. The CPT member who maintains a complete, up-to-date
documentation of the project is the
a.   technical development analyst
b.   librarian
c.   chief programmer
d.   assistant to the chief programmer

11-54. The CPT member who enhances communication among team
members is the
a.   technical development analyst
b.   librarian
c.   chief programmer
d.   assistant to the chief programmer

11-55. A lead analyst working with a CPT would work most closely
with the
a. technical development analyst
b. librarian
c. chief programmer
d. assistant to the chief programmer

11-56. An informal design review is usually conducted
a. in the early phases of system development
b. after the program has been largely documented
c. after the program has been coded
d. after the program has been tested

11-57. A structured walk-through is the same as
a. a formal design review
b. an informal design review
c. an egoless program review
d. a CPT review

11-58. When the system design documentation is studied by
selected managers, analysts, and programmers before the
actual coding of program modules, this is called
a. a formal design review
b. an informal design review
c. an egoless program review
d. a mid-term program review

11-59. Which of the following is not true of "egoless
programming"?
a. predetermined coding standards established
b. increase in productivity
c. de-emphasis on program review process
d. applicable to environments using programming teams

APPLICATION

11-60. Armco Inc. employs _____ people in its data processing
center in Butler, Pa.
a. 15   c. 35
b. 25   d. 55

11-61. Armco's data processing department develops all computer
systems through
a. a system study
b. a defined project life cycle
c. scheduled basis operations
d. programming modules

11-62. Which of the following is not used by the Armco data
processing department?
a. diagrams
b. coding rules
c. detailed HIPOs
d. indentation and segmentation

11-63. Which language does the Armco data processing department
use in coding?
a. Pascal   c. COBOL
b. FORTRAN   d. RPG

11-64. Which of the following is not one of the standard items
that must be included in one of Armco's UDPs?
a. data definition list and flow plan
b. coding estimates
c. documentation plans
d. test run estimates

11-65. While the UDP is being developed, the team members meet
a. daily   c. bi-weekly
b. weekly   d. monthly

ANSWER KEY

11-1.	a	11-21.	a	11-41.	b	11-61.	b
11-2.	c	11-22.	a	11-42.	a	11-62.	c
11-3.	a	11-23.	b	11-43.	b	11-63.	a
11-4.	c	11-24.	c	11-44.	c	11-64.	d
11-5.	d	11-25.	d	11-45.	d	11-65.	b
11-6.	b	11-26.	c	11-46.	a		
11-7.	b	11-27.	b	11-47.	c		
11-8.	b	11-28.	d	11-48.	b		
11-9.	d	11-29.	d	11-49.	b		
11-10.	d	11-30.	a	11-50.	a		
11-11.	c	11-31.	c	11-51.	c		
11-12.	a	11-32.	d	11-52.	d		
11-13.	b	11-33.	d	11-53.	b		
11-14.	a	11-34.	b	11-54.	b		
11-15.	d	11-35.	d	11-55.	c		
11-16.	c	11-36.	b	11-56.	a		
11-17.	b	11-37.	b	11-57.	a		
11-18.	a	11-38.	b	11-58.	b		
11-19.	b	11-39.	c	11-59.	c		
11-20.	a	11-40.	b	11-60.	c		

Application Software

12

MULTIPLE CHOICE

WORD-PROCESSING SOFTWARE

12-1.   For _____ companies the expenses associated with developing and maintaining application software have become a very significant cost of doing business.
a. small   c. medium
b. small to medium   d. medium to large

12-2.   An application software package designed to allow the user to enter, manipulate, store, and retrieve text is called
a. a word processor
b. a word processing system
c. word processing
d. dedicated word processing

12-3.   The term used to describe the process of entering, manipulating, storing, and retrieving text is called
a. a word processor
b. a word processing system
c. word processing
d. dedicated word processing

12-4.   The computer system used for entering, manipulating, storing, and retrieving text is called
a. a word processor
b. a word processing system
c. word processing
d. dedicated word processing

12-5.   When a system is used solely for word processing, it is
        called
        a.   a word processor
        b.   a word processing system
        c.   word processing
        d.   dedicated word processing

12-6.   A screen editor can be used to edit as much as _____
        lines of text at a time.
        a.   12 to 13   c.   36 to 37
        b.   24 to 25   d.   48 to 49

12-7.   A _____ can be used to edit as much as 24 to 25 lines
        of text at a time.
        a.   edit mode   c.   line editor
        b.   screen editor   d.   page editor

12-8.   The word processing mode used to make changes in text is
        the _____ mode.
        a.   edit mode   c.   single mode
        b.   print mode   d.   page mode

12-9.   When using a page-oriented word processor the user can
        display and edit _____ at a time.
        a.   one page   c.   1 to 6 pages
        b.   two pages   d.   more than 6 pages

12-10. A page-oriented word processor will permit _____ of
        text to be in internal memory at one time.
        a.   one page   c.   1 to 6 pages
        b.   two pages   d.   more than 6 pages

12-11. The type of word processor that has a reduced need to
        access secondary storage for retrieving and storing text
        is called
        a.   page-oriented word processor
        b.   line editor word processor
        c.   document-oriented word processor
        d.   screen editor word processor

12-12. Print formatting is the _____ step of word processing.
        a.   first   c.   first or second
        b.   second   d.   third

12-13. The word processors most widely used in the home fall
        into the _____ price range.
        a. $25-$50   c. $75-$150
        b. $50-$100   d. $150-$500

12-14. The cost of word processors typically used for business
       purposes falls within the _____ price range.
       a. $25-$50   c. $75-$150
       b. $50-$100   d. $150-$500

12-15. Which of the following categories does the feature "cur-
       sor positioning" fall under?
       a. writing and editing   c. character formatting
       b. screen formatting   d. print formatting

12-16. Which of the following categories does the word proc-
       essing feature "character enhancement" fall under?
       a. writing and editing   c. character formatting
       b. screen formatting   d. print formatting

12-17. Which of the following categories does the word procesing
       feature "scrolling" fall under?
       a. writing and editing   c. character formatting
       b. screen formatting   d. print formatting

12-18. The word processing feature "headers and footers" falls
       under the category called
       a. writing and editing   c. character formatting
       b. screen formatting   d. print formatting

12-19. The word processing feature "display of upper and lower
       case letters" falls under the category called
       a. writing and editing   c. character formatting
       b. screen formatting   d. print formatting

12-20. The word processing feature "status of cursor location"
       falls under the category called
       a. writing and editing   c. character formatting
       b. screen formatting   d. print formatting

12-21. The cursor position that locates the upper left-hand
       corner of the display screen is called
       a. tab   c. home
       b. top of page   d. page up

12-22. The cursor position that displays the top portion of the
       current page and positions the cursor to the first
       character is called
       a. page up   c. previous page
       b. next page   d. page down

12-23. What is the feature of a word processor that allows the user to recover text that has been accidentally deleted?
- a. search
- b. undo
- c. insertion
- d. deletion

12-24. The placing of footnotes in a formal paper using a word processor would be accomplished using the _____ feature.
- a. footer
- b. header
- c. insertion
- d. search

12-25. The _____ feature allows for underlining, boldfacing, and the use of subscript.
- a. header
- b. centering
- c. footer
- d. character enhancement

DATA-MANAGEMENT SOFTWARE

12-26. The first type of data manager that was developed was called a
- a. file handler
- b. file package
- c. data base package
- d. data base handler

12-27. The type of data manager that can access only one data file at a time is called
- a. file handler
- b. file package
- c. data base package
- d. data base handler

12-28. A large, centrally located room with file cabinet after file cabinet of information can be likened to a
- a. file handler
- b. file package
- c. data base package
- d. data base handler

12-29. A single file cabinet kept in a particular department can be likened to a
- a. file handler
- b. file package
- c. data base package
- d. data base handler

12-30. The consolidation of various independent files into one integrated whole, from which all users can have access to the information they need is possible with a
- a. file handler
- b. file package
- c. data base package
- d. data base handler

12-31. Keeping organized, readily accessible records by computerizing a manual record-keeping task is called
- a. data management
- b. file package
- c. data base package
- d. data base handler

12-32. A file handler can access _____ file(s) at a time.
  a. two   c. only one
  b. an unlimited number of   d. ten

12-33. Which of the following is the best example of both a personal use and a business use of data managers?
  a. listings of customers and suppliers
  b. library holding listings
  c. keeping inventory
  d. accounts receivable file

12-34. The data manager feature that provides the user with a
way to alter the order of storage is called
  a. sort
  b. mathematical calculations
  c. add/delete
  d. search/update

12-35. The data manager feature that enables the user to add
data to the file after that file has been created is
called
  a. sort
  b. mathematical calculations
  c. add/delete
  d. search/update

12-36. The data manager feature that enables the user to get
totals, subtotals, and means is called
  a. sort
  b. mathematical calculations
  c. add/delete
  d. search/update

12-37. The data manager feature that allows the user to find and
change an existing data file for a record is called
  a. sort
  b. mathematical calculations
  c. add/delete
  d. search/update

12-38. Most data managers offer a standard group of features
that can be selected by the user through choices from
_____ display.
  a. a search/update   c. an add/delete
  b. a menu   d. a sort

MODELING SOFTWARE

12-39. Modeling software packages used with minicomputers and mainframes are called
   a. model electronic spreadsheets
   b. electronic spreadsheets
   c. planning packages
   d. electronic planning packages

12-40. Modeling software packages used with microcomputers are called
   a. model electronic spreadsheets
   b. electronic spreadsheets
   c. planning packages
   d. electronic planning packages

12-41. If an electronic spreadsheet is as large as 254 rows by 64 columns the user can view _____ at one time.
   a. only a portion of it
   b. the whole spreadsheet
   c. only about 1/2 of the spreadsheet
   d. about 3/4 of the spreadsheet

12-42. Which of the following does not appear as frequently as the others in typical spreadsheets?
   a. labels
   b. values
   c. formulas
   d. predefined math functions

12-43. The "status area" of a spreadsheet is found at the
   a. top   c. right side
   b. bottom   d. left side

12-44. The "command area" of a spreadsheet is found at the _____ of the spreadsheet.
   a. top   c. right side
   b. bottom   d. left side

12-45. The spreadsheet feature that is very helpful when large values, large variable names, or large formulas are required is called
   a. sliding cells   c. variable column width
   b. templates   d. locking cells

12-46. The spreadsheet feature that prevents cells from being altered or destroyed is called
   a. automatic spillover   c. variable column width
   b. templates   d. locking cells

12-47. The spreadsheet feature that allows extra-long labels to
go into the next cell is called
a. automatic spillover   c. variable column width
b. templates   d. locking cells

12-48. The spreadsheet feature that eliminates the need to enter
formulas each time calculations are required is
a. automatic spillover   c. variable column width
b. templates   d. locking cells

12-49. The spreadsheet feature that permits the user to divide
the display screen into several independent displays is
called
a. titles   c. copy
b. windows   d. sort

12-50. The spreadsheet feature that eliminates the need to
retype cells that must be duplicated throughout the
spreadsheet is called
a. titles   c. copy
b. windows   d. sort

12-51. The spreadsheet feature that provides for the ordering of
information contained within the spreadsheet is called
a. titles   c. copy
b. windows   d. sort

12-52. The spreadsheet feature that allows the first column of
the spreadsheet to stay locked in place while the
remainder of the columns scrolls as desired is called
a. titles   c. copy
b. windows   d. sort

GRAPHICS SOFTWARE

12-53. Which of the following options from a graphic software
package is the most simple?
a. creating images with data on the display screen
b. selecting choices from a menu of options
c. using pixels
d. developing bar charts

12-54. The graphics software feature that eliminates the need to
create a new display screen from scratch each time one is
needed is called
a. high-resolution graphics c. cursor positioning
b. save   d. animation

12-55. The graphics software feature that provides for a greater
total number of pixels is called
a. high-resolution graphics c. cursor positioning
b. save   d. animation

12-56. The graphics software feature that may use a Koala pad or
a mouse is called
a. high-resolution graphics c. cursor positioning
b. save   d. animation

INTEGRATED SOFTWARE

12-57. Currently there _____ of viewing software integration.
a. is one way   c. are several ways
b. are two ways   d. are only a few ways

12-58. A word processor designed for use in creating legal documents is an example of
a. horizontal software integration
b. vertical software integration
c. horizontal or vertical software integration
d. neither horizontal nor vertical software integration

12-59. A word processor that can be used by anyone who desires
to manipulate text is an example of
a. horizontal software integration
b. vertical software integration
c. horizontal or vertical software integration
d. neither horizontal nor vertical software integration

12-60. Adding a spelling program to a word processor is an
example of
a. horizontal software integration
b. vertical software integration
c. horizontal or vertical software integration
d. neither horizontal nor vertical software integration

12-61. Combining application packages such as word processor,
data manager, and spreadsheet is called
a. horizontal software integration
b. vertical software integration
c. horizontal or vertical software integration
d. neither horizontal nor vertical software integration

12-62. Which of the following statements is not true about
"windows"?
a. allow the user to move from one application to
another
b. designed to be used with a pointing device
c. can provide a consistent command structure
d. are currently found primarily with minicomputers and
mainframes

APPLICATION

12-63. Which company has the most extensive range of microcomputer software products of any company in the market?
a. Sunburst Communications   c. Triton Products Company
b. Computer Skill Builders   d. Microsoft Corporation

12-64. Following the release of System Card, Microsoft produced
an inexpensive hand-held input device called
a. a Microsoft light pen   c. a Microsoft mouse
b. a Microsoft track ball   d. a Microsoft joystick

12-65. Software designers assert that _____ will be a standard
part of all computers that cost over $1,000.
a. word processing   c. data managers
b. Logo   d. graphics

12-66. To increase productivity, developers need to build or
design
a. more powerful hardware
b. a new programming language
c. better input devices
d. new software packages

ANSWER KEY

12-1.	d	12-21.	c	12-41.	a	12-61.	a
12-2.	a	12-22.	a	12-42.	d	12-62.	d
12-3.	c	12-23.	b	12-43.	a	12-63.	d
12-4.	b	12-24.	a	12-44.	b	12-64.	c
12-5.	d	12-25.	d	12-45.	c	12-65.	d
12-6.	b	12-26.	a	12-46.	d	12-66.	d
12-7.	b	12-27.	a	12-47.	a		
12-8.	a	12-28.	c	12-48.	b		
12-9.	a	12-29.	a	12-49.	b		
12-10.	a	12-30.	c	12-50.	c		
12-11.	c	12-31.	a	12-51.	d		
12-12.	b	12-32.	c	12-52.	a		
12-13.	b	12-33.	c	12-53.	b		
12-14.	d	12-34.	a	12-54.	b		
12-15.	a	12-35.	c	12-55.	a		
12-16.	d	12-36.	b	12-56.	c		
12-17.	a	12-37.	d	12-57.	b		
12-18.	d	12-38.	b	12-58.	b		
12-19.	b	12-39.	c	12-59.	a		
12-20.	b	12-40.	b	12-60.	b		

System Analysis and Design

MULTIPLE CHOICE

SYSTEM THEORY

13-1.   Although an important concept in system theory, which of
        the following is not actually part of the system itself?
        a. inputs   c. feedback
        b. processes   d. outputs

13-2.   In system theory internal or external communication can
        be referred to as
        a. inputs   c. feedback
        b. processes   d. outputs

13-3.   In system theory, the purpose of feedback is
        a. survival of the system
        b. to transform inputs into outputs
        c. to let the system know if predetermined standards and
            goals are being met
        d. bring together a group of related elements

13-4.   In system theory, a system's primary goal is
        a. feedback
        b. survival
        c. to become larger
        d. to influence other systems

13-5.   Using the "trees in the forest" analogy from the text,
        which item below is not part of a system model?
        a. accurate representation of each tree
        b. the outline of trees in the forest
        c. countryside bordering the forest's edge
        d. overall pattern of trees

13-6. A system approach to an organization is to view it
       a. from the top down
       b. from the bottom up
       c. either from the top down or the bottom up
       d. neither from the top down or the bottom up

13-7. Which of the following components is not part of devel-
       oping a system?
       a. analysis   c. preprogramming
       b. design   d. implementation

SYSTEM ANALYSIS

13-8. Which of the following is not a part of a proposal to
       conduct system analysis?
       a. a clear, concise statement of the problem
       b. a statement defining the level of system analysis
       c. an identification of the information that must be
           collected
       d. a finalized schedule for conducting the analysis

13-9. If a particular manager is not getting a report at the
       time when it is needed, the reason for conducting a
       system analysis would be to
       a. solve a problem
       b. respond to new requirements
       c. implement new technology
       d. make broad system improvements

13-10. If an increase in size or sales or a competitive incen-
       tive leads a company to update its entire information
       system, the reason for conducting a system analysis would
       be to
       a. solve a problem
       b. respond to new requirements
       c. implement new technology
       d. make broad system improvements

13-11. If a company decides to change its information system
       because of changes in data-processing technology, the
       reason for conducting a system analysis would be to
       a. solve a problem
       b. respond to new requirements
       c. implement new technology
       d. make broad system improvements

13-12. If governmental or legal regulations change, the reason
        for conducting a system analysis would be to
        a. solve a problem
        b. respond to new requirements
        c. implement new technology
        d. make broad system improvements

13-13. Which of the following is not part of the system analysis
        report?
        a. a restatement of the scope and objectives of the
            system analysis
        b. a preliminary report of feasible alternatives
        c. an estimate of the resources needed
        d. an explanation of proposed designs in both flowchart
            and narrative form

13-14. Which of the following is not considered to be an inter-
        nal source for data gathering in a system analysis?
        a. interview
        b. system flowchart
        c. manufacturers' product specifications
        d. formal report

13-15. Which of the following is not an external source for data
        gathering in a system analysis?
        a. formal reports   c. periodicals
        b. books   d. brochures

13-16. Questionnaires can be very helpful data gathering tools,
        especially if they are related to
        a. interviews   c. books
        b. formal reports   d. system flowcharts

13-17. The focus in the data gathering stage of system analysis
        is on
        a. who   c. why
        b. what   d. how

13-18. The focus in the data analysis stage of system analysis
        is on
        a. who   c. why
        b. what   d. how

13-19. Creating and maintaining an effective data base requires
        that data items be
        a. independent
        b. dependent
        c. interdependent
        d. dependent or independent but not simultaneously

13-20. System flowcharts emphasize the flow of data through the
entire data-processing system _____ describing details
of internal computer operations.
a. instead of   c. by way of
b. enumerating and   d. while

13-21. System flowcharting utilizes a _____ as a symbol for
representing input/output.
a. parallelogram   c. diamond
b. trapezoid   d. rectangle

13-22. In system flowcharting a _____ is used to represent a
manual operation such as key-to-tape data entry.
a. circle   c. triangle
b. square   d. trapezoid

13-23. In system flowcharting _____ to represent many
operations.
a. two or more process symbols must be used
b. one process symbol must be used
c. one process symbol can be used
d. many process symbols must be used

13-24. In system flowcharting the smallest number of process
symbols that can be used to represent multiple operations
is
a. 1   c. 3
b. 2   d. 4 or more

13-25. A system flowchart is to a program flowchart as
a. a world globe is to a map of the U.S.A.
b. a map of the U.S.A. is to a world globe
c. print is to newspaper
d. newspaper is to print

13-26. Which of the following is not part of a decision logic
table?
a. condition stub   c. action stub
b. flowcharting   d. action entry

13-27. Which of the following about decision logic tables is false?
    a. They are used to record facts collected during the investigation of the old system.
    b. They can be used to summarize aspects of the new system.
    c. They can be used to guide programmers in writing programs for the new system.
    d. The first step in constructing them is to determine what actions can take place.

SYSTEM DESIGN

13-28. Which of the following does not apply to system design?
    a. time consuming   c. creativity required
    b. inexpensive   d. planning required

13-29. The focus in the system design phase is on
    a. who   c. why
    b. what   d. how

13-30. Asking the question, "Are too many functions included within one subsystem?" is an example of which step in the system design phase?
    a. reviewing goals and objectives
    b. developing system model
    c. evaluating organizational constraints
    d. developing alternative designs

13-31. Restating the users' information requirements so that they reflect the needs of the majority of users, is an example of which step in the system design phase?
    a. reviewing goals and objectives
    b. developing system model
    c. evaluating organizational constraints
    d. developing alternative designs

13-32. Analyzing the human factors of system design, is an example of which step in the system design phase?
    a. reviewing goals and objectives
    b. developing system model
    c. evaluating organizational constraints
    d. developing alternative designs

13-33. Designing several possible systems in order to discover valuable parts in each that can be integrated into an entirely new system, is an example of which step in the system design phase?
   a.   reviewing goals and objectives
   b.   developing system model
   c.   evaluating organizational constraints
   d.   developing alternative designs

13-34. Observing the current sales level and predicting how much sales will increase if the new system is implemented is an example of which step in the system design phase?
   a.   performing feasibility analysis
   b.   performing cost/benefit analysis
   c.   preparing system design report and recommendation
   d.   preparing system design evaluation

13-35. Finding out that the design may require certain procedures that the organization is not staffed to handle, is an example of which step in the system design phase?
   a.   performing feasibility analysis
   b.   developing system model
   c.   evaluating organizational constraints
   d.   developing alternative designs

13-36. Explaining in general terms how the various systems will satisfy the information requirements determined in the analysis phase, is an example of which step in the system design phase?
   a.   preparing system design report
   b.   developing system model
   c.   evaluating organizational constraints
   d.   developing alternative designs

13-37. In which step of the system design phase would the analyst ask the following questions? "Are the major interactions among subsystems shown?", "Are the inputs, processes, and outputs identified appropriately?"
   a.   reviewing goals and objectives
   b.   developing system model
   c.   evaluating organizational constraints
   d.   developing alternative designs

13-38. _____ organizations request the optimal design for their information requirements.
   a.   no   c.   many
   b.   few   d.   most

13-39. The analyst may develop alternative systems in _____ of
complexity and cost for consideration by the management.
a. ascending order   c. equal order
b. descending order   d. equal amounts

13-40. In the development of alternative designs phase, _____
developed by the analyst must be technically feasible.
a. most designs   c. some designs
b. many designs   d. each design

13-41. When the analyst determines what processing is to occur
in each of the system designs, he or she often works in
conjunction with the _____ staff to determine these
requirements and to develop cost estimates.
a. managerial   c. clerical
b. programming   d. financial

13-42. Process-control measures were easier in the days
a. of batch processing
b. of online systems
c. of privacy legislation
d. before data-base specifications

13-43. Which of the following would not be found in a system
design report?
a. explanation of how the various designs will satisfy
the specific information requirements determined in
the analysis phase
b. review of the information requirements uncovered in
the system analysis
c. explanation of the proposed designs in flowchart and
narrative form
d. documentation of all designs, their subsystem, and
the function of each subsystem.

13-44. After evaluating the system design report, management can
do one of _____ things.
a. 2   c. 4
b. 3   d. 5

SYSTEM PROGRAMMING

13-45. Evaluation of software packages designed to perform tasks
similar to those required of the selected design should
be made on the basis of
a. cost
b. compatibility only
c. adaptability only
d. compatibility and adaptability

13-46. The lowest level of testing before a system becomes
operational is
a. system testing   c. desk-checking
b. program testing   d. processing test data

13-47. The level of testing before a system becomes operational
that involves checking all the application programs that
support the system is
a. system testing   c. desk-checking
b. program testing   d. processing test data

13-48. The type of testing that involves mentally tracing the
sequence of operations performed in a particular transaction is called
a. system testing   c. desk-checking
b. program testing   d. processing test data

13-49. The type of testing that involves taking a sample of
"live" data that has already been processed by the old
system and processing it in the new system is called
a. system testing   c. desk-checking
b. program testing   d. processing test data

13-50. During the _____ documentation was a very much
neglected part of system development.
a. early 1970s   c. late 1970s
b. mid-1970s   d. early 1980s

13-51. A _____ verifies that the data value is in the right
form.
a. input check   c. output check
b. type check   d. reasonableness

13-52. If the first program in the processing cycle has done
       extensive edit checks on the input data, later programs
       a. need only do very little verification
       b. need to verify also
       c. need not do verification
       d. need to verify extensively also

13-53. Edit checks must be made during the
       a. acceptance of data storage
       b. writing of data to the data base
       c. processing of data
       d. input of data

13-54. When is adequate documentation of a system most useful?
       a. during the system design stage
       b. when programmers are analyzing the situation before
          writing the programs
       c. when presenting the system design report to
          management
       d. when changes in the system are required after imple-
          mentation

SYSTEM IMPLEMENTATION

13-55. During system implementation, what two groups should be
       educated and trained with respect to the new system's
       operations?
       a. programmers and analysts
       b. operators and users
       c. operators and programmers
       d. users and managers

13-56. Operating the new system side-by-side with the old one
       for some period of time is called
       a. parallel conversion   c. phased conversion
       b. pilot conversion   d. direct conversion

13-57. Converting only a small portion of the organization to
       the new system is called
       a. parallel conversion   c. phased conversion
       b. pilot conversion   d. direct conversion

13-58. If the new system is completely different in structure
       then _____ is appropriate.
       a. parallel conversion   c. phased conversion
       b. pilot conversion   d. direct conversion

13-59. Gradually replacing the old system with the new system is
called
a. parallel conversion   c. phased conversion
b. pilot conversion   d. direct conversion

SYSTEM AUDIT AND REVIEW

13-60. After a system has been implemented entirely, which of
the following conditions is true?
a. Keeping information systems responsive to information
needs is a never-ending process.
b. Keeping information systems responsive to information
needs is performed automatically within the system.
c. It is too late to make any major changes in the
system.
d. A secret audit of the system should be performed.

13-61. Minor changes in the system should be easily accommodated
without large amounts of reprogrammng because
a. a thorough audit was completed
b. each program module is independent
c. continuous verification steps have been accomplished
d. only major errors require reprogramming

13-62. Which of the following about system maintenance is false?
a. It eliminates the need for verification procedures.
b. It detects and corrects errors.
c. It meets new information needs.
d. It responds to changes in the environment.

APPLICATION

13-63. The computer facility at Marathon Oil Company's international office in London, England is primarily concerned
with
a. the support of petroleum engineering, geophysical and
research work
b. maintenance of current systems and development of new
systems
c. updating an existing billing system
d. construction and operation of large offshore drilling
and production platforms

13-64. How many phases of system analysis and design are part of
PRIDE methodology?
a. 5   c. 4
b. 7   d. 8

13-65. Phase I of PRIDE is a feasibility study that is made up
of certain steps. Which of the following is not part of
Phase I?
a.   identifying major functions of the system
b.   project scope
c.   recommendations and concepts
d.   economics

ANSWER KEY

13-1.	c	13-21.	a	13-41.	b	13-61.	b
13-2.	c	13-22.	d	13-42.	a	13-62.	a
13-3.	c	13-23.	c	13-43.	d	13-63.	d
13-4.	b	13-24.	a	13-44.	b	13-64.	b
13-5.	a	13-25.	a	13-45.	d	13-65.	a
13-6.	a	13-26.	b	13-46.	b		
13-7.	c	13-27.	d	13-47.	a		
13-8.	d	13-28.	b	13-48.	c		
13-9.	a	13-29.	d	13-49.	d		
13-10.	d	13-30.	b	13-50.	a		
13-11.	c	13-31.	a	13-51.	b		
13-12.	b	13-32.	c	13-52.	c		
13-13.	d	13-33.	d	13-53.	d		
13-14.	c	13-34.	b	13-54.	d		
13-15.	a	13-35.	a	13-55.	b		
13-16.	a	13-36.	a	13-56.	a		
13-17.	b	13-37.	b	13-57.	b		
13-18.	c	13-38.	b	13-58.	d		
13-19.	a	13-39.	a	13-59.	c		
13-20.	a	13-40.	d	13-60.	a		

File Organization and Data Design

MULTIPLE CHOICE

FILE PROCESSING

14-1. Which of the following arrangements is correct by order
       of inclusiveness?
       a. field in record in file   c. file in field in record
       b. record in field in file   d. record in file in field

14-2. The customer file in a typical company's filing system
       would be accessed in one of _____ general ways.
       a. 2   c. 4
       b. 3   d. 5

SEQUENTIAL DESIGN

14-3. Which of the following sequences is the correct sequen-
       tial processing sequence?
       a. read the master file/process the transaction/update
           the master record/rewrite the master file
       b. update the master record/ process the
           transaction/rewrite the master file/update the master
           record
       c. process the transaction/read the master file/update
           master record/rewrite master file
       d. rewrite the master file/process the transaction/read
           the master file/update the master record

14-4.   Transactions are collected for a given time period and
        then processed against the master file in one run; this
        approach eliminates a lot of unneccessary processing and
        is called
        a.   real time processing
        b.   batch processing
        c.   online processing
        d.   direct-access processing

14-5.   In sequential processing the old master file and the
        transaction records are retained for a period of time
        because of
        a.   cost
        b.   security
        c.   historical interest and value
        d.   tradition

14-6.   In sequential processing the updated master record can be
        _____ it was before the updating occurred.
        a.   longer than
        b.   shorter than
        c.   longer, shorter, or the same as
        d.   the same as

14-7.   In sequential processing, an unmatched transaction causes
        a.   new records to be lost
        b.   old records to be verified
        c.   the program application to terminate
        d.   an entirely new record to be inserted between old
             master records or old records to be deleted from the
             master file

14-8.   Which of the following is not true about sequential
        processing?
        a.   The transaction file must be sequentially organized.
        b.   The master file must be sequentially organized.
        c.   The master file serves as input to the computer
             system.
        d.   The transaction file serves as input to the computer
             system.

14-9.   In sequential processing a "key" is used
        a.   with a master file only
        b.   with a transaction file only
        c.   with both master and transaction files
        d.   with neither master nor transaction files

14-10. Which statement is false about keys in sequential proc-
       essing?
       a. A key is used to locate a particular file.
       b. No two records have the same key value.
       c. A key must be unique.
       d. Keys are arranged sequentially.

14-11. _____ is an appropriate medium for the billing opera-
       tion application, because billing is done only at sche-
       duled intervals and the customer records can be arranged
       in customer number order.
       a. magnetic tape   c. magnetic diskette
       b. magnetic disk   d. floppy disk

14-12. Which of the following statements about sequential proc-
       essing is false?
       a. It is suitable for applications that require periodic
           updating of large numbers of records.
       b. Magnetic tape is not a suitable medium.
       c. It is simple in design.
       d. Input/output rates are higher than with direct
           keyboard input.

14-13. Which of the folowing statements about sequential proc-
       essing is true?
       a. Transactions do not have to be sorted in a particular
           sequence.
       b. It cannot handle unanticipated inquiries very well.
       c. The entire master file does not have to be processed.
       d. The design of sequential processing results in up-to-
           date current information in all cases.

14-14. Generally, it is considered efficient to use sequential
       processing when
       a. on a given processing run, at least half of the
           records are updated
       b. the records frequently need to be accessed directly
       c. it is not possible to put the records in order by
           their key
       d. inquiries on the file need to be answered quickly

DIRECT-ACCESS DESIGN

14-15. The chances of accidental destruction of data _____
       with direct-access design.
       a. are greater   c. are about the same
       b. are less   d. are minimal

14-16. Direct-access files must
   a. use inverted files
   b. be arranged in order by their key before processing
   c. be stored on magnetic disks
   d. be processed sequentially

14-17. Another name for hashing is
   a. volatility   c. updating
   b. inverting   d. randomizing

14-18. The frequency of changes to a file during a certain time
       period is called
   a. activity   c. change ratio
   b. activity records   d. volatility

14-19. A record may consist of any number of
   a. files   c. directories
   b. fields   d. lists

14-20. The proportion of records processed during an updating
       run is called
   a. activity   c. change ratio
   b. activity records   d. volatility

14-21. A direct-access system _____ that transaction records
       be sorted before they are processed.
   a. sometimes requires   c. never requires
   b. frequently requires   d. is based on the fact

14-22. The address used to find records in a direct-access
       system is usually a number from _____ digits in length
       that is related to the physical characteristics of the
       direct-access storage device.
   a. two to five   c. four to eight
   b. three to six   d. five to seven

14-23. Which of the following terms does not refer to a method
       of obtaining addresses for direct-access systems?
   a. directory   c. volatility
   b. hashing   d. randomizing

14-24. Duplicate addresses in direct-access systems is a problem
       with
   a. directory   c. tabling
   b. hashing   d. randomizing

14-25. Randomizing involves determining a disk address for a record by
   a. performing an arithmetic manipulation on the key field of the record
   b. using a directory
   c. using an inverted file
   d. searching a file sequentially until the record with the correct key is found

14-26. A _____ lists record keys along with their corresponding addresses in storage.
   a. hashing routine   c. randomizing routine
   b. directory   d. sequential file

14-27. Which of the following applications is not well suited to direct-access processing?
   a. airline reservation systems
   b. customer and supplier records
   c. savings accounts
   d. hotel-room reservation systems

14-28. Finding a particular landmark on a city map by means of coordinates is similar to
   a. using the direct-access method to processing
   b. using the sequential processing method
   c. using either the direct-access or the sequential processing method
   d. neither the direct-access nor the sequential processing method

14-29. Which of the following statements about direct-access processing is false?
   a. Transactions are processed as they occur.
   b. Chances for accidental destruction are greater.
   c. Confidential information could fall into unauthorized hands.
   d. Transactions are sorted before being processed through online terminals.

14-30. Which of the following statements is true about direct-access processing?
   a. It is somewhat inflexible in handling inquiries.
   b. It requires that the master file be read completely each time updating occurs.
   c. It takes only a fraction of a second to access to any record.
   d. Implementation is usually simple.

14-31. Using direct-access processing the original record is
_____ during processing.
a. destroyed
b. placed in a temporary file
c. modified
d. held for a maximum of two weeks

14-32. Direct-accessd processing can update _____ file(s)
concurrently.
a. only one   c. several
b. an unlimited number of   d. only two

14-33. In using _____ with direct-access file organization
some file locations may be unused.
a. directories   c. keys
b. tabling   d. randomization

14-34. _____ processing can use online terminals.
a. direct-access
b. sequential
c. direct-access and sequential
d. neither direct-access nor sequential

INDEXED-SEQUENTIAL DESIGN

14-35. When a single file must be used for both batch processing
and online processing,
a. direct-access file organization is appropriate
b. sequential file organization is appropriate
c. either direct-access or sequential file organization
is appropriate
d. neither direct-access nor sequential file organization is appropriate

14-36. In an indexed-sequential file organization an index is
the same as
a. record keys   c. corresponding addresses
b. a directory   d. divisional levels

14-37. In an indexed-sequential design the amount of searching
to locate the desired record can be reduced by
a. dividing the index into a matrix
b. adding more cells to the matirix
c. dividing the index into levels
d. adding more specific information

14-38. An indexed-sequential file allows
    a. efficient sequential processing only
    b. direct-access capability only
    c. efficient sequential processing and direct-access capability
    d. neither efficient sequential processing nor direct-access capability

14-39. The following step in preparing a customer order using an indexed-sequential processing system--"searching the customer file until a match is found between the number entered and the appropriate record"--is the _____ step in the process.
    a. first   c. third
    b. second   d. fourth

14-40. Which of the following statements about indexed-sequential design process is false?
    a. More direct-access storage place is required.
    b. They are well suited for both inquiries and large processing runs.
    c. Processing time for specific record selection is longer than in a direct-access system.
    d. Access time to specific records is apt to be somewhat slower than it would be if the file were sequentially searched.

14-41. In which of the following methods of file organization is a file not treated as a single entity?
    a. direct-access design
    b. indexed-sequential design
    c. data-base design
    d. sequential design

DATA-BASE CONCEPTS

14-42. Which of the following stores the organization's data in such a way that the same data can be accessed by multiple users for varied applications?
    a. direct-access design
    b. indexed-sequential design
    c. data-base design
    d. sequential design

14-43. A tree structure is also referred to as
    a. simple   c. inverted
    b. linear   d. hierarchical

14-44. Which of the following about the data-base approach is false?
   a. Data redundancy is minimized.
   b. An error in one input area does not impact on other data.
   c. Highly skilled and well-trained people are needed to operate it.
   d. Traditional processing jobs may run slower using it.

14-45. Which of the following is true about the data-base approach?
   a. Major attention must be given to the security of the system.
   b. Updating involves developing several copies of the data.
   c. Data can be stored for relatively few and specific applications.
   d. Data redundancy is a problem.

14-46. Which of the following serves as an interface between the data base and the data-base user?
   a. a record   c. an application program
   b. a file   d. magnetic disks

14-47. Data-base organization emphasizes
   a. logical structures
   b. physical structures
   c. logical and physical structures
   d. data dependence

14-48. Which of the following outcomes does not apply to data-base systems?
   a. reduces redundancies
   b. increases efficiency
   c. reduces flexibility
   d. increases data independence

14-49. The smallest unit in a data-base record is often called a(n)
   a. value   c. item
   b. attribute   d. file

14-50. How data is kept on storage devices and how it is accessed refers to
   a. logical design   c. physical design
   b. terminal design   d. integration design

14-51. How the data is viewed by application programmers or individual users refers to
a. logical design   c. physical design
b. terminal design   d. integration design

14-52. Which of the following concerns is addressed by the DBA team in the process of implementing the logical data design?
a. access time   c. data redundancy
b. storage constraints   d. all of the above

14-53. In data-base file organization, a logical unit can _____ physical file(s).
a. access one
b. extend across multiple
c. extend across only two
d. access no

14-54. In data-base file organization, a physical file may contain
a. up to three logical units of data
b. only one logical unit of data
c. parts of several logical units of data
d. parts of two logical units of data

14-55. A sequential record of data records is called a
a. simple structure   c. hierarchical structure
b. linear structure   d. inverted structure

14-56. A specific sequence of records is called a
a. simple structure   c. hierarchical structure
b. linear structure   d. inverted structure

14-57. In a tree structure how many owner records may a member record have?
a. 0   c. a maximum of 2
b. as many as are needed   d. 1

14-58. The structure that is well suited to responding to unanticipated inquiries is
a. simple structure   c. hierarchical structure
b. linear structure   d. inverted structure

14-59. The structure that subdivides lists into groups is
a. simple structure   c. hierarchical structure
b. linear structure   d. inverted structure

14-60. The structure that enables a variety of inquiries to be handled quickly and efficiently is called
    a. simple structure   c. hierarchical structure
    b. linear structure   d. inverted structure

14-61. The structure which is complex but suitable for applications that require multiple linkages among data items is
    a. network structure   c. tree structure
    b. inverted structure   d. linear structure

14-62. In a DBMS the programmer does not have to pay attention to
    a. the logical nature of a file
    b. the physical nature of a file
    c. the relationships among data items
    d. the user's needs

14-63. Which of the following is not a facility that is typically provided by DBMs?
    a. integration of data into physical structures that model the hypothetical relationships among data items
    b. provision for privacy controls
    c. provision for storing the volume of data required to meet needs of multiple uses
    d. controls to present unintended interaction among programs

APPLICATION

14-64. At the Spicer Transmission Division of Dana Corporation, most application programs are written in
    a. COBOL   c. Pascal
    b. FORTRAN   d. BASIC

14-65. An example of an online/direct-access system used by the Spicer Transmission Division is the one used to
    a. produce inventory shortage and overage reports
    b. develop the payroll system
    c. plan production schedules
    d. enter sales orders

ANSWER KEY

14-1.	a	14-21.	c	14-41.	c	14-61.	a
14-2.	a	14-22.	d	14-42.	c	14-62.	b
14-3.	c	14-23.	c	14-43.	d	14-63.	a
14-4.	b	14-24.	d	14-44.	b	14-64.	a
14-5.	b	14-25.	a	14-45.	a	14-65.	d
14-6.	c	14-26.	b	14-46.	c		
14-7.	d	14-27.	b	14-47.	a		
14-8.	a	14-28.	a	14-48.	c		
14-9.	c	14-29.	d	14-49.	b		
14-10.	a	14-30.	c	14-50.	c		
14-11.	a	14-31.	a	14-51.	a		
14-12.	b	14-32.	c	14-52.	d		
14-13.	b	14-33.	d	14-53.	b		
14-14.	a	14-34.	a	14-54.	c		
14-15.	a	14-35.	d	14-55.	a		
14-16.	c	14-36.	b	14-56.	b		
14-17.	d	14-37.	c	14-57.	d		
14-18.	d	14-38.	c	14-58.	d		
14-19.	b	14-39.	b	14-59.	c		
14-20.	a	14-40.	d	14-60.	d		

Management Information and Decision Support Systems

MULTIPLE CHOICE

ELEMENTS OF MANAGEMENT INFORMATION SYSTEMS

15-1.   Establishing goals and determining strategies is the
        responsibility of _____ management.
        a. lower-level   c. top-level
        b. middle-level   d. any level of

15-2.   Scheduling production and formulating budgets are
        examples of _____ management.
        a. lower-level   c. top-level
        b. middle-level   d. any level of

15-3.   Maintaining inventory records and assigning jobs to
        workers are examples of _____ management.
        a. lower-level   c. top-level
        b. middle-level   d. any level of

15-4.   Operational decision making is the responsibility of
        _____ management.
        a. lower-level   c. top-level
        b. middle-level   d. any level of

15-5.   Tactical decision making is the responsibility of _____
        management.
        a. lower-level   c. top-level
        b. middle-level   d. any level of

15-6. Strategic decision making is the responsibility of
       _____ management.
       a. lower-level   c. top-level
       b. middle-level   d. any level of

15-7. The needs of _____ management can be met through admin-
       istrative data processing activities such as the prep-
       aration of financial statements.
       a. lower-level   c. top-level
       b. middle-level   d. any level of

15-8. The high use of internal information characterizes the
       decision making process at the _____ management
       level.
       a. lower-level   c. top-level
       b. middle-level   d. any level of

15-9. If information is faulty at the _____ management level,
       the organization faces an immediate crisis.
       a. lower-level   c. top-level
       b. middle-level   d. any level of

15-10. The main problems of MIS design relate to the information
       requirements of _____ management.
       a. lower-level   c. top-level
       b. middle-level   d. any level of

15-11. The information needs of _____ management are not
       involved when data are organized to provide query capa-
       bilities across functional lines.
       a. lower-level   c. top-level
       b. middle-level   d. any level of

15-12. Well-designed management information systems can help
       _____ management.
       a. lower-level   c. top-level
       b. middle-level   d. any level of

15-13. Which of the following is not involved with typical data-
       processing activities?
       a. management information system
       b. collecting data
       c. producing reports
       d. manipulating data

15-14. Which of the following is false? Managers have found
       computers to be helpful in data processing because
       typical data-processing activities can be done
       a. faster
       b. more accurately
       c. completely by the computer
       d. at a lower cost

15-15. Which of the following is not a primary goal of MIS?
       a. provide correct information
       b. provide managers with appropriate information
       c. provide information in a timely manner
       d. reduce the cost of providing information

15-16. Which of the following adjectives does not necessarily
       describe information in a decision-oriented report?
       a. concise   c. complete
       b. inexpensive   d. timely

15-17. Which of the following is not a provision of an organiza-
       tion's management information system no matter what types
       of operations it performs?
       a. reports that are decision-oriented
       b. results that the user needs
       c. room for expansion and growth
       d. ability to handle at least a few of the potential
           increases in user requirements

15-18. The level of decision making which is characterized by
       the following description is found in _____ management.
           Time Horizon = weekly/monthly
           Degree of Structure = moderate
           Use of External Information = moderate
           Use of Internal Information = high
           Degree of Judgment = moderate
           Information Online = high
           Level of Complexity = moderate
           Information in Real Time = high
       a. lower-level   c. top-level
       b. middle-level   d. any level of

DECISION-ORIENTED REPORTING

15-19. The type of information report that is produced at regu-
       lar intervals and provides routine information to a wide
       variety of users is
       a. an exception report   c. a demand report
       b. a scheduled listing   d. a predictive report

15-20. The type of information report that is considered an action oriented management report and focuses attention on situations which require special handling is
   a. an exception report   c. a demand report
   b. a scheduled listing   d. a predictive report

15-21. The type of information report that projects future results based on decision models is
   a. an exception report   c. a demand report
   b. a scheduled listing   d. a predictive report

15-22. The type of information reports that are not required on a regular basis but are produced upon request are called
   a. exception reports   c. demand reports
   b. scheduled listings   d. predictive reports

15-23. The type of information report that is likely to be expensive is
   a. an exception report   c. a demand report
   b. a scheduled listing   d. a predictive report

15-24. "What if" models, suited to tactical and strategic decision making, are appropriate for
   a. an exception report   c. a demand report
   b. a scheduled listing   d. a predictive report

15-25. In designing MIS the analyst should rely on _____ to determine information requirements.
   a. his/her training
   b. his/her judgment
   c. the manager/user
   d. the system's technical manual

DECISION SUPPORT SYSTEMS

15-26. The relationship between DSS and MIS can be described as follows:
   a. MIS relates to systems that emphasize structured operations and DSS focuses on unstructured decision-making
   b. MIS's are only subsystems of the larger DSS
   c. MIS relates to systems that emphasize unstructured operations and DSS focuses on structured decision-making
   d. there is no relationship

15-27. Which of the following terms does not belong with the others?
   a. DSS
   b. tactical decision making
   c. operational decision making
   d. strategic decision making

15-28. Which of the following is the primary use of computer technology within DSS?
   a. increasing the speed at which large amounts of data can be processed
   b. improving the effectiveness of decision making
   c. improving the quality of decision making
   d. increasing the number of alternatives to be considered

15-29. Which of the following statements about a model is not true?
   a. the manager is responsible for its development
   b. it contains independent variables
   c. it represents the manager's perceptions of how the system works
   d. it is a conceptual representation of a hypothetical world

15-30. _____ is a commercial software package that models various marketing relationships using a predefined model.
   a. ADBUDG   c. MEDIAC
   b. BRANDAID   d. CALLPLAN

15-31. The commercial software package that aids in the allocation of a sales force is
   a. ADBUDG   c. MEDIAC
   b. BRANDAID   d. CALLPLAN

15-32. The commercial software package that helps to prepare advertising media schedules is
   a. ADBUDG   c. MEDIAC
   b. BRANDAID   d. CALLPLAN

15-33. The commercial software package that helps in preparing marketing plans is
   a. ADBUDG   c. MEDIAC
   b. BRANDAID   d. CALLPLAN

15-34. Such applications as balance sheet and income statement
       preparation, operating budgets, forecasting, and risk
       analysis are uses for
       a. IFPS
       b. EXECUCOM
       c. MEDIAC
       d. MARKETPLAN

15-35. A commercial software package which can be used in a
       similar fashion as IFPS is
       a. EXECUCOM
       b. VISICALC
       c. MEDIAC
       d. MUTPAN

15-36. Currently commercial software packages that can be used
       in a similar fashion as IFPS are available for
       a. microcomputers
       b. minicomputers
       c. mainframe computers
       d. microcomputers and minicomputers

15-37. Which of the following statements about simulation is
       false?
       a. It is used to identify all variables.
       b. It is used to identify optimal solutions for decision
          alternatives.
       c. It is used to analyze the effects of changing key
          variables.
       d. It eliminates the need to experiment with a real-
          world system.

15-38. The type of simulation that is used to identify those
       sensitive variables that warrant management's attention
       is called
       a. "what if" analysis
       b. sensitivity analysis
       c. goal seeking
       d. identity analysis

15-39. The type of simulation that allows the manager to
       interactively process various decision alternatives is
       called
       a. "what if" analysis
       b. sensitivity analysis
       c. goal seeking
       d. identity analysis

15-40. The type of simulation that allows the manager to select
       an independent variable that can be altered to achieve a
       given output from the decision model is called
       a. "what if" analysis
       b. sensitivity analysis
       c. goal seeking
       d. identity analysis

15-41. The type of simulation that allows the manager to select
an independent variable that can be altered to achieve
a given output from the decision model is called
a. "what if" analysis   c. goal seeking
b. sensitivity analysis   d. identity analysis

15-42. The key factor in the acceptance of DSS within business
is
a. cost   c. efficiency
b. management   d. accuracy

15-43. Which of the following is not a major obstacle to the
adoption of DSSs by businesses?
a. resistance
b. lack of sophistication
c. interdepartmental communication problems
d. incomplete software development

15-44. A DSS can be found
a. in each functional area of an organization
b. in most areas of an organization
c. usually in one area of an organization
d. typically in 50% of the organization's functional
areas

15-45. Simultaneous DSSs have begun to be referred to in the
past _____ years.
a. 2   c. 10
b. 5   d. 15

15-46. Another term used to refer to a simultaneous DSS is
a. combination planning model
b. corporate planning model
c. functional planning model
d. simultaneous planning model

15-47. Which of the following about a model is false?
a. must be all-inclusive
b. is a mathematical representation of an actual system
c. is the heart of a DSS
d. represents the perception of its developer

DESIGN ALTERNATIVES

15-48. There are _____ basic design structures to choose from
when designing a MIS.
a. 2   c. 6
b. 4   d. 8

15-49. The MIS basic design structures are
   a. checkpoints along a continuous range of design alternatives
   b. separate options
   c. mutually exclusive alternatives
   d. none of the above

15-50. The most traditional design approach is
   a. hierarchical   c. centralized
   b. distributed   d. decentralized

15-51. The design used when the organization consists of multiple levels with varying degrees of responsibility and decision making authority is called
   a. hierarchical   c. centralized
   b. distributed   d. decentralized

15-52. The MIS design alternative that identifies the existence of independent operating units but recognizes the benefits of central coordination and control is called
   a. hierarchical   c. centralized
   b. distributed   d. decentralized

15-53. The MIS design alternative that places authority and responsibility for computer support in relatively autonomous organizational units is called
   a. hierarchical   c. centralized
   b. distributed   d. decentralized

15-54. The MIS design alternative that breaks the organization into the smallest activity centers requiring computer support is called
   a. hierarchical   c. centralized
   b. distributed   d. decentralized

15-55. The MIS design alternative in which the authority for computer operations goes directly to the managers in charge of the operating units is called
   a. hierarchical   c. centralized
   b. distributed   d. decentralized

15-56. The MIS design alternative in which all program development is controlled by the EDP group is called
   a. hierarchical   c. centralized
   b. distributed   d. decentralized

15-57. The MIS design alternative in which each management level
is given the computer power necessary to support its task
objectives is called
a. hierarchical   c. centralized
b. distributed   d. decentralized

15-58. The MIS design alternative in which data bases are
usually segregated along regional or functional lines is
called
a. hierarchical   c. centralized
b. distributed   d. decentralized

15-59. The MIS design alternative that permits economies of
scale, eliminates redundancy and duplication of data, and
results in efficient utilization of data-processing capability is called
a. hierarchical   c. centralized
b. distributed   d. decentralized

15-60. The MIS design alternative in which communication among
units is limited, thereby ruling out the possibility of
common or shared applications, is
a. hierarchical   c. centralized
b. distributed   d. decentralized

15-61. The MIS design alternative that is not highly compatible
with the MIS concept is called
a. hierarchical   c. centralized
b. distributed   d. decentralized

APPLICATION

15-62. Most of the computers used by Ford Motor Company for
business applications are
a. super computers   c. mainframes
b. microcomputers   d. minicomputers

15-63. A system has been developed by Ford Parts and Service
Division to get parts from PDCs to dealers quickly. An
individual dealer has four ordering alternatives. Which
one is not a choice?
a. monthly stock order   c. a priority order
b. an interim order   d. inoperable vehicle order

15-64. The development of Computer Systems has helped Ford management to improve operations related to
a. research and development c. future designs
b. customer service   d. increased sales

15-65. The Ford parts distribution system was designed for real time operation to help dealers. For which function was it not designed?
a.   normal stock reordering
b.   to help dealers get out-of-stock parts
c.   to provide up-to-date inventory information
d.   to order newly designed parts for stock

ANSWER KEY

15-1.	c	15-21.	d	15-41.	c	15-61.	d
15-2.	b	15-22.	c	15-42.	b	15-62.	b
15-3.	a	15-23.	c	15-43.	d	15-63.	a
15-4.	a	15-24.	d	15-44.	a	15-64.	b
15-5.	b	15-25.	c	15-45.	c	15-65.	d
15-6.	c	15-26.	a	15-46.	b		
15-7	b	15-27.	c	15-47.	a		
15-8.	b	15-28.	a	15-48.	b		
15-9	a	15-29.	d	15-49.	a		
15-10.	c	15-30.	a	15-50.	c		
15-11.	a	15-31.	d	15-51.	a		
15-12.	d	15-32.	c	15-52.	b		
15-13.	a	15-33.	b	15-53.	d		
15-14.	c	15-34.	a	15-54.	b		
15-15.	d	15-35.	b	15-55.	d		
15-16.	b	15-36.	a	15-56.	c		
15-17.	d	15-37.	a	15-57.	a		
15-18.	b	15-38.	b	15-58.	a		
15-19.	b	15-39.	a	15-59.	c		
15-20.	a	15-40.	c	15-60.	d		

The Impact of Computers on People and Organizations

MULTIPLE CHOICE

BEHAVIOR ASPECTS

16-1.   The computer revolution has had _____ negative effects
on people and organizations.
a. some   c. totally
b. many   d. no

16-2.   Which of the following phenomena has been found not to be
related to computer anxiety?
a. jargon
b. depersonalization
c. age
d. all of the above are related

16-3.   Women with degrees in computer science earn nearly
_____ percent of the salary that men holding a similar
position earn.
a. 75   c. 100
b. 50   d. 150

16-4.   Women account for about _____ percent of computer professionals.
a. 10   c. 50
b. 25   d. 75

16-5.   In 1980 the National Science Foundation reported that
there were approximately _____ female computer specialists.
a. 90,000   c. 50,000
b. 75,000   d. 25,000

16-6. Between 1978 and 1980 the number of women who were identified as computer specialists by the National Science
Foundation grew _____ percent.
a. 12   c. 33
b. 22   d. 44

16-7. Which of the following components is not considered
necessary for one to be computer literate?
a. knowledge of the functions of hardware components
b. knowledge of COBOL, FORTRAN, or PL/I
c. knowledge of basic programming techniques
d. knowledge of the effects of computers on society

16-8. The Federal Commission on Excellence in Education recommended in 1983 that all students be required to take
a. a full year of computer science in high school
b. computer literacy classes in grades K-12
c. a half year of computer science in high school
d. computer literacy classes in grades 9-12

16-9. The Excellence in Education Commission's recommendation
relative to computer literacy was
a. highly controversial
b. agreed to readily by the general public
c. rejected by the majority of school board members
d. rejected by the general public

16-10. Research evidence over the last _____ years does not
indicate that increased automation leads to increased
unemployment.
a. 75   c. 30
b. 60   d. 50

16-11. People who fear the effects computers have on their lives
and on society in general are said to be suffering from
a. computer literacy   c. ergonomics
b. computer anxiety   d. displacement

16-12. Which of the following is not a major factor influencing
worker displacement?
a. the goals that are sought from the use of the computer
b. the availability of formal retraining opportunities
c. the organization's growth rate
d. the planning that has gone into the acquisition and
use of the computer

16-13. The method of researching and designing computer hardware
and software to enhance employee productivity and comfort
is called
a. ergonomics
b. job displacement
c. computer phobia
d. system analysis and design

16-14. The area of work that has seen the greatest change and
offers the greatest potential for automation is
a. the office   c. the schools
b. the factory   d. the military

16-15. The agricultural business that seems to be most likely to
benefit from computerization is
a. fruit raising   c. dairy farming
b. crop raising   d. cattle ranching

16-16. The biggest complaint of office workers in automated
offices is
a. potential dangers from radiation
b. backstrain
c. neck pain
d. eyestrain

16-17. In order to reduce physical problems, it is recommended
that the time a worker spends at a CRT be reduced to a
maximum of _____ hours of continuous screen work per
day.
a. 2   c. 4
b. 3   d. 5

16-18. The application of ergonomics to workstations has
resulted in a _____ percent improvement in performance
in some offices.
a. 5-10   c. 10-25
b. 10-15   d. 25-50

OFFICE AUTOMATION

16-19. It is estimated that _____ percent of U.S. companies
employ some type of word processing.
a. 25   c. 75
b. 50   d. 90

16-20. The use of word processing can increase a secretary's
       productivity _____ percent.
       a. 10-50   c. 50-100
       b. 25-50   d. 25-200

16-21. Current word-processing techniques apply _____ of com-
       puter capabilities.
       a. about 90%   c. about 50%
       b. a tiny fraction   d. about 75%

16-22. There are _____ basic forms of electronic mail.
       a. 2   c. 6
       b. 4   d. 8

16-23. Which of the following is not a form of electronic mail?
       a. teletypewriter systems   c. teleconferencing systems
       b. facsimile systems   d. voice message systems

16-24. Which of the following statements about electronic mail
       is false?
       a. It is used primarily for internal communications.
       b. It stores messages in a special storage area for up
           to 24 hours before canceling if it has not been
           received.
       c. It is used primarily for routine communication.
       d. It may replace the traditional post office in the
           future.

16-25. There are currently _____ forms of teleconferencing.
       a. 2   c. 4
       b. 3   d. 5

16-26. The form of teleconferencing that is a conference call
       linking two or three people is called
       a. computer conferencing   c. video seminars
       b. audio conferencing   d. video conferencing

16-27. The form of teleconferencing that is well suited to
       ongoing meetings among a number of people where par-
       ticipants need not attend at the same time is called
       a. computer conferencing   c. video seminars
       b. audio conferencing   d. video conferencing

16-28. The form of teleconferencing that employs one-way, full-
       motion video with two-way audio is called
       a. computer conferencing   c. video seminars
       b. audio conferencing   d. video conferencing

16-29. The form of teleconferencing that employs a two-way, full-motion video plus a two-way audio system is called
    a. computer conferencing   c. video seminars
    b. audio conferencing   d. video conferencing

16-30. The form of teleconferencing that has been found to reduce decision-making time considerably is called
    a. computer conferencing   c. video seminars
    b. audio conferencing   d. video conferencing

16-31. The form of teleconferencing that provides an effective simulation of face-to-face communication and is well suited for use by planning groups who want a full sense of participation is called
    a. computer conferencing   c. video seminars
    b. audio conferencing   d. video conferencing

16-32. Using a computer connected to the office from home via leased phone lines is called
    a. telecommuting   c. computer conferencing
    b. audio conferencing   d. teleconferencing

16-33. Saving research time by accessing online data bases through subscriptions to online information services is called
    a. telecommuting   c. telecomputing
    b. telecommunicating   d. teleconferencing

16-34. Which of the following is not an example of an online information service?
    a. CompuServe   c. AccuServe
    b. The Source   d. Dow Jones News/Retrieval

16-35. Service time from an online information service typically costs _____ per hour depending on the time of day.
    a. from $2 to $5   c. from $5 to $25
    b. from $50 to $100   d. from $50 to $75

16-36. Which of the following pieces of equipment is not needed to use an online information service?
    a. printer
    b. modem
    c. communications software package
    d. computer

16-37. A local area network (LAN) has stations that are linked by
    a. telephone lines   c. telegraph lines
    b. cable   d. satellite

16-38. Typically workstations in LANs cannot be located more
       than
       a. one mile apart   c. three miles apart
       b. two miles apart   d. four miles apart

16-39. LANs are classified on_____ different bases.
       a. two   c. four
       b. three   d. five

16-40. The LAN that is comprised of a central station with
       multiple stations connected to it is a _____ network.
       a. bus   c. star
       b. ring   d. center

16-41. The LAN that has multiple stations connected to a main
       communication line is a _____ network.
       a. bus   c. star
       b. ring   d. center

16-42. The LAN that is comprised of multiple stations each con-
       nected to its adjacent station is a _____ network.
       a. bus   c. star
       b. ring   d. center

COMPUTERS IN BUSINESS AND INDUSTRY

16-43. The greatest impact of computers on our society has been
       in
       a. government   c. the home
       b. education   d. business and industry

16-44. Which of the following is not an area in which computers
       are used in most businesses?
       a. marketing and sales
       b. personnel recruitment and selection
       c. accounting and finance
       d. management

16-45. The first business software to be offered for personal
       computers was in
       a. accounting   c. finance
       b. marketing   d. management

16-46. The most common use of the computer in financial analysis
       is
       a. electronic mail   c. electronic spreadsheet
       b. word processing   d. teleconferencing

16-47. Computerized graphic displays of data can help managers
to focus on the _____ percent core data that they need
to make decisions.
a.   10   c.   25
b.   20   d.   50

16-48. Industry uses computers in the designing and manufacturing of products through the use of robotics and
a.   CAD/CAM   c.   DSS
b.   teleconferencing   d.   electronic spreadsheets

16-49. American factories have over _____ robots at work.
a.   4,000   c.   10,000
b.   6,000   d.   20,000

16-50. It is expected that by 1990 there will be nearly _____
robots working in American factories.
a.   75,000   c.   150,000
b.   100,000   d.   200,000

16-51. Which of the following companies is not one of the three
leading users of industrial robots?
a.   General Motors   c.   Westinghouse
b.   General Electric   d.   Ford

16-52. When the industrial engineer uses the computer to analyze
the product and in the manufacturing process, he/she is
using
a.   CAD   c.   CAD/CAM
b.   CAM   d.   CAI

16-53. How many generations of robots have evolved so far?
a.   one   c.   three
b.   two   d.   four

16-54. Robots that possess tactile sense or crude vision are
part of the _____ generation.
a.   first   c.   third
b.   second   d.   fourth

16-55. The largest single user of computers in the U.S.A. is
a.   the federal government
b.   business
c.   industry
d.   the country's colleges and universities

16-56. Using a computer to forecast weather is an example of
a.   CAD/CAM   c.   robotics
b.   computer modeling   d.   an MIS system

16-57. How many satellites does the National Weather Service
       employ to send pictures revealing the movement and shape
       of the clouds?
       a.   two   c.   four
       b.   three   d.   five

16-58. The National Weather Service's "brain" consists of
       _____ computers housed at the meteorological center.
       a.   three   c.   ten
       b.   seven   d.   fourteen

16-59. Computers enable the National Weather Service to make
       _____ weather reports daily to local weather offices.
       a.   100   c.   1,000
       b.   500   d.   2,000

16-60. Which of the following is not one of the federal govern-
       ment's three largest data bases?
       a.   FBI   c.   CIA
       b.   IRS   d.   Library of Congress

16-61. The computer system used by the Library of Congress con-
       verts library cards into digital images on optical disks
       developed by
       a.   Xerox   c.   Burroughs
       b.   IBM   d.   Control Data

16-62. Each of the optical disks used by the Library of Congress
       holds about _____ library cards.
       a.   50,000   c.   200,000
       b.   100,000   d.   300,000

16-63. The FBI plans to have all of its offices connected to
       computer-accessed data bases by
       a.   the end of the 1980s   c.   1995
       b.   mid 1980s   d.   the year 2000

APPLICATION

16-64. Prudential Property and Casualty Insurance Company
       (PRUPAC) maintains certain information in online data
       bases. Which is not included?
       a.   claims files
       b.   policy holder records
       c.   billing systems
       d.   information about other insurance companies' rates

16-65. When word processors were introduced in a noncomputer environment in PRUPAC, the people using the new equipment went through a variety of emotional stages in relation to the equipment. Which one was not a stage discussed in the application?
    a.   rejection   c.   anger
    b.   high anxiety   d.   delighted acceptance

16-66. Which item does not describe the "hand-held computer"?
    a.   "user friendly"
    b.   small size
    c.   quick speed in calculating data
    d.   very expensive

ANSWER KEY

16-1.	a	16-21.	b	16-41.	a	16-61.	a
16-2.	d	16-22.	a	16-42.	b	16-62.	c
16-3.	c	16-23.	c	16-43.	d	16-63.	a
16-4.	b	16-24.	b	16-44.	b	16-64.	d
16-5.	a	16-25.	d	16-45.	a	16-65.	a
16-6.	d	16-26.	b	16-46.	c	16-66.	d
16-7	b	16-27.	a	16-47.	b		
16-8.	c	16-28.	c	16-48.	a		
16-9	b	16-29.	d	16-49.	b		
16-10.	c	16-30.	a	16-50.	c		
16-11.	b	16-31.	d	16-51.	d		
16-12.	b	16-32.	a	16-52.	c		
16-13.	a	16-33.	c	16-53.	b		
16-14.	a	16-34.	c	16-54.	b		
16-15.	c	16-35.	c	16-55.	a		
16-16.	d	16-36.	a	16-56.	b		
16-17.	a	16-37.	b	16-57.	a		
16-18.	b	16-38.	b	16-58.	d		
16-19.	c	16-39.	b	16-59.	d		
16-20.	d	16-40.	c	16-60.	c		

Computer Security, Crime, Ethics, and the Law

MULTIPLE CHIOCE

COMPUTER CRIME AND SECURITY

17-1. Many crimes committed with a computer
     a.   are never reported and are hard to discover
     b.   are extremely violent
     c.   are usually performed by hardened criminals
     d.   cause very little monetary damage

17-2. Which response is not a true statement about computer crime?
     a.   A criminal act that poses a greater threat to a computer user than it would to a noncomputer user.
     b.   A criminal act that poses a greater threat to a noncomputer user than a computer user.
     c.   Computer crime is generally classified as white-collar crime.
     d.   The computer is used to perpetrate acts of deceit and theft.

17-3. Which characteristic does not generally describe the computer criminal?
     a.   young and ambitious   c.   well educated
     b.   technically competent   d.   blue collar worker

17-4. Which response is not one of the four broad categories of computer crimes?
     a.   sabotage   c.   violent crimes
     b.   property crimes   d.   theft of services

17-5.   _____ of computers results in destruction or damage of computer hardware.
    a. property crimes   c. sabotage
    b. financial crimes   d. theft of services

17-6.   Which of the following is false in regards to the occurrence of sabotage to a computer system?
    a. It can occur during periods of political unrest.
    b. Dissatisfied or fired employees may sabotage a company's sytem.
    c. It requires technical competence to sabotage a computer system.
    d. It results in destruction of damage of computer hardware.

17-7.   _____ crimes involve unauthorized computer use after or during working hours.
    a. theft of services   c. property crimes
    b. financial crimes   d. sabotage

17-8.   _____ systems have been exposed to great amounts of abuse because of poor security precautions.
    a. time-sharing   c. employee financial
    b. time-management   d. information

17-9.   Which response about a time-sharing system is false?
    a. It is easy to gain access to a time-sharing system.
    b. Most require passwords to gain access.
    c. Access codes are changed regularly.
    d. Security precautions are minimal.

17-10. _____ is another technique used to gain access to a time-sharing system.
    a. wiretapping
    b. a special password
    c. a special program
    d. use of an add-on peripheral

17-11. Besides using a password, another way to gain access to a time-sharing system is to
    a. encrypt the system's code
    b. conduct a free-lance service
    c. request the system's data base
    d. wiretap the system

17-12. _____ includes theft of the computer equipment itself.
    a. financial crime   c. theft of services
    b. property crime   d. wiretapping

434   COMPUTERS AND DATA PROCESSING

17-13. Which response about theft of property is false?
    a. It frequently involves merchandise of a company whose
        orders are processed by a computer.
    b. These crimes are usually committed by internal
        personnel.
    c. The theft may extend to software.
    d. This type of theft does not include money actually
        paid by the company for nonexistent merchandise.

17-14. _____ is the most serious in terms of monetary loss
    a. property crime   c. theft of services
    b. financial crime   d. sabotage

17-15. Concerning theft of property, different courts have come
    to different conclusions about
    a. whether "round-off fraud" should be considered a
        theft of property crime
    b. whether actual merchandise should be included in this
        form of crime
    c. whether this kind of theft is limited to those within
        a company's structure
    d. the definition of the property to be included in this
        category

17-16. Which response is a false statement about the use of
    checks and financial crimes?
    a. Checks can be manipulated in a number of ways.
    b. Multiple checks can be made out to the same person.
    c. Checks can be rerouted to a false address.
    d. This is not a common method of committing financial
        crime.

17-17. "Round-off fraud" is a form of _____ computer crime.
    a. property   c. sabotage
    b. financial   d. theft of services

17-18. Which response is a false statement about electronic
    crime?
    a. Input to the computer is manipulated.
    b. Computer programs are altered.
    c. Data is stolen.
    d. Computer time remains intact.

17-19. Possibilities for computer crime seem
    a. almost nonexistent   c. to be increasing
    b. on the down side   d. to be endless

17-20. Solving computer crime, according to lawmakers, seems to depend on
a.   luck
b.   the number of convictions
c.   the computer's ability to make statistical analyses
d.   wiretapping capabilities

17-21. Businesses that have suffered losses due to computer crimes
a.   fear disclosure will undermine investor confidence
b.   often publicize the details of the crime
c.   seldom discover the loss
d.   oppose laws restricting computer use

17-22. The computer's capability _____ has been called on in New York City to help authorities determine which buildings are likely targets for arson.
a.   in graphics
b.   in voice recognition
c.   in expert systems
d.   to make statistical analysis

17-23. A computerized crime predictor that has been the object of criticism and is maintained by the FBI
a.   is part of a worldwide communication network
b.   tracks known criminals and monitors those considered to be threats to officials
c.   works in conjunction with the IRS
d.   has been used to track unpopular politicians

17-24. What worries people about the Justice Department's use of the FBI's National Crime Information Center is that
a.   it is not adequate in predicting who could be a dangerous criminal
b.   the Justice Department uses the system to check up on people who are considered threats to officials, but who have never committed a crime
c.   it is a new untested system and could provide incorrect results
d.   it is not available to state and local justice agencies

17-25. The Atlanta police force set up a(n) _____ to help solve a series of 28 murders.
a.   evidence analysis system   c.   data base
b.   polygraph testing system   d.   computer graphics system

17-26. Which response is not a physical threat to computer security?
a. fire
b. natural disaster
c. environmental problems
d. data tampering

17-27. Which response about fire as a physical threat to computer security is false?
a. Water cannot be used to extinguish fire.
b. Carbon-dioxide fire-extinguisher systems are hazardous to employees.
c. Combustible materials are not used around computer installations.
d. Halon extinguishers are expensive.

17-28. Which of the following is not considered a natural disaster that might threaten computer centers?
a. flood
b. cyclone
c. power failures
d. earthquakes

17-29. Which of the following is not classified as an environmental problem that threatens computer centers?
a. bursting pipes
b. magnetic fields made by electric motors
c. external radiation
d. wiretapping

17-30. Which physical threat poses the greatest risk to computer installations?
a. environmental problems
b. fire
c. sabotage
d. natural disaster

17-31. Which of the following is not an example of sabotage?
a. magnets used to scramble codes on tapes
b. planting bombs
c. using someone's password
d. cutting communication lines

17-32. Which response is not an example of data security?
a. backup copies
b. special passwords
c. codes that are frequently changed
d. 24-hour computer usage

17-33. Data that is encrypted and decrypted is a form of
a. data security
b. new computer programming language
c. voice pattern for the computer
d. a new code for a data base

17-34. Which institutions are especially susceptible to sabotage, fraud, or embezzlement?
a. universities
b. banks and insurance companies
c. oil companies
d. U.S. government agencies

17-35. Which of the following would an organization not do to establish computer security?
a. recognize their role in security
b. employ a well-trained security force
c. carefully screen people who have access to computers, terminals, and computer-stored data
d. retain employees who go beyond legal and ethical boundaries

ETHICS AND PRIVACY

17-36. _____ is a term used to refer to the standard of moral conduct in computer use.
a. computer ethics   c. computer applications
b. computer law   d. computer security

17-37. Protection in the areas of computer crime, security, privacy, and ethics in the final analysis is largely dependent upon
a. wiretapping capabilities
b. data encryption
c. human nature
d. criminal nature

17-38. Which of the following is not a topic being addressed under the issue of ethics?
a. employee loyalty
b. employee bargaining rights
c. software piracy
d. hacking

17-39. Which of the following statements about employee loyalty is true?
- a. The many job opportunities in the computer field have increased the temptation for employees to switch jobs taking company information with them.
- b. The courts do not recognize any degree of duty of loyalty to the employees on the part of the employee.
- c. Employee loyalty has not been a problem in the area of data processing.
- d. The employee's duty of loyalty is not considered an ethical issue.

17-40. _____ is the unauthorized copying of a computer program that has been written by someone else.
- a. software piracy
- b. wiretapping
- c. encryption
- d. word processing

17-41. Because computers are being used as a means of storing personal information relating to aspects of a person's life, the issue of _____ is a growing concern.
- a. individual personality
- b. privacy
- c. power
- d. computer access

17-42. As a result of computers, information is both easier to _____ and _____.
- a. obtain, store
- b. obtain, lose
- c. store, lose
- d. obtain, sell

17-43. Because information is easier to obtain many organizations
- a. no longer bother to keep good records
- b. replace their data yearly
- c. store files in several locations
- d. collect more information than necessary

17-44. Which of the following is not a concern about privacy?
- a. Accuracy of information compiled may be low.
- b. Personal information data may be irrelevant for the purposes for which it is used.
- c. Irreplaceable data may be lost.
- d. Security of stored data may be a problem.

17-45. The accuracy, completeness, and currency of information about individuals is a concern of computer
- a. law
- b. ethics
- c. security
- d. privacy

17-46. To maintain privacy, there must be an appropriate balance
between _____ and _____.
a. needs of an organization, rights of an individual
b. government, industry
c. government, law
d. cost, efficiency

17-47. Efforts to protect our privacy led the government to
a. restrict data bases
b. enact privacy legislation
c. reduce computer use by the IRS
d. limit the use of computers for data collection

17-48. The major legislation enacted to protect the privacy of
private citizens is
a. Privacy Rights of 1970
b. The Rights Act of 1981
c. The Privacy Act of 1974
d. The Computer Act of 1979

17-49. The Privacy Act of 1974 was adopted by _____
government(s).
a. city   c. county
b. state   d. the federal

17-50. The Privacy Act of 1974 provides for all but which of the
following?
a. Individuals must be able to determine what information is being recorded and how it will be used.
b. A way must be made to correct mistakes.
c. Information collected for one purpose should not be
used for another.
d. Individuals whose privacy is violated are entitled to
financial compensation.

17-51. The lawmaking process is moving slowly on the issue of
privacy partly because
a. legislators do not recognize the problem
b. few people feel concerned
c. there is a lack of litigation over privacy
d. states are in conflict with federal agencies

17-52. When privacy has been violated due to unauthorized access or use of a data base, few instances become court cases and few new laws result. All but one of the following are reasons for this.
   a. Most people are not aware when their privacy has been violated.
   b. Organizations are careful to correct the matter immediately.
   c. Court cases would make public the information people wish to keep private.
   d. Laws vary from state to state.

COMPUTERS AND THE LAW

17-53. The Uniform Commercial Code (UCC) is a set of provisions proposed by legal experts to promote uniformity among the _____ courts in their legal treatment of commercial transactions.
   a. state
   b. federal
   c. county
   d. district

17-54. By using Article Two of the UCC, the courts have a common basis for rendering decisions concerning the sale of _____ and _____ by vendors.
   a. hardware, software
   b. robots, biochips
   c. RAM chips, magnetic bubbles
   d. impact, nonimpact printers

17-55. _____ is based on customs and past judicial decisions in similar cases.
   a. basic law
   b. common law
   c. ethical law
   d. user's law

17-56. _____ are created when a seller makes any promises or statement of fact concerning the goods being sold; they are also found in the written contract.
   a. express warranties
   b. implied warranties
   c. implied warranty of merchantability
   d. implied warranty of fitness

17-57. _____ provides that a contract for the sale of goods automatically contains certain warranties that exist by law.
   a.   implied warranty of fitness
   b.   implied warranty of merchantability
   c.   express warranties
   d.   implied warranties

17-58. _____ only exists if the seller is considered a merchant.
   a.   express warranties
   b.   implied warranties
   c.   implied warranty of fitness
   d.   implied warranty of merchantability

17-59. To create an _____ for a particualr purpose, the purchaser must communicate to the supplier the specific purpose for which the product will be used.
   a.   implied warranties
   b.   express warranties
   c.   implied warranty of fitness
   d.   implied warranty of merchantability

17-60. All but which of the following is contained in a notice of copyright?
   a.   name of the copyright owner
   b.   the © symbol, the word copyright or the abbreviation copr.
   c.   the year of the work's first publication
   d.   the current year

17-61. Copyright law
   a.   protects against copying programs from magazines
   b.   protects against unauthorized use of programs
   c.   protects against the right to sue for copyright infringement
   d.   protects against unauthorized copying of programs

APPLICATION

17-62. The concept of information security has certain basic components. Which one is not a component?
   a.   computer security
   b.   telecommunications security
   c.   personal security
   d.   supporting systems security

17-63. One area that threatens federal information systems is
       "unintentional actions." Which item is not an uninten-
       tional action?
       a. improper design of systems failures
       b. personnel errors
       c. equipment failures
       d. attacks on equipment

17-64. Which of the following is not an influence to the level
       of protection in today's technological environment?
       a. expanded use of remote terminals
       b. telecommunications networks
       c. increased numbers of microcomputers in use
       d. creation of new programming languages

17-65. All of the following are key factors affecting informa-
       tion security but one.
       a. legislation   c. auditing
       b. lobbying   d. policy

ANSWER KEY

17-1.	a	17-21.	a	17-41.	b	17-61.	a
17-2.	b	17-22.	d	17-42.	a	17-62.	c
17-3.	d	17-23.	b	17-43.	d	17-63.	d
17-4.	c	17-24.	b	17-44.	c	17-64.	d
17-5.	c	17-25.	c	17-45.	d	17-65.	b
17-6.	c	17-26.	d	17-46.	a		
17-7.	a	17-27.	c	17-47.	b		
17-8.	a	17-28.	c	17-48.	c		
17-9.	c	17-29.	d	17-49.	d		
17-10.	a	17-30.	c	17-50.	d		
17-11.	d	17-31.	c	17-51.	c		
17-12.	b	17-32.	d	17-52.	b		
17-13.	d	17-33.	a	17-53.	a		
17-14.	b	17-34.	b	17-54.	a		
17-15.	d	17-35.	d	17-55.	b		
17-16.	d	17-36.	a	17-56.	a		
17-17.	b	17-37.	c	17-57.	d		
17-18.	d	17-38.	b	17-58.	d		
17-19.	d	17-39.	a	17-59.	c		
17-20.	a	17-40.	a	17-60.	d		

Computers in Our Lives: Today and Tomorrow

MULTIPLE CHOICE

COMPUTERS AT HOME

18-1. Studies show shopping at home by computer is successful
       but movement in that direction is slower than expected.
       Which response is not a reason for this slow movement?
       a. use of computers is still too expensive
       b. shopping at home does not allow one to touch the
           product
       c. you cannot judge whether quality of item is good
       d. you are not able to see all the choices

18-2. Which response is a reason for banking at home by
       computer?
       a. transaction is too impersonal
       b. personal finances may be revealed to unauthorized
           eyes
       c. widespread use of computers is still too expensive
       d. saves time by allowing user to instantly make a
           transaction without going out to the bank

18-3. Data-base producers
       a. design data-base software
       b. compile and store data in soft-copy data bases
       c. compile and store data in hard-copy data bases
       d. design the physical layout of a data base

18-4.   There are many benefits to in-home banking. Which
        response is not a benefit?
        a.   users can pay bills automatically by instructing
             bank's computers to transfer money out of a certain
             account and send it
        b.   faster
        c.   possibility of personal computer code being erased
             from banking code list
        d.   more convenient

18-5.   Which one is not a major data base that provides in-home
        information?
        a.   The Source   c.   Dow Jones News/Retrieval
        b.   Compu Serve   d.   Accu Serve

18-6.   Information services are accessed by
        a.   a phone call   c.   ham radio
        b.   mail   d.   parcel post

18-7.   Which of the following is not a major telecommunications
        network?
        a.   Telenet   c.   Uninet
        b.   Tymnet   d.   Special Net

18-8.   The computer-controlled house Ahwatukee is described as
        state of the art in three areas. Which response is not
        one of these areas?
        a.   technology   c.   sociology
        b.   ecology   d.   psychology

18-9.   How many microcomputers run the systems in Ahwatukee?
        a.   two   c.   ten
        b.   six   d.   five

18-10. How many systems are controlled by microcomputers in
        Ahwatukee?
        a.   two   c.   ten
        b.   five   d.   six

18-11. In Ahwatukee heating, cooling, and the opening and
        shutting of doors and windows is the primary function of
        the _____ system.
        a.   environmental control
        b.   security
        c.   electrical switching
        d.   information storage and retrieval

18-12. In Ahwatukee, the _____ system protects against intruders with use of television cameras, sensors, and
password-controlled front door.
a. information storage and retrieval
b. electrical switching
c. security
d. energy management

18-13. In Ahwatukee, the _____ system uses sensors to note
people moving through the house and adjusts lights.
a. electrical switching
b. security
c. energy management
d. information storage and retrieval

18-14. In Ahwatukee, cost-efficient use of electricity is
assured with the _____ system.
a. environmental control   c. security
b. electrical switching   d. energy management

18-15. In Ahwatukee, the _____ system provides for personal
and home business needs.
a. information storage and retrieval
b. environmental control
c. security
d. energy management

18-16. Which task is a home robot not able to perform so far?
a. welcome guests   c. retrieve objects
b. act as a sentinel   d. do the laundry

18-17. Home robot B.O.B. (Brains-On-Board) is housed with
microprocessors and _____ million bytes of memory.
a. 3   c. 8
b. 1   d. 4

18-18. B.O.B. is programmed with a high-level programming
language called
a. BASIC   c. ACL
b. Logo   d. LISP

18-19. Heath Company's robot Hero I can be ordered about by a
a. joystick   c. graphics tablet
b. mouse   d. track ball

THE IMPACT ON EDUCATION

18-20. Which response is a false statement about computer-assisted instruction?
   a. Instruction is adapted to a student's learning pace.
   b. Immediate feedback is given on progress.
   c. Motivation is provided with sound and graphics.
   d. It usually presents material in an unusual manner.

18-21. Which item is a false statement about computer-assisted instruction?
   a. Students who use this mode of learning are becoming computer literate.
   b. Computer-assisted instruction helps the student to overcome computer anxiety.
   c. A majority of students using CAI cover required material in less time than in traditional classroom settings.
   d. The teacher-learner relationship is an unintimidating one.

18-22. At computer camps, children are placed in levels based on their age and computer skills. Which one is not a level of placement?
   a. pre-beginner   c. intermediate
   b. beginner   d. advanced

18-23. Which response does not describe the computer camp experience?
   a. individual lessons in programming languages
   b. experience in using peripherals
   c. no recreational activities
   d. hands-on experience in computer use

18-24. The uses of computers in education appear to be
   a. none at all   c. almost to the limit
   b. just beginning   d. endless

18-25. Which statement is false about the specialized learning tool Urban Adventure?
   a. Children explored the landmarks of the city.
   b. With a light pen and Apple Graphics Tablet, they drew landmarks and stored them in the computer's memory.
   c. English was the only language used.
   d. They learned to work with others on a complex project.

18-26. Which statement is false about computer and videodisk technology?
a.   Videodisk can be accessed at a chosen print.
b.   Motion sequences can be shown in slow motion.
c.   through computerized controls, students have access on disks to visual skills, sound tracks and so on.
d.   It is not possible to overlay computer text and graphics on top of projected videodisk images.

COMPUTERS IN MEDICINE AND SCIENCE

18-27. Computers have many uses in medicine. Most of these applications are found in _____ settings.
a.   hospital   c.   private doctor's office
b.   local pharmacy   d.   neighborhood clinic

18-28. Computers have become essential for the health care profession since the
a.   1940s   c.   1960s
b.   1950s   d.   1980s

18-29. Which response is a false statement about MPHT?
a.   Questions are asked about family history.
b.   Test results from the patient are computerized.
c.   Results compare a given test value against established normal limits.
d.   A printout of test findings and physician's recommendations is given to the patient.

18-30. With CT or CAT scanning units linked to a central computer, costs are
a.   decreased
b.   increased
c.   the same as without linkage
d.   somewhat increased

18-31. The CT scan is a _____ procedure in today's hospitals.
a.   common   c.   rare
b.   unused   d.   dangerous

18-32. Using computers to evaluate medical data to show variations from normal is called
a.   CAD
b.   CAM
c.   computer-assisted diagnosis
d.   health testing

18-33. MPHT stands for
     a.   multiphasic home testing
     b.   multipurpose health testing
     c.   multipurpose hospital testing
     d.   multiphasic health testing

18-34. In a MPHT program, tests are administered by
     a.   the patients themselves c.   nurses
     b.   doctors   d.   computers

18-35. Combining X-ray techniques with a computer for quick and
     accurate physical diagnosis is
     a.   impossible   c.   fast scanning
     b.   computerized tomography   d.   relatively inexpensive

18-36. An example in the text described computerized tomography
     that was used on a child to
     a.   correct a congenital skull deformity
     b.   correct a cleft palate
     c.   reconstruct a crushed pelvis
     d.   remove a spinal tumor

18-37. Which statement is false about computerized life support?
     a.   It monitors physiological variables.
     b.   It digests patient information.
     c.   It increases the time nurses must spend with the
          critically ill.
     d.   It monitors urine output.

18-38. Using computers makes work easier for scientists because
     a.   They no longer need to record data.
     b.   Data can be retrieved, classified, and displayed more
          quickly.
     c.   Computers can design a model with no inputs from
          humans.
     d.   The computer model does not need to be precise.

18-39. EM stands for
     a.   emergency medicine   c.   electron molecule
     b.   electronic magnetic   d.   electron microscopy

18-40. An EM used with a computer can
     a.   view material about the thickness of a baby's eyelash
     b.   take pictures of the surface of the moon
     c.   produce a three-dimensional image
     d.   view material the thickness of a dime

18-41. EM techniques are used to determine
    a. the need for cataract surgery
    b. the curvature of contact lens
    c. the three-dimensional structure of a two-dimensional drawing
    d. the three-dimensional structure of biological specimens

18-42. The technique of using an EM with a computer is called
    a. electron graphics
    b. electro-graphics
    c. tomographic scanning
    d. electron microscope tomography

18-43. A recent innovation in science has been the use of _____ in place of animal testing in laboratories.
    a. computer printouts   c. computer software
    b. computer modeling   d. computer projections

COMPUTERS IN THE ARTS, RECREATION, AND ENTERTAINMENT

18-44. Computers have _____ uses in the arts.
    a. many   c. no
    b. some   d. few

18-45. Which area is word processing not used in the arts?
    a. writing   c. choreography
    b. editing   d. painting

18-46. A computer artist must
    a. be knowledgeable about programming
    b. know all the details about computers
    c. be prepared to give up creativity for technology
    d. know all his or her brush strokes

18-47. Reaction to portraits of Queen Elizabeth and Prince Phillip, by the computer artist Berstein, in comparison to photographs was that
    a. the Queen had difficulty telling them apart (images and photographs)
    b. the Queen did not like the computer art
    c. the Prince did not like his image
    d. the Queen thought the photograph was much better than the computer art

18-48. Pierre Boulez uesd computer technology to produce a work
in what field?
a. literature   c. dance
b. art   d. music

18-49. Pierre Boulez used a computer to
a. compose a symphony
b. store and retrieve original compositions
c. edit musical scores
d. alter and transform musical sounds

18-50. In his last album, <u>Double Fantasy</u>, John Lennon used a
computer to
a. alter and transform musical sounds
b. compose two songs
c. edit the music
d. compose the score

18-51. Which statement about computers in music is false?
a. very expensive
b. used to edit recordings
c. used to design music for television commercials
d. used to store special effect sounds

18-52. At the COTO Research Center,_____ is used to analyze
human movement.
a. biomechanics   c. CAD
b. X-ray   d. CAM

18-53. Which is not used in the science of biomechanics to
study human movement?
a. high-speed cameras c. CAM
b. computers   d. digitizer pens

18-54. Which response is not a benefit from the research at COTO
center?
a. prevention and treating of sport injury
b. study of human motion at work
c. motion study of racing horses
d. improvements in CAD

18-55. Which response is false about EPCOT Center at Walt Disney
World?
a. Visitors become accustomed to computers.
b. Visitors gain confidence in their own ability to
manage computers.
c. Visitors are surrounded by computerization in Future
World.
d. Visitors do not have available hands-on experience
with computers.

18-56. At Computer Central at EPCOT, visitors are given explanations about how the wide variety of _____ computer
systems work.
a. Sperry   c. DEC
b. IBM   d. Honeywell

18-57. At Computer Central in EPCOT, which specific computer
application is not highlighted?
a. manufacturing   c. CAM
b. CAD   d. airline operations

18-58. EPCOT World Key Information Service allows guests to
seek instant information through
a. touch-sensitive screens c. a track ball
b. joysticks   d. a mouse

FUTURE TECHNOLOGY

18-59. Brain-wave interface is
a. a very simple process
b. in the theoretical stages
c. very slow for a computer
d. not feasible financially

18-60. Brain-wave interface would be especially useful
a. in intelligence operations
b. for the handicapped
c. for making rapid calculations
d. in robotics

18-61. A problem in the development of brain-wave interface is
a. interference from tense neck muscles
b. resistence of public opinion
c. the need for using lights
d. regulation of the uses of the process

18-62. A major effort in the field of software is being made to
        develop computers with
        a. biochips   c. artificial intelligence
        b. electrical chips   d. brain-wave interface

18-63. The ability of computers to reason and think like human
        is called
        a. robotics   c. artificial intelligence
        b. script theory   d. expert systems

18-64. A system designed to imitate how expert humans in a cer-
        tain field think through a problem is called
        a. brain-wave interface   c. artificial intelligence
        b. script theory   d. expert systems

18-65. A well-known experimental expert system called CADUCEUS
        a. is used in CAD engineering
        b. diagnoses medical problems
        c. forecasts tornadoes
        d. is used to design robots

18-66. _____ allows conclusions to be drawn from assumptions,
        and if more assumptions are added, the new conclusions
        will not make the previous conclusions wrong.
        a. script theory   c. nonmonotonic logic
        b. monotonic logic   d. artificial intelligence

18-67. _____ adapts to monotonic logic to allow for unusual
        situations.
        a. expert system theory
        b. artificial intelligence
        c. nonmonotonic logic theory
        d. script theory

18-68. _____ states that in any particular situation humans
        have an idea of how thinking or dialogue would go.
        a. script theory   c. brain-wave interface
        b. monotonic logic theory d. artificial intelligence

APPLICATION

18-69. At NASA, early command and control systems were _____
        devices.
        a. analog   c. hand-held
        b. digital   d. dedicated systems

18-70. All aspects of a NASA space mission can now be
        a. eliminated   c. executed
        b. simulated   d. repeated

18-71. The embedded nature of computing systems in ground-based
        space mission operations has grown _____ to the on-
        board systems.
        a. in a greater degree   c. parallel
        b. in a lesser degree   d. not at all in relation

18-72. The technological advances of the computing industry and
        the space industry are
        a. interdependent   c. dependent
        b. independent   d. autonomous

ANSWER KEY

18-1.	d	18-21.	a	18-41.	d	18-61.	a
18-2.	d	18-22.	a	18-42.	d	18-62.	c
18-3.	c	18-23.	c	18-43.	b	18-63.	c
18-4.	c	18-24.	d	18-44.	a	18-64.	d
18-5.	d	18-25.	c	18-45.	d	18-65.	b
18-6.	a	18-26.	d	18-46.	a	18-66.	b
18-7	d	18-27.	a	18-47.	a	18-67.	c
18-8.	d	18-28.	b	18-48.	d	18-68.	a
18-9	d	18-29.	d	18-49.	d	18-69.	a
18-10.	b	18-30.	a	18-50.	c	18-70.	b
18-11.	a	18-31.	a	18-51.	a	18-71.	c
18-12.	c	18-32.	c	18-52.	a	18-72.	a
18-13.	a	18-33.	d	18-53.	c		
18-14.	d	18-34.	c	18-54.	d		
18-15.	a	18-35.	b	18-55.	d		
18-16.	d	18-36.	a	18-56.	a		
18-17.	a	18-37.	c	18-57.	c		
18-18.	c	18-38.	b	18-58.	a		
18-19.	a	18-39.	d	18-59.	b		
18-20.	d	18-40.	a	18-60.	b		

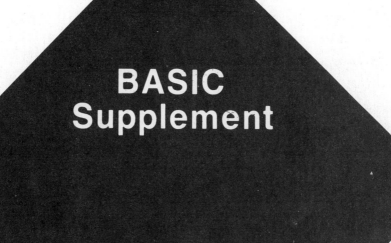

BASIC
Supplement

SECTION I
Introduction to BASIC

ANSWERS TO TEXTBOOK REVIEW QUESTIONS

1.   BASIC is short for Beginner's All-purpose Symbolic Instruction Code. BASIC is a programming language that can be used for a wide variety of tasks and is well suited for interactive processing.

2.   a.   Define the problem
      b.   Design a solution
      c.   Write the program
      d.   Compile, debug, and test the program
      e.   Document the program

3.   Documentation consists of all written descriptions and explanations of the instructions and statements in a program. It is important because it helps others to understand what the program is doing. Documentation also makes modification or updating of the program easier.

4.   System and editing commands are immediate-mode commands which are used by the programmer to communicate with the operating system of the computer. NEW, SAVE, LOAD, LIST, RUN, and DELETE are all examples of system commands.

SECTION II
BASIC Fundamentals

ANSWERS TO TEXTBOOK REVIEW QUESTIONS

1.   A BASIC instruction contains a line number and a BASIC statement.

2.   BASIC statements contain special reserved words (programming commands), numeric or character string constants, numeric or string variables, and formulas (expressions).

3.   Line numbers serve as labels by which statements can be referenced and as instructions to specify the order of execution of the program statements. Using line numbers in increments of five or ten allows easy insertion of additional instructions.

4.   A variable is the name of the location or address in memory where the value is stored. There are numeric variables and string variables. Numeric variables represent numeric values, and string variables represent character strings. String variable names are distinguished from numeric variable names by the use of a dollar sign preceding at least one alphabetic character.

ANSWERS TO STUDY GUIDE WORKSHEET PROBLEMS

2.   Constants are values that do not change throughout a
program's execution.   Variables are storage locations which contain values that may change as the program is executed.

4.   a.   8$--variable name must begin with a letter; change to B$
      b. $X--string variable name must begin with a letter and
                 end with a dollar sign; change to X$
      d.   7F--must begin with a letter; change to F7
      f.   3A$--must begin with a letter and end with a dollar
                 sign; change to A$ or A3$

6.   Reserved words are words that have a special meaning to the
translator program of a computer.   They may not be used as
variable names.

SECTION III
Getting Started with BASIC Programming

ANSWERS TO TEXTBOOK REVIEW QUESTIONS

1.   It is important to document your program to explain program segments, define variables used, and to note any special instructions for the programmer or anyone else reading the program.

2.   The LET statement can be used to assign values to numeric or string variables directly or to assign the results of calculations to numeric variables.

3.   Parentheses, exponentiation, multiplication or division, addition or subtraction

4.   The PRINT statement is used to print or display the results of computer processing. It also permits the formatting of output.

B-4

ANSWERS TO TEXTBOOK DEBUGGING EXERCISES

1.
```
10 *** THIS PROGRAM PRINTS A CITY ***
15 REM *** AND ITS POPULATION ***
20 LET C$ = 500
25 LET P = "HICTON"
30 PRINT C$,P
```
The REM statement is needed here

C$ should be a numeric variable (P)

P should be a character string variable (C$)

2.
```
40 LET 5 * X = B
45 LET C$ = 54.7
50 PRINT X B C$
```
B is on the wrong side of the equation, Line 40 should be: LET B = 5 * X

commas or semicolons must be used instead of blanks to separate the variables

C$ should be a numeric variable (C), change lines 45 and 50 to:

45 LET C = 54.7
50 PRINT X, B, C

ANSWER TO TEXTBOOK PROGRAMMING PROBLEM 1

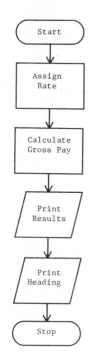

```
00100 REM *** CALCULATE GROSS PAY FOR THE YEAR ***
00110 REM *** R = RATE PER HOUR ***
00120 REM *** G = GROSS PAY ***
00130 LET R = 15.50
00140 LET G = R * 40 * 51
00150 PRINT
00160 PRINT "GROSS PAY","RATE PER HOUR"
00170 PRINT G,R
00999 END

READY
RUNNH

GROSS PAY     RATE PER HOUR
 31620            15.5
```

PSEUDOCODE

```
Start
Assign rate per hour to R
Calculate gross pay
Print headings
Print gross pay and rate per hour
Stop
```

MICROCOMPUTERS:	
Apple	No space is reserved before the numbers for a sign.
Apple Macintosh	No space is reserved before the numbers for a sign.
IBM/Microsoft	No differences.
PET/Commodore 64	No differences.
TRS-80	No differences.

ANSWER TO TEXTBOOK PROGRAMMING PROBLEM 2

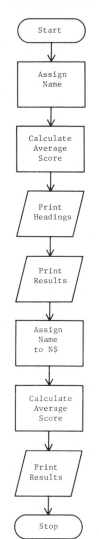

```
00100 REM *** THIS PROGRAM CALCULATES AVERAGE ***
00110 REM *** BOWLING SCORES ***
00120 REM *** N$ - BOWLER'S NAME ***
00130 REM *** A - BOWLERS AVERAGE ***
00140 LET N$ = "BILL DAVIS"
00150 LET A = (103 + 136 + 145) / 3
00160 PRINT
00170 PRINT "NAME","GAME 1","GAME 2","GAME 3","AVERAGE"
00180 PRINT N$,103,136,145,A
00190 LET N$ = "TONYA RAE"
00200 LET A = (150 + 172 + 167) / 3
00210 PRINT N$,150,172,167,A
00999 END

READY
RUNNH
```

NAME	GAME 1	GAME 2	GAME 3	AVERAGE
BILL DAVIS	103	136	145	128
TONYA RAE	150	172	167	163

PSEUDOCODE

```
Start
Assign bowler's name to N$
Calculate average bowling score
Print headings
Print bowler's name, game scores, and average
Assign another name to N$
Calculate the second bowler's average
Print name, game scores, and average
```

MICROCOMPUTERS:	
Apple	The fourth and fifth print zones will begin printing on the next line.
Apple Macintosh	AVERAGE does not fit on the screen, output must be reformatted.
IBM/Microsoft	No differences.
PET/Commodore 64	The fifth print zone will begin printing on the next line.
TRS-80	Same as PET/Commodore 64.

ANSWER TO STUDY GUIDE PROGRAMMING PROBLEM 2

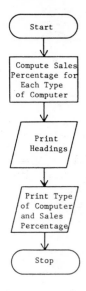

```
00010 REM ******************************
00020 REM *** COMPUTER SALES PROGRAM ***
00030 REM ******************************
00040 REM *** IIC = APPLE IIC      ***
00050 REM *** IIE = APPLE IIE      ***
00060 REM *** MAC = APPLE MACINTOSH ***
00070 REM *** PC = IBM PC          ***
00080 REM *** JR = IBM PCJR        ***
00090 REM *** CM = PET COMMODORE 64 ***
00100 REM ******************************
00110 REM ***    COMPUTE SALES %   ***
00120 REM ******************************
00130 LET IIC = 20 / 35
00140 LET IIE = 10 / 15
00150 LET MAC = 41 / 50
00160 LET PC = 19 / 30
00170 LET JR = 10 / 25
00180 LET CM = 8 / 15
00190 REM ******************************
00200 REM ***   PRINT THE RESULTS   ***
00210 REM ******************************
00220 PRINT
00230 PRINT "   COMPUTER",,"PERCENTAGE"
00240 PRINT
00250 PRINT "APPLE IIC",,IIC
00260 PRINT "APPLE IIE",,IIE
00270 PRINT "APPLE MACINTOSH",MAC
00280 PRINT "IBM PC",,PC
00290 PRINT "IBM PCJR",,JR
00300 PRINT "PET COMMODORE 63",CM
00999 END
```

```
RUNNH

   COMPUTER                  PERCENTAGE

APPLE IIC                    0.5714286
APPLE IIE                    0.6666667
APPLE MACINTOSH              0.82
IBM PC                       0.6333333
IBM PCJR                     0.4
PET COMMODORE 63             0.5333333
```

PSEUDOCODE

```
Start
Percentage of Apple IIc's sold equals 20 / 35
Percentage of Apple IIe's sold equals 10 / 15
Percentage of Apple Macintosh's sold equals 41 / 50
Percentage of IBM-PC's sold equals 19 / 30
Percentage of IBM-PCjr's sold equals 10 / 25
Percentage of Pet Commodore 64's sold equals 8 / 15
Percentage of Timex 1000's sold equals 16 / 41
Print the report headings
Print each computer and the percentage sold
Stop
```

MICROCOMPUTERS:	
Apple	Division will be carried 9 decimal places; no leading zeroes.
Apple Macintosh	Division will be carried 14 decimal places; no leading zeroes.
IBM/Microsoft	No leading zeroes.
PET/Commodore 64	Division will be carried 9 decimal places; no leading zeroes.
TRS-80	Division will be carried 6 decimal places; no leading zeroes.

ANSWERS TO STUDY GUIDE WORKSHEET PROBLEMS

2.   First priority is exponentiation; second priority is
multiplication or division; and addition or subtraction is third
priority. The first, or highest, priority operations are performed first.

4.   a.   5
      b.   27
      c.   37

6.   All of the LET statements in a, b, and c are invalid. The
LET statement in a is invalid because a character string must be
assigned to a string variable name. In b the variable name
must be on the left of the equal sign. In c the character
string "JANUARY" must be enclosed within quotation marks.

8.   b.   20 PRINT "BIRTHDAY"
      d.   40 PRINT "JANUARY NINTH"
      e.   50 PRINT "I = 90"
      f.   60 PRINT 99, "DOMINOS"

10.   The REM statement is used to document a program. It can be
used to explain program segments, define the variables used
within the program, or to note any special instructions. The
REM statement is necessary to provide information to the
programmer.

SUPPLEMENTARY PROGRAMMING PROBLEMS

Problem A

Mr. Kline needs to determine a grading scale for his computer classes. Mr. Kline gives four tests and a final exam each
semester. Each test is worth 75 points and the final exam is
worth 100 points. Mr. Kline also assigns six programs, each
worth 25 points.

Determine the grading scale for Mr. Kline's class. The
output should appear as follows:

GRADING SCALE

A	92-100%	XXX - XXX POINTS
B	85-91%	XXX - XXX POINTS
C	75-84%	XXX - XXX POINTS
D	65-74%	XXX - XXX POINTS
F	0-64%	XXX - XXX POINTS

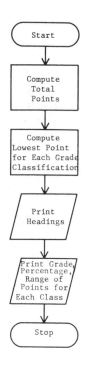

```
00100 REM ***********************************
00110 REM ***    GRADING SCALE PROGRAM    ***
00120 REM ***********************************
00130 REM *** T = TOTAL NUMBER OF POINTS   ***
00140 REM *** A = LOWEST POINTS FOR AN "A" ***
00150 REM *** B = LOWEST POINTS FOR A "B"  ***
00160 REM *** C = LOWEST POINTS FOR A "C"  ***
00170 REM *** D = LOWEST POINTS FOR A "D"  ***
00180 REM ***********************************
00190 REM ***    COMPUTE TOTAL POINTS AND   ***
00200 REM *** LOWEST POINT FOR EACH GRADE  ***
00210 REM ***********************************
00220 LET T = (4 * 75) + 100 + (6 * 25)
00230 LET A = 0.92 * T
00240 LET B = 0.85 * T
00250 LET C = 0.75 * T
00260 LET D = 0.65 * T
00270 REM ***********************************
00280 REM ***         PRINT THE RESULTS    ***
00290 REM ***********************************
00300 PRINT "               GRADING SCALE"
00310 PRINT
00320 PRINT "A","92-100%",A;"-";T;"POINTS"
00330 PRINT "B","85-91%",B;"-";A - 1;"POINTS"
00340 PRINT "C","75-84%",C;"-";B - 1;"POINTS"
00350 PRINT "D","65-74%",D;"-";C - 1;"POINTS"
00360 PRINT "F","0-64%",0;"-";D - 1;"POINTS"
00999 END
```

```
RUNNH
               GRADING SCALE

A          92-100%        506 - 550 POINTS
B          85-91%         467.5 - 505 POINTS
C          75-84%         412.5 - 466.5 POINTS
D          65-74%         357.5 - 411.5 POINTS
F          0-64%          0 - 356.5 POINTS
```

PSEUDOCODE

```
Start
Total points = (4 * 75) + (6 * 25) + 100
Lowest point for "A" = 0.91 * total points
Lowest point for "B" = 0.85 * total points
Lowest point for "C" = 0.75 * total points
Lowest point for "D" = 0.65 * total points
Print the report headings
Print points for "A"
Print points for "B"
Print points for "C"
Print points for "D"
Print points for "F"
Stop
```

MICROCOMPUTERS:	
Apple	No spaces between the number of points.
Apple Macintosh	No differences.
IBM/Microsoft	No differences.
PET/Commodore 64	No differences.
TRS-80	No differences.

Problem B

The President of Welcome, Inc. has asked you to write a program to total department costs for the accounting, finance, and computer services department. Use as many REM, LET, and PRINT statements as necessary. The costs are as follows:

Accounting	Finance	Computer Services
45750	67500	19900
25000	12500	35000

Use the following report format for your report:

```
               DEPARTMENT COSTS

               DEPARTMENT    COST
               XXXXXXX       #######
               XXXXXXX       #######
               XXXXXXX       #######
```

(Note: You can use comp services in the report instead of computer services.)

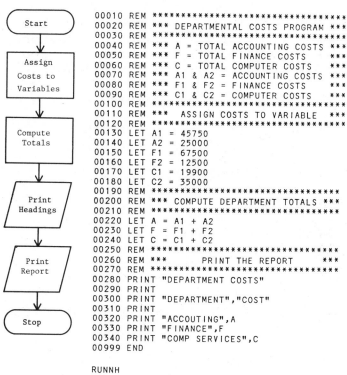

```
00010 REM ********************************
00020 REM *** DEPARTMENTAL COSTS PROGRAM ***
00030 REM ********************************
00040 REM *** A = TOTAL ACCOUNTING COSTS ***
00050 REM *** F = TOTAL FINANCE COSTS    ***
00060 REM *** C = TOTAL COMPUTER COSTS   ***
00070 REM *** A1 & A2 = ACCOUNTING COSTS ***
00080 REM *** F1 & F2 = FINANCE COSTS    ***
00090 REM *** C1 & C2 = COMPUTER COSTS   ***
00100 REM ********************************
00110 REM ***   ASSIGN COSTS TO VARIABLE ***
00120 REM ********************************
00130 LET A1 = 45750
00140 LET A2 = 25000
00150 LET F1 = 67500
00160 LET F2 = 12500
00170 LET C1 = 19900
00180 LET C2 = 35000
00190 REM ********************************
00200 REM *** COMPUTE DEPARTMENT TOTALS ***
00210 REM ********************************
00220 LET A = A1 + A2
00230 LET F = F1 + F2
00240 LET C = C1 + C2
00250 REM ********************************
00260 REM ***        PRINT THE REPORT    ***
00270 REM ********************************
00280 PRINT "DEPARTMENT COSTS"
00290 PRINT
00300 PRINT "DEPARTMENT","COST"
00310 PRINT
00320 PRINT "ACCOUTING",A
00330 PRINT "FINANCE",F
00340 PRINT "COMP SERVICES",C
00999 END


RUNNH
DEPARTMENT COSTS

DEPARTMENT    COST

ACCOUTING       70750
FINANCE         80000
COMP SERVICES   54900
```

PSEUDOCODE

```
Start
Assign 45750 to A1
Assign 25000 to A2
Assign 67500 to F1
Assign 12500 to F2
Assign 19900 to C1
Assign 35000 to C2
Add A1 and A2 and assign the result to A
Add F1 and F2 and assign the result to F
Add C1 and C2 and assign the result to C
Print the report headings
Print "Accounting" and total accounting costs
Print "Finance" and total finance costs
Print "Comp Services" and total computer costs
Stop
```

MICROCOMPUTERS:	
Apple	Space before each department cost.
Apple Macintosh	Space before each department cost.
IBM/Microsoft	No differences.
PET/Commodore 64	No differences.
TRS-80	No differences.

Problem C

The Accounting Department of the Roly-Poly Company needs a program to determine the amount due to each of the following companies. Each company is listed below with the amount due and a credit amount that Roly-Poly does not have to pay.

COMPANY NAME	AMOUNT DUE	CREDIT AMOUNT
AC&C	750.34	105.00
Berlex Industries	150.87	35.67
Repair Company	225.91	61.23
Wamat Enterprises	90.12	8.99
XYZ Corporation	101.33	15.06

Use the following guideline for the program output:

COMPANY NAME	AMOUNT DUE
XXXXXXXXXXXXXXX	###.##
XXXXXXXXXXXXXXX	###.##
XXXXXXXXXXXXXXX	###.##

(Hint: Amount due = Amount due - credit amount)

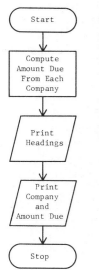

```
00100 REM ******************************
00110 REM ***   AMOUNT DUE PROGRAM   ***
00120 REM ******************************
00130 REM *** A = AC&C               ***
00140 REM *** B = BERLEX INDUSTRIES  ***
00150 REM *** R = REPAIR COMPANY     ***
00160 REM *** W = WAMAT ENTERPRISES  ***
00170 REM *** X = XYZ CORPORATION    ***
00180 REM ******************************
00190 REM ***   COMPUTE AMOUNT DUE   ***
00200 REM ******************************
00210 LET A = 750.34 - 105.00
00220 LET B = 150.87 - 35.67
00230 LET R = 225.91 - 61.23
00240 LET W = 90.12 - 8.99
00250 LET X = 101.33 - 15.06
00260 REM ******************************
00270 REM ***    PRINT THE RESULTS   ***
00280 REM ******************************
00290 PRINT
00300 PRINT "COMPANY NAME",,"AMOUNT DUE"
00310 PRINT
00320 PRINT "AC&C",,A
00330 PRINT "BERLEX INDUSTRIES",B
00340 PRINT "REPAIR COMPANY",R
00350 PRINT "WAMAT ENTERPRISES",W
00360 PRINT "XYZ CORPORATION",X
00999 END

RUNNH

COMPANY NAME              AMOUNT DUE

AC&C                      645.34
BERLEX INDUSTRIES         115.2
REPAIR COMPANY            164.68
WAMAT ENTERPRISES         81.13
XYZ CORPORATION           86.27
```

PSEUDOCODE

```
Start
Amount due to AC&C equals 750.34 - 105.00
Amount due to Berlex Industries equals 150.87 - 35.67
Amount due to Repair Company equals 225.91 - 61.23
Amount due to Wamat Enterprises equals 90.12 - 8.99
Amount due to XYZ Corporation equals 101.33 - 15.06
Print the report headings
Print each company and the amount due
Stop
```

MICROCOMPUTERS:	
Apple	No space before the amount due.
Apple Macintosh	No differences.
IBM/Microsoft	No differences.
PET/Commodore 64	No differences.
TRS-80	No differences.

Problem D

Currently, tuition at Famous University is $900 and room
and board fees are $1500. Next fall, tuition is expected to
rise by 15 percent and room and board fees are expected to rise
by 10 percent.

Karl Perry wants to know what the fees are expected to be
and if he will have enough money to cover his fees at Famous
University. Karl earns approximately $3000 over the summer and
gets no additional help for his college expenses. Write a
program to help Karl. The output should have the following
format:

```
TUITION     ROOM/BOARD     TOTAL     EXCESS
 XXXX          XXXX         XXXX       XXXX
```

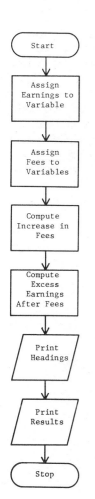

```
00100 REM ************************************************
00110 REM *** FAMOUS UNIVERSITY FEE INCREASE PROGRAM ***
00120 REM ************************************************
00130 REM *** T = TUITION FEES                       ***
00140 REM *** R = ROOM AND BOARD FEES                ***
00150 REM *** E = KARL'S EARNINGS                    ***
00160 REM *** A = KARL'S EXCESS EARNINGS AFTER FEES  ***
00170 REM ************************************************
00180 REM *** ASSIGN FEES AND EARNINGS TO VARIABLES  ***
00190 REM ************************************************
00200 LET E = 3000
00210 LET T = 900
00220 LET R = 1500
00230 REM ************************************************
00240 REM *** COMPUTE NEW FEE COST AND EXCESS AMOUNT ***
00250 REM ************************************************
00260 LET T1 = T * 1.15
00270 LET R1 = R * 1.10
00280 LET A = E - (T1 + R1)
00290 REM ************************************************
00300 REM ***              PRINT THE RESULTS         ***
00310 REM ************************************************
00320 PRINT "TUITION","ROOM/BOARD","TOTAL","EXCESS"
00330 PRINT T1,R1,T1 + R1,A
00999 END


RUNNH
TUITION        ROOM/BOARD      TOTAL           EXCESS
 1035            1650          2685            315
```

PSEUDOCODE

```
Start
Earnings equals 3000
Present tuition is 900
Present room and board fees are 1500
Compute new tuition
Compute new room and board fees
Compute amount left over from earnings
Print the headings
Print the results for Karl
Stop
```

MICROCOMPUTERS:	
Apple	Output must be reformatted.
Apple Macintosh	No differences.
IBM/Microsoft	No differences.
PET/Commodore 64	Output must be reformatted.
TRS-80	Output must be reformatted.

SECTION IV
Input and Output

1.   The INPUT statement allows the user to enter data at the
terminal while the program is running. The INPUT statement
should therefore be used whenever an inquiry-and-response or
user-friendly mode is desired. The purpose of the prompt is to
explain to the user what data is to be entered.

2.   The READ/DATA statements are best used when there are many
data values to be entered into a program.

3.   LET statements are most often used for entering small
amounts of data or for initializing variables.

4.   The TAB function causes the printer to be spaced to the
column specified in parentheses to print the value following the
semicolon after the TAB. The column numbers in parentheses must
increase from right to left because the TAB function does not
backspace the printer. Once a column has been passed the
printer cannot go back to it.

ANSWERS TO TEXTBOOK DEBUGGING EXERCISES

1.
```
10 REM ***   READ IN DATA   ***
20 READ P,A,T$
30 PRINT P,A,T$
40 READ P,T$,A
60 DATA 5,10,Z00,8,16
99 END
```
another character string must be included between 8 and 16, in order that the data will correspond to the variable names in the READ statements

2.
```
10 INPUT "ENTER YOUR NAME",N$
20 INPUT "ENTER YOUR AGE";A$
30 PRINT TAB(10),"NAME",TAB(25),"AGE"
40 PRINT TAB(10);N$;TAB(5);A$
```
There should be a semicolon instead of a comma before N$

The commas in this line should be semicolons

The computer cannot backspace to column 5 (column numbers must increase from left to right)

ANSWER TO TEXTBOOK PROGRAMMING PROBLEM 1

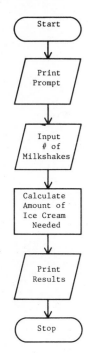

```
00100 REM *** CALCULATE # OF OUNCES OF ICE CREAM NEEDED ***
00110 REM *** N - NUMBER OF SHAKES ***
00120 REM *** I - # OF OUNCES OF ICE CREAM ***
00130 PRINT
00140 INPUT "ENTER THE NUMBER OF SHAKES YOU WISH TO MAKE";N
00150 LET I = N * 6
00160 PRINT
00170 PRINT "FOR";N;"MILKSHAKES YOU WILL NEED";I;"OUNCES OF ICE CREAM"
00999 END

READY
RUNNH

ENTER THE NUMBER OF SHAKES YOU WISH TO MAKE ? 67

FOR 67 MILKSHAKES YOU WILL NEED 402 OUNCES OF ICE CREAM
```

PSEUDOCODE

```
Start
Print prompt requesting # of shakes
Enter the number of shakes
Calculate the # of ounces of ice cream needed
Print the results
Stop
```

MICROCOMPUTERS:	
Apple	Output must be reformatted; output lines carry over to next line.
Apple Macintosh	No differences.
IBM/Microsoft	No differences.
PET/Commodore 64	Output must be reformatted; output lines carry over to next line.
TRS-80	No differences.

ANSWER TO TEXTBOOK PROGRAMMING PROBLEM 2

```
00100 REM *** FIND AVERAGE HEIGHT OF PATIENTS ***
00110 DATA "JIM GERFER",67
00120 DATA "FRED PFIEFER",74
00130 DATA "HENRY HOLLOW",72
00140 REM *** READ IN NAMES AND HEIGHTS ***
00150 READ A$,H1,B$,H2,C$,H3
00160 REM *** FIND AVERAGE HEIGHT ***
00170 LET X = (H1 + H2 + H3) / 3
00180 REM *** PRINT RESULTS ***
00190 PRINT
00200 PRINT TAB(10);"NAME";TAB(25);"HEIGHT"
00210 PRINT TAB(10);A$;TAB(25);H1
00220 PRINT TAB(10);B$;TAB(25);H2
00230 PRINT TAB(10);C$;TAB(25);H3
00240 PRINT
00250 PRINT TAB(10);"AVERAGE HEIGHT IS";X;"INCHES"
00999 END

READY

RUNNH

          NAME            HEIGHT
          JIM GERFER        67
          FRED PFIEFER      74
          HENRY HOLLOW      72

          AVERAGE HEIGHT IS 71 INCHES
```

PSEUDOCODE

Start
Read in patient's names and heights
Calculate average height of patients
Print the headings "NAME" and "HEIGHT"
Print patient's names and height
Print the average height
Stop

```
MICROCOMPUTERS:

Apple               No space is reserved for
                    sign before height.
Apple Macintosh     No differences.
IBM/Microsoft       No differences.
PET/Commodore 64    No differences.
TRS-80              No differences.
```

ANSWER TO STUDY GUIDE PROGRAMMING PROBLEM 2

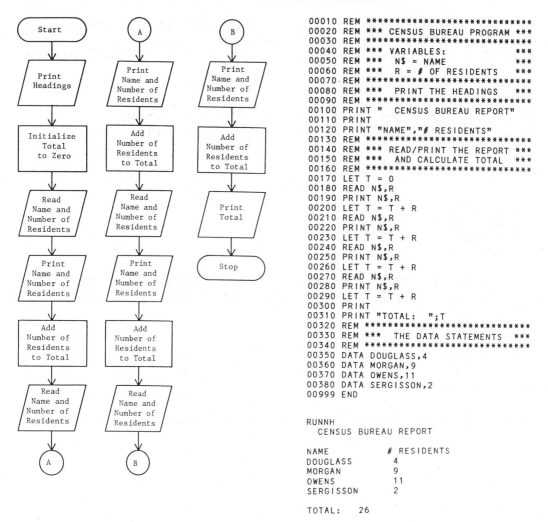

```
00010 REM *******************************
00020 REM *** CENSUS BUREAU PROGRAM ***
00030 REM *******************************
00040 REM *** VARIABLES:            ***
00050 REM ***   N$ = NAME           ***
00060 REM ***   R = # OF RESIDENTS  ***
00070 REM *******************************
00080 REM ***  PRINT THE HEADINGS   ***
00090 REM *******************************
00100 PRINT "  CENSUS BUREAU REPORT"
00110 PRINT
00120 PRINT "NAME","# RESIDENTS"
00130 REM *******************************
00140 REM *** READ/PRINT THE REPORT ***
00150 REM ***   AND CALCULATE TOTAL ***
00160 REM *******************************
00170 LET T = 0
00180 READ N$,R
00190 PRINT N$,R
00200 LET T = T + R
00210 READ N$,R
00220 PRINT N$,R
00230 LET T = T + R
00240 READ N$,R
00250 PRINT N$,R
00260 LET T = T + R
00270 READ N$,R
00280 PRINT N$,R
00290 LET T = T + R
00300 PRINT
00310 PRINT "TOTAL:   ";T
00320 REM *******************************
00330 REM ***   THE DATA STATEMENTS  ***
00340 REM *******************************
00350 DATA DOUGLASS,4
00360 DATA MORGAN,9
00370 DATA OWENS,11
00380 DATA SERGISSON,2
00999 END


RUNNH
   CENSUS BUREAU REPORT

NAME            # RESIDENTS
DOUGLASS        4
MORGAN          9
OWENS           11
SERGISSON       2

TOTAL:   26
```

PSEUDOCODE

```
Start
Print the report headings
Initialize total to zero
Read name and number of residents
Print name and number of residents
Add number of residents to total
Read name and number of residents
Print name and number of residents
Add number of residents to total
Read name and number of residents
Print name and number of residents
Add number of residents to total
Read name and number of residents
Print name and number of residents
Add number of residents to total
Print the total number of residents
Stop
```

MICROCOMPUTERS:	
Apple	No space before the number of residents.
Apple Macintosh	No differences.
IBM/Microsoft	No differences.
PET/Commodore 64	No differences.
TRS-80	No differences.

ANSWERS TO STUDY GUIDE WORKSHEET PROBLEMS

2.   Prompts are used to indicate to the user of the program
what data the program needs to continue execution.
    Method 1:   precede the INPUT statement with a PRINT state-
ment.
    10 PRINT "WHAT IS THE COLOR OF YOUR HAIR"
    20 INPUT H$
    Method 2:   include prompt within INPUT statement.
    10 INPUT "WHAT IS THE COLOR OF YOUR HAIR";H$

4.   X = 9   Z$ = JASON
      Y = 10   A = -393

6.   (1) 10 LET X$ = "CHAIRS"
          20 LET X1 = 8
          30 LET Y$ = "TABLES"
          40 LET Y1 = 2

      (2) 10 INPUT "ENTER NAME OF ITEM AND QUANTITY";X$,X1
          20 INPUT "ENTER NAME OF ITEM AND QUANTITY";Y$,Y1

      (3) 10 READ X$,X1,Y$,Y1
          20 DATA "CHAIRS",8
          30 DATA "TABLES",2

8.   PRINT USING

10.   a, b, and d will result in the same output.

SUPPLEMENTARY PROGRAMMING PROBLEMS

Problem A

The president of a newly formed company needs an employee report listing its three employees, their home address, and their telephone numbers. The information needed is listed below:

```
Sam Snead
61 Rolling Ridge Road
Hackensack, New Jersey    07465
(201)   652-8977

Mark Spitz
16-56 202nd Street
Whitestone, New York   12107
(212)   679-9794

John Carson
51 Madison Avenue Apartment #76
New York, New York   10017
(212)   499-7281
```

Use READ/DATA statements when writing the program, and use the following format for the report:

```
NAME                ADDRESS                PHONE

XXXXXXXXXXXX        XXXXXXXXXXXXXX         (###)  ###-####
                    XXXXXXXXXXXXXX

XXXXXXXXXXXX        XXXXXXXXXXXXXX         (###)  ###-####
                    XXXXXXXXXXXXXX

XXXXXXXXXXXX        XXXXXXXXXXXXXX         (###)  ###-####
                    XXXXXXXXXXXXXX
```

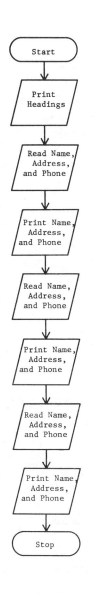

```
00100 REM ********************************
00110 REM *** EMPLOYEE REPORT PROGRAM ***
00120 REM ********************************
00130 REM *** VARIABLES:              ***
00140 REM ***    N$ = EMPLOYEE'S NAME ***
00150 REM ***    A1$ = STREET ADDRESS ***
00160 REM ***    A2$ = CITY ADDRESS   ***
00170 REM ***    T$ = TELEPHONE NUMBER ***
00180 REM ********************************
00190 REM ***   PRINT REPORT HEADINGS  ***
00200 REM ********************************
00210 PRINT
00220 PRINT " ","     EMPLOYEE REPORT"
00230 PRINT
00240 PRINT "NAME","ADDRESS"," ","PHONE"
00250 PRINT
00260 REM ********************************
00270 REM *** READ/PRINT 1ST DATA SET ***
00280 REM ********************************
00290 READ N$,A1$,A2$,T$
00300 PRINT N$,A1$,T$
00310 PRINT " ",A2$
00320 PRINT
00330 REM ********************************
00340 REM *** READ/PRINT 2ND DATA SET ***
00350 REM ********************************
00360 READ N$,A1$,A2$,T$
00370 PRINT N$,A1$,T$
00380 PRINT " ",A2$
00390 PRINT
00400 REM ********************************
00410 REM *** READ/PRINT 3RD DATA SET ***
00420 REM ********************************
00430 READ N$,A1$,A2$,T$
00440 PRINT N$,A1$,T$
00450 PRINT " ",A2$
00460 REM ********************************
00470 REM ***    DATA STATEMENTS       ***
00480 REM ********************************
00490 DATA "SAM SNEAD"
00500 DATA "61 ROLLING RIDGE ROAD"
00510 DATA "WAYNE, NEW JERSEY  07465"
00520 DATA "(201)  652-8977"
00530 DATA "MARK SPITZ","16-56 202ND STREET"
00540 DATA "WHITESTONE, NEW YORK  12107"
00550 DATA "(212)  679-9794"
00560 DATA "JOHN CARSON"
00570 DATA "51 MADISON AVENUE #76"
00580 DATA "NEW YORK, NEW YORK  10017"
00590 DATA "(212)  499-7281"
00999 END
RUNNH
```

```
                    EMPLOYEE REPORT

NAME          ADDRESS                      PHONE

SAM SNEAD     61 ROLLING RIDGE ROAD        (201)  652-8977
              WAYNE, NEW JERSEY  07465

MARK SPITZ    16-56 202ND STREET           (212)  679-9794
              WHITESTONE, NEW YORK  12107

JOHN CARSON   51 MADISON AVENUE #76        (212)  499-7281
              NEW YORK, NEW YORK  10017
```

PSEUDOCODE

Start
Print the report headings
Read name, first address line, second address line,
    and telephone number
Print name, first address line, and telephone number
Print second address line
Read name, first address line, second address line,
    and telephone number
Print name, first address line, and telephone number
Print second address line
Read name, first address line, second address line,
    and telephone number
Print name, first address line, and telephone number
Print second address line
Stop

MICROCOMPUTERS:	
Apple	Output must be reformatted.
Apple Macintosh	No differences.
IBM/Microsoft	No differences.
PET/Commodore 64	Output must be reformatted.
TRS-80	No differences.

Problem B

The manager of Craigmeyer ski resort area needs a report listing all of the nearby competition. He has asked you to write a program to print out the daily revenues of the ski resorts in the area, the average daily revenue of all ski resorts, and to print the amount Craigmeyer is from the average. Use the following information:

SKI RESORT	DAILY REVENUE
Craigmeyer	$805.00
Great Gorge	$750.00
The Ski Place	$675.00
Sussex Valley	$890.00

The report should be formatted as follows:

```
CRAIGMEYER SKI REPORT

SKI RESORT      REVENUE

XXXXXXXXXXXX    $###.##

AVERAGE DAILY REVENUE = $###.##

DIFFERENCE FROM AVERAGE = $###.##
```

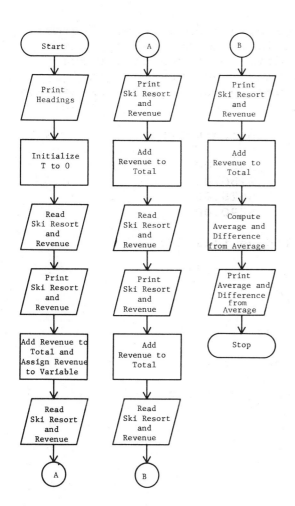

```
00100 REM ***********************************
00110 REM ***        SKI RESORT PROGRAM      ***
00120 REM ***********************************
00130 REM *** VARIABLES:                     ***
00140 REM ***    S$ = SKI RESORT             ***
00150 REM ***    R = DAILY REVENUE           ***
00160 REM ***    C = CRAIGMEYER REVENUE      ***
00170 REM ***    T = TOTAL DAILY REVENUE     ***
00180 REM ***    A = AVERAGE REVENUE         ***
00190 REM ***    D = DIFFERENCE FROM AVERAGE ***
00200 REM ***                                ***
00210 REM ***        PRINT THE HEADINGS      ***
00220 REM ***********************************
00230 PRINT
00240 PRINT "CRAIGMEYER SKI REPORT"
00250 PRINT
00260 PRINT "SKI RESORT","REVENUE"
00270 PRINT
00280 REM ***********************************
00290 REM ***   COMPUTE AND PRINT REVENUE    ***
00300 REM ***      AVERAGE, AND DIFFERENCE   ***
00310 REM ***              FROM AVERAGE      ***
00320 REM ***********************************
00330 LET T = 0
00340 READ S$,R
00350 PRINT S$,"$";R
00360 LET T = T + R
00370 LET C = R
00380 READ S$,R
00390 PRINT S$,"$";R
00400 LET T = T + R
00410 READ S$,R
00420 PRINT S$,"$";R
00430 LET T = T + R
00440 READ S$,R
00450 PRINT S$,"$";R
00460 LET T = T + R
00470 LET A = T / 4
00480 LET D = C - A
00490 PRINT
00500 PRINT "AVERAGE DAILY REVENUE = $";A
00510 PRINT
00520 PRINT "DIFFERENCE FROM AVERAGE = $";D
00530 REM ***********************************
00540 REM ***        THE DATA STATEMENTS     ***
00550 REM ***********************************
00560 DATA CRAIGMEYER,805.00
00570 DATA GREAT GORGE,750.00
00580 DATA THE SKI PLACE,675.00
00590 DATA SUSSEX VALLEY,890.00
00999 END

RUNNH

CRAIGMEYER SKI REPORT

SKI RESORT      REVENUE

CRAIGMEYER      $ 805
GREAT GORGE     $ 750
THE SKI PLACE $ 675
SUSSEX VALLEY $ 890

AVERAGE DAILY REVENUE = $ 780

DIFFERENCE FROM AVERAGE = $ 25
```

PSEUDOCODE

Start
Print the report headings
Total equals zero
Read ski resort and daily revenue
Print ski resort and daily revenue
Add revenue to total
Craigmeyer's revenue equals daily revenue
Read ski resort and daily revenue
Print ski resort and daily revenue
Add revenue to total
Read ski resort and daily revenue
Print ski resort and daily revenue
Add revenue to total
Read ski resort and daily revenue
Print ski resort and daily revenue
Add revenue to total
Compute average
Compute difference from average
Print average
Print difference from average
Stop

```
MICROCOMPUTERS:

Apple              No space after dollar signs.
Apple Macintosh    No differences.
IBM/Microsoft      No differences.
PET/Commodore 64   No differences.
TRS-80             No differences.
```

Problem C

The owner of a local pet store is increasing the prices of his dogs by 8 percent. The owner has asked you to write a program to list the types of dogs it sells, their prices after the increase, and the amount of the increase. Listed below are the dogs and their prices.

DOGS	PRICE
1. Irish Setter	$ 50.00
2. Pekinese	$ 75.00
3. Corgi	$125.00
4. Poodle	$ 45.00
5. Mutt	$ 30.00

Write a program using READ/DATA statements that prints a report listing the type of dog, the new price, and price increase. Use the format shown below:

DOG	PRICE	INCREASE
XXXXXXXXX	$###.##	$##.##
XXXXXXXXX	$###.##	$##.##
XXXXXXXXX	$###.##	$##.##

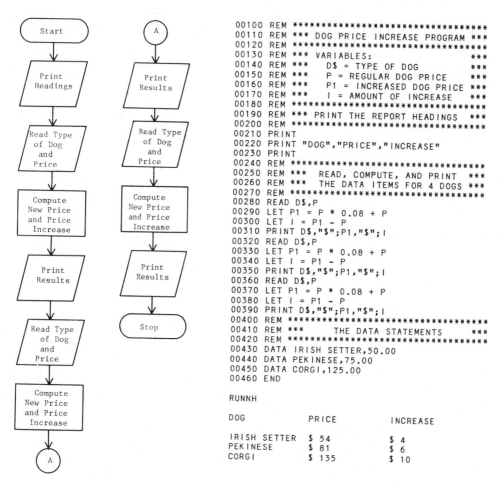

```
00100 REM *************************************
00110 REM *** DOG PRICE INCREASE PROGRAM ***
00120 REM *************************************
00130 REM *** VARIABLES:                  ***
00140 REM ***    D$ = TYPE OF DOG         ***
00150 REM ***    P  = REGULAR DOG PRICE   ***
00160 REM ***    P1 = INCREASED DOG PRICE ***
00170 REM ***    I  = AMOUNT OF INCREASE  ***
00180 REM *************************************
00190 REM *** PRINT THE REPORT HEADINGS   ***
00200 REM *************************************
00210 PRINT
00220 PRINT "DOG","PRICE","INCREASE"
00230 PRINT
00240 REM *************************************
00250 REM ***   READ, COMPUTE, AND PRINT  ***
00260 REM ***   THE DATA ITEMS FOR 4 DOGS ***
00270 REM *************************************
00280 READ D$,P
00290 LET P1 = P * 0.08 + P
00300 LET I = P1 - P
00310 PRINT D$,"$";P1,"$";I
00320 READ D$,P
00330 LET P1 = P * 0.08 + P
00340 LET I = P1 - P
00350 PRINT D$,"$";P1,"$";I
00360 READ D$,P
00370 LET P1 = P * 0.08 + P
00380 LET I = P1 - P
00390 PRINT D$,"$";P1,"$";I
00400 REM *************************************
00410 REM ***     THE DATA STATEMENTS      ***
00420 REM *************************************
00430 DATA IRISH SETTER,50.00
00440 DATA PEKINESE,75.00
00450 DATA CORGI,125.00
00460 END

RUNNH

DOG            PRICE          INCREASE

IRISH SETTER   $ 54           $ 4
PEKINESE       $ 81           $ 6
CORGI          $ 135          $ 10
```

PSEUDOCODE

```
Start
Print the headings
Read type of dog and price
New price equals price * 1.08
Price increase equals new price - price
Print type of dog, new price, and price increase
Read type of dog and price
New price equals price * 1.08
Price increase equals new price - price
Print type of dog, new price, and price increase
Read type of dog and price
New price equals price * 1.08
Price increase equals new price - price
Print type of dog, new price, and price increase
Stop
```

MICROCOMPUTERS:	
Apple	No space after dollar sign.
Apple Macintosh	No differences.
IBM/Microsoft	No differences.
PET/Commodore 64	No differences.
TRS-80	No differences.

Problem D

The University Health Department needs you to write a program for them. The Department needs a program that prints a student report listing the student's name, an emergency number, and any medical problems the student might have. The program should work for any number of students and should use READ/DATA statements to enter the data. Use an appropriate format for the report. The input data is as follows:

NAME	EMERGENCY NUMBER	MEDICAL PROBLEMS
Candi Mullen	(716) 459-0989	none
Joy Jones	(614) 787-8382	none
Polly Cracker	(222) 321-1234	asthma
Larry Illsen	(716) 938-2739	none
Sam Travers	(614) 244-3500	diabetes

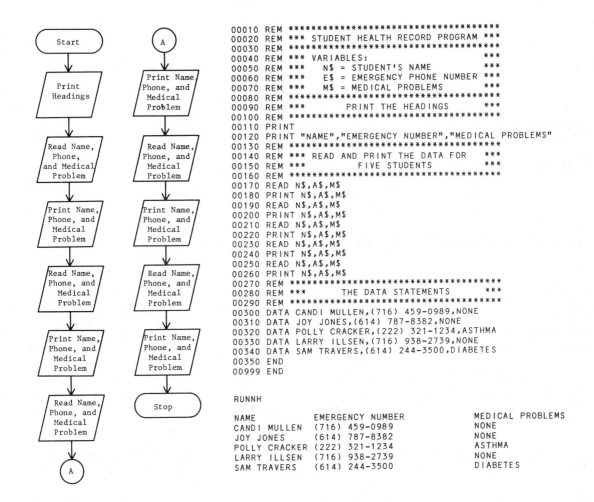

```
00010 REM *****************************************
00020 REM *** STUDENT HEALTH RECORD PROGRAM ***
00030 REM *****************************************
00040 REM *** VARIABLES:                        ***
00050 REM ***    N$ = STUDENT'S NAME            ***
00060 REM ***    E$ = EMERGENCY PHONE NUMBER    ***
00070 REM ***    M$ = MEDICAL PROBLEMS          ***
00080 REM *****************************************
00090 REM ***        PRINT THE HEADINGS         ***
00100 REM *****************************************
00110 PRINT
00120 PRINT "NAME","EMERGENCY NUMBER","MEDICAL PROBLEMS"
00130 REM *****************************************
00140 REM *** READ AND PRINT THE DATA FOR       ***
00150 REM ***            FIVE STUDENTS          ***
00160 REM *****************************************
00170 READ N$,A$,M$
00180 PRINT N$,A$,M$
00190 READ N$,A$,M$
00200 PRINT N$,A$,M$
00210 READ N$,A$,M$
00220 PRINT N$,A$,M$
00230 READ N$,A$,M$
00240 PRINT N$,A$,M$
00250 READ N$,A$,M$
00260 PRINT N$,A$,M$
00270 REM *****************************************
00280 REM ***        THE DATA STATEMENTS        ***
00290 REM *****************************************
00300 DATA CANDI MULLEN,(716) 459-0989,NONE
00310 DATA JOY JONES,(614) 787-8382,NONE
00320 DATA POLLY CRACKER,(222) 321-1234,ASTHMA
00330 DATA LARRY ILLSEN,(716) 938-2739,NONE
00340 DATA SAM TRAVERS,(614) 244-3500,DIABETES
00350 END
00999 END

RUNNH
```

NAME	EMERGENCY NUMBER	MEDICAL PROBLEMS
CANDI MULLEN	(716) 459-0989	NONE
JOY JONES	(614) 787-8382	NONE
POLLY CRACKER	(222) 321-1234	ASTHMA
LARRY ILLSEN	(716) 938-2739	NONE
SAM TRAVERS	(614) 244-3500	DIABETES

PSEUDOCODE

```
Start
Print the report headings
Read name, emergency number, and medical problem
Print name, emergency number, and medical problem
Read name, emergency number, and medical problem
Print name, emergency number, and medical problem
Read name, emergency number, and medical problem
Print name, emergency number, and medical problem
Read name, emergency number, and medical problem
Print name, emergency number, and medical problem
Read name, emergency number, and medical problem
Print name, emergency number, and medical problem
Stop
```

MICROCOMPUTERS:	
Apple	Output must be reformatted.
Apple Macintosh	No differences.
IBM/Microsoft	No differences.
PET/Commodore 64	Output must be reformatted.
TRS-80	No differences.

SECTION V
Control Statements

ANSWERS TO TEXTBOOK REVIEW QUESTIONS

1.   An unconditional transfer transfers control or causes branching to occur everytime the statement is executed. When a conditional transfer is executed branching only occurs when the condition is evaluated to be true.   The GOTO statement is an unconditional transfer, and the IF/THEN and ON/GOTO statements are both conditional transfers.

2.   The IF/THEN statement is a conditional transfer because branching only occurs when the condition is evaluated to be true. If the condition is evaluated to false, control is transferred to the next statement in the program.

3.   270 divided by 90 is 3 so control would be transferred to the third line number following the GOTO, which is line 310.

4.   A menu is a listing that displays the choices of functions in which the user can instruct the computer to do.

5.   Trailer values and the use of counters are two ways of controlling the number of times a loop is executed.

ANSWERS TO TEXTBOOK DEBUGGING EXERCISES

1.
```
50 LET C = 4
55 ON C GOTO 60,70,80
60 PRINT "C = ";1
65 GOTO 99
70 PRINT "C = ";2
75 GOTO 100
80 PRINT "C = ";3
99 END
```
C should not be equal to 4 since the ON/GOTO statement in line 55 does not contain 4 line numbers. C should be equal to 1, 2, or 3 instead.

There is no line 100, change to GOTO 99

2.
```
05 REM *** PRINT THE EVEN NUMBERS FROM 10 DOWN THROUGH Z ***
10 LET Z = -6
15 LET X = 10
20 IF X THEN 99
25 PRINT X * 10
30 LET X = x - 2
35 GOTO 10
99 END
```
no condition is being tested, change to: IF X < Z THEN 99

to print the even numbers from 10 to Z, you do not need to multiply X by 10

should be uppercase

should be GOTO 20, otherwise the value of X will always be 10 and an infinite loop has been created

ANSWER TO TEXTBOOK PROGRAMMING PROBLEM 1

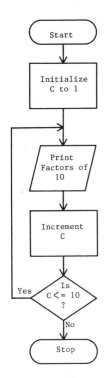

```
00100 REM *** THIS PROGRAM PRINTS THE FACTORS OF 10 ***
00110 REM *** FROM 10 THROUGH 120 ***
00120 REM *** C = COUNTER ***
00130 LET C = 1
00140 PRINT
00150 PRINT C * 10,(C + 1) * 10,(C + 2) * 10
00160 LET C = C + 3
00170 IF C <= 10 THEN 150
00999 END

READY
RUNNH
```
PP VI

```
10              20              30
40              50              60
70              80              90
100             110             120
```

PSEUDOCODE

```
Start
Initialize counter to 1
Print factors of ten
Increment C by three
If C <= 10 then
  Repeat the last three steps
Else
  Stop
```

MICROCOMPUTERS:	
Apple	No space is reserved before the number for sign.
Apple Macintosh	Same as Apple.
IBM/Microsoft	No differences.
PET/Commodore 64	No differences.
TRS-80	No differences.

ANSWER TO TEXTBOOK PROGRAMMING PROBLEM 2

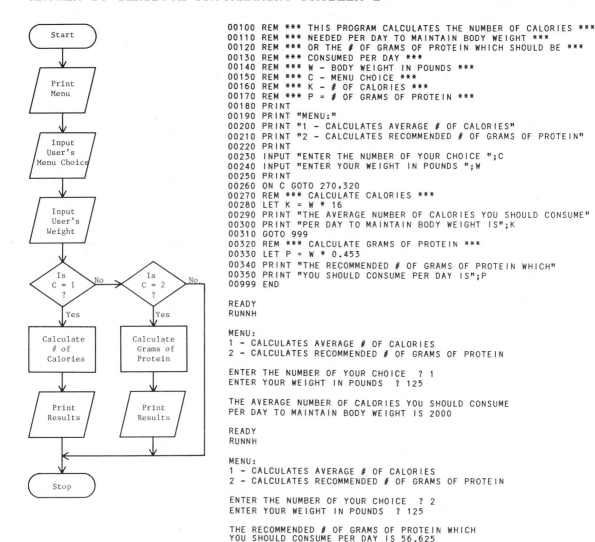

```
00100 REM *** THIS PROGRAM CALCULATES THE NUMBER OF CALORIES ***
00110 REM *** NEEDED PER DAY TO MAINTAIN BODY WEIGHT ***
00120 REM *** OR THE # OF GRAMS OF PROTEIN WHICH SHOULD BE ***
00130 REM *** CONSUMED PER DAY ***
00140 REM *** W - BODY WEIGHT IN POUNDS ***
00150 REM *** C - MENU CHOICE ***
00160 REM *** K - # OF CALORIES ***
00170 REM *** P = # OF GRAMS OF PROTEIN ***
00180 PRINT
00190 PRINT "MENU:"
00200 PRINT "1 - CALCULATES AVERAGE # OF CALORIES"
00210 PRINT "2 - CALCULATES RECOMMENDED # OF GRAMS OF PROTEIN"
00220 PRINT
00230 INPUT "ENTER THE NUMBER OF YOUR CHOICE ";C
00240 INPUT "ENTER YOUR WEIGHT IN POUNDS ";W
00250 PRINT
00260 ON C GOTO 270,320
00270 REM *** CALCULATE CALORIES ***
00280 LET K = W * 16
00290 PRINT "THE AVERAGE NUMBER OF CALORIES YOU SHOULD CONSUME"
00300 PRINT "PER DAY TO MAINTAIN BODY WEIGHT IS";K
00310 GOTO 999
00320 REM *** CALCULATE GRAMS OF PROTEIN ***
00330 LET P = W * 0.453
00340 PRINT "THE RECOMMENDED # OF GRAMS OF PROTEIN WHICH"
00350 PRINT "YOU SHOULD CONSUME PER DAY IS";P
00999 END

READY
RUNNH

MENU:
1 - CALCULATES AVERAGE # OF CALORIES
2 - CALCULATES RECOMMENDED # OF GRAMS OF PROTEIN

ENTER THE NUMBER OF YOUR CHOICE  ? 1
ENTER YOUR WEIGHT IN POUNDS  ? 125

THE AVERAGE NUMBER OF CALORIES YOU SHOULD CONSUME
PER DAY TO MAINTAIN BODY WEIGHT IS 2000

READY
RUNNH

MENU:
1 - CALCULATES AVERAGE # OF CALORIES
2 - CALCULATES RECOMMENDED # OF GRAMS OF PROTEIN

ENTER THE NUMBER OF YOUR CHOICE  ? 2
ENTER YOUR WEIGHT IN POUNDS  ? 125

THE RECOMMENDED # OF GRAMS OF PROTEIN WHICH
YOU SHOULD CONSUME PER DAY IS 56.625
```

PSEUDOCODE

```
Start
Print menu
Input user's choice
Input user's weight
If choice = 1 then
   Calculate number of calories
   Print results
   Goto stop
If choice = 2 then
   Calculate grams of protein
   Print results
Stop
```

MICROCOMPUTERS:	
Apple	Output must be reformatted; output lines carry over to next line.
Apple Macintosh	No differences.
IBM/Microsoft	No differences.
PET/Commodore 64	Output must be reformatted; output lines carry over to next line.
TRS-80	No differences.

ANSWER TO STUDY GUIDE PROGRAMMING PROBLEM 2

```
00100 REM ***************************************
00110 REM *** HAPPY HAMBURGER MENU PROGRAM ***
00120 REM ***************************************
00130 REM *** VARIABLES:                    ***
00140 REM ***    T = THE TOTAL BILL         ***
00150 REM ***    S = CUSTOMER'S SELECTION   ***
00160 REM ***    N = NUMBER OF ITEMS WANTED ***
00170 REM ***************************************
00180 REM ***    PRINT HAPPY HAMBURGER MENU   ***
00190 REM ***************************************
00200 PRINT
00210 PRINT
00220 PRINT "WELCOME TO THE HAPPY HAMBURGER"
00230 PRINT
00240 PRINT "OUR MENU:"
00250 PRINT "  1)   HAMBURGER ................. $ .80"
00260 PRINT "  2)   CHEESEBURGER .............. $1.00"
00270 PRINT "  3)   FRENCH FRIES .............. $ .40"
00280 PRINT "  4)   COLA ..................... $ .50"
00290 PRINT "  5)   COOKIES ................... $ .60"
00300 PRINT "  6)   NO MORE, THANK YOU"
00310 PRINT
00320 PRINT "WHAT WOULD YOU LIKE? (PICK A NUMBER)"
00330 INPUT S
00340 PRINT "HOW MANY WOULD YOU LIKE?  (INPUT 0 IF THROUGH)"
00350 INPUT N
00360 REM ***************************************
00370 REM ***   COMPUTE TOTAL BILL SO FAR    ***
00380 REM ***************************************
00390 ON S GOTO 400,420,440,460,480,500
00400 LET T = T + (N * 0.80)
00410 GOTO 490
00420 LET T = T + (N * 1.00)
00430 GOTO 490
00440 LET T = T + (N * 0.40)
00450 GOTO 490
00460 LET T = T + (N * 0.50)
00470 GOTO 490
00480 LET T = T + (N * 0.60)
00490 GOTO 230
00500 LET T = T + (T * 0.04)
00510 REM ***************************************
00520 REM ***    PRINT THE CUSTOMER'S BILL    ***
00530 REM ***************************************
00540 PRINT
00550 PRINT "YOUR TOTAL BILL IS $";T
00560 PRINT
00570 PRINT "THANK YOU FOR COMING TO THE HAPPY HAMBURGER"
00999 END
```

```
RUNNH

WELCOME TO THE HAPPY HAMBURGER

OUR MENU:
    1)   HAMBURGER .................. $ .80
    2)   CHEESEBURGER ............... $1.00
    3)   FRENCH FRIES ............... $ .40
    4)   COLA ....................... $ .50
    5)   COOKIES .................... $ .60
    6)   NO MORE, THANK YOU

WHAT WOULD YOU LIKE? (PICK A NUMBER)
 ? 2
HOW MANY WOULD YOU LIKE?  (INPUT 0 IF THROUGH)
 ? 1
OUR MENU:
    1)   HAMBURGER .................. $ .80
    2)   CHEESEBURGER ............... $1.00
    3)   FRENCH FRIES ............... $ .40
    4)   COLA ....................... $ .50
    5)   COOKIES .................... $ .60
    6)   NO MORE, THANK YOU

WHAT WOULD YOU LIKE? (PICK A NUMBER)
 ? 4
HOW MANY WOULD YOU LIKE?  (INPUT 0 IF THROUGH)
 ? 1
OUR MENU:
    1)   HAMBURGER .................. $ .80
    2)   CHEESEBURGER ............... $1.00
    3)   FRENCH FRIES ............... $ .40
    4)   COLA ....................... $ .50
    5)   COOKIES .................... $ .60
    6)   NO MORE, THANK YOU

WHAT WOULD YOU LIKE? (PICK A NUMBER)
 ? 6
HOW MANY WOULD YOU LIKE?  (INPUT 0 IF THROUGH)
 ? 0

YOUR TOTAL BILL IS $ 1.56

THANK YOU FOR COMING TO THE HAPPY HAMBURGER
```

PSEUDOCODE

```
Start
Print the menu
Print prompt to enter selection
Enter number of selection
Print prompt to enter the number of items
Enter the number of items
Start loop, do until selection 6 has been entered
  If selection equals 1
    Then
    Add number of items multiplied by 0.80 to total bill
  Endif
  If selection equals 2
    Then
    Add number of items multiplied by 1.00 to total bill
  Endif
  If selection equals 3
    Then
    Add number of items multiplied by 0.40 to total bill
  Endif
  If selection equals 4
    Then
    Add number of items multiplied by 0.50 to total bill
  Endif
  If selection equals 5
    Then
    Add number of items multiplied by 0.60 to total bill
  Endif
End loop
Print the customer's total
Print thank you message
Stop
```

MICROCOMPUTERS:	
Apple	Output must be reformatted; no space after dollar sign in total line.
Apple Macintosh	No differences.
IBM/Microsoft	No differences.
PET/Commodore 64	Output must be reformatted.
TRS-80	No differences.

ANSWERS TO STUDY GUIDE WORKSHEET PROBLEMS

2.

```
5 LET T = 0
10 PRINT
15 PRINT "SWIMMER","# OF LAPS"
20 PRINT
25 READ S$,L
30 IF S$ = "END" THEN 65
40 LET T = T + L
50 PRINT S$,L
60 GOTO 25
65 PRINT
70 PRINT "TOTAL NUMBER OF LAPS SWUM WAS";T
80 DATA "DOL FIN",72,"SWORD FISH",10
90 DATA "CHARLIE TUNA",49,"END",0
99 END

RUN

SWIMMER                # OF LAPS

DOL FIN                72
SWORD FISH             10
CHARLIE TUNA           49

TOTAL NUMBER OF LAPS SWAM WAS 131
```

4.   The counter is being reinitialized each time through the loop, creating an infinite loop. Change line 40 to
      40 IF Z < 15 THEN 20

6.   Looping is the processing of the same sequence of steps repeatedly. Looping saves typing the same sequence of steps over and over again.

8.   Line 99; the END statement

10. A trailer value or dummy value is a value read into the program which indicates the end of the data has been reached. The programmer should be careful to select trailer values that will not be confused as actual data values.

SUPPLEMENTARY PROGRAMMING PROBLEMS

Problem A

The principal of the grade school in your hometown would like you to put your computer knowledge to work for the second grade students at her school. She has asked you to write an educational program for the students using the first six states of the Union. The students will type in a number from 1 to 6 and then tell the computer the corresponding state. For example, if the student puts a 1 in, he or she must then tell the computer which state was the first to join the Union. If the student is wrong, the computer must give an appropriate message and ask the student to try again. If the student is right, the computer must again give an appropriate message and then ask the student if he or she wants to try another one. Use the ON/GOTO statement in this program. In order to end the program a number greater than 6 should be entered instead of the usual 1 to 6. The first six states to join the Union were:

1. Delaware
2. Pennsylvania
3. New Jersey
4. Georgia
5. Connecticut
6. Massachusetts

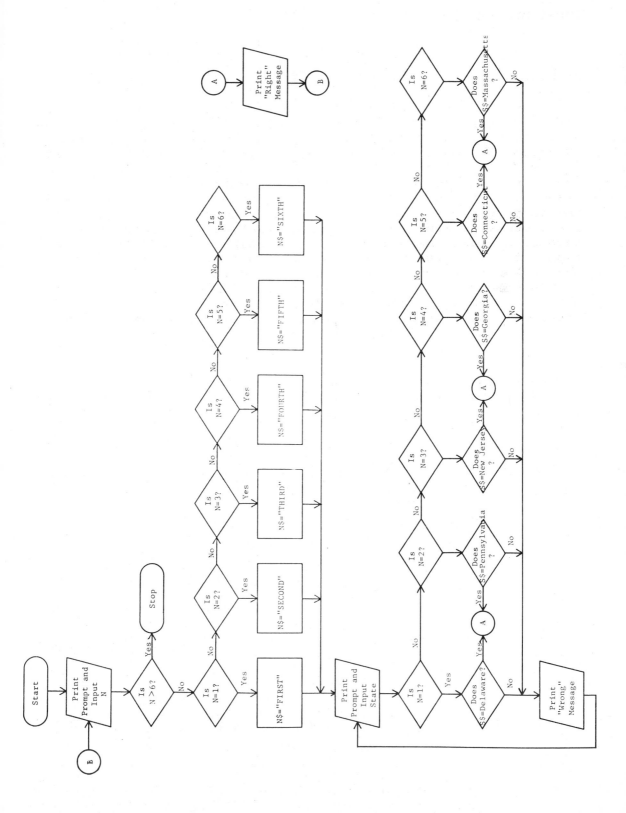

```
00100 REM *********************************
00110 REM *** FIRST SIX STATES PROGRAM ***
00120 REM *********************************
00130 REM *** VARIABLES:               ***
00140 REM ***   S$ = NAME OF THE STATE ***
00150 REM ***   N = NUMBER OF STATE'S  ***
00160 REM ***        ADMITTANCE TO UNION ***
00170 REM ***   N$ = WRITTEN NUMBER OF ***
00180 REM ***        STATE'S ADMITTANCE ***
00190 REM ***        TO THE UNION       ***
00200 REM *********************************
00210 REM ***       ENTER A NUMBER     ***
00220 REM *********************************
00230 PRINT "ENTER A NUMBER FROM 1 TO 6"
00240 PRINT "ENTER A NUMBER GREATER"
00250 PRINT "THAN 6 TO END"
00260 INPUT N
00270 PRINT
00280 IF N > 6 THEN 999
00290 REM *********************************
00300 REM ***    PLACE NUMBER INTO     ***
00310 REM ***        WRITTEN FORM       ***
00320 REM *********************************
00330 ON N GOTO 350,370,390,410,430,450
00340 GOTO 490
00350 LET N$ = "FIRST"
00360 GOTO 490
00370 LET N$ = "SECOND"
00380 GOTO 490
00390 LET N$ = "THIRD"
00400 GOTO 490
00410 LET N$ = "FOURTH"
00420 GOTO 490
00430 LET N$ = "FIFTH"
00440 GOTO 490
00450 LET N$ = "SIXTH"
00460 REM *********************************
00470 REM *** ENTER CORRESPONDING STATE***
00480 REM *********************************
00490 PRINT "WHICH STATE WAS THE ";N$
00500 PRINT "STATE TO ENTER THE UNION?"
00510 INPUT S$
00520 PRINT
00530 REM *********************************
00540 REM ***   DETERMINE IF IT IS THE ***
00550 REM ***      RIGHT ANSWER         ***
00560 REM *********************************
00570 ON N GOTO 580,600,620,640,660,680
00580 IF S$ = "DELAWARE" THEN 740
00590 GOTO 800
00600 IF S$ = "PENNSYLVANIA" THEN 740
00610 GOTO 800
00620 IF S$ = "NEW JERSEY" THEN 740
00630 GOTO 800
00640 IF S$ = "GEORGIA" THEN 740
00650 GOTO 800
00660 IF S$ = "CONNECTICUT" THEN 740
00670 GOTO 800
00680 IF S$ = "MASSACHUSETTS" THEN 740
00690 GOTO 800
00700 GOTO 800
00710 REM *********************************
00720 REM ***   PRINT "RIGHT" MESSAGE   ***
00730 REM *********************************
00740 PRINT "VERY GOOD, YOU WERE RIGHT!"
00750 PRINT
00760 GOTO 230
00770 REM *********************************
00780 REM ***   PRINT "WRONG" MESSAGE   ***
00790 REM *********************************
00800 PRINT "SORRY, YOUR ANSWER WAS WRONG."
00810 PRINT "TRY AGAIN."
00820 PRINT
00830 GOTO 490
00999 END
```

```
RUNNH
ENTER A NUMBER FROM 1 TO 6
ENTER A NUMBER GREATER
THAN 6 TO END
? 1

WHICH STATE WAS THE FIRST
STATE TO ENTER THE UNION?
? NEW YORK

SORRY, YOUR ANSWER WAS WRONG.
TRY AGAIN.

WHICH STATE WAS THE FIRST
STATE TO ENTER THE UNION?
? DELAWARE

VERY GOOD, YOU WERE RIGHT!

ENTER A NUMBER FROM 1 TO 6
ENTER A NUMBER GREATER
THAN 6 TO END
? 9
```

PSEUDOCODE

```
Start
Start loop, do until number is greater than 6
  Print prompt to enter a number
  Enter a number
  If number = 1
     Then N$ = "FIRST"
  End if
  If number = 2
     Then N$ = "SECOND"
  End if
  If number = 3
     Then N$ = "THIRD"
  End if
  If number = 4
     Then N$ = "FOURTH"
  End if
  If number = 5
     Then N$ = "FIFTH"
  End if
  If number = 6
     Then N$ = "SIXTH"
  End if
  Print prompt with N$ to enter corresponding state's name
  Enter corresponding state's name
  If number = 1
     Then
        If state's name = "Delaware"
           Then
              Print correct message
              Repeat loop
           Else
              Print wrong message
              Enter another state until it equals "Delaware" the
                repeat loop
        Endif
  Endif
  If number = 2
     Then
        If state's name = "Pennsylvania"
           Then
              Print correct message
              Repeat loop
           Else
              Print wrong message
              Enter another state until it equals "Pennsylvania'
                then repeat loop
```

```
    Endif
    If number = 3
      Then
        If state's name = "New Jersey"
          Then
            Print correct message
            Repeat loop
          Else
            Print wrong message
            Enter another state until it equals "New Jersey" then
              repeat loop
        Endif
    Endif
    If number = 4
      Then
        If state's name = "Georgia"
          Then
            Print correct message
            Repeat loop
          Else
            Print wrong message
            Enter another state until it equals "Georgia" then
              repeat loop
        Endif
    Endif
    If number = 5
      Then
        If state's name = "Connecticut"
          Then
            Print correct message
            Repeat loop
          Else
            Print wrong message
            Enter another state until it equals "Connecticut" then
              repeat loop
        Endif
    Endif
    If number = 6
      Then
        If state's name = "Massachusetts"
          Then
            Print correct message
            Repeat loop
          Else
            Print wrong message
            Enter another state until it equals "Massachusetts"
              then repeat loop
        Endif
    Endif
Endloop
Stop
```

```
MICROCOMPUTERS:

Apple                No differences.
Apple Macintosh      No differences.
IBM/Microsoft        No differences.
PET/Commodore 64     No differences.
TRS-80               No differences.
```

Problem B

A building contractor has asked you to help him. In this building he needs to have an electrical socket every four feet in each room. He has asked you to write a program to give the number of sockets that should be included in a room of any size. The input to this program will be the length and width of the room. Use INPUT statements because the size of the room is going to change often. To determine the number of sockets needed just divide the area of the room by 4. Here is some test data:

LENGTH	WIDTH
4	3
8.5	7
9	6
11	8.5

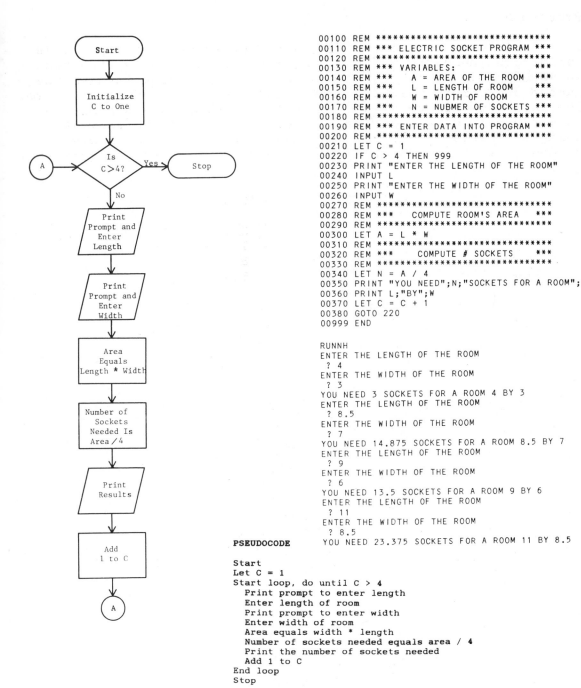

```
00100 REM ********************************
00110 REM *** ELECTRIC SOCKET PROGRAM ***
00120 REM ********************************
00130 REM *** VARIABLES:              ***
00140 REM ***    A = AREA OF THE ROOM ***
00150 REM ***    L = LENGTH OF ROOM   ***
00160 REM ***    W = WIDTH OF ROOM    ***
00170 REM ***    N = NUBMER OF SOCKETS ***
00180 REM ********************************
00190 REM *** ENTER DATA INTO PROGRAM ***
00200 REM ********************************
00210 LET C = 1
00220 IF C > 4 THEN 999
00230 PRINT "ENTER THE LENGTH OF THE ROOM"
00240 INPUT L
00250 PRINT "ENTER THE WIDTH OF THE ROOM"
00260 INPUT W
00270 REM ********************************
00280 REM ***    COMPUTE ROOM'S AREA   ***
00290 REM ********************************
00300 LET A = L * W
00310 REM ********************************
00320 REM ***    COMPUTE # SOCKETS     ***
00330 REM ********************************
00340 LET N = A / 4
00350 PRINT "YOU NEED";N;"SOCKETS FOR A ROOM";
00360 PRINT L;"BY";W
00370 LET C = C + 1
00380 GOTO 220
00999 END

RUNNH
ENTER THE LENGTH OF THE ROOM
 ? 4
ENTER THE WIDTH OF THE ROOM
 ? 3
YOU NEED 3 SOCKETS FOR A ROOM 4 BY 3
ENTER THE LENGTH OF THE ROOM
 ? 8.5
ENTER THE WIDTH OF THE ROOM
 ? 7
YOU NEED 14.875 SOCKETS FOR A ROOM 8.5 BY 7
ENTER THE LENGTH OF THE ROOM
 ? 9
ENTER THE WIDTH OF THE ROOM
 ? 6
YOU NEED 13.5 SOCKETS FOR A ROOM 9 BY 6
ENTER THE LENGTH OF THE ROOM
 ? 11
ENTER THE WIDTH OF THE ROOM
 ? 8.5
YOU NEED 23.375 SOCKETS FOR A ROOM 11 BY 8.5
```

PSEUDOCODE

```
Start
Let C = 1
Start loop, do until C > 4
  Print prompt to enter length
  Enter length of room
  Print prompt to enter width
  Enter width of room
  Area equals width * length
  Number of sockets needed equals area / 4
  Print the number of sockets needed
  Add 1 to C
End loop
Stop
```

MICROCOMPUTERS:	
Apple	No differences.
Apple Macintosh	No differences.
IBM/Microsoft	No differences.
PET/Commodore 64	No differences.
TRS-80	No differences.

Problem C

The Financial Aid Officer at your school needs your help. She has many loan applications to look at and determine if the student is eligible for financial aid. She has asked you to write a program to help her. She wants the program to determine if the student meets the basic eligibility requirements. The requirements are as follows:

1. If the student is male, has he registered for the draft?
2. Does the student have a combined income total of $40,000 or less?
3. Does the student have at least a 2.2 GPA?
4. Is the student registered for at least 12 hours?

If the student is eligible, she wants you to write "ELIGIBLE" next to the student's name. If the student is not eligible, she wants you to write "NOT ELIGIBLE" next to the student's name. The printed report should look like this:

```
              STUDENT LOAN ELIGIBILITY REPORT
                    FOR YEAR 1985-86

         NAME                        LOAN STATUS

         XXXXXXXXXXXXXXXXX           NOT ELIGIBLE
         XXXXXXXXXXXXXXXXX           ELIGIBLE
         XXXXXXXXXXXXXXXXX           ELIGIBLE
         XXXXXXXXXXXXXXXXX           NOT ELIGIBLE
```

The input data consists of the student's name, sex (M for male and F for female), draft registration (Y for Yes and N for No), combined income, GPA, and number of registered class hours. The input data is as follows:

NAME	SEX	DRAFT?	INCOME	GPA	HOURS
Shawn Gregory	M	Y	30000	2.3	14
Patricia Olmstead	F	N	25000	3.0	11
Connie DelVecchio	F	N	41000	2.5	17
David Pollio	M	N	40000	3.4	15
Robert Lin	M	Y	32000	2.1	15
Jody Thelms	F	N	21500	2.0	12
Pauline Lewis	F	N	37500	3.5	14

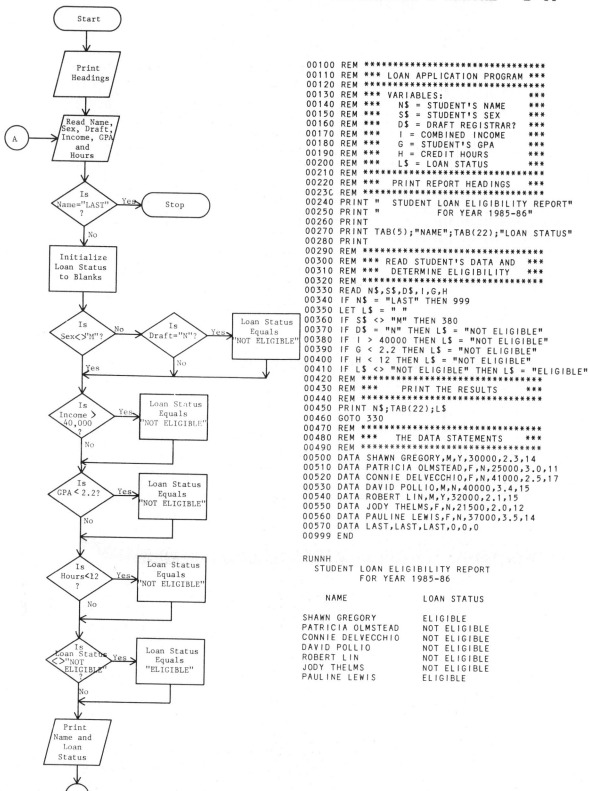

```
00100 REM *********************************
00110 REM *** LOAN APPLICATION PROGRAM ***
00120 REM *********************************
00130 REM *** VARIABLES:                ***
00140 REM ***    N$ = STUDENT'S NAME    ***
00150 REM ***    S$ = STUDENT'S SEX     ***
00160 REM ***    D$ = DRAFT REGISTRAR?  ***
00170 REM ***    I = COMBINED INCOME    ***
00180 REM ***    G = STUDENT'S GPA      ***
00190 REM ***    H = CREDIT HOURS       ***
00200 REM ***    L$ = LOAN STATUS       ***
00210 REM *********************************
00220 REM ***   PRINT REPORT HEADINGS   ***
00230 REM *********************************
00240 PRINT "   STUDENT LOAN ELIGIBILITY REPORT"
00250 PRINT "           FOR YEAR 1985-86"
00260 PRINT
00270 PRINT TAB(5);"NAME";TAB(22);"LOAN STATUS"
00280 PRINT
00290 REM *********************************
00300 REM *** READ STUDENT'S DATA AND   ***
00310 REM ***   DETERMINE ELIGIBILITY   ***
00320 REM *********************************
00330 READ N$,S$,D$,I,G,H
00340 IF N$ = "LAST" THEN 999
00350 LET L$ = " "
00360 IF S$ <> "M" THEN 380
00370 IF D$ = "N" THEN L$ = "NOT ELIGIBLE"
00380 IF I > 40000 THEN L$ = "NOT ELIGIBLE"
00390 IF G < 2.2 THEN L$ = "NOT ELIGIBLE"
00400 IF H < 12 THEN L$ = "NOT ELIGIBLE"
00410 IF L$ <> "NOT ELIGIBLE" THEN L$ = "ELIGIBLE"
00420 REM *********************************
00430 REM ***    PRINT THE RESULTS      ***
00440 REM *********************************
00450 PRINT N$;TAB(22);L$
00460 GOTO 330
00470 REM *********************************
00480 REM ***    THE DATA STATEMENTS    ***
00490 REM *********************************
00500 DATA SHAWN GREGORY,M,Y,30000,2.3,14
00510 DATA PATRICIA OLMSTEAD,F,N,25000,3.0,11
00520 DATA CONNIE DELVECCHIO,F,N,41000,2.5,17
00530 DATA DAVID POLLIO,M,N,40000,3.4,15
00540 DATA ROBERT LIN,M,Y,32000,2.1,15
00550 DATA JODY THELMS,F,N,21500,2.0,12
00560 DATA PAULINE LEWIS,F,N,37000,3.5,14
00570 DATA LAST,LAST,LAST,0,0,0
00999 END
```

```
RUNNH
   STUDENT LOAN ELIGIBILITY REPORT
           FOR YEAR 1985-86

    NAME                LOAN STATUS

SHAWN GREGORY          ELIGIBLE
PATRICIA OLMSTEAD      NOT ELIGIBLE
CONNIE DELVECCHIO      NOT ELIGIBLE
DAVID POLLIO           NOT ELIGIBLE
ROBERT LIN             NOT ELIGIBLE
JODY THELMS            NOT ELIGIBLE
PAULINE LEWIS          ELIGIBLE
```

PSEUDOCODE

```
Start
Print the report headings
Start loop, do until name equals "LAST"
  Read name, sex, draft registrar?, combined income, GPA, and
    hours
  Initialize loan status to blanks
  If sex = "M"
    Then
      If draft registrar = "N"
        Then
        Loan status = "NOT ELIGIBLE"
      Endif
  Endif
  If income > 40000
    Then
    Loan status = "NOT ELIGIBLE"
  Endif
  If GPA < 2.2
    Then
    Loan status = "NOT ELIGIBLE"
  Endif
  If hours < 12
    Then
    Loan status = "NOT ELIGIBLE"
  Endif
  If loan status not equal to "NOT ELIGIBLE"
    Then
    Loan status equals "ELIGIBLE"
  Endif
  Print name and loan status
End loop
Stop
```

MICROCOMPUTERS:	
Apple	No differences.
Apple Macintosh	No differences.
IBM/Microsoft	No differences.
PET/Commodore 64	No differences.
TRS-80	No differences.

Problem D

The Record Place is having a sale on albums. All albums marked "D" are marked 20 percent off and all albums marked "C" are ten percent off. The Manager of The Record Place wants you to write a program to input albums and print out a report of the albums, the artist, the regular price, and the sales price. Since some albums are not on sale, the report would list the albums's sale price as the album's regular price. Use READ/DATA statements to enter the data. The report should be formatted with the PRINT USING statements as shown below:

```
                      ALBUM SALES PRICES

ALBUM                ARTIST            REGULAR PRICE    SALES PRICE

XXXXXXXXXXXXXXXXXX   XXXXXXXXXXXXXXX      ##.##            ##.##
XXXXXXXXXXXXXXXXXX   XXXXXXXXXXXXXXX      ##.##            ##.##
XXXXXXXXXXXXXXXXXX   XXXXXXXXXXXXXXX      ##.##            ##.##
```

The input data will consist of the name of the album, the artist, the regular price, and the price marking (A, B, C, or D). Use the following for the input data:

ALBUM	ARTIST	REGULAR PRICE	PRICE MARKING
Extended Play	The Pretenders	7.99	C
Bad Company	Bad Company	7.99	A
Departure	Journey	6.99	D
Face Dances	The Who	7.99	B
Greatest Hits	Blondie	8.99	C

```
00100 REM ****************************
00110 REM *** ALBUM SALE PROGRAM  ***
00120 REM ****************************
00130 REM *** N$ = ALBUM'S NAME    ***
00140 REM *** A$ = ARTIST'S NAME   ***
00150 REM *** R  = REGULAR PRICE   ***
00160 REM *** S  = SALES PRICE     ***
00170 REM *** M  = PRICE MARKING   ***
00180 REM ****************************
00190 REM *** PRINT THE HEADINGS   ***
00200 REM ****************************
00210 PRINT TAB(25);"ALBUM SALES PRICES"
00220 PRINT
00230 PRINT "ALBUM";TAB(18);"ARTIST";
00240 PRINT TAB(35);"REGULAR PRICE";TAB(50);"SALES PRICE"
00250 PRINT
00260 REM ****************************
00270 REM ***   READ THE DATA AND   ***
00280 REM *** COMPUTE SALES PRICE ***
00290 REM ****************************
00300 READ N$,A$,R,M$
00310 IF N$ = "END" THEN 999
00320 IF M$ = "C" THEN 360
00330 IF M$ = "D" THEN 380
00340 LET S = R
00350 GOTO 390
00360 LET S = R * 0.90
00370 GOTO 390
00380 LET S = R * 0.80
00390 PRINT USING 410,N$,A$,R,S
00400 GOTO 300
00410:'LLLLLLLLLLLLLL    'LLLLLLLLLLLLLL    ##.##        ##.##
00420 REM ****************************
00430 REM *** THE DATA STATEMENTS ***
00440 REM ****************************
00450 DATA EXTENDED PLAY,PRETENDERS,7.99,C
00460 DATA BAD COMPANY,BAD COMPANY,7.99,A
00470 DATA DEPARTURE,JOURNEY,6.99,D
00480 DATA FACE DANCES,THE WHO,7.99,B
00490 DATA GREATEST HITS,BLONDIE,8.99,C
00500 DATA END,END,0,END
00999 END

RUNNH
```

```
                         ALBUM SALES PRICES

ALBUM              ARTIST          REGULAR PRICE   SALES PRICE

EXTENDED PLAY      PRETENDERS          7.99           7.19
BAD COMPANY        BAD COMPANY         7.99           7.99
DEPARTURE          JOURNEY             6.99           5.59
FACE DANCES        THE WHO             7.99           7.99
GREATEST HITS      BLONDIE             8.99           8.09
```

MICROCOMPUTERS:	
Apple	No PRINT USING statement.
Apple Macintosh	PRINT USING statement is different; see Section IV of text.
IBM/Microsoft	PRINT USING statement is different; see Section IV of text.
PET/Commodore 64	No PRINT USING statement.
TRS-80	PRINT USING statement is different; see Section IV of text.

PSEUDOCODE

```
Start
Print the report headings
Do until album name equals "END"
   Read the album name, artist, regular price, and price marking
   If price marking equals "C"
      Then
         Sales price equals regular price * 0.90
      Else
         If price marking equals "D"
            Then
               Sales price equals regular price * 0.80
            Else
               Sales price equals regular price
         Endif
   Endif
   Print album name, artist, regular price, and sales price
End loop
Stop
```

SECTION VI
More About Looping

ANSWERS TO TEXTBOOK REVIEW QUESTIONS

1. ● The loop variable is set to the initial value indicated.
    ● The first time the loop is executed, the loop variable is tested to see if it exceeds the terminal value. If the value of the loop variable doesn't exceed the terminal value, the loop is executed. If the value of the loop variable exceeds the terminal value, control is transferred to the statement following the NEXT statement.

2. ● The step value is added to the loop variable.
    ● The loop variable is tested to see if it exceeds the terminal value.
    ● If the value of the loop variable doesn't exceed the terminal value the statements within the loop are executed.
    ● If the value of the loop variable exceeds the terminal value, control is transferred to the statement following the statement immediately following.

3. True

4. Be careful not to mix the FOR of one loop with the NEXT of another. Also, do not to use the same loop variable for both loops.

ANSWERS TO TEXTBOOK DEBUGGING EXERCISES

1.
```
10 FOR I = 1 TO 20 STEP -2
15    READ N
20    IF N > 15 THEN 10
25    PRINT N
30 NEXT I
```
step must be a positive value. otherwise an infinite loop is created

control should be transferred to line 30

2.
```
10 FOR J = 1 TO 5
15    FOR K = 3 TO 9
20      LET J = J + 2
25    NEXT J
30 NEXT K
```
The value of the loop variable may not be changed within the loop

The loops have been interchanged, Line 25 should be NEXT K and Line 30 should be NEXT J

ANSWER TO TEXTBOOK PROGRAMMING PROBLEM 1

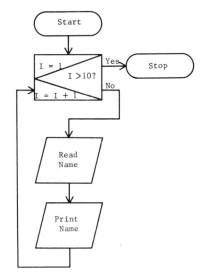

```
00100 REM *** READ AND PRINT A LIST OF 10 NAMES ***
00110 REM *** N$ - NAME ***
00120 PRINT
00130 FOR I = 1 TO 10
00140   READ N$
00150   PRINT N$
00160 NEXT I
00170 DATA "JOHN","KAREN","EDWARD","DAVID","TONYA"
00180 DATA "CANDY","ROBERT","MIKE","JOSE","LISA"
00999 END

READY
RUNNH

JOHN
KAREN
EDWARD
DAVID
TONYA
CANDY
ROBERT
MIKE
JOSE
LISA
```

PSEUDOCODE

```
Start
Do ten times
  Read and print name
  Repeat
Stop
```

MICROCOMPUTERS:	
Apple	No differences.
Apple Macintosh	No differences.
IBM/Microsoft	No differences.
PET/Commodore 64	No differences.
TRS-80	No differences.

ANSWER TO TEXTBOOK PROGRAMMING PROBLEM 2

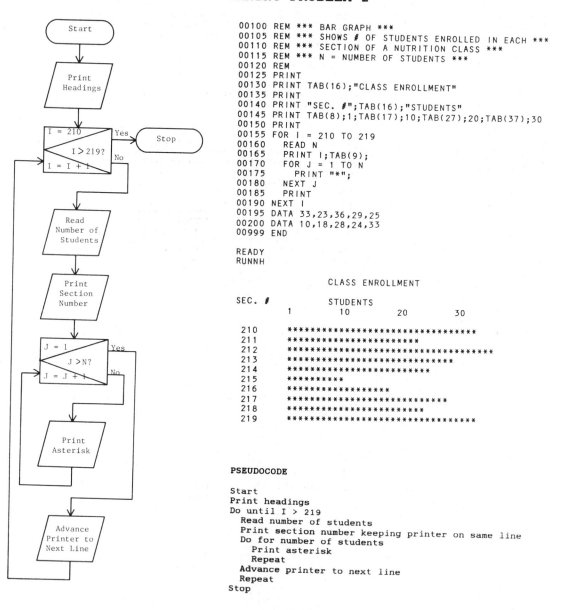

```
00100 REM *** BAR GRAPH ***
00105 REM *** SHOWS # OF STUDENTS ENROLLED IN EACH ***
00110 REM *** SECTION OF A NUTRITION CLASS ***
00115 REM *** N = NUMBER OF STUDENTS ***
00120 REM
00125 PRINT
00130 PRINT TAB(16);"CLASS ENROLLMENT"
00135 PRINT
00140 PRINT "SEC. #";TAB(16);"STUDENTS"
00145 PRINT TAB(8);1;TAB(17);10;TAB(27);20;TAB(37);30
00150 PRINT
00155 FOR I = 210 TO 219
00160    READ N
00165    PRINT I;TAB(9);
00170    FOR J = 1 TO N
00175       PRINT "*";
00180    NEXT J
00185    PRINT
00190 NEXT I
00195 DATA 33,23,36,29,25
00200 DATA 10,18,28,24,33
00999 END

READY
RUNNH
```

```
                    CLASS ENROLLMENT

SEC. #              STUDENTS
                1       10       20       30

   210       ********************************
   211       ***********************
   212       ************************************
   213       *****************************
   214       *************************
   215       **********
   216       ******************
   217       ***************************
   218       *************************
   219       ********************************
```

PSEUDOCODE

```
Start
Print headings
Do until I > 219
  Read number of students
  Print section number keeping printer on same line
  Do for number of students
    Print asterisk
    Repeat
  Advance printer to next line
  Repeat
Stop
```

MICROCOMPUTERS:	
Apple	Screen width differences; lines carry over to next line.
Apple Macintosh	No differences.
IBM/Microsoft	No differences.
PET/Commodore 64	Screen width differences; lines carry over to next line.
TRS-80	No differences.

ANSWER TO STUDY GUIDE PROGRAMMING PROBLEM 2

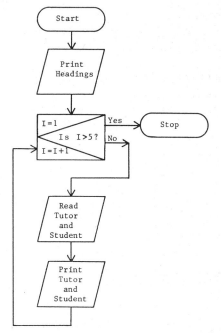

```
00100 REM ****************************
00110 REM *** STUDENT TUTOR PROGRAM ***
00120 REM ****************************
00130 REM *** VARIABLES:          ***
00140 REM ***   T$ = NAME OF TUTOR   ***
00150 REM ***   S$ = NAME OF STUDENT ***
00160 REM ****************************
00170 REM ***   PRINT THE HEADINGS   ***
00180 REM ****************************
00190 PRINT TAB(12);"TUTOR LIST"
00200 PRINT
00210 PRINT TAB(3);"TUTOR";TAB(23);"STUDENT"
00220 PRINT
00230 REM ****************************
00240 REM *** READ & PRINT THE DATA ***
00250 REM ****************************
00260 FOR I = 1 TO 5
00270    READ T$,S$
00280    PRINT T$;TAB(20);S$
00290 NEXT I
00300 REM ****************************
00310 REM ***   THE DATA STATEMENTS   ***
00320 REM ****************************
00330 DATA KATHI JOHNSON,LONNIE MACARTHUR
00340 DATA PAT WILLIS,BARRY MOORE
00350 DATA ALAN RATH,KAREN HOLLAND
00360 DATA JENNIFER LORING,MARTHA EDISON
00370 DATA DONNA CORNELL,RANDY PARSONS
00999 END


RUNNH
            TUTOR LIST

    TUTOR              STUDENT

KATHI JOHNSON      LONNIE MACARTHUR
PAT WILLIS         BARRY MOORE
ALAN RATH          KAREN HOLLAND
JENNIFER LORING    MARTHA EDISON
DONNA CORNELL      RANDY PARSONS
```

PSEUDOCODE

```
Start
Print the report headings
Start loop, do 5 times
   Read tutor's name and student's name
   Print tutor's name and student's name
End loop
Stop
```

MICROCOMPUTERS:	
Apple	No differences.
Apple Macintosh	No differences.
IBM/Microsoft	No differences.
PET/Commodore 64	No differences.
TRS-80	No differences.

ANSWERS TO STUDY GUIDE WORKSHEET PROBLEMS

2.    ```
10 FOR I = 100 TO 75 STEP -5
20   PRINT I
30 NEXT I
99 END
```

4.    ```
10 INPUT "ENTER A POSITIVE INTEGER";N
20 LET S = 1
30 FOR I = N TO (N - N + 1) STEP -1
40   LET S = S * N
50 NEXT I
60 PRINT S
99 END
```

6.   a.   ```
10 FOR I = 10 TO 1 STEP -1
   .
   .
   .
50 NEXT I
```

    b.    ```
20 FOR J = 2 TO 12 STEP 2
30   LET S = S + J
40 NEXT J
```

    c.   ```
50 FOR K = 1 TO 10 STEP 2
60   LET S = K + 1
70   PRINT S
80 NEXT K
```

    d.    ```
10 FOR X = 1 TO 10 STEP 1
20   PRINT X
30   LET S = X * S
40 NEXT X
```

8.   a.   ```
10 FOR I = 1 TO 10
20   FOR J = 2 TO 4
30   IF (I + J) = 6 THEN 50
40   PRINT I,J
50   NEXT J
60 NEXT I
```

    b.    ```
10 FOR I = 10 TO 5 STEP -1
20   FOR J = 3 TO 1 STEP -1
30     FOR K = 9 TO 12
         .
         .
         .
80     NEXT K
90   NEXT J
100 NEXT I
```

10.   1 1 8   1 1 10
       1 2 8   1 2 10
       1 3 8   1 3 10
       2 1 8   2 1 10
       2 2 8   2 2 10
       2 3 8   2 3 10

SUPPLEMENTARY PROGRAMMING PROBLEMS

Problem A

Washington College needs a program to determine the late enrollment for its CS 101 class. The input data consists of the student's name, his or her class rank, and the class he or she registered late to take. From this information Washington College needs a report containing a horizontal bar graph depicting the late enrollment of its CS 101 class by the student's class rank and by the total as a whole. An example is shown below:

```
        LATE ENROLLMENT FOR CS 101
              SPRING, 1985

            1        10       20       30       40

FRESHMEN:      ++++++++++++++
SOPHOMORES:    ??????????????
JUNIORS:       //////
SENIORS:       $

TOTAL:         ************************************************
```

The input data is listed below. Note there are twenty students.

Herman Roberts	Sophomore	CS 101
Donald Kreischer	Senior	CS 101
Kelly Pollack	Junior	MGMT 300
Valerie Long	Senior	CS 101
Helen McDonald	Freshman	CS 101
Patrick Dunbar	Freshman	SOC 100
Julie Travers	Senior	CS 101
Lucy Rivers	Sophomore	MIS 200
Lionel Travers	Senior	CS 101
William Wilson	Junior	CS 101
Darryl Hanson	Freshman	CS 101
Ronald Chapman	Senior	CS 101
Dwight Anderson	Junior	CS 101
Holly Compton	Sophomore	CS 101
Rhoda Olsen	Freshman	MATH 124
Gregory Harmon	Junior	CS 101
Mary Mooney	Senior	CS 101
Carrie Sanders	Sophomore	CS 101
Theodore Rogers	Freshman	CS 101
Tracy Smith	Junior	CS 101

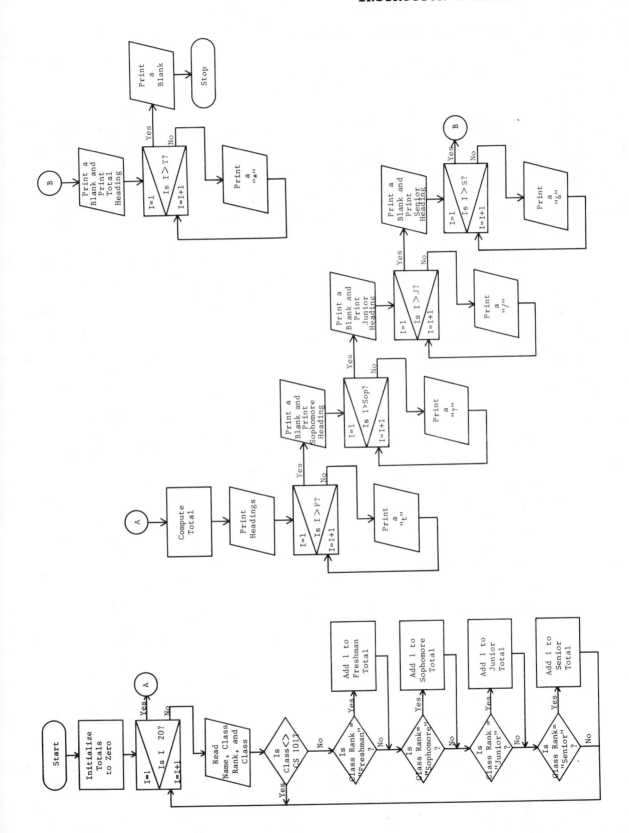

```
00100 REM ********************************
00110 REM *** CS 101 ENROLLMENT PROGRAM ***
00120 REM ********************************
00130 REM *** VARIABLES:              ***
00140 REM ***     F = # FRESHMEN       ***
00150 REM ***     SOP = # SOPHOMORES   ***
00160 REM ***     J = # JUNIORS        ***
00170 REM ***     S = # SENIORS        ***
00180 REM ***     T = TOTAL ENROLLMENT ***
00190 REM ***     N$ = STUDENT'S NAME  ***
00200 REM ***     S$ = CLASS RANK      ***
00210 REM ***     C$ = NAME OF THE CLASS ***
00220 REM ********************************
00230 LET F = 0
00240 LET SOP = 0
00250 LET J = 0
00260 LET S = 0
00270 REM ********************************
00280 REM ***        READ THE DATA     ***
00290 REM ********************************
00300 FOR I = 1 TO 20
00310   READ N$,S$,C$
00320   REM ********************************
00330   REM ***     COMPUTE THE TOTALS   ***
00340   REM ********************************
00350   IF C$ <> "CS 101" THEN 400
00360   IF S$ = "FRESHMAN" THEN F = F + 1
00370   IF S$ = "SOPHOMORE" THEN SOP = SOP + 1
00380   IF S$ = "JUNIOR" THEN J = J + 1
00390   IF S$ = "SENIOR" THEN S = S + 1
00400 NEXT I
00410 LET T = F + SOP + J + S
00420 REM ********************************
00430 REM ***       PRINT THE BAR GRAPH  ***
00440 REM ********************************
00450 PRINT
00460 PRINT "ENROLLMENT FOR CS 101"
00470 PRINT "     SPRING, 1985"
00480 PRINT
00490 PRINT "              1    5   10   15   20"
00500 PRINT
00510 PRINT "FRESHMEN:     ";
00520 FOR I = 1 TO F
00530   PRINT "+";
00540 NEXT I
00550 PRINT
00560 PRINT "SOPHOMORES:   ";
00570 FOR I = 1 TO SOP
00580   PRINT "?";
00590 NEXT I
00600 PRINT
00610 PRINT "JUNIORS:      ";
00620 FOR I = 1 TO J
00630   PRINT "/";
00640 NEXT I
00650 PRINT
00660 PRINT "SENIORS:      ";
00670 FOR I = 1 TO S
00680   PRINT "$";
00690 NEXT I
00700 PRINT
00710 PRINT "TOTAL:        ";
00720 FOR I = 1 TO T
00730   PRINT "*";
00740 NEXT I
00750 PRINT
```

```
00760 REM ********************************
00770 REM ***     THE DATA STATEMENTS   ***
00780 REM ********************************
00790 DATA HERMAN ROBERTS,SOPHOMORE,CS 101
00800 DATA DONALD KREISCHER,SENIOR,CS 101
00810 DATA KELLY POLLACK,JUNIOR,MGMT 300
00820 DATA VALERIE LONG,SENIOR,CS 101
00830 DATA HELEN MCDONALD,FRESHMAN,CS 101
00840 DATA PATRICK DUNBAR,FRESHMAN,SOC 100
00850 DATA JULIE WYLAN,SENIOR,CS 101
00860 DATA LUCY RIVERS,SOPHOMORE,MIS 200
00870 DATA LIONEL TRAVERS,SENIOR,CS 101
00880 DATA WILLIAM WILSON,JUNIOR,CS 101
00890 DATA DARRYL HANSON,FRESHMAN,CS 101
00900 DATA RONALD CHAPMAN,SENIOR,CS 101
00910 DATA DWIGHT ANDERSON,JUNIOR,CS 101
00920 DATA HOLLY COMPTON,SOPHOMORE,CS 101
00930 DATA RHODA OLSEN,FRESHMAN,MATH 124
00940 DATA GREGORY HARMON,JUNIOR,CS 101
00950 DATA MARY MOONE,SENIOR,CS 101
00960 DATA CARRIE SANDERS,SOPHOMORE,CS 101
00970 DATA THEODORE ROGERS,FRESHMAN,CS 101
00980 DATA TRACY SMITH,JUNIOR,CS 101
00999 END

RUNNH

ENROLLMENT FOR CS 101
     SPRING, 1985

              1    5   10   15   20

FRESHMEN:     +++
SOPHOMORES:   ???
JUNIORS:      ////
SENIORS:      $$$$$
TOTAL:        ***************
```

PSEUDOCODE

```
Start
Set all totals equal to zero
Start loop, do twenty times
  Read student's name, class rank, and class
  If class equals CS 101
    Then go to endloop
  Endif
  If class rank equals "Freshman"
    Then add one to Freshman counter
  Endif
  If class rank equals "Sophomore"
    Then add one to Sophomore counter
  Endif
  If class rank equals "Junior"
    Then add one to Junior counter
  Endif
  If class rank equals "Senior"
    Then add one to Senior counter
  Endif
End loop
Total equals freshman counter + sophomore counter + junior
  counter + senior counter
Print the report headings
Start loop, do until I = freshman counter
  Print "+"
End loop
Print a blank
Start loop, do until I = sophomore counter
  Print "?"
End loop
Print a blank
Start loop, do until I = junior counter
  Print "/"
End loop
Print a blank
Start loop, do until I = senior counter
  Print "$"
End loop
Print a blank
Start loop, do until I = total
  Print "*"
End loop
Stop
```

MICROCOMPUTERS:	
Apple	No differences.
Apple Macintosh	No differences.
IBM/Microsoft	No differences.
PET/Commodore 64	No differences.
TRS-80	No differences.

Problem B

   The Stay-Slim Health Club has opened recently in your
college town. The Club is offering two types of membership,
"weight training" membership and "all facilities" membership.
The manager of Stay-Slim has asked you to write a program to
print out a list of the new members of the club and the type of
membership they hold. The program should use at least one
FOR/NEXT loop. The report should look as follows:

                    STAY-SLIM HEALTH CLUB

           MEMBER   MEMBERSHIP

           XXXXXXXXXXXXXXXXX   XXXXXXXXXXXXX
           XXXXXXXXXXXXXXXXX   XXXXXXXXXXXXX
           XXXXXXXXXXXXXXXXX   XXXXXXXXXXXXX
           XXXXXXXXXXXXXXXXX   XXXXXXXXXXXXX
           XXXXXXXXXXXXXXXXX   XXXXXXXXXXXXX
           XXXXXXXXXXXXXXXXX   XXXXXXXXXXXXX
           XXXXXXXXXXXXXXXXX   XXXXXXXXXXXXX

   The input data to be used is listed below:

            Shelley Longsmith, all facilities
            Kenneth Upjohn, all facilities
            Wallace Turner, weight training
            Laura Placid, all facilities
            Bethany Wooster, weight training
            Colleen Oversight, all facilities
            Paul Kruzich, weight facilities

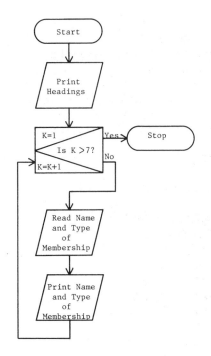

```
00100 REM **************************************
00110 REM *** HEALTH CLUB MEMBERSHIP PROGRAM ***
00120 REM **************************************
00130 REM *** VARIABLES:                     ***
00140 REM ***   N$ = THE MEMBER'S NAME        ***
00150 REM ***   M$ = TYPE OF MEMBERSHIP       ***
00160 REM **************************************
00170 REM ***        PRINT THE HEADINGS       ***
00180 REM **************************************
00190 PRINT
00200 PRINT TAB(5);"STAY-SLIM HEALTH CLUB"
00210 PRINT
00220 PRINT "MEMBER";TAB(20);"MEMBERSHIP"
00230 PRINT
00240 REM **************************************
00250 REM *** READ/PRINT NAME AND MEMBERSHIP ***
00260 REM **************************************
00270 FOR K = 1 TO 7
00280   READ N$,M$
00290   PRINT N$;TAB(20);M$
00300 NEXT K
00310 REM **************************************
00320 REM ***        THE DATA STATEMENTS      ***
00330 REM **************************************
00340 DATA SHELLEY LONGSMITH,ALL FACILITIES
00350 DATA KENNETH UPJOHN,ALL FACILITIES
00360 DATA WALLACE TURNER,WEIGHT TRAINING
00370 DATA LAURA PLACID,ALL FACILITIES
00380 DATA BETHANY WOOSTER,WEIGHT TRAINING
00390 DATA COLLEEN OVERSIGHT,ALL FACILITIES
00400 DATA PAUL KRUZICH,WEIGHT TRAINING
00999 END

RUNNH

     STAY-SLIM HEALTH CLUB

MEMBER              MEMBERSHIP

SHELLEY LONGSMITH   ALL FACILITIES
KENNETH UPJOHN      ALL FACILITIES
WALLACE TURNER      WEIGHT TRAINING
LAURA PLACID        ALL FACILITIES
BETHANY WOOSTER     WEIGHT TRAINING
COLLEEN OVERSIGHT   ALL FACILITIES
PAUL KRUZICH        WEIGHT TRAINING
```

PSEUDOCODE

```
Start
Print the report headings
Start loop, do 7 times
  Read name and type of membership
  Print name and type of membership
End loop
Stop
```

MICROCOMPUTERS:	
Apple	No differences.
Apple Macintosh	No differences.
IBM/Microsoft	No differences.
PET/Commodore 64	No differences.
TRS-80	No differences.

Problem C

The administration at Playground University have asked you
to help them write a program to print out a report of all
business teachers returning in the fall. The administration has
also asked you to print out the classes each teacher will be
teaching (only one class per teacher). The program should use
a FOR/NEXT loop. Use the following format for the report:

                    BUSINESS PROFESSORS

         NAME   CLASS

         XXXXXXXXXXXXXXXXX   XXXXXX
         XXXXXXXXXXXXXXXXX   XXXXXX
         XXXXXXXXXXXXXXXXX   XXXXXX

The input data consists of the professor's name and the
class he or she will teach in the fall. There will be six pro-
fessors returning. The input data is listed below:

              Gonsalves, Frank - Acct 221
              Smith, Tom - Stat 212
              Juniper, Pat - Econ 200
              Preech, Laura - Acct 321
              Kruger, Brian - Stat 211
              VanDerWalle, Sherry - Econ 305

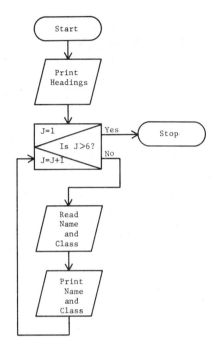

```
00100 REM **********************************
00110 REM *** BUSINESS PROFESSOR PROGRAM ***
00120 REM **********************************
00130 REM *** VARIABLES:                 ***
00140 REM ***  P$ = PROFESSOR'S NAME     ***
00150 REM ***  C$ = CLASS NAME           ***
00160 REM **********************************
00170 REM ***      PRINT THE HEADINGS    ***
00180 REM **********************************
00190 PRINT
00200 PRINT
00210 PRINT TAB(5);"BUSINESS PROFESSORS"
00220 PRINT
00230 PRINT "PROFESSOR";TAB(20);"CLASS"
00240 PRINT
00250 REM **********************************
00260 REM ***    PRINT OUT THE REPORT    ***
00270 REM **********************************
00280 FOR J = 1 TO 6
00290    READ P$,C$
00300    PRINT P$;TAB(20);C$
00310 NEXT J
00320 REM **********************************
00330 REM ***     THE DATA STATEMENTS    ***
00340 REM **********************************
00350 DATA FRANK GONSALVES,ACCT 221,TOM SMITH,STAT 212
00360 DATA PAT JUNIPER,ECON 200,LAURA PREECH,ACCT 321
00370 DATA BRIAN KRUGER,STAT 211,SHERRY VANDERWALL
00380 DATA ECON 305
00999 END


RUNNH


      BUSINESS PROFESSORS

PROFESSOR           CLASS

FRANK GONSALVES     ACCT 221
TOM SMITH           STAT 212
PAT JUNIPER         ECON 200
LAURA PREECH        ACCT 321
BRIAN KRUGER        STAT 211
SHERRY VANDERWALL   ECON 305
```

PSEUDOCODE

```
Start
Print the report headings
Start loop, do six times
  Read Professor's name and class
  Print Professor's name and class
End loop
Stop
```

MICROCOMPUTERS:	
Apple	No differences.
Apple Macintosh	No differences.
IBM/Microsoft	No differences.
PET/Commodore 64	No differences.
TRS-80	No differences.

Problem D

    The University Ice Arena sponsors hockey intramurals during
each semester. The manager of the Ice Arena needs a listing of
each team and its captain. The manager has asked you to write a
program to print out each team listing. The program will only
be run once for each hockey team. The first player on the list
must be the captain of the team and the last player on the list
is the goalie. Each team has twelve players including the captain and the goalie. Use INPUT statements to enter the players'
names and the team's name. Use appropriate prompts when
entering the data. Also, use FOR/NEXT loops in the program.
The report should look as follows:

<pre>
                    TEAM NAME

          XXXXXXXXXXXXXXXXX   CAPTAIN
          XXXXXXXXXXXXXXXXX
          XXXXXXXXXXXXXXXXX
          XXXXXXXXXXXXXXXX
                   .
                   .
                   .
          XXXXXXXXXXXXXXXXX   GOALIE
</pre>

    Use the following as input to your program:

        TEAM NAME - Knights

        PLAYERS - Kevin Luce (Captain)
                Brian Cranston
                Larry Conroy
                Paul Holly
                Rick VanGoerder
                Matt Lysack
                Terry Jon
                Sam Hamilton
                Scott Curtiss
                Issac Wolfly
                Ed Court
                Jay Brown (Goalie)

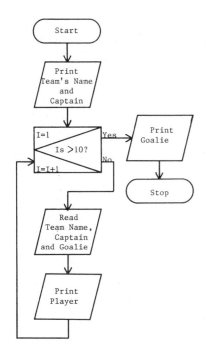

```
00100 REM ******************************
00110 REM *** HOCKEY INTRAMURAL PROGRAM ***
00120 REM ******************************
00130 REM *** VARIABLES:              ***
00140 REM ***   T$ = TEAM'S NAME      ***
00150 REM ***   P$ = PLAYER'S NAME    ***
00160 REM ***   C$ = CAPTAIN'S NAME   ***
00170 REM ***   G$ = GOALIE'S NAME    ***
00180 REM ******************************
00190 REM ***        READ THE DATA    ***
00200 REM ******************************
00210 READ T$,C$,G$
00220 REM ******************************
00230 REM ***    PRINT THE HEADINGS   ***
00240 REM ******************************
00250 PRINT
00260 PRINT
00270 PRINT "TEAM NAME - ";T$
00280 PRINT
00290 PRINT "PLAYERS - ";C$;TAB(30);"CAPTAIN"
00300 REM ******************************
00310 REM *** PRINT REST OF THE REPORT ***
00320 REM ******************************
00330 FOR I = 1 TO 10
00340   READ P$
00350   PRINT TAB(10);P$
00360 NEXT I
00370 REM ******************************
00380 REM ***   PRINT THE GOALIE'S NAME ***
00390 REM ******************************
00400 PRINT TAB(10);G$;TAB(30);"GOALIE"
00410 REM ******************************
00420 REM ***     THE DATA STATEMENTS  ***
00430 REM ******************************
00440 DATA KNIGHTS,KEVIN LUCE,JAY BROWN
00450 DATA BRIAN CRANSTON,LARRY CONROY
00460 DATA PAUL HOLLY,RICK VANGOERDER
00470 DATA MATT LYSACK,TERRY JON
00480 DATA SAM HAMILTON,SCOTT CURTISS
00490 DATA ISSAC WOLFLY,ED COURT
00999 END


RUNNH


TEAM NAME - KNIGHTS

PLAYERS - KEVIN LUCE        CAPTAIN
          BRIAN CRANSTON
          LARRY CONROY
          PAUL HOLLY
          RICK VANGOERDER
          MATT LYSACK
          TERRY JON
          SAM HAMILTON
          SCOTT CURTISS
          ISSAC WOLFLY
          ED COURT
          JAY BROWN          GOALIE
```

PSEUDOCODE

```
Start
Read the team's name, captain's name, and goalie's name
Print the team's name and the captain's name
Start loop, do ten times
  Read the player's name
  Print the player's name
End loop
Print the goalie's name
Stop
```

MICROCOMPUTERS:	
Apple	No differences.
Apple Macintosh	No differences.
IBM/Microsoft	No differences.
PET/Commodore 64	No differences.
TRS-80	No differences.

SECTION VII
Functions

ANSWERS TO TEXTBOOK REVIEW QUESTIONS

1.   Library functions are functions that are included in the
BASIC language library so they can be easily referenced.

2.   The four trigonometric functions are SIN(X), COS(X),
TAN(X), and ATN(X). Angles are always used as an argument to
these functions. The angles are measured in radians.

3.   EXP(X) - makes the calculation e^X.
      LOG(X) - the reverse of EXP(X); it finds the power e is
               raised in order to find X.
      SQR(X) - finds the square root of a positive argument.

4.   INT(X) - computes the greatest integer less than or equal
               value of the argument.
      SGN(X) - yields a + 1 if X > 0, 0 if X = 0, and -1 if X < 0.
      ABS(X) - returns the absolute value of the argument.
      RND   - generates a random number between 0 and 1.

5.   General format of a user-defined function:

          line# DEF function name(argument) = expression

The function name consists of the letters FN followed by any one
of the twenty-six alphabetic characters. The user-defined function can be located anywhere in the program but it must be
before the first reference to the function.

ANSWERS TO TEXTBOOK DEBUGGING EXERCISES

1.
```
10 REM ***              GENERATE A RANDOM NUMBER              ***
15 REM ***                 BETWEEN 5 AND 15                   ***
20 LET R = RND
```
*This creates any random number, should be   LET R = RND * (5 - 15) + 15*

2.
```
10 LET R = FNAB(Y)
15 REM ***              FUNCTION TO ROUND NUMBER              ***
20 REM ***                 NEAREST TENTH                      ***
25 FNAB(X) = INT ((X + 0.005) * 100) / 100
```
This function must be defined before it is referenced

Function name must be FN followed by a single letter, change FNAB to FNA

The letters DEF must be included here

*This rounds a number to the nearest hundredth should be INT((X + 0.05) * 10)/10*

ANSWER TO TEXTBOOK PROGRAMMING PROBLEM 1

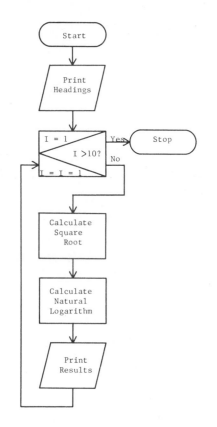

```
00100 REM *** CALCULATE SQUARE ROOTS AND NATURAL LOGARITHMS ***
00110 REM *** S - SQUARE ROOT ***
00120 REM *** L - NATURAL LOGARITHM ***
00130 PRINT
00140 PRINT "NUMBER","SQUARE ROOT","NATURAL LOGARITHM"
00150 FOR I = 1 TO 10
00160    LET S = INT((SQR(I) + 0.0005) * 1000) / 1000
00170    LET L = INT((LOG(I) + 0.0005) * 1000) / 1000
00180    PRINT I,S,L
00190 NEXT I
00999 END

READY
RUNNH

NUMBER          SQUARE ROOT     NATURAL LOGARITHM
1               1               0
2               1.414           0.693
3               1.732           1.099
4               2               1.386
5               2.236           1.609
6               2.449           1.792
7               2.646           1.946
8               2.828           2.079
9               3               2.197
10              3.162           2.303
```

PSEUDOCODE

```
Start
Print headings
Do ten times
   Calculate square root and natural logarithm
     of I
   Print results
   Repeat
Stop
```

MICROCOMPUTERS:	
Apple	Column headings carry over to next line.
Apple Macintosh	No differences.
IBM/Microsoft	No differences.
PET/Commodore 64	Change statement 160 to: 160 LET S = SQR(I) + 0.0005 160 LET S = INT(S * 1000) / 1000 Change statement 170 to: 170 LET L = LOG(I) + 0.0005 170 LET L = INT(L * 1000) / 1000 Print zones are also smaller, so headings continue on next line.
TRS-80	No differences.

ANSWER TO TEXTBOOK PROGRAMMING PROBLEM 2

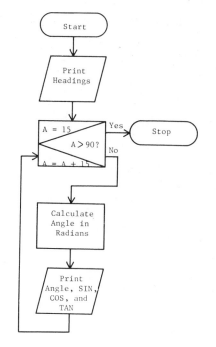

```
00100 REM *** TABLE GIVING SINE, COSINE, AND TANGENT ***
00110 REM *** A - ANGLE IN DEGREES ***
00120 REM *** R - ANGLE IN RADIANS ***
00130 PRINT
00140 PRINT "ANGLE","SINE","COSINE","TANGENT"
00150 FOR A = 15 TO 90 STEP 15
00160    LET R = A * 0.01745
00170    PRINT A,SIN(R),COS(R),TAN(R)
00180 NEXT A
00999 END

READY
RUNNH
```

ANGLE	SINE	COSINE	TANGENT
15	0.2587713	0.9659386	0.2678963
30	0.4999144	0.8660748	0.5772186
45	0.707002	0.7072116	0.9997037
60	0.8659266	0.5001711	1.731261
75	0.9658619	0.2590576	3.728368
90	1	0.0002963287	3374.498

PSEUDOCODE

```
Start
Print headings
Do until A > 90
  Calculate angle in radians
  Print angle in degrees, sine, cosine, and tangent
    of radian angle
  Repeat
Stop
```

MICROCOMPUTERS:	
Apple	Rounds to 9 digits; lines are too long, so they are continued on the next line.
Apple Macintosh	Rounds to 14 digits; no leading zeroes.
IBM/Microsoft	Rounds to 7 digits; print zones are lined up in their column.
PET/Commodore 64	Rounds to 9 digits; print zones are smaller, so lines continue on next line.
TRS-80	Rounds output to 6 digits.

ANSWER TO STUDY GUIDE PROGRAMMING PROBLEM 2

```
00010 REM ******************************************
00020 REM *** COSINE, SINE, AND TANGENT PROGRAM ***
00030 REM ******************************************
00040 REM *** VARIABLES:                        ***
00050 REM ***    C = COSINE OF THE ANGLE        ***
00060 REM ***    S = SINE OF THE ANGLE          ***
00070 REM ***    T = TANGENT OF THE ANGLE       ***
00080 REM ***    A = DEGREE OF THE ANGLE        ***
00090 REM ******************************************
00100 REM ***      PRINT THE REPORT HEADINGS    ***
00110 REM ******************************************
00120 PRINT
00130 PRINT
00140 PRINT "ANGLE";TAB(16);"COSINE";TAB(31);"SINE";TAB(44);"TANGENT"
00150 PRINT
00160 REM ******************************************
00170 REM *** COMPUTE COSINE, SINE, AND TANGENT ***
00180 REM ***      AND THEN PRINT THE RESULTS   ***
00190 REM ******************************************
00200 FOR I = 1 TO 20
00210   READ A
00220   LET C = COS(A)
00230   LET S = SIN(A)
00240   LET T = TAN(A)
00250   PRINT A,C,S,T
00260 NEXT I
00270 REM ******************************************
00280 REM ***        THE DATA STATEMENTS        ***
00290 REM ******************************************
00300 DATA 63.5,34.9,78,90.5,50,45
00310 DATA -89,-54,-72,-65,-12,128
00320 DATA 175,289,301,345,215,222,109,199
00999 END


RUNNH

ANGLE          COSINE          SINE            TANGENT

 63.5          0.7849716       0.6195323       0.7892421
 34.9         -0.9419244      -0.3358247       0.3565308
 78           -0.8578029       0.5139787      -0.5991794
 90.5         -0.8218261       0.5697384      -0.693258
 50            0.9649659      -0.2623752      -0.2719006
 45            0.5253219       0.8509034       1.619776
-89            0.5101772      -0.8600693      -1.685825
-54           -0.8293103       0.558789       -0.6737999
-72           -0.9672506      -0.253824        0.2624173
-65           -0.5624533      -0.826829        1.470038
-12            0.8438539       0.5365729       0.63586
 128          -0.6928953       0.7210382      -1.040613
 175           0.5984848      -0.8011351      -1.338604
 289           0.9996482      -0.02652098     -0.02653031
 301           0.8293262      -0.5587647      -0.6737575
 345           0.8390879      -0.5439958      -0.648318
 215           0.1977842       0.9802456       4.956138
 222          -0.4948989       0.868952       -1.755814
 109          -0.5770017       0.8167429      -1.415495
 199          -0.4716253      -0.8817984       1.869703
```

PSEUDOCODE

```
Start
Print the headings
Start loop, do twenty times
  Read angle
  Compute Cosine of angle
  Compute Sine of angle
  Compute Tangent of angle
  Print Angle, Cosine, Sine, and Tangent
End loop
Stop
```

MICROCOMPUTERS:	
Apple	No differences.
Apple Macintosh	No differences.
IBM/Microsoft	No differences.
PET/Commodore 64	No differences.
TRS-80	No differences.

ANSWERS TO STUDY GUIDE WORKSHEET PROBLEMS

2.   a.   99   c.   −5
      b.   99   d.   −6

4.   50 LET X = INT((X + .005) * 100) / 100

6.   Library functions are functions included in the BASIC
language library. Examples: LOG(X), EXP(X), SQR(X), INT(X),
RND, SGN(X), COS(X), SIN(X), TAN(X), ATN(X)

8.   a.   10 LET X = 5 * TAN(R)
      b.   20 PRINT SQR(16)
      c.   30 IF ABS(X) = 0 THEN 60
      d.   40 DEF FNA(X) = X * 3 * X∧2

10.   10 DEF FNR = RND * (1− 10) + 10

SUPPLEMENTARY PROGRAMMING PROBLEMS

Problem A

    WOPO radio station is having a special contest. If the
station calls your phone and you answer "HELLO WOPO!" you will
win $15,000 in cash. The radio station will be holding the con-
test next week and they want you to write a program to pick random phone numbers. All phones in the area begin with a 728 so
the program needs to determine the following four numbers.
Write the program so that it may be run as many times as
necessary.

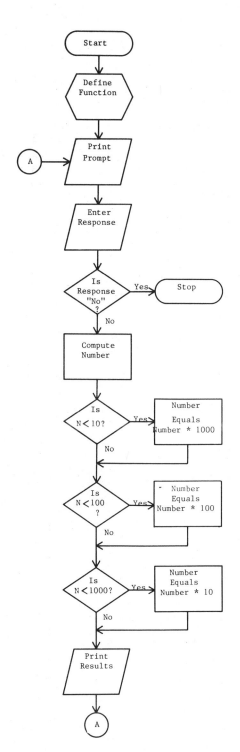

```
00010 REM ********************************
00020 REM *** TELEPHONE CONTEST PROGRAM ***
00030 REM ********************************
00040 REM *** N = THE TELEPHONE NUMBER  ***
00050 REM ********************************
00060 REM ***   DETERMINE PHONE NUMBER    ***
00070 REM ********************************
00080 RANDOMIZE
00090 DEF FNT = RND * 10000
00100 PRINT "DO YOU NEED A TELEPHONE NUMBER?  (YES OR NO)"
00110 INPUT R$
00120 IF R$ = "NO" THEN 999
00130 LET N = INT(FNT)
00140 REM ********************************
00150 REM ***      ADD TRUNCATED ZEROS     ***
00160 REM ********************************
00170 IF N < 10 THEN N = N * 1000
00180 IF N < 100 THEN N = N * 100
00190 IF N < 1000 THEN N = N * 10
00200 REM ********************************
00210 REM ***    PRINT THE PHONE NUMBER   ***
00220 REM ********************************
00230 PRINT
00240 PRINT
00250 PRINT
00260 PRINT "THE PHONE NUMBER IS 728 -";N
00270 PRINT
00280 PRINT
00290 REM ********************************
00300 REM ***            REPEAT LOOP         ***
00310 REM ********************************
00320 GOTO 100
00999 END
```

```
RUNNH
DO YOU NEED A TELEPHONE NUMBER?  (YES OR NO)
? YES


THE PHONE NUMBER IS 728 - 4606

DO YOU NEED A TELEPHONE NUMBER?  (YES OR NO)
? YES


THE PHONE NUMBER IS 728 - 1379

DO YOU NEED A TELEPHONE NUMBER?  (YES OR NO)
? NO
```

PSEUDOCODE

```
Start
Start loop, do until response is "NO"
   Print prompt
   Enter response
   If response is "YES"
      Then
         Compute a four digit random number
         Print phone number
      Else
         Stop
   Endif
End loop
```

MICROCOMPUTERS:	
Apple	No RANDOMIZE statement is needed; RND needs an argument.
Apple Macintosh	Asks for a random number seed.
IBM/Microsoft	Asks for a random number seed.
PET/Commodore 64	RND must contain an argument; no RANDOMIZE statement is needed.
TRS-80	A RANDOM statement is needed instead of a RANDOMIZE statement; RND must contain an argument.

Problem B

The Bureau of Statistics and Labor has asked you to write a program to determine the supply and demand of a certain type of ore for the next ten years. Both the supply and demand should be rounded to the next largest unit. The supply and demand for the first year are given below:

        Supply = 9500 units
        Demand = 500 units

The demand increases each year by 10 percent. Use a user-defined function to compute the demand. The supply equals the supply minus the increased demand. The output for your program should give the year, the supply for the year, and the demand for the next ten years. The report should look as follows:

YEAR	SUPPLY	DEMAND
1	XXXXX	XXXXX
2	XXXXX	XXXXX
3	XXXXX	XXXXX
.	.	.
.	.	.
.	.	.
10	XXXXX	XXXXX

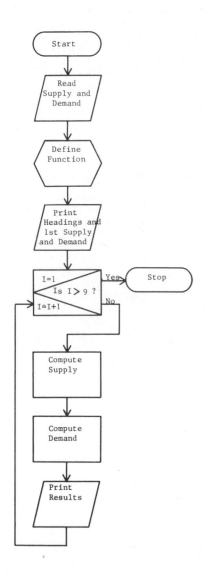

```
00100 REM *********************************
00110 REM *** SUPPLY AND DEMAND PROGRAM ***
00120 REM *********************************
00130 REM *** VARIABLES:               ***
00140 REM ***   S = SUPPLY             ***
00150 REM ***   D = DEMAND             ***
00160 REM *********************************
00170 REM *** READ FIRST YEAR DATA AND ***
00180 REM ***   DEFINE DEMAND FUNCTION ***
00190 REM *********************************
00200 READ S,D
00210 DEF FND(D) = D * 1.10
00220 REM *********************************
00230 REM *** PRINT THE REPORT HEADINGS ***
00240 REM *********************************
00250 PRINT
00260 PRINT
00270 PRINT "YEAR","SUPPLY","DEMAND"
00280 PRINT
00290 REM *********************************
00300 REM *** COMPUTE SUPPLY AND DEMAND ***
00310 REM ***    THEN PRINT THE RESULTS ***
00320 REM *********************************
00330 PRINT 1,S,D
00340 FOR I = 1 TO 9
00350    LET S = S - D
00360    LET D = FND(D)
00370    PRINT I + 1,S,D
00380 NEXT I
00390 DATA 9500,500
00999 END
```

RUNNH

YEAR	SUPPLY	DEMAND
1	9500	500
2	9000	550
3	8450	605
4	7845	665.5
5	7179.5	732.05
6	6447.45	805.255
7	5642.195	885.7805
8	4756.415	974.3585
9	3782.056	1071.794
10	2710.262	1178.974

PSEUDOCODE

```
Start
Print the report headings
Define demand function
Read the supply and demand for the first year
Print the supply and demand for the first year
Start loop, do nine times
   Compute supply
   Compute demand
   Print the year, supply, and demand
End loop
```

MICROCOMPUTERS:	
Apple	No differences.
Apple Macintosh	No differences.
IBM/Microsoft	No differences.
PET/Commodore 64	No differences.
TRS-80	No differences.

Problem C

A nearby company has decided to sell three new products. The accounting department of the company has asked you to write a program to determine the breakeven quantities of each of the products. The Breakeven Formula is given as:

Breakeven Quantity:

$$SP * n = FC + (VC * n)$$

where: SP = Selling Price/Unit
FD = Fixed Costs
VC = Variable Costs/Unit
n = Breakeven Quantity

The program should contain FOR/NEXT loops and arrays. Use an appropriate format to print out the breakeven quantities of the products. The following information will be necessary in your program:

PRODUCT	SELLING PRICE	FIXED COSTS	VARIABLE COSTS
A	$25.00/unit	$ 750.00	$10.00/unit
B	$10.00/unit	$ 300.00	$ 5.00/unit
C	$50.00/unit	$1500.00	$20.00/unit

The output should be formatted as follows

BREAKEVEN ANALYSIS

PRODUCT	S. PRICE	FIXED COSTS	V. COSTS	B/E QUANTITY
X	XX	XXXX	XX	XX

(S. PRICE is selling price and V. COSTS is variable costs)

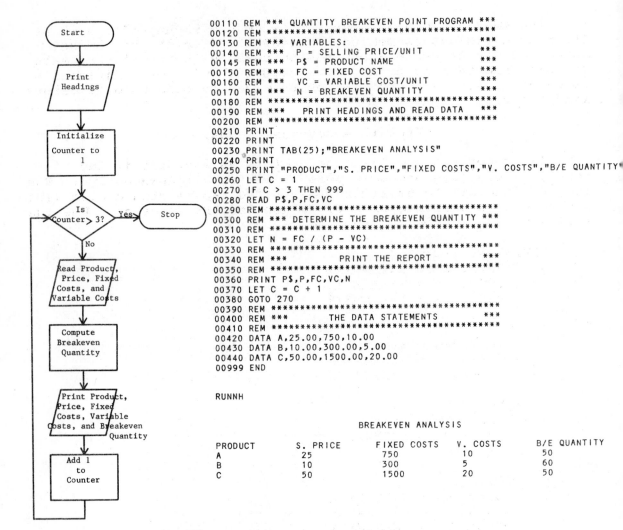

```
00110 REM *** QUANTITY BREAKEVEN POINT PROGRAM ***
00120 REM **********************************************
00130 REM *** VARIABLES:                            ***
00140 REM ***   P = SELLING PRICE/UNIT              ***
00145 REM ***   P$ = PRODUCT NAME                   ***
00150 REM ***   FC = FIXED COST                     ***
00160 REM ***   VC = VARIABLE COST/UNIT             ***
00170 REM ***   N = BREAKEVEN QUANTITY              ***
00180 REM **********************************************
00190 REM ***    PRINT HEADINGS AND READ DATA       ***
00200 REM **********************************************
00210 PRINT
00220 PRINT
00230 PRINT TAB(25);"BREAKEVEN ANALYSIS"
00240 PRINT
00250 PRINT "PRODUCT","S. PRICE","FIXED COSTS","V. COSTS","B/E QUANTITY"
00260 LET C = 1
00270 IF C > 3 THEN 999
00280 READ P$,P,FC,VC
00290 REM **********************************************
00300 REM *** DETERMINE THE BREAKEVEN QUANTITY ***
00310 REM **********************************************
00320 LET N = FC / (P - VC)
00330 REM **********************************************
00340 REM ***          PRINT THE REPORT            ***
00350 REM **********************************************
00360 PRINT P$,P,FC,VC,N
00370 LET C = C + 1
00380 GOTO 270
00390 REM **********************************************
00400 REM ***        THE DATA STATEMENTS           ***
00410 REM **********************************************
00420 DATA A,25.00,750,10.00
00430 DATA B,10.00,300.00,5.00
00440 DATA C,50.00,1500.00,20.00
00999 END


RUNNH


                        BREAKEVEN ANALYSIS

PRODUCT        S. PRICE       FIXED COSTS    V. COSTS    B/E QUANTITY
A              25             750            10          50
B              10             300            5           60
C              50             1500           20          50
```

PSEUDOCODE

```
Start
Print the report headings
Let counter equal one
Start loop, do until counter is greater than three
  Read product name, selling price, fixed costs, and variable
    costs
  Compute Breakeven Quantity
  Print product's name, selling price, fixed costs, and variable
    costs
  Add one to counter
End loop
Stop
```

MICROCOMPUTERS:	
Apple	No differences.
Apple Macintosh	No differences.
IBM/Microsoft	No differences.
PET/Commodore 64	No differences.
TRS-80	No differences.

Problem D

The Regional Company wants to know how much profit each of its four divisions is making. The head office of the company has asked you to write a program to compute the profits of each division and then to print out a report showing each division's revenues, costs, and profits/losses. The formula used to determine the profit is:

$$\text{Profits} = \text{Revenues} - \text{Costs}$$

The report should list the profits as a profit if the result is positive and as a loss if the result is negative. Use the SGN function to determine this. The report should also list the loss as a positive amount, so use the ABS function. Use the following as a guideline for the report:

```
DIVISION:  1
     REVENUES = XXXXXXXXX
     COSTS    = XXXXXXXXX
     PROFIT   = XXXXXXXXX

DIVISION:  2
     REVENUES = XXXXXXXXX
     COSTS    = XXXXXXXXX
     PROFITS  = XXXXXXXXX

DIVISION:  3
     REVENUES = XXXXXXXXX
     COSTS    = XXXXXXXXX
     PROFITS  = XXXXXXXXX

DIVISION:  4
     REVENUES = XXXXXXXXX
     COSTS    = XXXXXXXXX
     PROFITS  = XXXXXXXXX
```

Use the following as input to the program:

DIVISION	REVENUES	COSTS
1	934300	920000
2	795200	832870
3	929100	692200
4	750000	740000

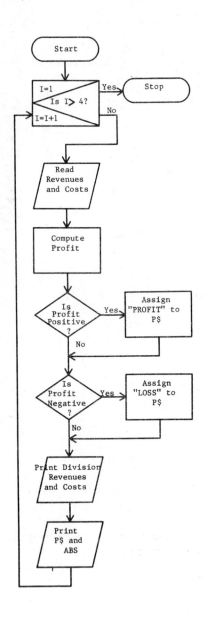

```
00100 REM *********************************
00110 REM *** DIVISONAL PROFITS PROGRAM ***
00120 REM *********************************
00130 REM *** VARIABLES:                ***
00140 REM ***   P = PROFIT/LOSS AMOUNT  ***
00150 REM ***   C = COSTS               ***
00160 REM ***   R = REVENUES            ***
00170 REM ***   P$ = PROFIT OR LOSS     ***
00180 REM *********************************
00190 REM *** COMPUTE PROFIT/LOSS AND   ***
00200 REM ***      PRINT THE RESULTS    ***
00210 REM *********************************
00220 FOR I = 1 TO 4
00230    READ R,C
00240    LET P = R - C
00250    IF SGN(P) > -1 THEN P$ = "PROFIT"
00260    IF SGN(P) < 1 THEN P$ = "LOSS"
00270    PRINT "DIVISION: ";I
00280    PRINT TAB(5);"REVENUES =";R
00290    PRINT TAB(5);"COSTS    =";C
00300    PRINT TAB(5);P$;TAB(13);" =";ABS(P)
00310 NEXT I
00320 DATA 934300,920000,795200,832870
00330 DATA 929100,692200,750000,740000
00999 END

RUNNH
DIVISION: 1
     REVENUES = 934300
     COSTS    = 920000
     PROFIT   = 14300
DIVISION: 2
     REVENUES = 795200
     COSTS    = 832870
     LOSS     = 37670
DIVISION: 3
     REVENUES = 929100
     COSTS    = 692200
     PROFIT   = 236900
DIVISION: 4
     REVENUES = 750000
     COSTS    = 740000
     PROFIT   = 10000
```

PSEUDOCODE

```
Start
Start loop, do 4 times
  Read sales revenues and costs
  Profit equals sales revenues - costs
  If profit is positive
    Then assign "PROFIT" to P$
  Endif
  If profit is negative
    Then assign "LOSS" to P$
  Endif
  Print division, revenues, costs, and profit (or loss)
End loop
Stop
```

MICROCOMPUTERS:	
Apple	No differences.
Apple Macintosh	No differences.
IBM/Microsoft	No differences.
PET/Commodore 64	No differences.
TRS-80	No differences.

SECTION VIII
Subroutines and String Functions

ANSWERS TO TEXTBOOK REVIEW QUESTIONS

1.   A subroutine is a sequence of statements that performs a particular function. Generally, subroutines are located at the end of the main program body. Subroutines are useful because although they can be used in several different parts of the main program, the set of instructions need only be typed in once.

2.   The GOSUB statement transfers control from the main logic of a program to a subroutine. The RETURN statement transfers control from a subroutine to the main program and to the statement immediately following the most recently executed GOSUB statement. The RETURN statement is placed at the end of a subroutine.

3.   The STOP statement is placed before a subroutine to prevent unnecessary execution of the subroutine when the program comes to its logical end. The STOP statement differs from the END statement in that a STOP can occur as many times as necessary in a program and the END statement may only appear once and must have the highest line number.

4.   A string is a series of alphanumeric characters, which are usually required to be enclosed in quotation marks.

5.   e

ANSWERS TO TEXTBOOK DEBUGGING EXERCISES

1.
```
10 READ N$,B$          should be A$ instead of N$
15 LET A = STR$(A$)
20 LET A = A + 3       should be VAL function,
25 LET A$ = VAL(A)        not STR$ function
30 LET C$ = A$ + B$    should be STR$ function
35 DATA 10,30             not VAL function
```

2.
```
10 REM *** PRINT THE FIRST 4 CHARACTERS ***
15 REM *** AND THE LAST 3 CHARACTERS OF A STRING ***
20 LET A$ = "GOOD FRIDAY"
25 PRINT LEFT(A$,4)
30 PRINT RIGHT(A$,3)    Dollar signs must be included
                                              here
```
After including the dollar sign, this line would
be correct for the microcomputers but on the
DEC, this line should be: PRINT RIGHT$(A$,9)

ANSWER TO TEXTBOOK PROGRAMMING PROBLEM 1

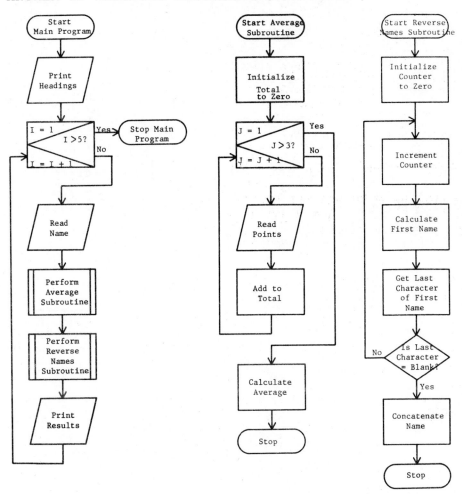

```
00100 REM *** REVERSE PLAYER'S NAMES AND CALCULATE ***
00110 REM *** THEIR AVERAGE NUMBER OF POINTS ***
00120 REM *** N$ - PLAYER'S NAME ***
00130 REM *** P - # OF POINTS SCORED IN A GAME ***
00140 REM *** T - TOTAL POINTS FOR A PLAYER ***
00150 REM *** A - AVERAGE POINTS SCORED ***
00160 REM *** L$,R$ - USED TO REVERSE NAME ***
00170 REM
00180 PRINT
00190 PRINT "NAME","AVERAGE"
00200 PRINT
00210 FOR I = 1 TO 5
00220    READ N$
00230    GOSUB 310
00240    GOSUB 400
00250    PRINT N$,A
00260 NEXT I
00270 PRINT
00280 STOP
00290 REM
00300 REM
00310 REM *** SUBROUTINE TO CALCULATE AVERAGE POINTS ***
00320 LET T = 0
00330 FOR J = 1 TO 3
00340    READ P
00350    LET T = T + P
00360 NEXT J
00370 LET A = T / 3
00380 RETURN
00390 REM
00400 REM *** SUBROUTINE TO REVERSE NAMES ***
00410 LET K = 0
00420 LET K = K + 1
00430 LET L$ = LEFT$(N$,K)
00440 LET R$ = RIGHT$(L$,K)
00450 IF R$ = CHR$(32) THEN 470
00460 GOTO 420
00470 LET N$ = RIGHT$(N$,K + 1) + ", " + L$
00480 RETURN
00490 REM
00500 DATA "ED MILLER",22,20,18
00510 DATA "JOHN LONG",12,19,17,"JOE BARROS",7,3,5
00520 DATA "MIKE HAWN",15,12,12,"GARY STORTS",10,13,7
00999 END

READY
RUNNH

NAME        AVERAGE

MILLER, ED      20
LONG, JOHN      16
BARROS, JOE     5
HAWN, MIKE      13
STORTS, GARY    10

STOP at line 00280 of MAIN PROGRAM
```

PSEUDOCODE

Start main program
Print headings
Perform average points calculation subroutine
Perform reverse names subroutine
Print results
Stop main program

Start average points calculation subroutine
Initialize T to zero
Start loop, to three times
  Read number of points
  Add number of points to total
Endloop
Average equals total divided by 3
Stop average points calculation subroutine

Start reverse names subroutine
Initialize K to zero
Start loop, do until a blank is found
  Assign defined character to L$
  Assign last character of L$ to R$
  Check to see if R$ is a blank
Endloop
Concatenate first name and last name
Stop reverse names as subroutine

MICROCOMPUTERS:	
Apple	Line 440 should be: 440 LET R$ = RIGHT$(L$,1) Line 470 should be: 470 LET N = LEN(N$) - K 475 LET N$ = RIGHT$(N$,N) +", "+L$
Apple Macintosh	Same as Apple.
IBM/Microsoft	Same as Apple.
PET/Commodore 64	Same as Apple.
TRS-80	Same as Apple.

ANSWER TO TEXTBOOK PROGRAMMING PROBLEM 2

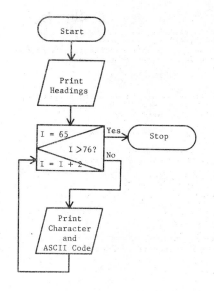

```
00100 REM *** PRINT CHART OF LETTERS AND THEIR ***
00110 REM *** CORRESPONDING ASCII VALUES ***
00120 PRINT
00130 PRINT "CHAR","VALUE","CHAR","VALUE"
00140 PRINT
00150 FOR I = 65 TO 76 STEP 2
00160   PRINT CHR$(I),I,CHR$(I + 1),I + 1
00170 NEXT I
00999 END

READY
RUNNH
```

CHAR	VALUE	CHAR	VALUE
A	65	B	66
C	67	D	68
E	69	F	70
G	71	H	72
I	73	J	74
K	75	L	76

PSEUDOCODE

```
Start
Print headings
Repeat six times
  Print the character corresponding to the
    ASCII value its ASCII value, the succeeding character, and
      its ASCII value
  Repeat
Stop
```

MICROCOMPUTERS:	
Apple	No differences.
Apple Macintosh	No differences.
IBM/Microsoft	No differences.
PET/Commodore 64	No differences.
TRS-80	No differences.

ANSWER TO STUDY GUIDE PROGRAMMING PROBLEM 2

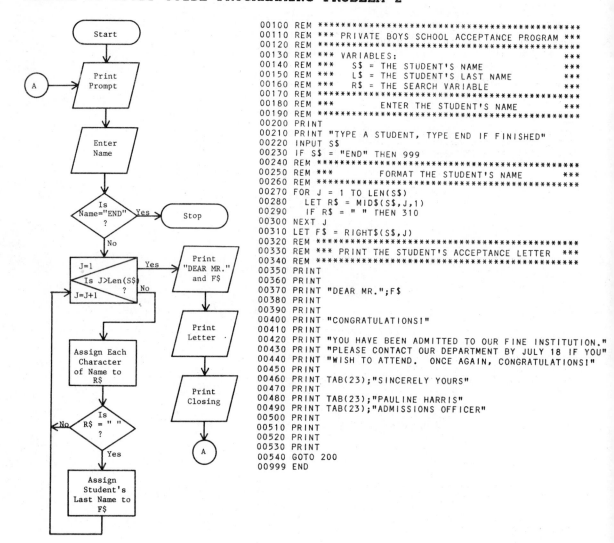

```
00100 REM ******************************************************
00110 REM *** PRIVATE BOYS SCHOOL ACCEPTANCE PROGRAM ***
00120 REM ******************************************************
00130 REM *** VARIABLES:                                    ***
00140 REM ***    S$ = THE STUDENT'S NAME                    ***
00150 REM ***    L$ = THE STUDENT'S LAST NAME               ***
00160 REM ***    R$ = THE SEARCH VARIABLE                   ***
00170 REM ******************************************************
00180 REM ***          ENTER THE STUDENT'S NAME             ***
00190 REM ******************************************************
00200 PRINT
00210 PRINT "TYPE A STUDENT, TYPE END IF FINISHED"
00220 INPUT S$
00230 IF S$ = "END" THEN 999
00240 REM ******************************************************
00250 REM ***          FORMAT THE STUDENT'S NAME            ***
00260 REM ******************************************************
00270 FOR J = 1 TO LEN(S$)
00280    LET R$ = MID$(S$,J,1)
00290    IF R$ = " " THEN 310
00300 NEXT J
00310 LET F$ = RIGHT$(S$,J)
00320 REM ******************************************************
00330 REM *** PRINT THE STUDENT'S ACCEPTANCE LETTER ***
00340 REM ******************************************************
00350 PRINT
00360 PRINT
00370 PRINT "DEAR MR.";F$
00380 PRINT
00390 PRINT
00400 PRINT "CONGRATULATIONS!"
00410 PRINT
00420 PRINT "YOU HAVE BEEN ADMITTED TO OUR FINE INSTITUTION."
00430 PRINT "PLEASE CONTACT OUR DEPARTMENT BY JULY 18 IF YOU"
00440 PRINT "WISH TO ATTEND.  ONCE AGAIN, CONGRATULATIONS!"
00450 PRINT
00460 PRINT TAB(23);"SINCERELY YOURS"
00470 PRINT
00480 PRINT TAB(23);"PAULINE HARRIS"
00490 PRINT TAB(23);"ADMISSIONS OFFICER"
00500 PRINT
00510 PRINT
00520 PRINT
00530 PRINT
00540 GOTO 200
00999 END
```

```
RUNNH

TYPE A STUDENT, TYPE END IF FINISHED
 ? GREG ALLGAIR


DEAR MR. ALLGAIR


CONGRATULATIONS!

YOU HAVE BEEN ADMITTED TO OUR FINE INSTITUTION.
PLEASE CONTACT OUR DEPARTMENT BY JULY 18 IF YOU
WISH TO ATTEND.  ONCE AGAIN, CONGRATULATIONS!

               SINCERELY YOURS

               PAULINE HARRIS
               ADMISSIONS OFFICER




TYPE A STUDENT, TYPE END IF FINISHED
 ? BILL HAIDLE


DEAR MR. HAIDLE


CONGRATULATIONS!

YOU HAVE BEEN ADMITTED TO OUR FINE INSTITUTION.
PLEASE CONTACT OUR DEPARTMENT BY JULY 18 IF YOU
WISH TO ATTEND.  ONCE AGAIN, CONGRATULATIONS!

               SINCERELY YOURS

               PAULINE HARRIS
               ADMISSIONS OFFICER




TYPE A STUDENT, TYPE END IF FINISHED
 ? END
```

PSEUDOCODE

```
Start
Start loop, do until student's name equals "END"
  Print prompt
  Enter student's name
  Start loop to search student's name for a blank
    If a blank is found
      Then assign student's last name to F$
    End if
  End loop
  Print "DEAR MR." and F$
  Print letter
  Print closing
  Print blank lines
End loop
Stop
```

MICROCOMPUTERS:	
Apple	Line 310: LET F$ = RIGHT$ (S$,LEN(S$) − J)
Apple Macintosh	Same as Apple.
IBM/Microsoft	Same as Apple.
PET/Commodore 64	Same as Apple.
TRS-80	Same as Apple.

ANSWERS TO STUDY GUIDE WORKSHEET PROBLEMS

2.   10 INPUT "ENTER A WORD";W$
       20 PRINT LEN(W$)

4.   10 LET D$ = "DAYTONA BEACH"
       20 FOR J = 1 TO LEN(D$)
       30   PRINT MID$(D$,J,1)
       40 NEXT J

6.   a

8.   The ASCII function returns the decimal ASCII value of the
first character of the string in the argument. The CHR$ func-
tion returns the character corresponding to the decimal ASCII
value in the argument.

10. a.   20 LET A = ASCII("HOME")
     b.   30 LET B = VAL("123.9")
     c.   40 LET X$ = CHR$(62)
     d.   correct as is

SUPPLEMENTARY PROGRAMMING PROBLEMS

Problem A

The Allied Company located in Mahwah, New Jersey ships
goods to other companies in the New York-New Jersey Metro area.
The shipping manager needs a program to determine a shipping
code for the company's deliveries. The shipping code will be
determined by adding 10000 to the city's zip code. A list of
all cities Allied ships to is shown below. Write a program that
prints a report listing each city and its shipping code.

```
Fairfield, 07324
Paramus, 07643
West New York, 07652
Paterson, 08431
Grand Central Station, 10017
Astoria, 11321
Hicksville, 11433
Woodside, 11890
```

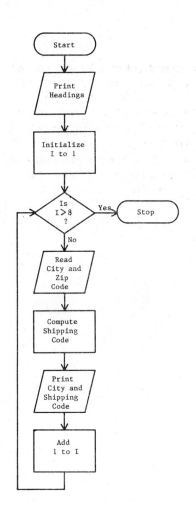

```
00010 REM ********************************
00020 REM *** SHIPPING CODE PROGRAM  ***
00030 REM ********************************
00040 REM *** VARIABLES:              ***
00050 REM ***   C = THE CITY          ***
00060 REM ***   Z$ = CITY'S ZIP CODE  ***
00070 REM ***   S = THE SHIPPING CODE ***
00080 REM ********************************
00090 REM *** PRINT REPORT HEADINGS   ***
00100 REM ********************************
00110 PRINT
00120 PRINT
00130 PRINT TAB(8);"SHIPPING CODE LIST"
00140 PRINT
00150 PRINT "CITY";TAB(23);"SHIPPING CODE"
00160 PRINT
00170 REM ********************************
00180 REM *** COMPUTE SHIPPING CODE   ***
00190 REM ***   FOR THE EIGHT CITIES  ***
00200 REM ********************************
00210 LET I = 1
00220 IF I > 8 THEN 999
00230 READ C$,Z$
00240 LET S = VAL(Z$) + 10000
00250 PRINT C$;TAB(26);S
00260 LET I = I + 1
00270 GOTO 220
00280 REM ********************************
00290 REM ***  THE DATA STATEMENTS    ***
00300 REM ********************************
00310 DATA FAIRFIELD,07234,PARAMUS,07643
00320 DATA WEST NEW YORK,07652,PATERSON,08431
00330 DATA GRAND CENTRAL STATION,10017
00340 DATA ASTORIA,11321,HICKSVILLE,11433
00350 DATA WOODSIDE,11890
00999 END


RUNNH


            SHIPPING CODE LIST

  CITY                    SHIPPING CODE

  FAIRFIELD                  17234
  PARAMUS                    17643
  WEST NEW YORK              17652
  PATERSON                   18431
  GRAND CENTRAL STATION      20017
  ASTORIA                    21321
  HICKSVILLE                 21433
  WOODSIDE                   21890
```

PSEUDOCODE

```
Start
Print the report headings
Initialize I to one
Start loop, do until I is greater than eight
  Read city and zip code
  Shipping code = numeric zip code + 10000
  Print city and shipping code
  Add one to I
End loop
Stop
```

MICROCOMPUTERS:	
Apple	One less space before shipping code.
Apple Macintosh	No differences.
IBM/Microsoft	No differences.
PET/Commodore 64	No differences.
TRS-80	No differences.

Problem B

The Computer Company is switching its computer files to a
new system.   The manager of Computer Services has asked you to
write a program that truncates names over 15 characters long
(the files will only facilitate names of 15 characters or less).
For example, if the name is MacNaughton, Richard, the name will
be truncated to MacNaughton, Ri.   Next, Computer Services
manager has asked you to print out a list of names and the names
after they have been truncated.   Use an appropriate format for
the report.   The input data is as follows:

                    Lawerance, Oliver
                    Kainsinger, Kathleen
                    Harrison, Mary Ann
                    Garrett, Lewis
                    Smith, Samantha
                    Newman, Terrence
                    Prentice, Larry
                    Trough, Wayne
                    Alcott, Missy
                    Evans, Franklin

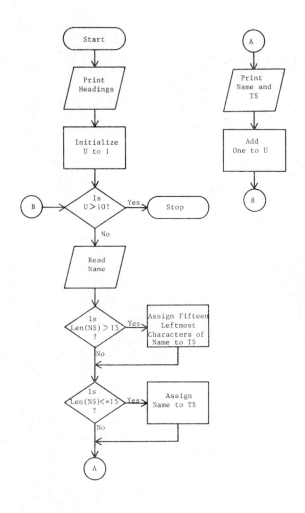

```
00010 REM *******************************
00020 REM *** NAME TRUNCATING PROGRAM ***
00030 REM *******************************
00040 REM *** VARIABLES:              ***
00050 REM ***   N$ = EMPLOYEE'S NAME  ***
00060 REM ***   T$ = TRUNCATED NAME   ***
00070 REM *******************************
00080 REM ***   PRINT REPORT HEADINGS  ***
00090 REM *******************************
00100 PRINT TAB(12);"NEW NAMES REPORT"
00110 PRINT
00120 PRINT TAB(2);"OLD NAME";TAB(27);"NEW NAME"
00130 PRINT
00140 REM *******************************
00150 REM *** READ THE DATA AND THEN  ***
00160 REM *** TRUNCATE NAME IF NEEDED ***
00170 REM *******************************
00180 LET U = 1
00190 IF U > 10 THEN 999
00200 READ N$
00210 IF LEN(N$) > 15 THEN LET T$ = LEFT$(N$,15)
00220 IF LEN(N$) <= 15 THEN LET T$ = N$
00230 PRINT N$;TAB(25);T$
00240 LET U = U + 1
00250 GOTO 190
00260 REM *******************************
00270 REM ***   THE DATA STATEMENTS    ***
00280 REM *******************************
00290 DATA "LAWERANCE, OLIVER"
00300 DATA "KAINSINGER, KATHLEEN"
00310 DATA "HARRISON, MARY ANN"
00320 DATA "GARRETT, LEWIS"
00330 DATA "SMITH, SAMANTHA"
00340 DATA "NEWMAN, TERRENCE"
00350 DATA "PRENTICE, LARRY"
00360 DATA "TROUGH, WAYNE"
00370 DATA "ALCOTT, MISSY"
00380 DATA "EVANS, FRANKLIN"
00999 END

RUNNH
              NEW NAMES REPORT

  OLD NAME                NEW NAME

LAWERANCE, OLIVER       LAWERANCE, OLIV
KAINSINGER, KATHLEEN    KAINSINGER, KAT
HARRISON, MARY ANN      HARRISON, MARY
GARRETT, LEWIS          GARRETT, LEWIS
SMITH, SAMANTHA         SMITH, SAMANTHA
NEWMAN, TERRENCE        NEWMAN, TERRENC
PRENTICE, LARRY         PRENTICE, LARRY
TROUGH, WAYNE           TROUGH, WAYNE
ALCOTT, MISSY           ALCOTT, MISSY
EVANS, FRANKLIN         EVANS, FRANKLIN
```

PSEUDOCODE

```
Start
Print the report headings
Initialize U to one
Start loop, do until U is greater than ten
  Read name
  If length of name is greater than fifteen
    Then assign the fifteen leftmost characters to T$
  Endif
  If length of name is less than or equal to fifteen
    Then assign name to T$
  Endif
  Print name and T$
  Add one to U
End loop
Stop
```

MICROCOMPUTERS:	
Apple	No differences.
Apple Macintosh	No differences.
IBM/Microsoft	No differences.
PET/Commodore 64	No differences.
TRS-80	No differences.

Problem C

The telephone company in your area wants to print out a new
telephone service roster. Use READ/DATA statements to enter the
data. The program should contain two subroutines, one to print
the report headings and one to print the names and numbers of
the new customer. Use the following as a guideline to the format of the report:

                    NEW SERVICE ROOSTER

          NAME   NUMBER

     XXXXXXXXXXXX   ###-####
     XXXXXXXXXXXX   ###-####
     XXXXXXXXXXXX   ###-####

Here are the names and phone numbers for your report:

          Jerry Johnson, 843-0938
          Thomas Magnum, 833-3849
          Kimberly Parson, 393-3403

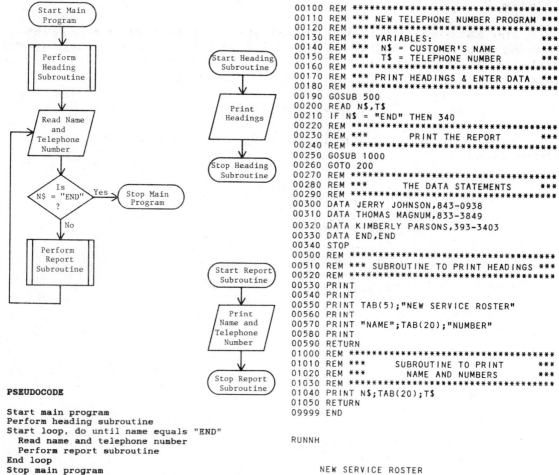

```
00100 REM ***********************************
00110 REM *** NEW TELEPHONE NUMBER PROGRAM ***
00120 REM ***********************************
00130 REM *** VARIABLES:                  ***
00140 REM ***   N$ = CUSTOMER'S NAME       ***
00150 REM ***   T$ = TELEPHONE NUMBER      ***
00160 REM ***********************************
00170 REM *** PRINT HEADINGS & ENTER DATA  ***
00180 REM ***********************************
00190 GOSUB 500
00200 READ N$,T$
00210 IF N$ = "END" THEN 340
00220 REM ***********************************
00230 REM ***       PRINT THE REPORT       ***
00240 REM ***********************************
00250 GOSUB 1000
00260 GOTO 200
00270 REM ***********************************
00280 REM ***      THE DATA STATEMENTS     ***
00290 REM ***********************************
00300 DATA JERRY JOHNSON,843-0938
00310 DATA THOMAS MAGNUM,833-3849
00320 DATA KIMBERLY PARSONS,393-3403
00330 DATA END,END
00340 STOP
00500 REM ***********************************
00510 REM *** SUBROUTINE TO PRINT HEADINGS ***
00520 REM ***********************************
00530 PRINT
00540 PRINT
00550 PRINT TAB(5);"NEW SERVICE ROSTER"
00560 PRINT
00570 PRINT "NAME";TAB(20);"NUMBER"
00580 PRINT
00590 RETURN
01000 REM ***********************************
01010 REM ***     SUBROUTINE TO PRINT      ***
01020 REM ***       NAME AND NUMBERS       ***
01030 REM ***********************************
01040 PRINT N$;TAB(20);T$
01050 RETURN
09999 END


RUNNH


          NEW SERVICE ROSTER

NAME                NUMBER

JERRY JOHNSON       843-0938
THOMAS MAGNUM       833-3849
KIMBERLY PARSONS    393-3403
STOP at line 00340 of MAIN PROGRAM
```

PSEUDOCODE

Start main program
Perform heading subroutine
Start loop, do until name equals "END"
  Read name and telephone number
  Perform report subroutine
End loop
Stop main program

Start heading subroutine
Print the report headings
Stop heading subroutine

Start report subroutine
Print name and telephone number
Stop report subroutine

MICROCOMPUTERS:	
Apple	No differences.
Apple Macintosh	No differences.
IBM/Microsoft	No differences.
PET/Commodore 64	No differences.
TRS-80	No differences.

Problem D

The National Guard has hired you to clean up their files. Some of the files start with the last name first and some start with the first name first. The National Guard would like to have all files start in the following format:

Last Name, First Name

Write a program to print all of the following names, last names first:

John Randolph
Bitter, Cheryl
Stafford, Lance
Sally Turner
Steve Lewis
Lin, Thomas
Packard, Oliver
Smith, Travis
Bob Berrios
Paula Vern

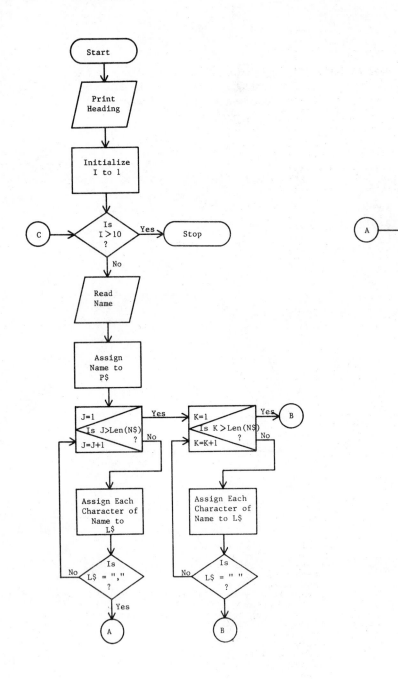

```
00100 REM **************************************
00110 REM *** NATIONAL GUARD ROSTER PROGRAM ***
00120 REM **************************************
00130 REM *** VARIABLES:                     ***
00140 REM ***    N$ = PERSON'S NAME AS INPUT ***
00150 REM ***    P$ = FORMATTED NAME         ***
00160 REM ***    I  = NAME COUNTER           ***
00170 REM ***    L$ = THE SEARCH VARIABLE    ***
00180 REM **************************************
00190 REM ***     PRINT THE REPORT HEADINGS  ***
00200 REM **************************************
00210 PRINT
00220 PRINT "NATIONAL GUARD ROSTER"
00230 PRINT
00240 REM **************************************
00250 REM ***          READ THE NAMES        ***
00260 REM **************************************
00270 LET I = 1
00280 IF I > 10 THEN 999
00290 READ N$
00300 REM **************************************
00310 REM *** DETERMINE IF NAME IS FORMATTED ***
00320 REM **************************************
00330 LET P$ = N$
00340 FOR J = 1 TO LEN(N$)
00350   LET L$ = MID$(N$,J,1)
00360   IF L$ = "," THEN 460
00370 NEXT J
00380 REM **************************************
00390 REM ***    FORMAT THE PERSON'S NAME    ***
00400 REM **************************************
00410 FOR K = 1 TO LEN(N$)
00420   LET L$ = MID$(N$,K,1)
00430   IF L$ = " " THEN 450
00440 NEXT K
00450 LET P$ = RIGHT$(N$,K + 1) + ", " + LEFT$(N$,K)
00460 PRINT P$
00470 LET I = I + 1
00480 GOTO 280
00490 REM **************************************
00500 REM ***      THE DATA STATEMENTS       ***
00510 REM **************************************
00520 DATA "JOHN RANDOLPH","BITTER, CHERYL"
00530 DATA "STAFFORD, LANCE","SALLY TURNER"
00540 DATA "STEVE LEWIS","LIN, THOMAS"
00550 DATA "PACKARD, OLIVER","SMITH, TRAVIS"
00560 DATA "BOB BERRIOS","PAULA VERN"
00999 END
```

```
RUNNH

NATIONAL GUARD ROSTER

RANDOLPH, JOHN
BITTER, CHERYL
STAFFORD, LANCE
TURNER, SALLY
LEWIS, STEVE
LIN, THOMAS
PACKARD, OLIVER
SMITH, TRAVIS
BERRIOS, BOB
VERN, PAULA
```

PSEUDOCODE

```
Start
Print the report headings
Initialize I to one
Start loop, do until I is greater than ten
  Read name
  Assign name to P$
  Start loop, search length of name until a comma is found
    If a comma is not found
      Then assign last name, first name to P$
    Endif
  End loop
  Print P$
  Add one to I
End loop
Stop
```

MICROCOMPUTERS:	
Apple	Line 450 should be: LET P$(I) = RIGHT$(N$(I), LEN(N$(I)) - K) + ", " + LEFT$(N$(I),K)
Apple Macintosh	Same as Apple.
IBM/Microsoft	Same as Apple.
PET/Commodore 64	Same as Apple.
TRS-80	Same as Apple.

SECTION IX
Arrays

ANSWERS TO TEXTBOOK REVIEW QUESTIONS

1.   An array is a group of related values assigned to a single
variable name. There are one-dimensional (lists) and two-
dimensional (tables or matrices) arrays. Arrays allow storage
of many related values without having to use a separate variable
for every value; also they are useful in sorting values,
searching for values, and file processing.

2.   Subscripts

   Three steps:

   ● The expression inside the parentheses is evaluated.
   ● The result of the expression is translated to the
     nearest integer.
   ● The indicated element of the array is accessed.

3.   The DIM statement indicates the number of elements in an
array for which space must be reserved. It must be located
before the first reference to the array(s) it describes,
although it is good programming practice to group all DIM statements together at the beginning of the program.

4.   FOR/NEXT statements

ANSWERS TO TEXTBOOK DEBUGGING EXERCISES

1.
```
10 DIM T$(25)
15 FOR I = 1 TO 30 — the terminal value should be 25
20   READ T$(I)      because array T$ only contains
25   PRINT T$(I)     25 data items
30 NEXT I
```

2.
```
100 REM ***    TOTAL THE ELEMENTS IN    ***
105 REM ***    ROW THREE OF ARRAY G     ***
110 DIM G(5,6)
115 LET T = 0
120 FOR I = 1 TO 5 —— the terminal value should be 6
125    LET T = T + G(I,6) — this totals the sixth
130 NEXT I                column. Line 125 should
                          be changed to
                              LET T = T + G(3,I)
```

ANSWER TO TEXTBOOK PROGRAMMING PROBLEM 1

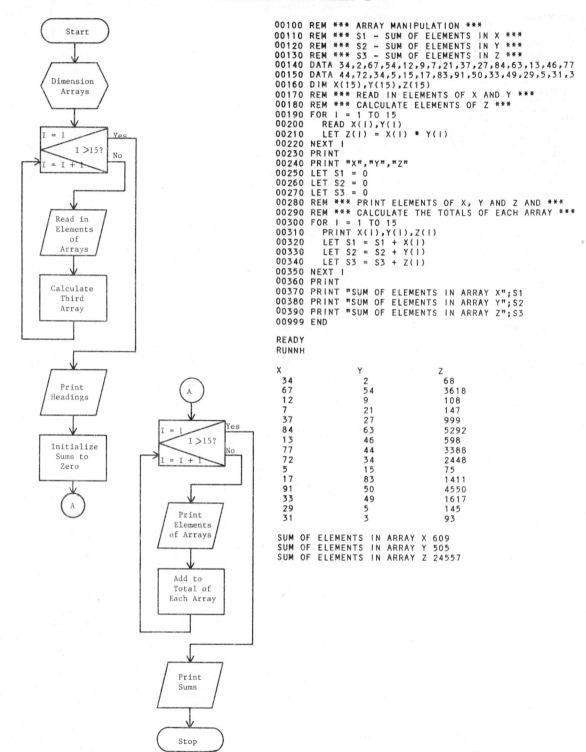

```
00100 REM *** ARRAY MANIPULATION ***
00110 REM *** S1 - SUM OF ELEMENTS IN X ***
00120 REM *** S2 - SUM OF ELEMENTS IN Y ***
00130 REM *** S3 - SUM OF ELEMENTS IN Z ***
00140 DATA 34,2,67,54,12,9,7,21,37,27,84,63,13,46,77
00150 DATA 44,72,34,5,15,17,83,91,50,33,49,29,5,31,3
00160 DIM X(15),Y(15),Z(15)
00170 REM *** READ IN ELEMENTS OF X AND Y ***
00180 REM *** CALCULATE ELEMENTS OF Z ***
00190 FOR I = 1 TO 15
00200   READ X(I),Y(I)
00210   LET Z(I) = X(I) * Y(I)
00220 NEXT I
00230 PRINT
00240 PRINT "X","Y","Z"
00250 LET S1 = 0
00260 LET S2 = 0
00270 LET S3 = 0
00280 REM *** PRINT ELEMENTS OF X, Y AND Z AND ***
00290 REM *** CALCULATE THE TOTALS OF EACH ARRAY ***
00300 FOR I = 1 TO 15
00310   PRINT X(I),Y(I),Z(I)
00320   LET S1 = S1 + X(I)
00330   LET S2 = S2 + Y(I)
00340   LET S3 = S3 + Z(I)
00350 NEXT I
00360 PRINT
00370 PRINT "SUM OF ELEMENTS IN ARRAY X";S1
00380 PRINT "SUM OF ELEMENTS IN ARRAY Y";S2
00390 PRINT "SUM OF ELEMENTS IN ARRAY Z";S3
00999 END

READY
RUNNH

X               Y               Z
 34              2               68
 67             54             3618
 12              9              108
  7             21              147
 37             27              999
 84             63             5292
 13             46              598
 77             44             3388
 72             34             2448
  5             15               75
 17             83             1411
 91             50             4550
 33             49             1617
 29              5              145
 31              3               93

SUM OF ELEMENTS IN ARRAY X 609
SUM OF ELEMENTS IN ARRAY Y 505
SUM OF ELEMENTS IN ARRAY Z 24557
```

PSEUDOCODE

```
Start
Dimension arrays
Start loop, do fifteen times
  Read element of x and element of y
  Multiply element of x by element of y and assign
    to corresponding position in z
Endloop
Print headings
Initialize sums of each array to zero
Start loop, do fifteen times
  Print elements of x, y, and z
  Add element of x to sum for x array
  Add element of y to sum for y array
  Add element of z to sum for z array
Endloop
Print sums for each array
Stop
```

MICROCOMPUTERS:	
Apple	No space is reserved before the numbers for a sign.
Apple Macintosh	No space is reserved before the numbers for a sign.
IBM/Microsoft	No differences.
PET/Commodore 64	No differences.
TRS-80	No differences.

ANSWER TO TEXTBOOK PROGRAMMING PROBLEM 2

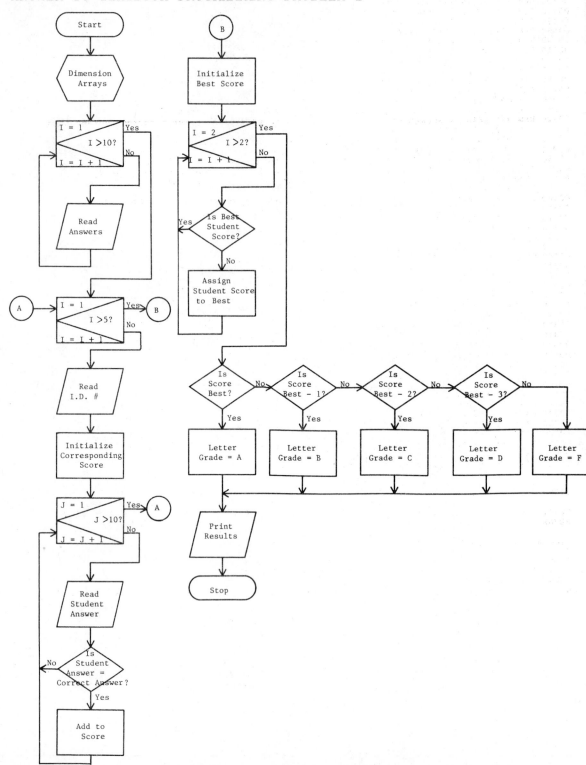

```
00100 REM *** DETERMINE STUDENT'S GRADES ***
00110 REM *** B - BEST SCORE ***
00120 REM *** L$ - LETTER GRADE ***
00130 DIM N$(5),S(5),G(5,10),A(10)
00140 REM *** READ IN ANSWERS ***
00150 FOR I = 1 TO 10
00160   READ A(I)
00170 NEXT I
00180 REM *** READ IN I.D. #'S ***
00190 FOR I = 1 TO 5
00200   READ N$(I)
00210   LET S(I) = 0
00220 REM *** READ IN SCORES ***
00230   FOR J = 1 TO 10
00240     READ G(I,J)
00250     IF G(I,J) <> A(J) THEN 270
00260     S(I) = S(I) + 1
00270   NEXT J
00280 NEXT I
00290 LET B = S(1)
00300 FOR I = 2 TO 5
00310   IF B > S(I) THEN 330
00320   LET B = S(I)
00330 NEXT I
00340 PRINT
00350 PRINT "I.D. #","GRADE"
00360 FOR I = 1 TO 5
00370   IF S(I) <> B THEN 400
00380   LET L$ = "A"
00390   GOTO 500
00400   IF S(I) <> B - 1 THEN 430
00410   LET L$ = "B"
00420   GOTO 500
00430   IF S(I) <> B - 2 THEN 460
00440   LET L$ = "C"
00450   GOTO 500
00460   IF S(I) <> B - 3 THEN 490
00470   LET L$ = "D"
00480   GOTO 500
00490   LET L$ = "F"
00500   PRINT N$(I),L$
00510 NEXT I
00520 DATA 0,1,1,1,0,1,0,0,1,1
00530 DATA "0009",0,0,1,0,0,1,0,0,1,0
00540 DATA "0108",0,1,0,1,0,0,0,0,1,1
00550 DATA "0187",0,1,1,1,0,1,0,0,1,1
00560 DATA "0309",1,1,0,1,0,1,0,1,0,1
00570 DATA "0256",0,1,1,1,0,1,0,0,1,0

00999 END

READY
RUNNH

I.D. #         GRADE
0009           D
0108           C
0187           A
0309           F
0256           B
```

PSEUDOCODE

```
Start
Dimension arrays
Start loop, do ten times
  Read correct answers
Endloop
Start loop, do five times
  Read student ID number
  Initialize corresponding score to zero
  Start loop, do ten times
    Read student's answer
    If student's answer = correct answer then
      Add 1 to score
  Endloop
    Repeat
  Endloop
Assign first student's score to best
Start loop, do five times
  If next student's score > Best then
    Best = next student's score
  End if
Endloop
Print headings
Start loop, do five times
  If score = Best then
    Letter grade = "A"
  Else if score = Best - 1 then
    Letter grade = "B"
  Else if score = Best - 2 then
    Letter grade = "C"
  Else if score = Best - 3 then
    Letter grade = "D"
  Else
    Letter grade = "F"
  End if
Endloop
Stop
```

MICROCOMPUTERS:	
Apple	No differences.
Apple Macintosh	No differences.
IBM/Microsoft	No differences.
PET/Commodore 64	No differences.
TRS-80	No differences.

ANSWER TO STUDY GUIDE PROGRAMMING PROBLEM 2

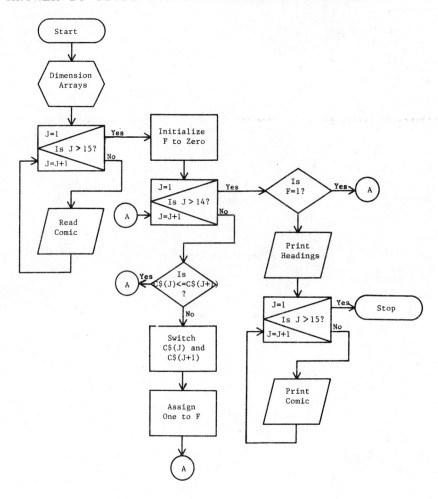

```
00100 REM *******************************
00110 REM *** COMIC STRIP SORT PROGRAM ***
00120 REM *******************************
00130 REM *** VARIABLES:              ***
00140 REM ***   C$ = COMIC STRIP NAME ***
00150 REM ***   F,H$ = SORT VARIABLES ***
00160 REM *******************************
00170 REM *** DIM ARRAYS & READ COMICS ***
00180 REM *******************************
00190 DIM C$(15)
00200 FOR J = 1 TO 15
00210   READ C$(J)
00220 NEXT J
00230 REM *******************************
00240 REM ***   SORT THE COMIC STRIPS  ***
00250 REM *******************************
00260 LET F = 0
00270 FOR J = 1 TO 14
00280   IF C$(J) <= C$(J + 1) THEN 330
00290   LET H$ = C$(J)
00300   LET C$(J) = C$(J + 1)
00310   LET C$(J + 1) = H$
00320   LET F = 1
00330 NEXT J
00340 IF F = 1 THEN 260
00350 REM *******************************
00360 REM ***   PRINT THE COMIC STRIPS ***
00370 REM *******************************
00380 PRINT
00390 PRINT
00400 PRINT "COMIC STRIPS"
00410 PRINT
00420 FOR J = 1 TO 15
00430   PRINT C$(J)
00440 NEXT J
00450 REM *******************************
00460 REM ***   THE DATA STATEMENTS    ***
00470 REM *******************************
00480 DATA PEANUTS,HEATHCLIFF,HERMAN
00490 DATA DENNIS THE MENACE,DICK TRACY
00500 DATA FAMILY CIRCUS,MARY WORTH
00510 DATA LI'L ABNER,SUPERMAN
00520 DATA BEETLE BAILEY,HAGAR THE HORRIBLE
00530 DATA THE WIZARD OF ID,SPIDERMAN
00540 DATA BRENDA STARR,BC
00999 END


RUNNH


COMIC STRIPS

BC
BEETLE BAILEY
BRENDA STARR
DENNIS THE MENACE
DICK TRACY
FAMILY CIRCUS
HAGAR THE HORRIBLE
HEATHCLIFF
HERMAN
LI'L ABNER
MARY WORTH
PEANUTS
SPIDERMAN
SUPERMAN
THE WIZARD OF ID
```

PSEUDOCODE

```
Start
Dimension the arrays
Start loop, do fifteen times
  Read comic strip
End loop
Start loop, do until flag is not equal to one
  Initialize flag to zero
  Start loop, do fourteen times
    If C$(I) > C$(I + 1)
      Then
        Switch C$(I) and C$(I + 1)
        Assign one to flag
    End if
  End loop
End loop
Print the report headings
Start loop, do fifteen times
  Print comic strip
End loop
Stop
```

MICROCOMPUTERS:	
Apple	No differences.
Apple Macintosh	No differences.
IBM/Microsoft	No differences.
PET/Commodore 64	No differences.
TRS-80	No differences.

ANSWERS TO STUDY GUIDE WORKSHEET PROBLEMS

2.   A(10) = 10   A(4) = 5
      A(8) = 2   A(2) = 12
      A(6) = 9

4.   9   8   7
      6   5   4

6.   a.   105   d.   155
      b.   475   e.   155
      c.   385   f.   205

8.   10 DIM 2(4,3)
      20 FOR I = 1 TO 4
      30   FOR J = 1 TO 3
      40   READ Z(I,J)
      50   NEXT J
      60 NEXT I
      70 LET S = 0
      80   FOR J = 1 to 4
      90   LET S = S + Z(J,2)
      100   NEXT J
      110   PRINT J
      120 DATA 1,3,9,12,15,18
      130 DATA 21,24,27,30,33,36
      999 END
      RUNNH
       75

10.   10 LET T = 0
      20 FOR I = 1 TO 4
      30   FOR J = 1 TO 3
      40   LET T = T + W(I,1)
      50   NEXT J
      60 NEXT I

SUPPLEMENTARY PROGRAMMING PROBLEMS

Problem A

Tommorrow marks the first annual University Beauty Contest. The judges have asked you to write a report showing each con- testant (in order of her score) and the score she received. Use the bubble sort making sure the scores are arranged from highest to lowest. The following format should be used when printing the report:

UNIVERSITY BEAUTY CONTEST

CONTESTANT   SCORE

XXXXXXXXXXXXXXXX   ##.##
XXXXXXXXXXXXXXXX   ##.##
XXXXXXXXXXXXXXXX   ##.##
XXXXXXXXXXXXXXXX   ##.##

The input data consists of the contestant's name and her score. There were eight contestants in the contest. The names and scores are:

Cheryl Ilyack, 73.9
Tamara Smythe, 81.02
Honor Heatherly, 79.88
Julie Barnes, 47.00
Gail Boller, 89.76
Denise Kowalski, 86.1
Frances Klinner, 65.89
Angela Young, 57.9

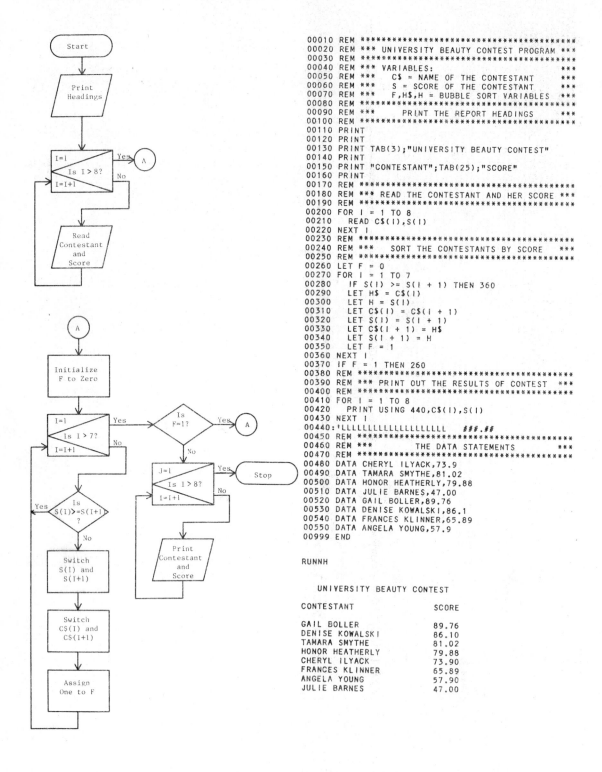

```
00010 REM *****************************************
00020 REM *** UNIVERSITY BEAUTY CONTEST PROGRAM ***
00030 REM *****************************************
00040 REM *** VARIABLES:                        ***
00050 REM ***   C$ = NAME OF THE CONTESTANT     ***
00060 REM ***   S = SCORE OF THE CONTESTANT     ***
00070 REM ***   F,H$,H = BUBBLE SORT VARIABLES  ***
00080 REM *****************************************
00090 REM ***      PRINT THE REPORT HEADINGS    ***
00100 REM *****************************************
00110 PRINT
00120 PRINT
00130 PRINT TAB(3);"UNIVERSITY BEAUTY CONTEST"
00140 PRINT
00150 PRINT "CONTESTANT";TAB(25);"SCORE"
00160 PRINT
00170 REM *****************************************
00180 REM *** READ THE CONTESTANT AND HER SCORE ***
00190 REM *****************************************
00200 FOR I = 1 TO 8
00210    READ C$(I),S(I)
00220 NEXT I
00230 REM *****************************************
00240 REM ***   SORT THE CONTESTANTS BY SCORE   ***
00250 REM *****************************************
00260 LET F = 0
00270 FOR I = 1 TO 7
00280    IF S(I) >= S(I + 1) THEN 360
00290    LET H$ = C$(I)
00300    LET H = S(I)
00310    LET C$(I) = C$(I + 1)
00320    LET S(I) = S(I + 1)
00330    LET C$(I + 1) = H$
00340    LET S(I + 1) = H
00350    LET F = 1
00360 NEXT I
00370 IF F = 1 THEN 260
00380 REM *****************************************
00390 REM *** PRINT OUT THE RESULTS OF CONTEST  ***
00400 REM *****************************************
00410 FOR I = 1 TO 8
00420    PRINT USING 440,C$(I),S(I)
00430 NEXT I
00440:'LLLLLLLLLLLLLLLLLLLLLLL    ###.##
00450 REM *****************************************
00460 REM ***       THE DATA STATEMENTS         ***
00470 REM *****************************************
00480 DATA CHERYL ILYACK,73.9
00490 DATA TAMARA SMYTHE,81.02
00500 DATA HONOR HEATHERLY,79.88
00510 DATA JULIE BARNES,47.00
00520 DATA GAIL BOLLER,89.76
00530 DATA DENISE KOWALSKI,86.1
00540 DATA FRANCES KLINNER,65.89
00550 DATA ANGELA YOUNG,57.9
00999 END


RUNNH


       UNIVERSITY BEAUTY CONTEST

CONTESTANT              SCORE

GAIL BOLLER             89.76
DENISE KOWALSKI         86.10
TAMARA SMYTHE           81.02
HONOR HEATHERLY         79.88
CHERYL ILYACK           73.90
FRANCES KLINNER         65.89
ANGELA YOUNG            57.90
JULIE BARNES            47.00
```

PSEUDOCODE

```
Start
Print the report headings
Start loop, do eight times
  Read contestant's name and score
End loop
Sort the contestants from highest score to lowest score
Start loop, do eight times
  Print the contestant's name and score
End loop
Stop
```

MICROCOMPUTERS:	
Apple	No differences.
Apple Macintosh	No differences.
IBM/Microsoft	No differences.
PET/Commodore 64	No differences.
TRS-80	No differences.

B-112   BASIC

Problem B

The Charity Company approaches celebrities on behalf of several charities for donations. The president of the company has asked you to provide a report listing the celebrity's name, his or her contribution to Charity One, his or her contribution to Charity Two, his or her contribution to Charity Three, and his or her total contribution. The program should use two-dimensional arrays for the contributions and should total donations to Charity One, donations to Charity Two, and donations to Charity Three as well as the total contribution. The following table is a good format for the report:

CHARITY REPORT

CELEBRITY	CANCER	DIABETES	MS	TOTAL
XXXXXXXXXXXXXX	$#,###.##	$#,###.##	$#,###.##	$##,###.##
XXXXXXXXXXXXXX	$#,###.##	$#,###.##	$#,###.##	$##,###.##
XXXXXXXXXXXXXX	$#,###.##	$#,###.##	$#,###.##	$##,###.##

TOTAL DONATIONS: $##,###.## $#,###.## $##,###.## $###,###.##

The input data is as follows:

CELEBRITY	CANCER	DIABETES	MS
James Garner	$3490.75	$ 44.98	$ 234.87
Harrison Ford	$ 23.15	$1974.78	$ 918.84
Edward Koch	$ 894.56	$ 8.00	$ 90.43
Joan Rivers	$4075.90	$ 0.00	$2348.00
Goldie Hawn	$ 78.52	$ 874.50	$7878.00
Sally Field	$9028.00	$9959.75	$ 990.50

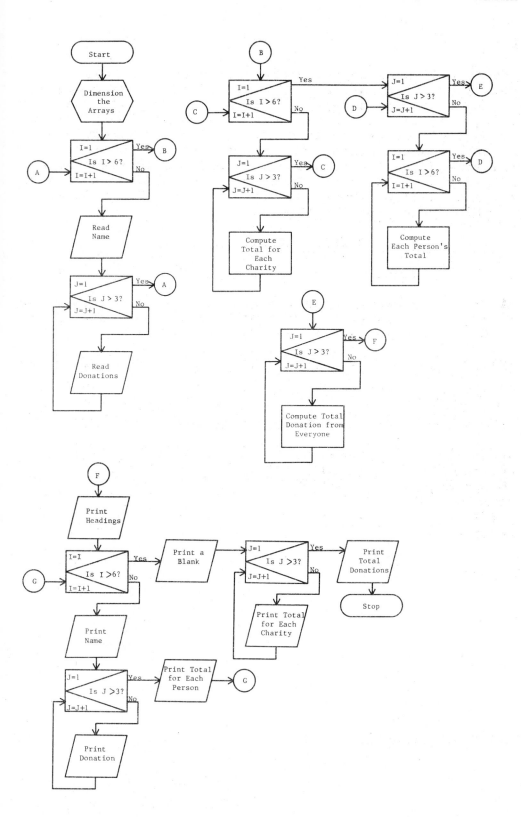

```
'00100 REM *************************************
 00110 REM ***   DONATION TO CHARITY PROGRAM  ***
 00120 REM *************************************
 00130 REM *** VARIABLES:                    ***
 00140 REM ***    N$ = CELEBRITY'S NAME      ***
 00150 REM ***    C = EACH CONTRIBUTION      ***
 00160 REM ***    TC = TOTAL FOR EACH PERSON ***
 00170 REM ***    TR = TOTAL FOR EACH CHARITY ***
 00180 REM ***    T = TOTAL CONTRIBUTION     ***
 00190 REM *************************************
 00200 REM *** DIMENSION ARRAYS & READ DATA  ***
 00210 REM *************************************
 00220 DIM N$(6),C(6,3),TC(6),TR(3)
 00230 FOR I = 1 TO 6
 00240   READ N$(I)
 00250   FOR J = 1 TO 3
 00260     READ C(I,J)
 00270   NEXT J
 00280 NEXT I
 00290 REM *************************************
 00300 REM ***       COMPUTE THE TOTALS      ***
 00310 REM *************************************
 00320 FOR I = 1 TO 6
 00330   FOR J = 1 TO 3
 00340     LET TC(I) = TC(I) + C(I,J)
 00350   NEXT J
 00360 NEXT I
 00370 FOR J = 1 TO 3
 00380   FOR I = 1 TO 6
 00390     LET TR(J) = TR(J) + C(I,J)
 00400   NEXT I
 00410 NEXT J
 00420 FOR J = 1 TO 3
 00430   LET T = T + TR(J)
 00440 NEXT J
 00450 REM *************************************
 00460 REM ***       PRINT THE REPORT        ***
 00470 REM *************************************
 00480 PRINT
 00490 PRINT
 00500 PRINT TAB(28);"CHARITY REPORT"
 00510 PRINT
 00520 PRINT "CELEBRITY";TAB(15);"CANCER";TAB(29);"DIABETES";
 00530 PRINT TAB(45);"MS";TAB(57);"TOTALS"
 00540 PRINT
 00550 FOR I = 1 TO 6
 00560   PRINT N$(I),
 00570   FOR J = 1 TO 3
 00580     PRINT C(I,J),
 00590   NEXT J
 00600   PRINT TC(I)
 00610 NEXT I
 00620 PRINT " ",
 00630 FOR J = 1 TO 3
 00640   PRINT TR(J),
 00650 NEXT J
 00660 PRINT T
 00670 REM *************************************
 00680 REM ***      THE DATA STATEMENTS      ***
 00690 REM *************************************
 00700 DATA JAMES GARNER,3490.75,44.98,234.87
 00710 DATA HARRISON FORD,23.15,1974.78,918.84
 00720 DATA EDWARD KOCH,894.56,8.00,90.43
 00730 DATA JOAN RIVERS,4075.90,0,2348.00
 00740 DATA GOLDIE HAWN,78.52,874.50,7878.00
 00750 DATA SALLY FIELD,9028,9959.75,990.50
 00999 END
```

RUNNH

```
                            CHARITY REPORT

CELEBRITY       CANCER       DIABETES      MS         TOTALS

JAMES GARNER    3490.75      44.98         234.87     3770.6
HARRISON FORD   23.15        1974.78       918.84     2916.77
EDWARD KOCH     894.56       8             90.43      992.99
JOAN RIVERS     4075.9       0             2348       6423.9
GOLDIE HAWN     78.52        874.5         7878       8831.02
SALLY FIELD     9028         9959.75       990.5      19978.25
                17590.88     12862.01      12460.64   42913.53
```

PSEUDOCODE

```
Start
Dimension the arrays
Start loop, do six times
  Read celebrity's name
  Start loop, do three times
    Read contribution to each charity
  End loop
End loop
Compute total contribution for each celebrity
Compute total contribution to each fund
Compute total contributions
Print the report headings
Print each celebrity, his contribution to each fund, and his
  total contribution
Print the total contribution for each fund and the total contri-
  butions
Stop
```

MICROCOMPUTERS:	
Apple	Output must be reformatted.
Apple Macintosh	Output must be reformatted.
IBM/Microsoft	No differences.
PET/Commodore 64	Output must be reformatted.
TRS-80	Output must be reformatted.

Problem C

The Movie-Goers Association is conducting a survey of 100 movie goers to see which movie they would pick as their all-time favorite. The Association would like you to write a program to show the results of the survey. The program should use input statements to enter the data into the program. Also, the program should print out a report of the survey, giving the name of the movie, the percentage of votes it received, and the number of votes it received. At the end of the report, print the total number of votes (100). The program should use the print using statement. Use the following as a guideline to the report:

```
                  FAVORITE MOVIE SURVEY

            MOVIE                    # VOTES        % VOTES

      XXXXXXXXXXXXXXXXXXXXXXXXX        ##             ##

      XXXXXXXXXXXXXXXXXXXXXXXXX        ##             ##
      XXXXXXXXXXXXXXXXXXXXXXXXX        ##             ##

      TOTAL VOTES                     100            100%
```

Use the following data:

Raiders of The Lost Ark, 25 votes
Star Wars, 24 votes
Ghostbusters, 21 votes
E.T., 15 votes
Gremlins, 8 votes
Star Trek, 4 votes
Indiana Jones, 3 votes

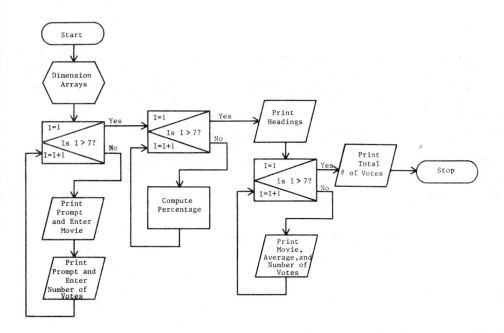

```
00100 REM *********************************
00110 REM ***   FAVORITE MOVIE PROGRAM   ***
00120 REM *********************************
00130 REM *** VARIABLES:                 ***
00140 REM ***    M$ = NAME OF THE MOVIE  ***
00150 REM ***    V = NUMBER OF VOTES     ***
00160 REM ***    A = VOTE PERCENTAGE     ***
00170 REM *********************************
00180 REM *** ENTER MOVIE AND # VOTES    ***
00190 REM *********************************
00200 DIM M$(7),V(7),A(7)
00210 FOR I = 1 TO 7
00220    PRINT "WHAT'S THE NAME OF THE MOVIE?"
00230    INPUT M$(I)
00240    PRINT "HOW MANY VOTES DID IT GET?"
00250    INPUT V(I)
00260 NEXT I
00270 REM *********************************
00280 REM *** COMPUTE VOTE PERCENTAGE   ***
00290 REM *********************************
00300 FOR I = 1 TO 7
00310    LET A(I) = V(I) / 100
00320 NEXT I
00330 REM *********************************
00340 REM ***      PRINT THE RESULTS     ***
00350 REM *********************************
00360 PRINT
00370 PRINT
00380 PRINT
00390 PRINT
00400 PRINT TAB(20);"FAVORITE MOVIE SURVEY"
00410 PRINT
00420 PRINT TAB(6);"MOVIE";TAB(32);"PERCENTAGE";
00430 PRINT TAB(45);"TOTAL VOTES"
00440 PRINT
00450 FOR I = 1 TO 7
00460    PRINT USING 500,M$(I),A(I),V(I)
00470 NEXT I
00480 PRINT
00490 PRINT "TOTAL VOTES";TAB(47);100
00500 :'LLLLLLLLLLLLLLLLLLLLLLLLLLLL    #.##        ##
00999 END
```

```
RUNNH
WHAT'S THE NAME OF THE MOVIE?
 ? RAIDERS OF THE LOST ARK
HOW MANY VOTES DID IT GET?
 ? 25
WHAT'S THE NAME OF THE MOVIE?
 ? STAR WARS
HOW MANY VOTES DID IT GET?
 ? 24
WHAT'S THE NAME OF THE MOVIE?
 ? GHOSTBUSTERS
HOW MANY VOTES DID IT GET?
 ? 21
WHAT'S THE NAME OF THE MOVIE?
 ? E. T.
HOW MANY VOTES DID IT GET?
 ? 15
WHAT'S THE NAME OF THE MOVIE?
 ? GREMLINS
HOW MANY VOTES DID IT GET?
 ? 8
WHAT'S THE NAME OF THE MOVIE?
 ? STAR TREK
HOW MANY VOTES DID IT GET?
 ? 4
WHAT'S THE NAME OF THE MOVIE?
 ? INDIANA JONES
HOW MANY VOTES DID IT GET?
 ? 3
```

```
                    FAVORITE MOVIE SURVEY

        MOVIE                PERCENTAGE    TOTAL VOTES

RAIDERS OF THE LOST ARK        0.25            25
STAR WARS                      0.24            24
GHOSTBUSTERS                   0.21            21
E. T.                          0.15            15
GREMLINS                       0.08             8
STAR TREK                      0.04             4
INDIANA JONES                  0.03             3

TOTAL VOTES                                   100
```

PSEUDOCODE

```
Start
Dimension arrays
Start loop, do seven times
  Print prompt
  Input movie and number of votes
End loop
Start loop, do seven times
  Percentage of each movie equals votes / 100
End loop
Print the report headings
Start loop, do seven times
Print the movie, the percentage of votes, and the number of
  votes
End loop
Print the total number of votes
Stop
```

MICROCOMPUTERS:	
Apple	Output must be reformatted; no PRINT USING statement.
Apple Macintosh	PRINT USING statement differs.
IBM/Microsoft	PRINT USING statement differs.
PET/Commodore 64	Output must be reformatted; no PRINT USING statement.
TRS-80	PRINT USING statement differs.

Problem D

The computer department has asked you to produce a computer dictionary for them. The department has given you a list of the words and definitions to print out in an alphabetical list. The department has not specified a format for the output, so you can use whatever format you wish. The list of words is as follows:

```
BASIC - a programming language for beginners
Byte - a unit of storage made up of bits
Microcomputer - a very small computer
Secondary Storage - external storage such as disk
ANSI BASIC - universally accepted rules for BASIC
Input - data submitted to the computer for processing
Record - a collection of fields related to a single unit
Bit - a binary digit that is the smallest unit of storage
Output - information from the computer as a result of proc-
          essing
Field - a meaningful item of data
```

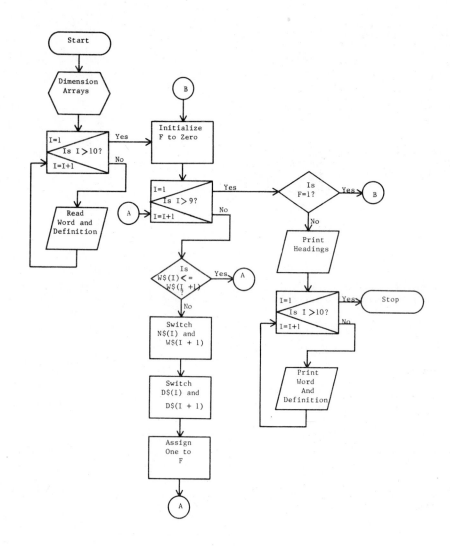

```
00100 REM *************************************
00110 REM *** COMPUTER TERM SORT PROGRAM  ***
00120 REM *************************************
00130 REM *** VARIABLES:                   ***
00140 REM ***   W$ = WORD                  ***
00150 REM ***   D$ = DEFINITION            ***
00160 REM ***   F,H1$,H2$ = SORT VARIABLES ***
00170 REM *************************************
00180 REM ***   DIM ARRAYS AND READ DATA   ***
00190 REM *************************************
00200 DIM W$(10),D$(10)
00210 FOR I = 1 TO 10
00220   READ W$(I),D$(I)
00230 NEXT I
00240 REM *************************************
00250 REM ***    SORT THE COMPUTER WORDS   ***
00260 REM *************************************
00270 LET F = 0
00280 FOR I = 1 TO 9
00290   IF W$(I) <= W$(I + 1) THEN 370
00300   LET H1$ = W$(I)
00310   LET H2$ = D$(I)
00320   LET W$(I) = W$(I + 1)
00330   LET D$(I) = D$(I + 1)
00340   LET W$(I + 1) = H1$
00350   LET D$(I + 1) = H2$
00360   LET F = 1
00370 NEXT I
00380 IF F = 1 THEN 270
00390 REM *************************************
00400 REM ***       PRINT THE RESULTS      ***
00410 REM *************************************
00420 PRINT
00430 PRINT
00440 PRINT "COMPUTER DICTIONARY"
00450 PRINT
00460 PRINT
00470 FOR I = 1 TO 10
00480   PRINT W$(I);" - ";D$(I)
00490   PRINT
00500 NEXT I
00510 REM *************************************
00520 REM ***      THE DATA STATEMENTS     ***
00530 REM *************************************
00540 DATA BASIC,A PROGRAMMING LANGUAGE FOR BEGINNERS
00550 DATA BYTE,A UNIT OF STORAGE MADE UP OF BITS
00560 DATA MICROCOMPUTER,A VERY SMALL COMPUTER
00570 DATA SECONDARY STORAGE,EXTERNAL STORAGE SUCH AS DISK
00580 DATA ANSI BASIC,UNIVERSALLY ACCEPTED RULES FOR BASIC
00590 DATA INPUT,DATA SUBMITTED TO THE COMPUTER FOR PROCESSING
00600 DATA RECORD,A COLLECTION OF FIELDS RELATED TO A SINGLE UNIT
00610 DATA BIT,A BINARY DIGIT THAT IS THE SMALLEST UNIT OF STORAGE
00620 DATA OUTPUT,INFORMATION FROM THE COMPUTER AS A RESULT OF PROCESSING
00630 DATA FIELD,A MEANINGFUL ITEM OF DATA
00999 END

RUNNH


COMPUTER DICTIONARY


ANSI BASIC - UNIVERSALLY ACCEPTED RULES FOR BASIC

BASIC - A PROGRAMMING LANGUAGE FOR BEGINNERS

BIT - A BINARY DIGIT THAT IS THE SMALLEST UNIT OF STORAGE

BYTE - A UNIT OF STORAGE MADE UP OF BITS

FIELD - A MEANINGFUL ITEM OF DATA

INPUT - DATA SUBMITTED TO THE COMPUTER FOR PROCESSING

MICROCOMPUTER - A VERY SMALL COMPUTER

OUTPUT - INFORMATION FROM THE COMPUTER AS A RESULT OF PROCESSING


RECORD - A COLLECTION OF FIELDS RELATED TO A SINGLE UNIT

SECONDARY STORAGE - EXTERNAL STORAGE SUCH AS DISK
```

PSEUDOCODE

```
Start
Dimension the arrays
Start loop, do ten times
  Read the word and its definition
End loop
Start loop, do until flag is not equal to zero
  Initialize flag to zero
  Start loop, do nine times
    If W$(I) > W$(I + 1)
      Then
        Switch W$(I) and W$(I + 1)
        Switch D$(I) and D$(I + 1)
        Assign one to flag
    End if
  End loop
End loop
Print the report headings
Start loop, do ten times
  Print the word and its definition
End loop
Stop
```

```
MICROCOMPUTERS:

Apple                No differences.
Apple Macintosh      No differences.
IBM/Microsoft        No differences.
PET/Commodore 64     No differences.
TRS-80               No differences.
```

SECTION X
File Processing

1.   A file is a way of organizing and storing data. Files
allow users to access data without having to retype it each time
the program is run. They also allow different programs to be
executed using the same data. A field is an individual data
item, a record is a group of related fields, and a file is a
group of related records.

2.   To record data in a sequential file these steps are needed:

    1. open sequential data file for writing to the file
    2. write data to the sequential file
    3. close the sequential file

To read data from a sequential file Step 1 above should be open
sequential data file for reading from the file, and Step 2
should be read data from sequential data file. Step 3 remains
the same.

3.   The closing of a data file prevents the loss of the file's
contents and also indicates to the computer that the use of the
file is finished for the present time.

4.   Records in sequential files must be written and read one
after the other starting with Record 1, whereas records in random files may be written and read in any order desired.

ANSWERS TO TEXTBOOK DEBUGGING EXERCISES

1.
```
100 OPEN CUSTOMER AS FILE #4    filename must be enclosed in
105 FOR I = 1 TO 100           quotation marks, change to
110    READ X                  "CUSTOMER"
115    PRINT #2,X
120 NEXT I
125 CLOSE #4      file number 4 was opened, change the 2
                  to 4
```

2.
```
50 REM *** READ DATA FROM FILE ***
55 OPEN PAYROLL FILE #3        filename must be enclosed in
60 FOR I = 1 TO 5             quotation marks, change to
65    READ #3 A$(I)            "PAYROLL"
70    PRINT A$(I)
75 NEXT I          a comma
80 CLOSE #2        must be inserted here

          file number 3 was opened therefore file number
          3 must be closed, change the 2 to 3
```

ANSWER TO TEXTBOOK PROGRAMMING PROBLEM 1

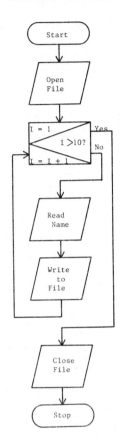

```
00010 REM *** CREATE SEQUENTIAL FILE ***
00015 OPEN "BODYBUILDERS" AS FILE #1
00020 FOR I = 1 TO 10
00025   READ N$
00030    PRINT #1,N$
00035 NEXT I
00040 CLOSE #1
00045 DATA "HANEY","BERTIL","PLATZ","FULLER","ZANE"
00050 DATA "BANNOUT","MAKKAWY","WILKOSZ","BECKLES","METZ"
00999 END

READY
RUNNH
```

PSEUDOCODE

```
Start
Open the file
Start loop, do ten times
   Read bodybuilder's name
   Write name to file
End loop
Close the file
Stop
```

MICROCOMPUTERS:		
Apple	Insert: 12 LET D$ = CHR$(4)	
	Line 15 should be:	
	15 PRINT D$;"OPEN BODYBUILDERS"	
	Insert: 17 PRINT N$	
	Line 30 should be:	
	30 PRINT D$;"WRITE BODYBUILDERS"	
Apple Macintosh	Line 15 should be:	
	15 OPEN "O",1,"BODYBUILDERS"	
IBM/Microsoft	Line 15 should be:	
	15 OPEN "BODYBUILDERS" FOR OUTPUT AS #1	
	Line 30 should be: 30 PRINT #1,N$	
PET/Commodore 64	Line 15 should be:	
	15 OPEN 1,8,2"O:BODYBUILDERS,S,W"	
	Line 30 should be: 30 PRINT#1,N$	
	Line 40 should be: 40 CLOSE#1	
TRS-80	Line 15 should be:	
	15 OPEN "O",1,"BODYBUILDERS"	

ANSWER TO TEXTBOOK PROGRAMMING PROBLEM 2

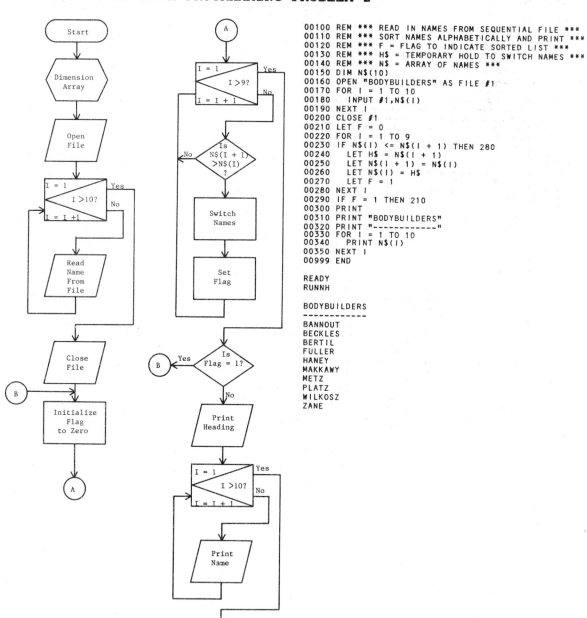

```
00100 REM *** READ IN NAMES FROM SEQUENTIAL FILE ***
00110 REM *** SORT NAMES ALPHABETICALLY AND PRINT ***
00120 REM *** F = FLAG TO INDICATE SORTED LIST ***
00130 REM *** H$ = TEMPORARY HOLD TO SWITCH NAMES ***
00140 REM *** N$ = ARRAY OF NAMES ***
00150 DIM N$(10)
00160 OPEN "BODYBUILDERS" AS FILE #1
00170 FOR I = 1 TO 10
00180    INPUT #1,N$(I)
00190 NEXT I
00200 CLOSE #1
00210 LET F = 0
00220 FOR I = 1 TO 9
00230 IF N$(I) <= N$(I + 1) THEN 280
00240    LET H$ = N$(I + 1)
00250    LET N$(I + 1) = N$(I)
00260    LET N$(I) = H$
00270    LET F = 1
00280 NEXT I
00290 IF F = 1 THEN 210
00300 PRINT
00310 PRINT "BODYBUILDERS"
00320 PRINT "------------"
00330 FOR I = 1 TO 10
00340    PRINT N$(I)
00350 NEXT I
00999 END

READY
RUNNH

BODYBUILDERS
------------
BANNOUT
BECKLES
BERTIL
FULLER
HANEY
MAKKAWY
METZ
PLATZ
WILKOSZ
ZANE
```

PSEUDOCODE

```
Start
Dimension array for names
Open file of bodybuilders
Start loop, do ten times
  Read bodybuilder's name into array
End loop
Close the file
(A) Set flag = zero
Start loop, do nine times
  If name should come after its successor then
    Assign successor to holding variable
    Assign name to position of successor
    Assign value in holding variable to the position
      where name was
    Set flag = one because switches were made
  End if
End loop
If flag = one (switches were made)
  Set flag back to zero
  Repeat the above steps starting with (A)
Otherwise
  Print headings
  Start loop, do ten times
    Print name
  End loop
End if
Stop
```

```
MICROCOMPUTERS:

Apple                Insert:   155 LET D$ = CHR$(4)
                     Line 160 should be:
                     160 PRINTDD$;"OPEN BODYBUILDERS"
                     Insert:
                     165 PRINT D$;"READ BODYBUILDERS"
                     Line 180 should be:  180 INPUT N$(I)
                     Line 200 should be:
                     200 PRINT D$;"CLOSE BODYBUILDERS"
Apple Macintosh      Line 160 should be:
                     160 OPEN "I",1,"BODYBUILDERS"
IBM/Microsoft        Line 160 should be:
                     160 OPEN "BODYBUILDERS" FOR INPUT AS #1
                     Line 180 should be:  180 INPUT#1,N$(I)
PET/Commodore 64     Line 160 should be:
                     160 OPEN 1,8,2,"0:BODYBUILDERS,S,R"
                     Line 180 should be:  180 INPUT#1,N$(I)
                     Line 200 should be:  200 CLOSE#1
TRS-80               Line 160 should be:
                     160 OPEN "I",1,"BODYBUILDERS"
```

ANSWER TO STUDY GUIDE PROGRAMMING PROBLEM 2

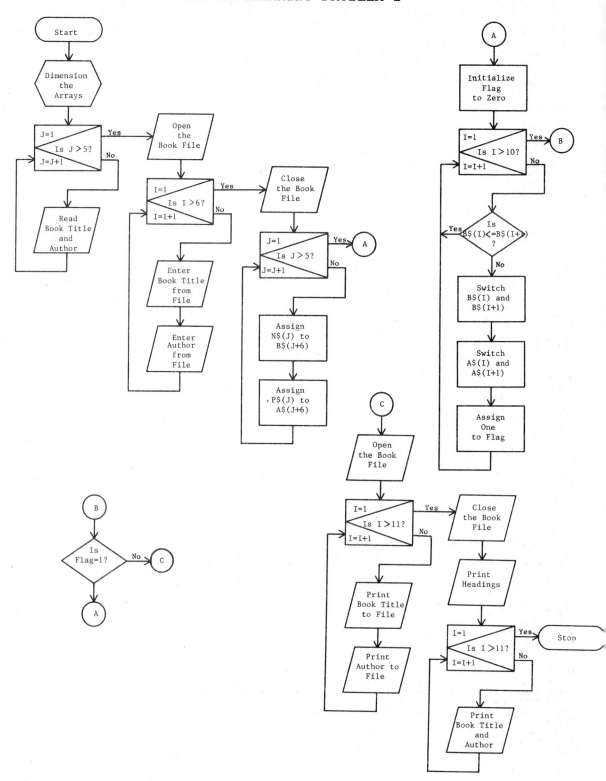

```
00100 REM *******************************************************
00110 REM *** FILE PROGRAM TO UPDATE BOOK COLLECTION FILE ***
00120 REM *******************************************************
00130 REM *** VARIABLES:                                    ***
00140 REM ***      N$ = TITLE OF THE BOOK TO BE ADDED       ***
00150 REM ***      P$ = AUTHOR OF THE BOOK TO BE ADDED      ***
00160 REM ***      B$ = TITLE OF THE BOOK FROM THE FILE     ***
00170 REM ***      A$ = AUTHOR OF THE BOOK FROM THE FILE    ***
00180 REM *******************************************************
00190 REM ***    DIMENSION THE ARRAYS AND READ THE DATA     ***
00200 REM *******************************************************
00210 DIM N$(15),P$(15),B$(20),A$(20)
00220 FOR J = 1 TO 5
00230    READ N$(J),P$(J)
00240 NEXT J
00250 REM *******************************************************
00260 REM ***   INPUT THE DATA FROM THE FILE INTO PROGRAM   ***
00270 REM *******************************************************
00280 OPEN "BOOK.FILE" AS FILE #1
00290 FOR I = 1 TO 6
00300    INPUT #1,B$(I)
00310    INPUT #1,A$(I)
00320 NEXT I
00330 CLOSE #1
00340 REM *******************************************************
00350 REM ***              ADD NEW BOOKS TO FILE            ***
00360 REM *******************************************************
00370 FOR J = 1 TO 5
00380    LET B$(J + 6) = N$(J)
00390    LET A$(J + 6) = P$(J)
00400 NEXT J
00410 REM *******************************************************
00420 REM ***          SORT THE BOOKS BY BOOK TITLE         ***
00430 REM *******************************************************
00440 LET F = 0
00450 FOR I = 1 TO 10
00460    IF B$(I) <= B$(I + 1) THEN 540
00470    LET H1$ = B$(I)
00480    LET H2$ = A$(I)
00490    LET B$(I) = B$(I + 1)
00500    LET A$(I) = A$(I + 1)
00510    LET B$(I + 1) = H1$
00520    LET A$(I + 1) = H2$
00530    LET F = 1
00540 NEXT I
00550 IF F = 1 THEN 440
00560 REM *******************************************************
00570 REM *** PRINT THE BOOK TITLES AND AUTHORS TO FILE  ***
00580 REM *******************************************************
00590 OPEN "BOOK.FILE" AS FILE #2
00600 FOR I = 1 TO 11
00610    PRINT #2,B$(I)
00620    PRINT #2,A$(I)
00630 NEXT I
00640 CLOSE #2
00650 REM *******************************************************
00660 REM ***          PRINT THE BOOK COLLECTION REPORT     ***
00670 REM *******************************************************
00680 PRINT
00690 PRINT
00700 PRINT TAB(15);"BOOK COLLECTION"
00710 PRINT
00720 PRINT "BOOK TITLE";TAB(35);"AUTHOR"
00730 PRINT
00740 OPEN "BOOK.FILE" AS FILE #2
00750 FOR I = 1 TO 11
00760    PRINT B$(I);TAB(35);A$(I)
00770 NEXT I
00780 REM *******************************************************
00790 REM ***               THE DATA STATEMENTS             ***
00800 REM *******************************************************
00810 DATA GONE WITH THE WIND,MARGARET MITCHELL
00820 DATA UNDERSTANDING COMPUTERS,STEVE MANDELL
00830 DATA A CHRISTMAS CAROL,CHARLES DICKENS
00840 DATA HAMLET,WILLIAM SHAKESPEARE
00850 DATA IN SEARCH OF EXECELLENCE,THOMAS PETERS
00999 END
```

RUNNH

BOOK COLLECTION

BOOK TITLE   AUTHOR

A CHRISTMAS CAROL   CHARLES DICKENS
COMPUTERS AND DATA PROCESSING   STEVE MANDELL
COST AND MANAGERIAL ACCOUNTING   RONALD HARTLEY
ECONOMICS   PAUL SAMUELSON
GONE WITH THE WIND   MARGARET MITCHELL
HAMLET   WILLIAM SHAKESPEARE
IN SEARCH OF EXECELLENCE   THOMAS PETERS
INFORMATION PROCESSING   MARILYN BOHL
THE SNOWS OF KILIMANJARO   ERNEST HEMINGWAY
THINK AND GROW RICH   NAPOLEON HILL
UNDERSTANDING COMPUTERS   STEVE MANDELL

PSEUDOCODE

```
Start
Dimension the arrays
Start loop, do five times
  Read new book title and author
End loop
Open the book file
Start loop, do six times
  Enter the book title from the file
  Enter the author from the file
End loop
Close the book file
Start loop, do five times
  Assign new book title to last position of the book title
    array
  Assign new author to last position of the author array
End loop
Start loop, do until flag is not equal to one
  Initialize flag to zero
  Start loop, do ten times
    If B$(I) > B$(I + 1)
      Then
        Switch B$(I) and B$(I + 1)
        Switch A$(I) and A$(I + 1)
        Switch one to flag
    End if
  End loop
End loop
Open the book file
Start loop, do eleven times
  Print book title to the file
  Print author to the file
End loop
Close the book file
Print the report headings
Start loop, do eleven times
  Print the book title and author
End loop
Stop
```

```
MICROCOMPUTERS:

Apple               See Section X of text.
Apple Macintosh     See Section X of text.
IBM/Microsoft       See Section X of text.
PET/Commodore 64    See Section X of text.
TRS-80              See Section X of text.
```

ANSWERS TO STUDY GUIDE WORKSHEET PROBLEMS

2.   30 PRINT #2,N$,S

4.   Fields are the individual data items such as a name.
Records are a group of one or more related fields and a file is
a group of one or more records.

6.   10 OPEN "GROCERIES" AS FILE #1
       20 FOR I = 1 TO 10
       30   READ G$
       40   PRINT #1,G$
       50 NEXT I
       60 CLOSE #1
       70 DATA "CARROTS", "POTATOES", "MILK","EGGS","CHEESE"
       80 DATA "LETTUCE","HAMBURGERS","BREAD","MUSTARD","APPLES"
       99 END

SUPPLEMENTARY PROGRAMMING PROBLEMS

Problem A

Mr. Jameson owns 12 apartments located near the campus of Watstown University. Mr. Jameson needs a program that will show which apartments have been rented for the coming school year, which have not been rented, and the number of persons leasing the apartment. Mr. Jameson has decided that the program should utilize disk data files. The apartments and their rental status are listed below. Store the apartment number, the number of persons leasing the apartment, and either an "V" or an "R" (for Vacant or Rented) on a file. Your program should print a report showing each apartment, the number of persons leasing the apartment, and the status of the apartment (either Vacant or Rented depending on if a "V" or an "R" is stored in the file).

Use the following to establish the original file.

Apartment	Status	# Leasees
1	Vacant	0
2	Vacant	0
3	Rented	3
4	Vacant	0
5	Rented	4
6	Rented	4
7	Vacant	0
8	Vacant	0
9	Vacant	0
10	Rented	4
11	Rented	3
12	Rented	4

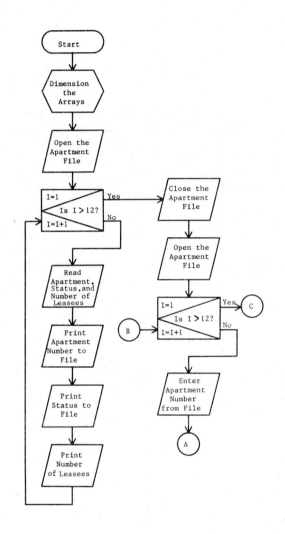

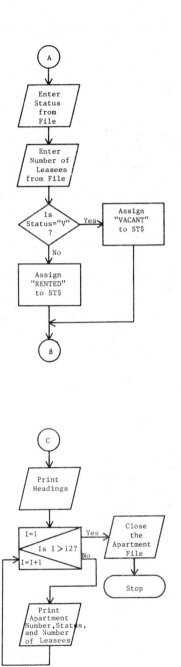

```
00100 REM ********************************************
00110 REM *** APARTMENT RENTAL PROGRAM USING FILES ***
00120 REM ********************************************
00130 REM *** VARIABLES:                          ***
00140 REM ***     A = APARTMENT NUMBER             ***
00150 REM ***     S$ = STATUS OF THE APARTMENT     ***
00160 REM ***     L = NUMBER OF PERSONS LEASING    ***
00170 REM ***     ST$ = NEW STATUS OF APARTMENT    ***
00180 REM ********************************************
00190 DIM A(12),S$(12),L(12),ST$(12)
00200 REM ********************************************
00210 REM ***      READ INITIAL VALUES INTO FILE   ***
00220 REM ********************************************
00230 OPEN "APART.FILE" AS FILE #1
00240 FOR I = 1 TO 12
00250    READ A(I),S$(I),L(I)
00260    PRINT #1,A(I)
00270    PRINT #1,S$(I)
00280    PRINT #1,I(I)
00290 NEXT I
00300 CLOSE #1
00310 REM ********************************************
00320 REM ***   PRINT OUT CURRENT APARTMENT STATUS ***
00330 REM ********************************************
00340 OPEN "APART.FILE" AS FILE #2
00350 FOR I = 1 TO 12
00360    INPUT #2,A(I)
00370    INPUT #2,S$(I)
00380    INPUT #2,L(I)
00390    IF S$(I) = "V" THEN 420
00400    ST$(I) = "RENTED"
00410    GOTO 430
00420    ST$(I) = "VACANT"
00430 NEXT I
00440 PRINT
00450 PRINT
00460 PRINT TAB(5);"CURRENT APARTMENT STATUS"
00470 PRINT
00480 PRINT "APARTMENT";TAB(14);"STATUS";TAB(24);"#LEASEES"
00490 PRINT
00500 FOR I = 1 TO 12
00510    PRINT TAB(3);A(I),ST$(I);TAB(26);L(I)
00520 NEXT I
00530 CLOSE #2
00532 REM ********************************************
00534 REM ***          THE DATA STATEMENTS        ***
00536 REM ********************************************
00540 DATA 1,V,0,2,V,0,3,R,3,4,V,0
00550 DATA 5,R,4,6,R,4,7,V,0,8,V,0
00560 DATA 9,V,0,10,R,4,11,R,3,12,R,4
00999 END
```

RUNNH

```
       CURRENT APARTMENT STATUS

APARTMENT     STATUS     #LEASEES

     1        VACANT        0
     2        VACANT        0
     3        RENTED        3
     4        VACANT        0
     5        RENTED        4
     6        RENTED        4
     7        VACANT        0
     8        VACANT        0
     9        VACANT        0
    10        RENTED        4
    11        RENTED        3
    12        RENTED        4
```

PSEUDOCODE

```
Start
Dimension the arrays
Open the apartment file
Start loop, do twelve times
    Read apartment number, status, and number of leasees
    Print apartment number to file
    Print status to file
    Print number of leasees to file
End loop
Close the apartment file
Open the apartment file
Start loop, do twelve times
    Enter apartment number from file
    Enter status from file
    Enter number of leasees from file
    If status = "V"
        Then
            Assign "VACANT" to ST$
        Else
            Assign "RENTED" to ST$
    Endif
End loop
Print the report headings
Start loop, do twelve times
    Print apartment number, ST$, and number of leasees
End loop
Close the apartment file
Stop
```

MICROCOMPUTERS:	
Apple	See Section X of text.
Apple Macintosh	See Section X of text.
IBM/Microsoft	See Section X of text.
PET/Commodore 64	See Section X of text.
TRS-80	See Section X of text.

Problem B

Mr. Jameson has rented five more of his apartments. Write
a program to update the file created in Problem A. Also, print
a report like the one in Problem A to show the new file data.
Use the following information to update the file:

Apartment	Status	#Leasees
1	Rented	4
4	Rented	2
7	Rented	5
8	Rented	4
9	Rented	3

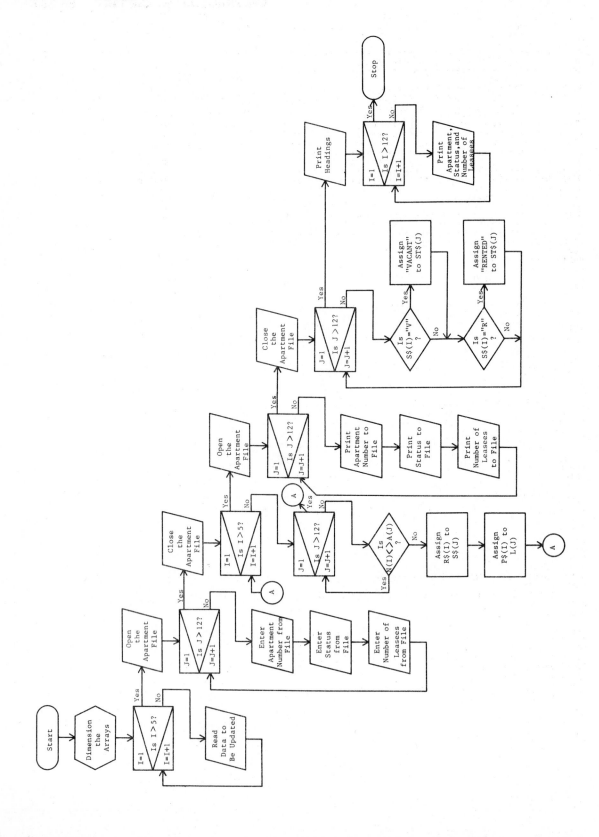

```
00010 REM ***********************************************
00020 REM *** FILE PROGRAM TO UPDATE APARTMENT FILE ***
00030 REM ***********************************************
00040 REM *** VARIABLES:                             ***
00050 REM ***   N = APARTMENT NUMBER TO BE UPDATED   ***
00060 REM ***   R$ = RENTAL STATUS TO BE UPDATED     ***
00070 REM ***   P = NUMBER OF LEASEES TO BE UPDATED  ***
00080 REM ***   A = APARTMENT NUMBER FROM FILE       ***
00090 REM ***   S$ = RENTAL STATUS FROM FILE         ***
00100 REM ***   L = NUMBER OF LEASEES FROM FILE      ***
00110 REM ***   ST$ = RENTAL STATUS FOR REPORT       ***
00120 REM ***********************************************
00130 REM ***      DIMENSION ARRAYS AND READ DATA    ***
00140 REM ***********************************************
00150 DIM N(12),R$(12),P(12),A(12),S$(12),L(12),ST$(12)
00160 FOR I = 1 TO 5
00170   READ N(I),R$(I),P(I)
00180 NEXT I
00190 REM ***********************************************
00200 REM ***   READ DATA FROM FILE INTO PROGRAM   ***
00210 REM ***********************************************
00220 OPEN "APART.FILE" AS FILE #1
00230 FOR J = 1 TO 12
00240   INPUT #1,A(J)
00250   INPUT #1,S$(J)
00260   INPUT #1,L(J)
00270 NEXT J
00280 CLOSE #1
00290 REM ***********************************************
00300 REM ***      DETERMINE NEW APARTMENT STATUS   ***
00310 REM ***********************************************
00320 FOR I = 1 TO 5
00330   FOR J = 1 TO 12
00340     IF N(I) <> A(J) THEN 380
00350     LET S$(J) = R$(I)
00360     LET L(J) = P(I)
00370     GOTO 390
00380   NEXT J
00390 NEXT I
00400 REM ***********************************************
00410 REM ***   PRINT NEW APARTMENT STATUS TO FILE  ***
00420 REM ***********************************************
00430 OPEN "APART.FILE" AS FILE #2
00440 FOR J = 1 TO 12
00450   PRINT #2,A(J)
00460   PRINT #2,S$(J)
00470   PRINT #2,L(J)
00480 NEXT J
00490 CLOSE #2
00500 REM ***********************************************
00510 REM ***   PRINT NEW APARTMENT STATUS REPORT   ***
00520 REM ***********************************************
00530 FOR J = 1 TO 12
00540   IF S$(J) = "V" THEN ST$(J) = "VACANT"
00550   IF S$(J) = "R" THEN ST$(J) = "RENTED"
00560 NEXT J
00570 PRINT
00580 PRINT
00590 PRINT TAB(8);"NEW APARTMENT STATUS"
00600 PRINT
00610 PRINT "APARTMENT";TAB(14);"STATUS";TAB(24);"#LEASEES"
00620 PRINT
00630 FOR I = 1 TO 12
00640   PRINT TAB(3);A(I),ST$(I);TAB(26);L(I)
00650 NEXT I
00660 REM ***********************************************
00670 REM ***          THE DATA STATEMENTS          ***
00680 REM ***********************************************
00690 DATA 1,R,4,4,R,2,7,R,5
00700 DATA 8,R,4,9,R,3
00999 END
```

```
RUNNH

        NEW APARTMENT STATUS

APARTMENT      STATUS    #LEASEES

    1          RENTED       4
    2          VACANT       0
    3          RENTED       3
    4          RENTED       2
    5          RENTED       4
    6          RENTED       4
    7          RENTED       5
    8          RENTED       4
    9          RENTED       3
   10          RENTED       4
   11          RENTED       3
   12          RENTED       4
```

PSEUDOCODE

```
Start
Dimension the arrays
Start loop, do five times
   Read new apartment number, new status, new number of leasees
End loop
Open the apartment file
Start loop, do twelve times
   Enter apartment number from file
   Enter status from file
   Enter number of leasees from file
End loop
Close the apartment file
Start loop, do five times
   Start loop, do twelve times
      If apartment number from file equals new apartment number
         Then
            Status from file equals new status
            Number of leasees from file equals new number of leasees
      End if
   End loop
End loop
Open the apartment file
Start loop, do twelve times
   Print the apartment number to the file
   Print the status to the file
   Print the number of leasees to the file
End loop
Close the apartment file
Start loop, do twelve times
   If the status equals "V"
      Then
         Assign "VACANT" to ST$
      Else
         Assign "RENTED" to ST$
   End if
End loop
Print the report headings
Start loop, do twelve times
   Print the apartment number, ST$, and the number of leasees
End loop
Stop
```

MICROCOMPUTERS:	
Apple	See Section X of text.
Apple Macintosh	See Section X of text.
IBM/Microsoft	See Section X of text.
PET/Commodore 64	See Section X of text.
TRS-80	See Section X of text.

Problem C

You have just graduated from college and you have received
a number of gifts. To keep the gifts and the persons who gave
them to you straight, you have decided to create a gift file.
Enter the gifts and names into the program using INPUT statements. Then create a disk file and write the gifts and names to
the file. After you have done this, reopen the file and print
the data in the following format:

GRADUATION GIFTS

GIFT   PERSON

XXXXXXXXXX   XXXXXXXXXX
XXXXXXXXXX   XXXXXXXXXX
XXXXXXXXXX   XXXXXXXXXX

Use the following data to create the file:

        Diamond Ring, Grandma and Grandpa
        Savings Bond, Ed
        Iron, Aunt Ruth and Uncle Punk
        Hair Dryer, The Kings
        $50.00, Aunt Martha and Uncle Jerry
        Necklace, The Thompsons
        $100.00, Aunt Pauline
        $30.00, The Stantons
        Car, Mom and Dad
        $25.00, Mr. and Mrs. Williams

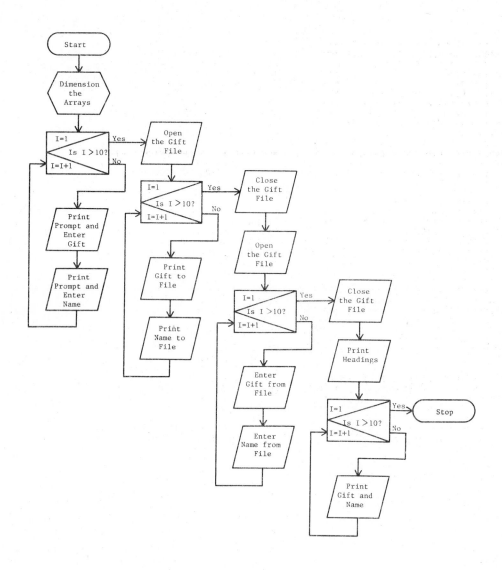

```
00100 REM ***********************************
00110 REM *** GRADUATION GIFT LIST PROGRAM ***
00120 REM ***********************************
00130 REM *** VARIABLES:                 ***
00140 REM ***    G$ = GIFT               ***
00150 REM ***    P$ = PERSON WHO GAVE GIFT ***
00160 REM ***********************************
00170 REM ***  DIM ARRAYS AND ENTER DATA  ***
00180 REM ***********************************
00190 DIM G$(10),P$(10)
00200 FOR I = 1 TO 10
00210    PRINT "WHAT GIFT DID YOU RECEIVE?"
00220    INPUT G$(I)
00230    PRINT "WHO GAVE YOU SUCH A NICE GIFT?"
00240    INPUT P$(I)
00250 NEXT I
00260 REM ***********************************
00270 REM ***    CREATE THE GIFT FILE     ***
00280 REM ***********************************
00290 OPEN "GIFT.FILE" AS FILE #1
00300 FOR I = 1 TO 10
00310    PRINT #1,G$(I)
00320    PRINT #1,P$(I)
00330 NEXT I
00340 CLOSE #1
00350 REM ***********************************
00360 REM ***  PUT FILE DATA INTO PROGRAM ***
00370 REM ***********************************
00380 OPEN "GIFT.FILE" AS FILE #2
00390 FOR I = 1 TO 10
00400    INPUT #2,G$(I)
00410    INPUT #2,B$(I)
00420 NEXT I
00430 CLOSE #2
00440 REM ***********************************
00450 REM ***     PRINT THE GIFT REPORT    ***
00460 REM ***********************************
00470 PRINT
00480 PRINT
00490 PRINT TAB(10);"GRADUATION GIFTS"
00500 PRINT
00510 PRINT "GIFT";TAB(20);"PERSON"
00520 PRINT
00530 FOR I = 1 TO 10
00540    PRINT G$(I);TAB(20);P$(I)
00550 NEXT I
00999 END
```

PSEUDOCODE

```
Start
Dimension the arrays
Start loop, do ten times
  Print prompt to enter gift
  Enter gift
  Print prompt to enter name
  Enter name
End loop
Open the gift file
Start loop, do ten times
  Print gift to the file
  Print name to the file
End loop
Close the gift file
Open the gift file
Start loop, do ten times
  Enter gift from the file
  Enter name from the file
End loop
Close the gift file
Print the headings
Start loop, do ten times
  Print gift and name
End loop
Stop
```

```
RUNNH
WHAT GIFT DID YOU RECEIVE?
? DIAMOND RING
WHO GAVE YOU SUCH A NICE GIFT?
? GRANDMA AND GRANDPA
WHAT GIFT DID YOU RECEIVE?
? SAVINGS BOND
WHO GAVE YOU SUCH A NICE GIFT?
? ED
WHAT GIFT DID YOU RECEIVE?
? IRON
WHO GAVE YOU SUCH A NICE GIFT?
? AUNT RUTH AND UNCLE PUNK
WHAT GIFT DID YOU RECEIVE?
? HAIR DRYER
WHO GAVE YOU SUCH A NICE GIFT?
? THE KINGS
WHAT GIFT DID YOU RECEIVE?
? $50.00
WHO GAVE YOU SUCH A NICE GIFT?
? AUNT MARTHA AND UNCLE JERRY
WHAT GIFT DID YOU RECEIVE?
? NECKLACE
WHO GAVE YOU SUCH A NICE GIFT?
? THE THOMPSONS
WHAT GIFT DID YOU RECEIVE?
? $100.00
WHO GAVE YOU SUCH A NICE GIFT?
? AUNT PAULINE
WHAT GIFT DID YOU RECEIVE?
? $30.00
WHO GAVE YOU SUCH A NICE GIFT?
? THE STANTONS
WHAT GIFT DID YOU RECEIVE?
? CAR
WHO GAVE YOU SUCH A NICE GIFT?
? MOM AND DAD
WHAT GIFT DID YOU RECEIVE?
? $25.00
WHO GAVE YOU SUCH A NICE GIFT?
? MR. AND MRS. WILLIAMS
```

```
              GRADUATION GIFTS

GIFT                  PERSON

DIAMOND RING          GRANDMA AND GRANDPA
SAVINGS BOND          ED
IRON                  AUNT RUTH AND UNCLE PUNK
HAIR DRYER            THE KINGS
$50.00                AUNT MARTHA AND UNCLE JERRY
NECKLACE              THE THOMPSONS
$100.00               AUNT PAULINE
$30.00                THE STANTONS
CAR                   MOM AND DAD
$25.00                MR. AND MRS. WILLIAMS
```

MICROCOMPUTERS:	
Apple	See Section X of text.
Apple Macintosh	See Section X of text.
IBM/Microsoft	See Section X of text.
PET/Commodore 64	See Section X of text.
TRS-80	See Section X of text.

Problem D

You have just written five thank-you notes for your graduation gifts; you want to reopen the gift file created in
Problem C and add the status of all the thank-you notes. The
status will be blank unless you've mailed the notes. After you
have mailed the thank-you notes, the status will be "MAILED."
Follow the instructions given in Problem C except add a new
column to the report called "THANK-YOU NOTE." You have mailed
thank-you notes to these people:

    Grandma and Grandpa
    The Kings
    The Thompsons
    The Stantons
    Mr. and Mrs. Williams

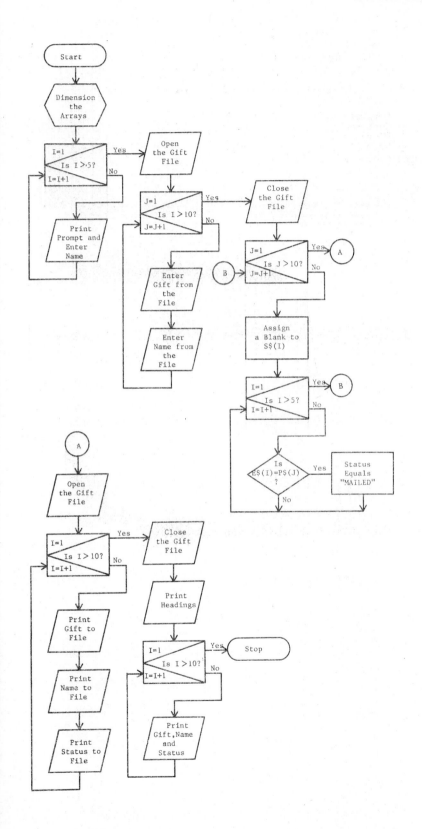

```
00100 REM ***************************************************
00110 REM ***      FILE PROGRAM TO UPDATE GIFT.FILE      ***
00120 REM ***************************************************
00130 REM *** VARIABLES:                                 ***
00140 REM ***   E$ = PERSON TO WHOM THANK-YOU WAS SENT   ***
00150 REM ***   G$ = GIFT FROM THE FILE                  ***
00160 REM ***   P$ = PERSON WHO GAVE GIFT FROM FILE      ***
00170 REM ***   S$ = STATUS OF THANK-YOU NOTE            ***
00180 REM ***************************************************
00190 REM *** DIMENSION THE ARRAYS AND ENTER THE DATA ***
00200 REM ***************************************************
00210 DIM E$(10),G$(10),P$(10),S$(10)
00220 FOR I = 1 TO 5
00230    PRINT "WHO DID YOU WRITE THE THANK-YOU NOTE TO?"
00240    INPUT E$(I)
00250 NEXT I
00260 REM ***************************************************
00270 REM *** ENTER DATA FROM GIFT.FILE INTO PROGRAM  ***
00280 REM ***************************************************
00290 OPEN "GIFT.FILE" AS FILE #1
00300 FOR J = 1 TO 10
00310    INPUT #1,G$(J)
00320    INPUT #1,P$(J)
00330 NEXT J
00340 CLOSE #1
00350 REM ***************************************************
00360 REM ***   COMPUTE STATUS OF THE THANK-YOU NOTE   ***
00370 REM ***************************************************
00380 FOR J = 1 TO 10
00390    LET S$(J) = " "
00400    FOR I = 1 TO 5
00410       IF E$(I) = P$(J) THEN S$(J) = "MAILED"
00420    NEXT I
00430 NEXT J
00440 REM ***************************************************
00450 REM ***      WRITE THE DATA TO THE GIFT.FILE      ***
00460 REM ***************************************************
00470 OPEN "GIFT.FILE" AS FILE #2
00480 FOR I = 1 TO 10
00490    PRINT #2,G$(I)
00500    PRINT #2,P$(I)
00510    PRINT #2,S$(I)
00520 NEXT I
00530 CLOSE #2
00540 REM ***************************************************
00550 REM ***            PRINT OUT THE GIFT REPORT      ***
00560 REM ***************************************************
00570 PRINT
00580 PRINT
00590 PRINT TAB(10);"GRADUATION GIFTS"
00600 PRINT
00610 PRINT "GIFT";TAB(20);"PERSON";TAB(45);"THANK-YOU NOTE"
00620 PRINT
00630 FOR I = 1 TO 10
00640    PRINT G$(I);TAB(20);P$(I);TAB(49);S$(I)
00650 NEXT I
00999 END
```

```
RUNNH
WHO DID YOU WRITE THE THANK-YOU NOTE TO?
? MR. AND MRS. WILLIAMS
WHO DID YOU WRITE THE THANK-YOU NOTE TO?
? GRANDMA AND GRANDPA
WHO DID YOU WRITE THE THANK-YOU NOTE TO?
? THE KINGS
WHO DID YOU WRITE THE THANK-YOU NOTE TO?
? THE STANTONS
WHO DID YOU WRITE THE THANK-YOU NOTE TO?
? THE THOMPSONS
```

```
            GRADUATION GIFTS

GIFT                PERSON                    THANK-YOU NOTE

DIAMOND RING        GRANDMA AND GRANDPA         MAILED
SAVINGS BOND        ED
IRON                AUNT RUTH AND UNCLE PUNK
HAIR DRYER          THE KINGS                   MAILED
$50.00              AUNT MARTHA AND UNCLE JERRY
NECKLACE            THE THOMPSONS               MAILED
$100.00             AUNT PAULINE
$30.00              THE STANTONS                MAILED
CAR                 MOM AND DAD
$25.00              MR. AND MRS. WILLIAMS       MAILED
```

PSEUDOCODE

```
Start
Dimension the arrays
Start loop, do five times
  Print prompt to enter name
  Enter name to be updated
End loop
Open the gift file
Start loop, do ten times
  Enter gift from the file
  Enter name from the file
End loop
Close the gift file
Start loop, do ten times
  Assign a blank to status
  Start loop, do five times
    If name to be updated equals the name from the file
      Then status equals "MAILED"
    Endif
  End loop
End loop
Open the gift file
Start loop, do ten times
  Print gift to the file
  Print name to the file
  Print status to the file
End loop
Close the gift file
Print the headings
Start loop, do ten times
  Print gift, name, and status
End loop
Stop
```

```
MICROCOMPUTERS:

Apple               See Section X of text.
Apple Macintosh     See Section X of text.
IBM/Microsoft       See Section X of text.
PET/Commodore 64    See Section X of text.
TRS-80              See Section X of text.
```

SECTION I
Introduction to BASIC

MULTIPLE CHOICE

B-1. The BASIC programming language
    a. doesn't adhere to syntax rules
    b. has never been altered
    c. stands for Beginner's All-Purpose Symbolic
        Instruction Code
    d. can be used on very few computers

B-2. BASIC contains
    a. words only the computer can understand
    b. easy to understand English words
    c. words only the programmer can understand
    d. little opportunity for documentation

B-3. Which of the following is not true of BASIC?
    a. easy to learn
    b. useful for a wide range of tasks
    c. there is only one version of the language
    d. well suited for classroom teaching

B-4. A universally accepted set of standard rules for BASIC is
    called
    a. ANSI BASIC   c. STANDARD BASIC
    b. UNIVERSAL BASIC   d. STANDARD BASIC RULES

B-5. Another name for software is
    a. computer hardware   c. computer paper
    b. computer keyboard   d. computer program

B-6.   The first step in the programming process is to
        a.   design a solution   c.   run the program
        b.   define the problem   d.   type the program

B-7.   Each computer instruction must be written precisely
        because the
        a.   computer must be able to read and interpret the
             instruction
        b.   programmer must be able to understand the program
        c.   flowchart must be written from the computer instruc-
             tions
        d.   programmer must use the computer instructions to
             design a solution to the problem

B-8.   The basic flow of all data processing is
        a.   input, processing, output
        b.   processing, input, output
        c.   output, processing, input
        d.   input, output, processing

B-9.   When defining the problem, one must analyze it by first
        determining the
        a.   programming statements needed
        b.   documentation
        c.   output that is needed
        d.   input

B-10.   The processing needed in programs is determined by the
        a.   computer
        b.   available input
        c.   required output
        d.   gap between the available input and the required out-
             put

B-11.   An algorithm is
        a.   the machinery used to solve a problem
        b.   a series of steps that enable you to produce the
             desired output
        c.   the input to a given problem
        d.   not used by a computer programmer

B-12.   An example of an algorithm is
        a.   computer input   c.   a computer program
        b.   computer output   d.   computer hardware

B-13.   Documentation is
        a.   written descriptions of the statements used to solve
             the problem
        b.   a report consisting of computer operations
        c.   also called computer input
        d.   a translation of the flowchart symbols into computer
             statements

B-14.   Good documentation
        a.   is necessary
        b.   makes the program easier for others to understand
        c.   consists of only a flowchart
        d.   makes it harder to update the program

B-15.   A flowchart contains
        a.   line numbers within the symbols
        b.   symbols that stand for system commands
        c.   symbols that are not shown in logical order
        d.   symbols that stand for program statements

B-16.   The flowchart makes it easy to see
        a.   the documentation of the program
        b.   the input and the output of the program
        c.   where the program has syntax errors
        d.   the input, processing, and output steps of the
             program

B-17.   In a flowchart, a rectangle stands for
        a.   processing   c.   documentation
        b.   preparation   d.   end of program

B-18.   Writing the program consists of
        a.   determining the inputs, outputs, and processing of
             the program
        b.   translating the flowchart into BASIC statements
        c.   debugging the program
        d.   testing the program

B-19.   Line numbers
        a.   mean nothing to the computer or to the programmer
        b.. tell the programmer the order the program statements
             were typed
        c.   tell the computer the order the program statements
             were typed
        d.   tell the computer the order in which to execute
             statements

B-20.   Interactive BASIC interpreters and compilers
        a.   document the program
        b.   type in the program
        c.   permit the user to input data during execution
        d.   draw flowcharts as the program is typed in

B-21.   Syntax refers to
        a.   English grammar rules
        b.   the logic of the program
        c.   documentation of the program
        d.   the way the instructions have to be written

B-22.   A syntax check
        a.   runs the program   c.   edits the program
        b.   saves debugging time   d.   documents the program

B-23.   The logic of the program is checked during which stage?
        a.   problem definition   c.   program testing
        b.   writing the program   d.   solution design

B-24.   Successful programming only comes
        a.   through diligent application of the five steps in the
             programming process
        b.   from knowing many programming languages
        c.   from using ANSI BASIC
        d.   from using programming languages other than BASIC

B-25.   Systems commands are used by programmers to
        a.   communicate with other programmers
        b.   communicate with the operating system of the computer
        c.   communicate with their programs
        d.   write their programs

B-26.   Which of the following system commands erases any
        programs currently in active memory?
        a.   NEW and SAVE   c.   SAVE and LOAD
        b.   NEW and LOAD   d.   LIST and SAVE

B-27.   NEW is a system command to
        a.   list all files on disk or tape
        b.   move a program from primary memory to secondary
             storage
        c.   erase any program on disk or tape
        d.   erase any program currently in active memory

B-28.   SAVE is a system command to
 a.   move a program from primary memory to secondary
       storage
 b.   move a program from secondary storage to primary
       memory
 c.   erase any program on disk or tape
 d.   erase aɪy program currently in active memory

B-29.   LIST is a system command to
 a.   move a program from secondary storage to primary
       memory
 b.   erase any program currently in active memory
 c.   list the program statements on the terminal
 d.   list all files on disk or tape

B-30.   LOAD is a system command to
 a.   move a program from secondary storage to primary
       memory
 b.   display program statements on the screen
 c.   move a program from primary memory
 d.   erase any program on disk or tape

B-31.   Computer programs
 a.   are also called computer hardware
 b.   define a problem
 c.   are composed of system commands
 d.   are step-by-step instructions to solve a problem

SECTION II
BASIC Fundamentals

MULTIPLE CHOICE

B-32. A sequence of instructions that tells the computer how to solve a problem is
  a. a flowchart   c. a BASIC program
  b. a text file   d. computer hardware

B-33. Basic statements are not composed of
  a. special programming commands
  b. flowcharting symbols
  c. constants
  d. variables

B-34. Line numbers must be
  a. integer values   c. exponential values
  b. decimal values   d. fractional values

B-35. Line numbers
  a. are executed in the order in which they were typed
  b. are not always used in the BASIC language
  c. can only be numbers from 10 to 100
  d. are executed in the sequence in which they are numbered

B-36. Line numbers can be used
  a. to document a program
  b. to represent certain flowchart symbols
  c. as labels to refer to specific statements in the program
  d. to highlight certain parts of the program

B-37.   A disadvantage of incrementing line numbers by one is
        a.   your program looks cluttered
        b.   you cannot insert new statements without renumbering
             the old statements
        c.   you will run out of line numbers
        d.   they cannot be renumbered

B-38.   Line numbers are arranged in _____ by the computer.
        a.   descending order
        b.   ascending order
        c.   the order in which they were typed
        d.   whatever order you wish

B-39.   An advantage of line numbers is that they
        a.   help determine flowcharting symbols
        b.   automatically check for logic errors
        c.   automatically run the program
        d.   permit changes to be made to the program as it is
             being typed in

B-40.   If two program statements are typed with the same line
        number, which line number will the computer recognize?
        a.   the first one typed
        b.   the last one typed
        c.   neither one of the statements
        d.   the computer will renumber both statements

B-41.   Two types of constants are
        a.   numeric and character string
        b.   numeric and exponential
        c.   numeric and alphabetic
        d.   alphabetic and literal

B-42.   Constants
        a.   change during a program's execution
        b.   contain the same values as their line numbers
        c.   must be changed more than once in a program
        d.   do not change during a program's execution

B-43.   In BASIC, numbers can be represented in two ways: as
        a.   numeric data or as character string data
        b.   fractional numbers or as decimal values
        c.   real numbers or in exponential notation
        d.   real numbers or as zero

B-44.   In BASIC, real numbers can be either
        a.   integers or decimal fractions
        b.   integers or exponents
        c.   decimals or fractions
        d.   decimals or zero

B-45.   Which of the following is not true when numbers are to be
        a part of a program?
        a.   All numbers must be preceded by a minus or a plus
             sign.
        b.   If no sign is included, the number is assumed to be
             positive.
        c.   No commas can be embedded within numbers.
        d.   If the number is negative, it must be preceded by a
             minus sign.

B-46.   The computer uses exponential notation for
        a.   all fractional values
        b.   all integer values
        c.   very large or very small numbers
        d.   all numbers

B-47.   In exponential notation a minus sign indicates a
        a.   very large number   c.   positive number
        b.   negative number   d.   very small number

B-48.   Character strings
        a.   cannot contain numbers
        b.   cannot contain any special character
        c.   must be enclosed in quotation marks
        d.   do not have to be enclosed in quotation marks

B-49.   Any data values that are to be used by a program must be
        a.   stored in computer memory either before or during
             execution
        b.   stored in computer memory before execution
        c.   enclosed in quotation marks
        d.   fractional values

B-50.   Computer memory locations are supplied with names by the
        a.   computer
        b.   programmer
        c.   systems programmer
        d.   manufacturer of the computer

B-51.   A variable
    a.   is constant throughout the program
    b.   can only change once during execution of the program
    c.   can only be changed by the computer's operating
          system
    d.   can change as many times as necessary during the exe-
          cution of a program

B-52.   A variable name is
    a.   also known as a constant
    b.   the name of the location in memory where a value is
          stored
    c.   the name of the location on disk or tape where a
          value is stored
    d.   a complete listing of the locations on disk or tape
          where programs are stored

B-53.   A variable can represent
    a.   many values at the same time
    b.   two values at the same time
    c.   only one value at a time
    d.   only one value during the entire program

B-54.   A numeric variable represents a number that
    a.   is always positive
    b.   can be changed only once
    c.   is constant throughout the program
    d.   can be either programmer-supplied or calculated by
          the computer

B-55.   Two types of variables are
    a.   alphabetic and numeric   c.   alphabetic and string
    b.   numeric and string   d.   numeric and alphanumeric

B-56.   A numeric variable is represented by
    a.   one letter followed by a dollar sign
    b.   one numeric digit
    c.   a dollar sign followed by one letter
    d.   one letter alone or one letter followed by one
          numeric digit

B-57.   Which of the following is a valid numeric variable name?
    a.   T1   c.   25
    b.   P$ d.   &1

B-58.   Which of the following is not a valid numeric variable
         name?
    a.   N$ c.   P9
    b.   Q   d.   T

B-59. String variable names are distinguished from numeric
       variable names by a(n)
       a. exclamation point   c. dollar sign
       b. asterisk   d. semicolon

B-60. Which of the following is a valid string variable name?
       a. *K   c. 8H
       b. N$ d. $P

B-61. Which of the following is not a valid string variable
       name?
       a. Z$ c. L$
       b. NA$ d. O

B-62. Reserved words are words that
       a. have a special meaning to the programmer
       b. can be used in a program only once
       c. can be used as variable names and constants
       d. have a special meaning to the translator program of
           the computer

SECTION III
Getting Started with BASIC Programming

MULTIPLE CHOICE

B-63. The REM statement is used to
    a. print the results of processing
    b. process information
    c. document the program
    d. perform arithmetic calculations

B-64. The REM statement provides information for the
    a. programmer and anyone else reading the program
    b. computer
    c. computer and anyone else reading the program
    d. translator program of the computer

B-65. The REM statement may be used
    a. only at the beginning of the program
    b. only at the end of the program
    c. only in the middle of the program
    d. anywhere in the program

B-66. The REM statement generally
    a. tells the computer that an arithmetic operation is to
        be performed
    b. explains program statements
    c. interprets the BASIC language for the computer
    d. ends the program

B-67.   The REM statement is usually surrounded by asterisks
        because
        a.   the format of the REM statement calls for it
        b.   the REM statement performs multiplication
        c.   they set the REM statement apart from the other
             programming statements
        d.   they are special characters used by the operation
             system of the computer

B-68.   Which of the following is not a form of documentation?
        a.   the REM statement   c.   the LET statement
        b.   a flowchart   d.   pseudocode

B-69.   The purpose of the LET statement is to
        a.   document the program
        b.   print data
        c.   assign values to variables
        d.   perform arithmetic operations

B-70.   Uses of the LET statement include
        a.   entering data into the program
        b.   the printing of headings
        c.   documenting variables
        d.   printing the results of calculations

B-71.   The expression in the LET statement assigns a value from
        a.   the right side of the equal sign to the variable on
             the left side
        b.   the left side of the equal sign to the variable on
             the right side
        c.   a memory location to the program
        d.   either side of the equal sign

B-72.   Only _____ can be on the left side of the equal sign in
        a LET statement
        a.   a constant   c.   a literal
        b.   a variable name   d.   the word LET

B-73.   The LET statement puts a
        a.   number into the program
        b.   numeric or character string value on to disk or tape
        c.   special character into the program for use by the
             programmer
        d.   numeric or character string value into a memory loca-
             tion

B-74.   Arithmetic operations are performed
         a.   any way the computer wants to perform them
         b.   from left to right
         c.   by a hierarchy of operations
         d.   from right to left

B-75.   Innermost parentheses are performed
         a.   last
         b.   first
         c.   second
         d.   whenever the computer wants to do them

B-76.   Which of the following arithmetic operations has the
         highest priority?
         a.   subtraction   c.   exponentiation
         b.   addition   d.   multiplication

B-77.   Which of the following has the lowest priority?
         a.   addition   c.   exponentiation
         b.   parentheses   d.   division

B-78.   If more than one operation is to be performed at the same
         level, the computer evaluates them
         a.   from left to right or from right to left
         b.   from left to right
         c.   from right to left
         d.   in whatever fashion it is programmed to

B-79.   What does a * mean in a LET statement?
         a.   documentation   c.   exponentiation
         b.   subtraction   d.   multiplication

B-80.   What does a / mean when used in a LET statement?
         a.   multiplication   c.   division
         b.   documentation   d.   subtraction

B-81.   If the value of an expression is very small, the computer
         will print it
         a.   in exponential notation c.   as a fraction
         b.   as a decimal number   d.   as a rounded number

B-82.   A PRINT statement with nothing after it will
         a.   print an error message   c.   print a blank line
         b.   bypass the statement   d.   print a special message

B-83.   To skip many lines one would
       a.   use the SKIP statement
       b.   use more than one PRINT statement
       c.   skip program lines
       d.   input blank data lines and then use a PRINT statement

B-84.   The END statement must be assigned
       a.   the lowest line number   c.   the highest line number
       b.   any line number   d.   to a decimal number

B-85.   The END statement indicates the
       a.   end of a program
       b.   beginning of a program
       c.   end of the documentation
       d.   end of the arithmetic operations only

B-86.   The END statement consists of
       a.   the word END
       b.   the highest line number of the program
       c.   the words END PROGRAM
       d.   the word END and the highest line number of the
           program

B-87.   All 9s are generally used for the line number of the END
       statement because they
       a.   look nice
       b.   serve as a reminder to the programmer to include the
           END statement
       c.   are part of the ANSI BASIC code
       d.   are the format of the END statement

B-88.   Which of the following is a valid LET statement?
       a.   20 LET N = "SALES"   c.   20 LET P$ = "TOTAL"
       b.   20 LET 25 * 0.8998 = K   d.   20 LET Y$ = 0.5

B-89.   Which of the following is not a valid LET statement?
       a.   150 LET U = 9
       b.   150 LET P * 2 = R
       c.   150 LET G$ = "THE BILL EQUALS"
       d.   150 LET H = E1 + E2 + E3

B-90.   What would be the result of the following expression if
       R = 2 and S = 3? $S \wedge 2 * (2 + R) - 10$
       a. 6   c.   16
       b. 20   d.   26

B-91.   If D = 10 and C = 20, what would be the result of the
        following expression?   (C - D) * (3 + 1) / 2
        a.   40   c.   20
        b.   10   d.   5

B-92.   Evaluate the following expression: 3∧2∧2 + 5 * 2
        a.   91   c.   170
        b.   172   d.   162

B-93.   Evaluate the following expression: 5 * 2 + 12 / 2 - 6
        a.   5   c.   10
        b.   12   d.   7

B-94.   Which of the following is not a valid PRINT statement?
        a.   10 PRINT HAPPY VALENTINE'S DAY
        b.   10 PRINT 44.33,N$,SL
        c.   10 PRINT 8.763 / 4R
        d.   10 PRINT "HELLO","THERE"

B-95.   Which of the following is not a valid PRINT statement?
        a.   30 PRINT "SALES","QUANTITY","TOTAL"
        b.   30 PRINT 658.94 * 374 - K
        c.   30 PRINT "THE TAX EQUALS";TAX
        d.   30 PRINT YESTERDAY

B-96.   What is the output of the following program segment?
                    10 LET Y = 8
                    20 LET X = 5
                    30 PRINT X * Y + 10 / 2
        a.   25   c.   20
        b.   45   d.   40

SECTION IV
Input and Output

MULTIPLE CHOICE

B-97.   The LET statement can be used
    a.   to enter large amounts of data into the program
    b.   as documentation for the program
    c.   in an interactive environment
    d.   to enter small amounts of data into the program

B-98.   The INPUT statement is used for
    a.   inquiry and response
    b.   reading data into the program during compilation
    c.   interaction between the system and the program
    d.   writing special characters

B-99.   The INPUT statement enters the data when the program is
    a.   written   c.   compiled
    b.   executed   d.   stored

B-100. The variables in the INPUT statement are
    a.   numeric variables   c.   constants
    b.   character strings   d.   either numeric or string

B-101. The _____ determines where the INPUT statement must be
        placed in the program.
    a.   computer   c.   logic of the program
    b.   user   d.   operating system

B-102. The type of data to be entered by the INPUT statement
       must be
       a.   the same as that designated by the variable
       b.   numeric
       c.   string
       d.   numeric or string

B-103. When the computer reaches an INPUT statement, it
       a.   reads the data
       b.   waits for the operating system to enter the data
       c.   waits for the user to enter the data
       d.   reads the data from disk or tape

B-104. A prompt tells the user
       a.   when to print the data
       b.   when to enter the data
       c.   that an error has occurred
       d.   that no more data are needed

B-105. The prompt is generated using a(n)
       a.   LET statement   c.   PRINT statement
       b.   REM statement   d.   error message

B-106. It is good to use prompts when using INPUT statements
       because the
       a.   programmer knows when an error has occurred
       b.   computer knows what data to enter
       c.   computer operator knows when to print a hard copy
       d.   user knows what data to enter and when to enter them

B-107. Most computers allow the prompt to
       a.   be integrated with the INPUT statement
       b.   enter any data
       c.   compute any arithmetic operation
       d.   determine if the data are numeric or string

B-108. The READ and DATA statements always work
       a.   apart   c.   together
       b.   side by side   d.   in the same line

B-109. The values contained in the DATA statement are assigned
       to
       a.   variables throughout the program
       b.   variables listed in the READ statement
       c.   literals listed in the READ statement
       d.   variables listed in the INPUT statement

B-110. The READ statement tells the
    a. user to enter the data values into the program
    b. computer to enter the values into the program
    c. programmer to enter the values into the program
    d. computer to search for the DATA statement

B-111. Each READ statement causes as many values to be taken
from the data list as there are
    a. values in the data list
    b. values that are needed in the program
    c. variables in the READ variable list
    d. variables in the program

B-112. Nondestructive read, destructive write means that once
values are read into the program they are not destroyed
until a new value is
    a. assigned to the storage location
    b. read
    c. entered into the program
    d. computed

B-113. If a READ statement tries to read the data after the data
have been exhausted, the computer will
    a. place blanks and/or zeroes into the variables
    b. bypass the READ statement
    c. not change the values of the variables
    d. produce an error message

B-114. DATA statements are
    a. executable by the computer
    b. non-executable
    c. a form of documentation
    d. always located at the end of the program

B-115. The BASIC interpreter takes all the values in the DATA
statements and
    a. places them into their respective storage locations
    b. forms a variable list
    c. forms a data list
    d. computes the values of the variables in the READ
        statement

B-116. Data values in the DATA statement are separated by
    a. semicolons   c. blank spaces
    b. commas   d. quotation marks

B-117. When character strings are placed in a DATA statement, they
a.   are never to be enclosed in quotation marks
b.   cannot contain commas
c.   must be enclosed in quotation marks if they contain semicolons
d.   must be enclosed in quotation marks if they contain commas

B-118. The READ statement string variables must be assigned to the _____ of the DATA statement.
a.   numeric variables   c.   string variables
b.   numeric values   d.   string values

B-119. The READ statement numeric variables must be assigned to the _____ of the DATA statement.
a.   numeric values   c.   character values
b.   numeric variables   d.   character variables

B-120. When the data to be entered into the program remain constant, the _____ statement should be used.
a.   READ   c.   REM
b.   INPUT   d.   LET

B-121. Initialization is when
a.   the INPUT statement is used to assign a value to a variable
b.   variables are assigned a beginning value
c.   constants are given their values
d.   literals are given values

B-122. When many values are to be entered into a program the _____ statement should be used.
a.   READ   c.   REM
b.   INPUT   d.   LET

B-123. When a question and answer mode is desired to enter data into a program, the _____ statement should be used.
a.   READ   c.   REM
b.   INPUT   d.   LET

B-124. The spacing of output can be controlled by
a.   commas   c.   commas and semicolons
b.   semicolons   d.   quotation marks

B-125. The comma directs the printing of output to the next
a.   space   c.   line
b.   column   d.   print zone

B-126. If there are more items listed in a PRINT statement than
there are print zones, the computer will
a.   start printing in the first zone of the next line
b.   not print those items
c.   print the items with a space between them
d.   give an error message

B-127. On most computers, a numeric value starts printing in the
second column of the print zone because the first column
is reserved for
a.   a space for easier readability
b.   the sign of the number
c.   the sign of the number preceding it
d.   documentation

B-128. A print zone can be skipped by using
a.   a semicolon
b.   a comma
c.   a blank character enclosed in quotation marks
d.   quotation marks

B-129. A semicolon causes the printer to go to the
a.   next column   c.   next line
b.   next print zone   d.   previous print zone

B-130. To avoid letters running together, a _____ is used.
a.   semicolon
b.   blank enclosed within the quotes
c.   comma
d.   comma or a semicolon

B-131. If a semicolon is used at the end of a PRINT statement,
the printer will
a.   advance to the next line
b.   advance to the next column
c.   advance to the next print zone
d.   stay where it is

B-132. The TAB function allows output to be printed
a.   on any line
b.   in any print zone
c.   in any column
d.   starting every fifth column

B-133. The expression in the TAB function cannot be a(n)
a.   numeric constant   c.   arithmetic expression
b.   numeric variable   d.   literal

B-134. Commas cannot be used to separate the values in the TAB function because the printer would
    a. default to the use of the predefined print zones
    b. think the commas separate the values
    c. print the commas
    d. print an error message

B-135. The columns specified in the parentheses of the TAB function must increase from left to right because the
    a. computer always increases from left to right
    b. printer will default
    c. printer cannot be backspaced
    d. computer will give an error message

B-136. The PRINT USING statement allows
    a. greater flexibility in formatting output
    b. the computer to use special formats for output
    c. the printer to use special formats for output
    d. the user to use special formats for output

B-137. Which of the following is a valid example of the INPUT statement?
    a. 50 INPUT 1
    b. 50 INPUT "ENTER YOUR NAME",N$
    c. 50 INPUT "ENTER YOUR NAME";N$
    d. 50 INPUT

B-138. Which of the following is not a valid example of the INPUT statement?
    a. 100 INPUT C$,K$,N
    b. 100 INPUT "ENTER THE AMOUNT OF THE CHECK"
    c. 100 INPUT N
    d. 100 INPUT "WHAT IS YOUR ADDRESS?";A$

B-139. Which of the following DATA statements is invalid?
    a. 200 DATA "PAUL MORALES"
    b. 200 DATA 67,78,89
    c. 200 DATA "THANKSGIVING","CHRISTMAS",
    d. 200 DATA 45,"HARRY KLINER",34

B-140. Which of the following DATA statements is valid?
    a. 350 DATA "JERRY SMITH"
    b. 350 DATA "THOMAS MAGNUM",367-90-9486
    c. 350 DATA 9,8,7,6
    d. 350 DATA "YOLANDA DOUGLASS","DAUGHTER"

B-141. What is the value of D in line 60?
```
10 LET A = 10
20 LET B = A / 2
30 LET C = B * 5
40 LET D = C + 4
50 LET C = A * 2
60 LET D = C + 8
```
a. 66   c. 64
b. 28   d. 36

B-142. What is the output from the following program?
```
10 READ N,K
20 READ C,T
30 PRINT N,T
40 PRINT K,C
50 DATA 5,15
60 DATA 25,35
```
a. 5   15   25   35
b. 5   35   15   25
c. 5   15
    25   35
d. 5   35
    15   25

B-143. What is the output from the following program?
```
10 READ S$,P$
20 PRINT S$;
30 PRINT P$
40 DATA GOOD,BYE
```
a. GOOD   BYE
b. GOOD BYE
c. GOODBYE
d. GOOD
    BYE

B-144. What is the value of A$ after the following program has
been executed?
```
10 LET A$ = "PRINT"
20 LET B$ = "REM"
30 READ A$,C$
40 DATA READ,LET
```
a. PRINT   c. REM
b. READ   d. LET

B-145. What is the output from the following program?
```
10 READ L,M,N$
20 LET L = M * 5
30 LET M = 2
40 PRINT N$,L,M
50 DATA 3,4,"TOTAL"
```
a.	TOTAL	20	2
b.	TOTAL	3	4
c.	TOTAL	3	2
d.	TOTAL	20	4

B-146. What is the output of the following program?
```
10 READ E,F,G
20 LET E = F * G
30 LET F = E + G
40 PRINT E,F,G
50 DATA 2,4,6
```
a.	2	4	6
b.	2	30	30
c.	24	4	30
d.	24	30	6

B-147. Which of the following lines has an error?
```
10 READ N$,L
20 LET L = L * 2
30 LET L = L + 1
40 PRINT N$,L
50 DATA 5,"PROGRAM"
```
a. 20   c. 40
b. 30   d. 50

B-148. What is wrong with the following program line?
```
10 PRINT TAB(5), "DAT", TAB(18), "PLACE"
```
a. Quotation marks are not needed.
b. Semicolons should be used instead of commas.
c. TAB function comes before the PRINT.
d. Line number is not needed.

B-149. What is wrong with the following program segment?
```
50 PRINT USING 60,352.35
60:    #.##
```
a. The control image is too small.
b. The data in the PRINT USING statement should be
    characters.
c. The decimal point is not needed.
d. The colon is not needed.

B-150. What is the value of P after the following program has been executed?

```
10 READ Q
20 LET P = 3 * Q
30 LET P = Q
40 DATA 1,5
```

a. 3   c. 1
b. 25   d. 5

SECTION V
Control Statements

MULTIPLE CHOICE

B-151. Branching is
    a. printing only a few of the required variables
    b. altering the flow of execution of the program
    c. the same as computing
    d. listing your program

B-152. The GOTO statement
    a. does not create a branch
    b. creates an error message when it tries to branch
    c. is a conditional transfer
    d. is an unconditional transfer

B-153. Every time the GOTO statement is encountered, the
    a. computer waits for the user to enter data
    b. computer skips over the statement unless a certain
        condition is met
    c. flow of execution is altered
    d. computer sends data to the printer

B-154. The IF/THEN statement transfers control
    a. if a certain condition is met
    b. every time it is encountered
    c. every other time it is encountered
    d. to the end of the program

B-155. Conditions included in the IF/THEN statement can involve
    a. numeric data only   c. LET statements
    b. string data only   d. numeric or string data

B-156. The symbol <> means
    a. less than   c. equal to
    b. not equal to   d. greater than

B-157. The flowcharting symbol for the IF/THEN statement is
    a. a rectangle   c. diamond-shaped
    b. a parallelogram   d. a circle

B-158. The ON/GOTO statement is
    a. a conditional transfer
    b. an unconditional transfer
    c. rarely used
    d   the same as the IF/THEN statement

B-159. The expression in the ON/GOTO statement is always evaluated as
    a. a fraction   c. a decimal fraction
    b. an integer   d. a character string

B-160. If the expression in the ON/GOTO statement evaluates to a number less than one, then
    a. control is passed to the statement before the ON/GOTO
    b. control is passed to the end of the program
    c. the ON/GOTO is bypassed
    d. the program becomes stuck in an infinite loop

B-161. A listing that displays the functions performed by a program is called a(n)
    a. documentation   c. algorithm
    b. ON/GOTO statement   d. menu

B-162. A loop controlled by a trailer value contains a(n)
    a. ON/GOTO statement
    b. IF/THEN statement
    c. counter
    d. an unconditional transfer

B-163. A dummy value is the
    a. end of data value, usually zero or "END"
    b. expression of the ON/GOTO statement
    c. number of times the loop is to be executed
    d. value of the loop variable when the execution of the loop has ceased

B-164. A counter is
    a. also called a dummy value
    b. tested only once by an IF/THEN statement
    c. incremented every time the loop is executed
    d. tested by an ON/GOTO statement

B-165. A counter is effective if the programmer
    a. is testing for the end of the data
    b. knows how many times the loop must be executed
    c. documents the program
    d. wants to determine the total of some quantity

B-166. Which of the following does not control the execution of
    the program?
    a. ON/GOTO   c. GOTO
    b. IF/THEN   d. END

B-167. Which of the following is an incorrect program statement?
    a. 10 IF G < 12 THEN 80
    b. 10 ON R GOTO 30,50,70,90
    c. 10 ON T$ GOTO 40,80,100
    d. 10 GOTO 90

B-168. Given the following BASIC statement, where will control
    be transferred if A = 500?
            70 ON A/100   GOTO 100, 120, 140, 160, 180
    a. 180   c. 120
    b. 100   d. 160

B-169. What is printed from the following program segment?
                10 LET L = 0
                20 LET M = 0
                30 IF L = 5 THEN 80
                40 READ G
                50 LET M = G * 2
                60 LET L = L + 1
                70 GOTO 30
                80 PRINT L,M,G
                90 DATA 10,20,30,40,50,60
                99 END
    a. 1   20   10
    b. 5   100   50
    c. 5   120   60
    d. 4   80   30

B-170. What is the value of T after execution of the following
    program?
                10 READ T
                20 IF T > 5 THEN 50
                30 LET T = T * 3
                40 GOTO 10
                50 LET T = 5
                60 DATA 3,4,5,6
    a. 15   c. 12
    b. 5   d. 3

B-171. If C = 3, what line will the following program line branch to?

```
30 ON C GOTO 100,150,200,250
```

 a. 100   c. 200
 b. 150   d. 30

B-172. What is the output from the following program?

```
10 LET U = 0
20 READ N$,P
30 IF U > 10 THEN 60
40 LET U = U + P
50 GOTO 20
60 LET U = U * 2
70 PRINT N$,P,U
80 DATA A,4,B,2,C,3,D,6,E,5
```

 a. E   5   30
 b. D   6   15
 c. E   5   15
 d. C   3   22

B-173. What is the value of L$ after the execution of the following program?

```
10 LET T = 0
20 READ L$
30 IF L$ = "END" THEN 99
45 LET T = T + 1
50 PRINT L$
65 GOTO 20
70 DATA "KATHY","BILLY","RAYMOND","END"
99 END
```

 a. KATHY   c. RAYMOND
 b. BILLY   d. END

B-174. What is the value of Q after execution of the following program?

```
10 READ Z
20 ON Z GOTO 30,40,50,60
30 LET Q = Z * 10
40 LET Q = Z * 20
50 LET Q = Z * 30
60 LET Q = Z * 40
70 DATA 3
99 END
```

 a. 60   c. 120
 b. 90   d. 30

B-175. What is the output from the following program?
```
10 READ Q,R,Y$
20 IF Y$ = "O" THEN X$ = "OPEN"
30 IF Y$ = "C" THEN X$ = "CLOSED"
40 PRINT X$;Q;R
50 DATA 1,215,"C",5,613,"O",12,7,"O"
99 END
```
  a.   CLOSED 1 215
  b.   OPEN 5 613
  c.   CLOSED   1   215
  d.   OPEN   12   7

B-176. How many times will the following loop be executed?
```
10 LET C = 0
20 IF C > 5 THEN 99
30 READ P,R
40 LET C = C + 1
50 LET Q = P * R
60 GOTO 20
70 DATA 5,10,15,20,6,11,16,21
80 DATA 4,9,14,19,3,8,13,18
99 END
```
  a. 3   c. 4
  b. 5   d. 6

SECTION VI
More About Looping

MULTIPLE CHOICE

B-177. The FOR statement does not
a. tell the computer how many times to execute the loop
b. set the initial value of the loop variable
c. test the value of the loop variable after the loop has been executed the first time
d. test the value of the loop variable the first time that the loop is executed

B-178. The NEXT statement
a. increments the loop variable
b. sets the initial value of the loop variable
c. is bypassed
d. only signifies the end of the loop

B-179. The FOR/NEXT loop
a. cannot contain a negative terminal value
b. cannot contain a negative initial value
c. can contain a negative terminal value, a positive initial value, and a positive step value
d. can contain a negative step value

B-180. An infinite loop is created when the step value is
a. zero   c. positive
b. negative   d. greater than ten

B-181. The FOR/NEXT loop should not contain a transfer statement
        which sends control to the
        a.   NEXT statement
        b.   statements inside the loop
        c.   FOR statement
        d.   statement following the FOR statement

B-182. The value of the loop variable should not be
        a.   a numeric variable
        b.   modified by the statements inside the loop
        c.   incremented by the NEXT statement
        d.   used again in the program

B-183. The loop variable indicated in the FOR statement must
        also be
        a.   accompanied by a step value equal to one
        b.   accompanied by a positive step value
        c.   specified in the NEXT statement
        d.   set equal to zero

B-184. The initial, terminal, and step expressions in the FOR
        statement cannot be
        a.   character variables   c.   numeric constants
        b.   numeric variables   d.   mathematical formulas

B-185. Which of the following is an invalid use of the FOR
        statement?
        a.   50 FOR K = 12 TO 1 STEP 2
        b.   50 FOR K = 1 TO 12 STEP 1
        c.   50 FOR K = 1 TO 12 STEP 2
        d.   50 FOR K = 12 TO 1 STEP -1

B-186. Nesting is
        a.   also called a FOR/NEXT loop
        b.   when one loop is inside another loop
        c.   the same as initializing variables
        d.   what birds do

B-187. The inner loop of nested loops is indented because
        a.   the format of nested loops calls for it
        b.   the computer will think that the two loops are the
              same loop
        c.   both loops have the same loop variable
        d.   it makes the program easier to read

B-188. Which of the following is not true of nested FOR/NEXT
loops?
a.   one loop must be completely inside the other loop
b.   the loops may have the same loop variable
c.   the loop variable(s) may not be changed inside either
     of the loops
d.   the inner loop variable is reinitialized every time
     the outer loop is executed

B-189. The FOR/NEXT loop
a.   can be written with one flowchart symbol
b.   must be written with at least three flowchart symbols
c.   is not a useful programming tool
d.   is used when the programmer does not know the number
     of times the loop is to be executed

B-190. What is the value of I after the following program is
executed?
```
10 FOR I = 1 TO 10 STEP 2
20    PRINT I
30 NEXT I
```
a.   12   c.   10
b.   9   d.   11

B-191. What is the output from the following program segment?
```
10 FOR J = 1 TO 5
20    LET P = J + 10
30 NEXT J
40 PRINT P
```
a.   10   c.   15
b.   11   d.   16

B-192. How many times is the inner loop of the following program
executed?
```
10 FOR I = 1 TO 2
20    FOR J = 1 TO 4
30       LET L = I * J
40    NEXT J
50 NEXT I
```
a.   8   c.   2
b.   4   d.   6

B-193. What is the output after the following program has been
       executed?
```
10 FOR I = 1 TO 3
20    READ T$
30 NEXT I
40 PRINT T$
50 DATA "MONDAY","TUESDAY","WEDNESDAY"
```
   a.   MONDAY   c.   WEDNESDAY
   b.   TUESDAY   d.   a blank line is printed

B-194. What is the value of T after the following program has
       been executed?
```
10 LET T = 0
20 FOR I = 1 TO 4 STEP 2
30    LET T = T + 1
40 NEXT I
```
   a.   0   c. 5
   b.   2   d. 4

B-195. What is the value of T after the following program has
       been executed?
```
10 LET T = 0
20 FOR J = 1 TO 6
30    LET T = J * 2
40    IF T > 10 THEN 60
50 NEXT J
60 LET T = 10
```
   a.   0   c.   6
   b.   4   d.   10

B-196. What is wrong with the following program?
```
10 FOR I = 1 TO 5 STEP 0
20    PRINT I
30    LET J = I
40 NEXT I
```
   a.   the value of I cannot be assigned to J
   b.   the step value does not have to be included
   c.   the loop variable has not been kept constant
   d.   an infinite loop has been created

B-197. What is wrong with the following program?
```
10 FOR J = 1 TO 10
20    LET P = 20 * J
30 NEXT I
40 PRINT "HELLO"
```
   a.   the loop variable has not been kept constant
   b.   an infinite loop has been created
   c.   the step value must be included
   d.   line 20 should read LET P = J * 20

B-198. Which line of the following program is invalid?

```
10 FOR M = 1 TO 20
20    FOR N = 1 TO 5
30       PRINT M,N
40    NEXT M
50 NEXT M
```

a. 10
b. 30

c. 40
d. 50

B-199. What is wrong with the following program?

```
10 FOR B = 1 TO 10
20    FOR B = 1 TO 10
30       PRINT B
40    NEXT B
50 NEXT B
```

a. the terminal values cannot be the same for both loops
b. the step values must be included
c. an infinite loop has been created
d. each loop must use separate loop variables

B-200. What is the value of C after the following program has been executed?

```
10 LET C = 0
   FOR A = 1 TO 12
      FOR B = 1 TO 2
40       LET C = C + 1
50    NEXT B
60 NEXT A
```

a. 14
b. 24

c. 0
d. 12

SECTION VII
Functions

MULTIPLE CHOICE

B-201. A function is
   a.   long and tedious to program
   b.   a type of loop useful to the programmer
   c.   built in to the BASIC language to perform specific mathematical operations
   d.   trigonometric only

B-202. Library functions are
   a.   found in the National Computer Library
   b.   included in the BASIC language library
   c.   obsolete
   d.   found in your college library

B-203. The argument of a function
   a.   is also called a library function
   b.   cannot be a mathematical expression
   c.   is not needed
   d.   can be another function

B-204. Which of the following is not a trigonometric function?
   a.   SIN   c.   TAN
   b.   COS   d.   INT

B-205. The SQR function determines the _____ of a number.
   a.   absolute value   c.   square root
   b.   sign   d.   logarithm

B-206. In most BASIC implementations, the argument of the SQR
functions must be
a. positive
b. negative
c. either positive or negative
d. another function

B-207. The INT function
a. determines the next greatest integer
b. computes the greatest integer less than or equal to a
    specified value
c. rounds a number
d. must have a positive argument

B-208. The INT function can be used to _____ a number.
a. return the sign of
b. return the absolute value of
c. compute
d. round

B-209. The SGN function returns a _____ if its argument is
positive.
a. 0   c. +1
b. -1   d. P

B-210. The ABS function returns the _____ value of its argument.
a. negative   c. positive
b. rounded   d. integer

B-211. The RND function generates
a. a random number between 0 and 1
b. any random number
c. a user-defined function
d. a random function determined by the computer

B-212. The DEF statement
a. is a trigonometric function
b. defines a function
c. does not contain an argument
d. is rarely used by scientists

B-213. The function name in the DEF statement consists of the
letters FN followed by any one of the
a. numbers from 0 to 9
b. twenty-six alphabetic characters
c. numbers from 1 to 9
d. special characters

B-214. A function definition cannot
    a.   contain another function
    b.   be used more than once in the program
    c.   contain a mathematical expression
    d.   exceed one line

B-215. What is the output from the following program?
```
10 READ X
20 LET Y = INT(X)
30 PRINT Y
40 DATA 3.99
```
    a. 4.0   c. 3
    b. 4   d. 3.99

B-216. What is the value of R after the following program has
been executed?
```
10 READ R
20 LET R = SQR(R)
30 PRINT R
40 DATA 16,4
```
    a. 2   c. 16
    b. 64   d. 4

B-217. What is the value of S after the following program has
been executed?
```
10 READ T
20 LET S = SGN(T)
30 PRINT S,T
40 DATA -13.25
```
    a. -13.25   c. 13.25
    b. -1   d. 1

B-218. What is the value of Y after the following program has
been executed?
```
10 LET Y = 0
20 READ A,B
30 IF B < 0 THEN LET Y = ABS(B)
40 IF A < 0 THEN LET Y = ABS(A)
50 DATA 0,-2.359
```
    a. 0   c. 2.359
    b. 1   d. -2.359

B-219. What line of the following program has an error?

```
10 READ P
20 LET X = COS(P)
30 LET Y = SIN
40 LET Z = ATN(P)
50 DATA 3.05
```

a. 30   c. 40
b. 20   d. 50

B-220. What line of the following program has an error?

```
10 LET Q = 1
20 LET Q$ = "TWO"
30 PRINT ABS(Q)
40 PRINT SGN(Q)
50 PRINT INT(Q$)
```

a. 50   c. 30
b. 40   d. 20

B-221. What is wrong with the following program?

```
10 FOR I = 1 TO 3
20    READ F
30    LET G = LOG(F)
40    LET H = EXP
50 NEXT I
60 DATA -3,2,6
```

a. the argument in line 30 is not needed
b. a negative number cannot be the argument for an expo-
    nential function
c. the argument must always be X, not F
d. no argument has been specified in line 40

SECTION VIII
Subroutines and String Functions

MULTIPLE CHOICE

B-222. The GOSUB statement transfers the flow of control from
the
a. beginning of a program to the end
b. main logic of a program to a subroutine
c. subroutine of a program to the main logic
d. end of a program to the beginning

B-223. The difference between the GOTO statement and the GOSUB
statement is that the
a. GOTO is an unconditional transfer while the GOSUB is
a conditional transfer
b. GOSUB is an unconditional transfer while the GOTO is
a conditional transfer
c. computer does not execute the GOSUB statement
d. computer remembers where to return after executing
the GOTO statement

B-224. Subroutines are typically assigned distinctive line numbers because the
a. subroutine format calls for it
b. computer will not execute the line numbers otherwise
c. subroutine is easier to locate
d. subroutine must be placed after the END statement

B-225. Subroutines are placed at the end of a program because
a. the subroutine format calls for it
b. the subroutine will not execute properly otherwise
c. this leaves room for additional program statements
d. the subroutine must be placed after the END statement

B-226. A RETURN statement is needed to tell the computer to
        return to the
        a. main logic of the program
        b. subroutine
        c. beginning of the program
        d. end of the program

B-227. No line number needs to follow the RETURN statement
        because the
        a. RETURN statement is a non-executable statement
        b. computer automatically goes to the END statement
        c. execution of the program terminates with the RETURN
            statement
        d. computer remembers to return to the statement
            following the most recently executed GOSUB statement

B-228. In the following example, to which line is control trans-
        ferred after the computer reaches the RETURN statement?

```
90 LET T = 1
100 GOSUB 500
110 LET T = 2
       .
       .
       .
500 REM ***SUBROUTINE***
       .
       .
       .
600 RETURN
610 LET T = 3
999 END
```

        a. 999   c. 110
        b. 610   d. 500

B-229. The STOP statement
        a. is used in place of the END statement
        b. halts execution of the program
        c. is non-executable by the computer
        d. is rarely used when the program contains a subroutine

B-230. The STOP statement can be used
        a. only once in the program
        b. twice in the program
        c. as many times as necessary
        d. as many times as there are GOSUB statements

B-231. A STOP statement is usually placed
       a.   after each subroutine
       b.   before the beginning of the first subroutine
       c.   at the end of the program
       d.   after the first GOSUB statement

B-232. A STOP statement is useful to stop program execution when
       a.   invalid data has been entered
       b.   the program has a logical error
       c.   a GOSUB has been executed
       d.   the program has a syntax error

B-233. Concatenation is
       a.   the joining together of two strings
       b.   the adding of two numbers
       c.   the comparing of two strings
       d.   also called sorting

B-234. The LEN function returns
       a.   the first letter of a string
       b.   blanks
       c.   the leftmost characters of a string
       d.   the length of a string

B-235. The LEFT$ function returns
       a.   the first letter of a string
       b.   the number of characters of the string specified in
            the argument beginning with the first character
       c.   blanks to the left of a string
       d.   the length of a string

B-236. The RIGHT$ function returns
       a.   the first letter of a string
       b.   blanks to the right of a string
       c.   a substring, starting with the character specified in
            the expression
       d.   the length of a string

B-237. The LEFT$ function is often used
       a.   in place of the LEN function
       b.   to compare character strings
       c.   when performing complex arithmetic operations
       d.   with the ASCII function

B-238. The MID$ function returns
     a. a specified number of characters starting from the last character of a specified string
     b. the length of a string
     c. blanks to the middle of a string
     d. a string in the middle of another string

B-239. The ASCII function returns
     a. the decimal value of the specified character value
     b. the character value of the specified numeric value
     c. the items in the DATA list into storage
     d. zeroes to a numeric variable

B-240. The CHR$ function returns
     a. the decimal value of the specified character value
     b. the character value of the specified numeric value
     c. program execution to the beginning of the program
     d. blanks to a character string variable

B-241. In BASIC programs, the ASCII and CHR$ functions are useful to
     a. determine a secret code
     b. print special words
     c. allow the program to respond to both uppercase and lowercase input
     d. concatenate

B-242. The VAL function converts a
     a. real number into a character string
     b. numeric string into a real number
     c. character string into lowercase letters
     d. character string into uppercase letters

B-243. The STR$ function converts a
     a. real number into a character string
     b. character string into a real number
     c. character string into lowercase letters
     d. character string into uppercase letters

B-244. What is the value of B after the following program has been executed?

```
10 READ A$
20 LET B = LEN(A$)
30 DATA "SEE JANE"
```

     a. 3   c. 8
     b. 7   d. 9

B-245. What is the value of C$ after the following program has
       been executed?

```
10 READ A$,B$
20 READ C$
30 LET C$ = A$ + B$
40 DATA WATER,MELON
50 DATA STR
```

a. WATER   c. STRAWBERRIES
b. MELON   d. WATERMELON

B-246. What is the value of L$ after the following program has
       been executed?

```
10 READ Z$
20 LET L$ = LEFT$(Z$,3)
30 DATA PIGLETS
```

a. PI   c. LETS
b. PIG   d. ETS

B-247. What is the value of R$ after the following program has
       been executed?

```
10 READ R$
20 LET R$ = RIGHT$(R$,6)
30 LET R$ = LEFT$(R$,2) + RIGHT$(R$,6)
40 DATA MARKETING
```

a. MARKETING   c. MATING
b. MAKE   d. RKETINGMARKET

B-248. What is the value of T after the following program has
       been executed?

```
10 READ L
20 GOSUB 100
30 STOP
40 LET T = T * L
50 DATA 20
60 STOP
100 REM ***SUBROUTINE***
110 LET T = L / 2
120 RETURN
999 END
```

a. 20   c. 400
b. 200   d. 10

B-249. What is the output of the following program?

```
10 READ S,R
20 LET Q = 3
30 GOSUB 100
40 LET Q = S * R
50 PRINT Q
60 DATA 2,5
70 STOP
100 REM ***SUBROUTINE***
110 LET Q = Q * S
120 RETURN
999 END
```

a. 15

b. 10

c. 30

d. 6

SECTION IX
Arrays

MULTIPLE CHOICE

B-250. An array is
   a.   one storage location in memory
   b.   also called a variable name
   c.   a group of storage locations in memory in which data elements can be stored
   d.   useful when the programmer has one or two values to be entered into the program

B-251. An array
   a.   can be given many names   c.   is not given a name
   b.   is given only one name   d.   is rarely used

B-252. A subscript
   a.   is the name of the array
   b.   reserves storage for the array
   c.   is rarely used when sorting
   d.   tells the computer which position in the array an item is stored

B-253. The DIM statement
   a.   tells the computer which position in the array an item is stored
   b.   is not used for arrays containing over fifty items
   c.   specifies the number of elements in an array
   d.   reserves a storage location for a variable

B-254. The computer will automatically reserve _____ memory locations if the DIM statement is not used
   a.   ten   c.   five
   b.   zero   d.   one

B-255. The DIM statement must be placed
     a.   at the beginning of the program
     b.   at the end of the program
     c.   before the first reference to the arrays it describes
     d.   anywhere in the program before the END statement

B-256. Which of the following is not an effective use of one-dimensional arrays?
     a.   printing tables   c.   reading data
     b.   printing data   d.   data computation

B-257. Two-dimensional arrays contain _____ subscripts.
     a.   one   c.   ten
     b.   two   d.   more than two

B-258. Two-dimensional arrays are not useful when
     a.   adding rows of data
     b.   adding columns of data
     c.   printing a single list of data
     d.   totaling rows and columns

B-259. Which of the following must be used when totaling a two-dimensional array?
     a.   two counters
     b.   nested FOR/NEXT loops
     c.   two one-dimensional arrays
     d.   two LET statements

B-260. Arrays are not useful to
     a.   merge data
     b.   search for a specific data item
     c.   sort data
     d.   serve as a counter

B-261. The bubble sort
     a.   is useful to compute
     b.   can be used to merge different arrays
     c.   works by comparing two adjacent values in an array
          and interchanging them according to the desired order
     d.   is not useful to alphabetize arrays

B-262. A flag
     a.   is used to test if the entire array has been sorted
     b.   is the terminal value of the sort FOR/NEXT loop
     c.   compares two values in an array and switches them if
          necessary
     d.   is used when totaling a two-dimensional array

B-263. The terminal value of the FOR/NEXT loop that sorts the
       array must be
       a.   a numeric variable
       b.   one less than the number of items to be sorted
       c.   equal to the number of items to be sorted
       d.   one more than the number of items to be sorted

B-264. Which of the following is invalid?
       a.   60 READ C(L,M)   c.   60 READ C(I + J,J)
       b.   60 READ C(I,-1)   d.   60 READ C(1,2)

B-265. Which of the following is valid?
       a.   90 READ T(-2)   c.   90 READ P$2(J)
       b.   90 READ X$(J,K$,L$,M)   d.   90 READ L$(Z + X)

B-266. Which of the following is not valid?
       a.   10 DIM L$(-2)
       b.   10 DIM L$(6),T$(22),Z$(3)
       c.   10 DIM L$(100)
       d.   10 DIM L$(1)

       For questions B-267 and B-268 use the following program
       segment:
```
            10 FOR I = 1 TO 5
            20    READ N$(I)
            30 NEXT I
            40 FOR I = 1 TO 4
            50    IF N$(I) <= N$(I + 1) THEN 100
            60    LET H$ = N$(I)
            70    LET N$(I) = N$(I + 1)
            80    LET N$(I + 1) = H$
            90    LET F = 1
            100 NEXT I
            110 IF F = 1 THEN 40
```

B-267. What is wrong with the preceding program segment?
       a.   the second FOR/NEXT loop cannot use the same loop
            variable as the first FOR/NEXT loop
       b.   the flag variable F must be set equal to zero
       c.   in line 60, H$ must be set equal to N$(I + 1)
       d.   in line 40, the terminal value must be b 5 instead
            of 4

B-268. Which of the following line numbers from the preceding
       program segment contains an error?
       a.   40   c.   90
       b.   50   d.   110

Use the following program segment to answer questions
B-269 through B-271. The segment should read in the
values for the array Q and then total them.

```
10 FOR I = 1 TO 3
20   READ Q(I)
30 NEXT I
40 LET Q = 0
50 FOR J = 1 TO 3
60   LET T = Q(I)
70 NEXT J
```

B-269. What is wrong with line 40 from the preceding program
segment?
a.   line 40 should be: 40 LET Q = 3
b.   line 40 should be: 40 LET Q = 1
c.   line 40 should be: 40 LET T = 0
d.   line 40 is correct

B-270. What is wrong with line 20 from the preceding program
segment?
a.   line 20 should be: 20 READ Q
b.   line 20 should be: 20 READ Q(J)
c.   line 20 should not be indented
d.   line 20 is correct

B-271. What is wrong with line 60 from the preceding program
segment?
a.   line 60 should be: 60 LET T = T + Q(I)
b.   line 60 should be: 60 LET T = Q(J)
c.   line 60 should be: 60 LET T = T + Q(J)
d.   line 60 is correct

Use the following program segment to answer questions
B-272 through B-274. The segment should read in the
values for the array L and then total them.

```
10 DIM L(5,15)
20 FOR M = 1 TO 15
30   FOR N = 1 TO 5
40     READ L(M,N)
50   NEXT N
60 NEXT M
70 LET T = 0
80 FOR M = 1 TO 15
90   LET T = T + L(M,N)
100 NEXT M
```

B-272. What is wrong with the preceding program segment?
    a.   the FOR/NEXT loop in lines 30 through 50 should be omitted
    b.   to total a two-dimensional array, another FOR/NEXT loop must be inserted between lines 80 and 100
    c.   T should not be initialized to zero
    d.   line 10 is not needed

B-273. What is wrong with line 10 from the preceding program segment?
    a.   line 10 should be: 10 DIM L(15,5)
    b.   line 10 should be: 10 DIM L(X,15)
    c.   line 10 should be: 10 DIM L(15,X)
    d.   line 10 is correct

B-274. What is wrong with line 90 from the preceding program segment?
    a.   line 90 should be: 90 LET T = L(M,N)
    b.   line 90 should be: 90 LET T = T + L(N,M)
    c.   line 90 should be indented
    d.   line 90 is correct

SECTION X
File Processing

MULTIPLE CHOICE

B-275. A file is
    a. an unrelated set of data
    b. a way of processing data
    c. rarely used for business applications
    d. a way of organizing data

B-276. A file contains
    a. general information
    b. data to be used by the President of a company only
    c. related information about one general topic
    d. unorganized data

B-277. A field is
    a. comprised of several non-related data items
    b. one or more related records
    c. one or more related files
    d. an individual data item

B-278. A record is
    a. comprised of several non-related data items
    b. one or more related fields
    c. one or more related files
    d. an individual data item

B-279. A file is
    a. comprised of several non-related data items
    b. one or more related fields
    c. one or more related records
    d. an individual data item

B-280. Two main types of file access methods are
       a.   sequential and random access
       b.   sequential and direct
       c.   direct and random access
       d.   direct and quick access

B-281. Accessing a file does not concentrate on _____ the
       file.
       a.   writing to
       b.   reading from
       c.   computing data to be stored in
       d.   opening and closing

B-282. Which of the following is used to store sequential files?
       a.   magentic tape only   c.   disk only
       b.   magnetic tape or disk   d.   punched cards

B-283. In a sequential file, the data items are stored
       a.   one after another
       b.   randomly
       c.   in different tracks on a disk
       d.   according to the key field of the record

B-284. The data items in a sequential file are read
       a.   starting with the specified data item
       b.   randomly
       c.   according to the key field of the record
       d.   starting with the first data item

B-285. Tracks are
       a.   each data item stored on tape
       b.   the number of data items stored in a sequential file
       c.   concentric circles on a disk, used to store data
       d.   the columns of a disk pack, used to store data

B-286. In a sequential file, each field
       a.   length must be the same
       b.   uses only the amount of space required by its length
       c.   must specify its length
       d.   cannot exceed twenty-five characters

B-287. Which of the following is not used to record data in a
       sequential file?
       a.   reading data from the sequential file
       b.   opening a sequential file
       c.   closing the sequential file
       d.   writing data to the sequential file

B-288. Which of the following is not used to read data from a
       sequential file?
       a. reading data from the sequential file
       b. opening a sequential file
       c. closing the sequential file
       d. writing data to the sequential file

B-289. When opening a file, the programmer must
       a. delete any existing files under the same file name
       b. name the file
       c. determine the storage location for the file
       d. empty the file

B-290. When writing data to a sequential file, the data are
       written to
       a. punched cards   c. the disk
       b. the screen   d. the printer

B-291. After the data have been written to the disk, the file
       must be closed to
       a. prevent loss of the file contents
       b. fulfill file requirements
       c. empty the file contents
       d. determine the storage location of the file

B-292. In a sequential file, data must always be
       a. grouped according to a key field
       b. read in the same order in which they were written
       c. written randomly
       d. written to the file before opening the file

B-293. Random data files allow the user to
       a. randomly open any file
       b. compute any data from the file in a random order
       c. close any file randomly
       d. write to or read from the file in a random order

B-294. All records in a random data file must be
       a. ordered by a key field   c. the same length
       b. of varying lengths   d. stored in magnetic tape

B-295. Random data files
       a. take up more storage space than do sequential files
       b. have slow access speeds
       c. are read starting with the first record
       d. do not contain fields

B-296. Which of the following is not true?
   a. records in a sequential file can be of varying lengths
   b. records in a random file must be the same length
   c. records in a random file must be read one after the other, starting with the first record
   d. records in a random file can be written in any order desired

B-297. A relative file
   a. stores its records randomly
   b. stores its records in numbered locations
   c. stores its records one after another
   d. is also called a sequential file

B-298. The number associated with a record in a relative file represents
   a. any random number
   b. the location of the record relative to the beginning of the disk track
   c. the print zone that the record will be printed in
   d. the location of the record relative to the beginning of the file

B-299. A relative file is accessed
   a. sequentially
   b. randomly
   c. sequentially or randomly by record number
   d. sequentially or directly

B-300. Random files must be _____ like sequential files.
   a. opened and closed   c. deleted
   b. read from and written to d. accessed

ANSWER KEY

B-1.	c	B-51.	d	B-101.	c	B-151.	b	B-201.	c
B-2.	b	B-52.	b	B-102.	a	B-152.	d	B-202.	b
B-3.	c	B-53.	c	B-103.	c	B-153.	c	B-203.	d
B-4.	a	B-54.	d	B-104.	b	B-154.	a	B-204.	d
B-5.	d	B-55.	b	B-105.	c	B-155.	d	B-205.	c
B-6.	b	B-56.	d	B-106.	d	B-156.	b	B-206.	a
B-7.	a	B-57.	a	B-107.	a	B-157.	c	B-207.	b
B-8.	a	B-58.	a	B-108.	c	B-158.	a	B-208.	d
B-9.	c	B-59.	c	B-109.	b	B-159.	b	B-209.	c
B-10.	d	B-60.	b	B-110.	d	B-160.	c	B-210.	c
B-11.	b	B-61.	d	B-111.	c	B-161.	d	B-211.	a
B-12.	c	B-62.	d	B-112.	a	B-162.	b	B-212.	b
B-13.	a	B-63.	c	B-113.	d	B-163.	a	B-213.	b
B-14.	b	B-64.	a	B-114.	b	B-164.	c	B-214.	d
B-15.	d	B-65.	d	B-115.	c	B-165.	b	B-215.	c
B-16.	d	B-66.	b	B-116.	b	B-166.	d	B-216.	d
B-17.	a	B-67.	c	B-117.	d	B-167.	c	B-217.	b
B-18.	b	B-68.	c	B-118.	d	B-168.	a	B-218.	c
B-19.	d	B-69.	c	B-119.	a	B-169.	b	B-219.	a
B-20.	c	B-70.	a	B-120.	d	B-170.	b	B-220.	a
B-21.	d	B-71.	a	B-121.	b	B-171.	c	B-221.	d
B-22.	b	B-72.	b	B-122.	a	B-172.	a	B-222.	b
B-23.	c	B-73.	d	B-123.	b	B-173.	d	B-223.	a
B-24.	a	B-74.	c	B-124.	c	B-174.	c	B-224.	c
B-25.	b	B-75.	b	B-125.	d	B-175.	a	B-225.	c
B-26.	b	B-76.	c	B-126.	a	B-176.	b	B-226.	a
B-27.	d	B-77.	a	B-127.	b	B-177.	c	B-227.	d
B-28.	a	B-78.	b	B-128.	c	B-178.	a	B-228.	c
B-29.	c	B-79.	d	B-129.	a	B-179.	d	B-229.	b
B-30.	a	B-80.	c	B-130.	b	B-180.	a	B-230.	c
B-31.	d	B-81.	a	B-131.	b	B-181.	b	B-231.	b
B-32.	c	B-82.	c	B-132.	c	B-182.	b	B-232.	a
B-33.	b	B-83.	b	B-133.	d	B-183.	c	B-233.	a
B-34.	a	B-84.	c	B-134.	a	B-184.	a	B-234.	d
B-35.	d	B-85.	a	B-135.	c	B-185.	a	B-235.	b
B-36.	c	B-86.	d	B-136.	a	B-186.	b	B-236.	c
B-37.	b	B-87.	b	B-137.	c	B-187.	d	B-237.	b
B-38.	b	B-88.	c	B-138.	b	B-188.	b	B-238.	d
B-39.	d	B-89.	b	B-139.	c	B-189.	a	B-239.	a
B-40.	b	B-90.	d	B-140.	b	B-190.	c	B-240.	b
B-41.	a	B-91.	c	B-141.	b	B-191.	c	B-241.	c
B-42.	d	B-92.	a	B-142.	d	B-192.	a	B-242.	b
B-43.	c	B-93.	c	B-143.	c	B-193.	c	B-243.	a
B-44.	a	B-94.	a	B-144.	b	B-194.	b	B-244.	c
B-45.	a	B-95.	d	B-145.	a	B-195.	d	B-245.	d
B-46.	c	B-96.	b	B-146.	d	B-196.	d	B-246.	b
B-47.	d	B-97.	d	B-147.	d	B-197.	a	B-247.	c
B-48.	c	B-98.	a	B-148.	b	B-198.	c	B-248.	d
B-49.	a	B-99.	b	B-149.	a	B-199.	d	B-249.	b
B-50.	b	B-100.	d	B-150.	c	B-200.	b	B-250.	c

Answer Key cont.

B-251.   b
B-252.   d
B-253.   c
B-254.   a
B-255.   c
B-256.   a
B-257.   b
B-258.   c
B-259.   b
B-260.   d
B-261.   c
B-262.   a
B-263.   b
B-264.   b
B-265.   d
B-266.   a
B-267.   b
B-268.   a
B-269.   c
B-270.   d
B-271.   c
B-272.   b
B-273.   a
B-274.   d
B-275.   d
B-276.   c
B-277.   d
B-278.   b
B-279.   c
B-280.   a
B-281.   c
B-282.   b
B-283.   a
B-284.   d
B-285.   c
B-286.   b
B-287.   a
B-288.   d
B-289.   b
B-290.   c
B-291.   a
B-292.   b
B-293.   d
B-294.   c
B-295.   a
B-296.   c
B-297.   b
B-298.   d
B-299.   c
B-300.   a

DATE DUE